TREASURES OF THE LIBRARY
Trinity College Dublin

TREASURES OF THE LIBRARY

Trinity College Dublin

EDITED BY PETER FOX

PUBLISHED FOR THE LIBRARY OF
TRINITY COLLEGE DUBLIN
BY THE ROYAL IRISH ACADEMY

ROYAL IRISH ACADEMY
19 Dawson Street,
Dublin 2

Editorial Committee:
Aidan Clarke, Peter Fox,
Vincent Kinane, Bernard Meehan,
Veronica Morrow

ISBN 0 901714 45 3 (hardback)
ISBN 0 901714 46 1 (paperback)

First published in 1986

Cataloguing in Publication Data

Trinity College *(Dublin), Library*
Treasures of the Library, Trinity College Dublin.
1. Trinity College *(Dublin), Library*
I. Title II. Fox, Peter, *1949-*
027.7418′ 35 Z792.5.T7

ISBN 0-901714-45-3
ISBN 0-901714-46-1 Pbk

Production Control: Tony Farmar
Design: Jacques Teljeur
Typeset by Printset & Design Ltd, Dublin
Printed in Ireland by Cahills, Dublin

PHOTOGRAPHS

Bibliothèque nationale, Paris: [62]; British Library, London: [59]; Anthony Cains: [9]; Cambridge University Library: [58]; Jonathan Gibson, Ripley, Surrey: [13]; Green Studio, Dublin: all manuscripts; Irish Times: Peter Brown; Pieterse Davison International: [4], [11]; Brendan Dempsey, Trinity College Photographic Centre: all other photographs.

ACKNOWLEDGEMENTS

The Editorial Committee wish to thank the following. For allowing the use of photographs and quotations: the Board of Trinity College Dublin; Mr Samuel Beckett; Bibliothèque nationale, Paris (illustration [62], from Bibl. nat. Vélins 700, fol.1); Blackstaff Press, Belfast (illustration [142], from H. Shields, *Shamrock, rose and thistle* (1981), p. 77; British Library (illustration [59], from BL. c.19.e.14, fol.2r); Syndics of Cambridge University Library (illustration [58], from CUL. Inc.1, B.3.2.); Professor F.B. Chubb (photograph of Mrs Margot Chubb); Country Life (illustration [13]); Ms Clare Craven; the Hon. Mr Justice Cahir Davitt; Professor J.M. Dillon; Dolmen Press, Mountrath; Irish Times (photograph of Mr Peter Brown); Mr Micheal Johnston; J.M. Synge Trust; Miss Anne Butler Yeats and Mr Michael Yeats. For the compilation of the index: Mrs Elizabeth Duffin. For typing, word processing and much running to and fro: Miss Janet Monaghan.

CONTENTS

CONTRIBUTORS

J.H. Andrews, *Associate Professor of Geography, Trinity College*
Lilian Armstrong, *Professor of Art, Wellesley College, Wellesley, Massachusetts*
Charles Benson, *Assistant Librarian, Department of Early Printed Books, Trinity College Library*
John Bowman, *Author of* De Valera and the Ulster question, 1917-1973
Aidan Clarke, *Associate Professor of Modern History, Trinity College*
Anne Crookshank, *Professor of the History of Art, Trinity College*
Peter Fox, *Librarian and College Archivist, Trinity College*
Nicholas Grene, *Lecturer in English, Trinity College*
F.J.E. Hurst, *Research Librarian, University of Ulster*
Vincent Kinane, *Assistant Librarian, Department of Early Printed Books, Trinity College Library*
R.B. McDowell, *Formerly Erasmus Smith's Professor of Oratory and History, Trinity College*
B.C. McGing, *Lecturer in Classics, Trinity College*
Gearóid Mac Niocaill, *Professor of History, University College Galway*
Bernard Meehan, *Keeper of Manuscripts, Trinity College Library*
Veronica Morrow, *Keeper (Technical Services), Trinity College Library*
Christine Nudds, *Library Assistant, Department of Early Printed Books, Trinity College Library*
Ann O'Brien, *Assistant Librarian, Department of Technical Services, Trinity College Library*
Felicity O'Mahony, *Assistant Librarian, Department of Manuscripts, Trinity College Library*
Stuart Ó Seanóir, *Assistant Librarian, Department of Manuscripts, Trinity College Library*
H.W. Parke,* *Formerly Louis Claude Purser Professor of Ancient History and Curator of the Library, Trinity College*
M. Pollard, *Formerly Keeper (Early Printed Books), Trinity College Library*
H. Robinson-Hammerstein, *Senior Lecturer in Modern History, Trinity College*
Hugh Shields, *Senior Lecturer in French, Trinity College*
George Otto Simms, *Formerly Archbishop of Armagh and Primate of all Ireland*
John Tedeschi, *Curator, Rare Books and Special Collections, University of Madison-Wisconsin*
James Woolley, *Assistant Professor of English, Lafayette College, Easton, Pennsylvania*

PREFACE

Open any guidebook to Dublin or read any description of that city and you will find a major section devoted to Trinity College and its Library. Mention Trinity College (or TCD as it is widely known) anywhere in the world and you will encounter people familiar with the Library and its most treasured possession, the Book of Kells.

This book, and the exhibition for which it was prepared, had their origins in a series of tragic events in 1984. In January of that year Peter Brown, who had been Librarian and College Archivist since 1970, died suddenly. In June Margot Chubb, the Keeper (Readers' Services), who had served on the Library staff for thirty-four years and had effectively created the Department of Readers' Services from nothing, died after an illness of many months.

The Library staff felt that a fitting tribute to the memory of their two senior colleagues would be to take the opportunity of bringing to the attention of a wider public some of the treasures of the Library's collections. A number are already well known; the great early Christian manuscripts attract visitors from all over the world. Others are more the province of specialists but deserve to be more widely appreciated. In a compilation such as this it is inevitable that important items will have been omitted. What has been attempted is to show varied facets of the collections: some of the oldest written materials of the age before printing; the transition from manuscript to print in the fifteenth and sixteenth centuries and its impact on the reading public; later manuscripts as source materials for scholars of history and literature; and the printed book as a source of enlightenment, entertainment and polemic. The Long Room, in which many of the Library's treasures are stored or displayed, is one of the finest library buildings in the world and is, in itself, one of our 'treasures'.

By its very nature this book concentrates on the treasures of the past. The chapter by the College Librarian shows that the Library is keeping abreast of the technological developments of the present. It is also collecting for the future, by purchase, by receiving modern books and journals under the terms of the Copyright Act and by collecting twentieth-century papers and records.

W.A. Watts, *Provost*
January 1986

PETER BROWN

3 DECEMBER 1925 – 7 JANUARY 1984

Peter Brown was a graduate of King's College London, where he read German and Medieval Latin. He then entered a career in librarianship, which brought him to three of the copyright libraries in the British Isles.

As a member of staff of the Department of Printed Books at the British Museum he edited the 263 volumes of the *British Museum catalogue of printed books*, the *Short title catalogue of books printed in German-speaking countries, 1455-1600* and the *Short title catalogue of books printed in the Netherlands, 1470-1600.*

This cataloguing work aroused an interest in the use of computers in libraries, and from 1964 be became involved in experiments in computerized cataloguing. He was invited to apply for the new post of Keeper of

Catalogues at the Bodleian Library in Oxford, a post he held from 1966 to 1970. During this time he began the task of converting the pre-1920 catalogue to machine-readable form. In 1970 he was appointed Librarian of Trinity College. Within a short time he set up a computer-based catalogue using the *British National Bibliography* machine-readable (MARC) records, thus making Trinity one of the earliest libraries in the British Isles to transfer all its current cataloguing to a computer-based system.

Peter Brown's other great professional interest was conservation. He set up a conservation laboratory at Trinity and he was Chairman of the IFLA Section on Conservation, which produced the 'Principles of conservation and restoration in libraries' (*IFLA Journal* 5 (1979) 292-300). He was also a member of the (British) Library Association's Sub-Committee on Conservation.

Peter Brown was a keen chess and croquet player and an accomplished musician. During his days in the Royal Navy, at the end of the Second World War, he was apparently a trumpeter of some distinction, this despite the fact that his trumpet had suffered considerably during differences of opinion with matelots of other ships of His Majesty's Fleet! His unflagging good-humour and equanimity, together with his great interest in people, are sorely missed by friends and colleagues across the world.

Peter Fox

MARGARET GERTRUDE CHUBB

15 JULY 1922 – 16 JUNE 1984

If ever there was a born 'front of house' librarian, it surely was Margot Chubb. She also successfully demonstrated that one can become a first-rate librarian without having any formal qualification in librarianship. She had all the necessary characteristics required by a good leader and administrator, including a perpetual cheerfulness, sense of humour, approachability, confidentiality, personal courage, and a way of dealing with people. Trinity College is extremely fortunate that – though at first almost by accident – Margot was on the Library scene (and serving, incidentally, under four Librarians) during thirty years that covered such a fundamental change in every aspect of the Library's activity and growth.

Margot Chubb was a history graduate of the University of London (Westfield College). She married Basil in 1946 and came to Dublin on his appointment as Lecturer in Political Science at Trinity College in 1948. She joined the College Library (in effect, in building terms, then the West Pavilion) in 1950 as secretary to Dr Parke, Vice-Provost and Librarian. In 1951 she became a Library Assistant, cataloguing, supervising the binding and (because she was a married woman, so the story goes) acting as custodian of banned books. No one who did not experience them can possibly imagine the conditions for working experienced in the old 'Classing Room' and the basement of the 1937 Reading Room. Margot thrived on them.

When the policy of opening up Trinity College Library's resources to a wider public and of making contacts with other libraries began, Margot enthusiastically responded. From 1961 she became Information Librarian, in 1967 took charge of Readers' Services, in 1968 became Sub-Librarian, and in 1976 Keeper of Printed Books – for technical reasons this post, with wide-ranging responsibilities, was renamed Keeper (Readers' Services) in 1981. She was one of the first members of the Library staff to be made an MA of Dublin University. She became a member of An Chomhairle Leabharlanna in 1968, was deeply interested in the work of the Library Association of Ireland, and was a member of the Committee on Library Co-operation in Ireland.

All of this professional work was combined with her life as the wife of Basil; their reputation for hospitality and kindliness to staff, newcomers and visitors to Dublin was unbeatable. Many of us have lost a great personal friend. Librarians in Ireland have lost an inspiring colleague. Trinity has lost an outstanding servant and ambassador. We all deeply regret her passing.

F.J.E. Hurst

TABULA AMICORUM MEMORUM

Aberdeen University Library
Muriel Allison, *Dublin*
Ronald Anderson, *Bective Village, County Meath*
J.H. Andrews, *Dublin*
Thomas Armitage, *Dublin*
Lilian Armstrong, *Wellesley, Massachusetts*
Kader Asmal, *Dublin*
Sheila Astbury, *Blackrock, County Dublin*
Jennefer Aston, *Dublin*
T.W. Atkinson, *Tandragee, County Armagh*
Ronald Ayling, *Edmonton, Alberta*

T.B. Barry, *Dublin*
John R. Bartlett, *Dublin*
Claire T. Baylis (née Dowling), *Aberystwyth*
Richard Bell, *Oxford*
C.J. Benson, *Dublin*
David Berman, *Dublin*
Birmingham University Library
R.M. Blackwell, *Oxford*
John Anthony Boland, *Kingston-upon-Thames*
Brotherton Library, *Leeds*
Peter Howard Boyle, *Dublin*
Hugh Brazier, *Dublin*
Leslie Bryan, *Dublin*
J.G. Byrne, *Dublin*
John Bowman, *Dublin*

Conor Cahill, *Dublin*
Mary Cahill, *Dublin*
Cambridge University Library
Thomas Gildea Cannon, *Milwaukee*
Agnes B. Cassidy, *Dublin*
Central Library Services, University of London
P.L. and C.M. Chambers, *Dublin*
Patricia A. Chapman (née McCarthy), *London*
Aidan Clarke, *Dublin*
George Clarke, *Dublin*
Davis Coakley, *Dublin*
Robert Grant Coleman, *Woodbridge, Suffolk*
Brid Conneely, *Dublin*
Al Connolly, *Dundalk, County Louth*
John Cooke, *Droichead Nua, County Kildare*
John Corish, *Dublin*
Owen I. Corrigan, *Dublin*
Anthony Coughlan, *Dublin*
Maurice Craig, *Dublin*
Anne Crookshank, *Dublin*
Michael Curran, *Dublin*

Marie Davis, *Mount Merrion, County Dublin*
Mary G. Davis, *Belfast*
William J. Davis, *Dublin*
John Dean, *Dublin*
Donnell J. Deeny, *Strangford, County Down*
Kenneth L. De Haven, *Sunnyvale, California*
Marisa and William Dieneman, *Aberystwyth*
John M. Dillon, *Dublin*
Michael Doherty, *Dublin*
Brigid Dolan, *Dublin*
Beatrice Doran, *Cork*
Robert O. Dougan, *Santa Barbara, California*
P.J. Drudy, *Dublin*
Urs Düggelin, *Luzern*
Elizabeth Duffin, *Dublin*
J.G. Duffy, *Dublin*

Austin Dunphy, *Dublin*

Rosa Pennick Edwards, *Oxford*
Bartholomew Egan, *Killiney, County Dublin*
Elizabeth A. L. Esteve-Coll, *London*

Norah Fahie, *Dublin*
John Feely, *Dublin*
W.E.C. Fleming, *Portadown, County Armagh*
Dermot Fleury, *Dublin*
Peter and Isobel Fox, *Dalkey, County Dublin*
Frances-Jane French, *Dublin*

Marie Geoghegan, *Dublin*
G.H.H. Giltrap, *Dublin*
John Graham, *Dublin*
W.H.B. Greenwood, *Dublin*
Stephen and Jane Gregory, *Cambridge*
Nicholas Grene, *Dublin*
Michael and Lucy Grose, *Leicester*
R. Geraint Gruffydd, *Aberystwyth*

David J. Hall, *Cambridge*
Frank X. Hanlon, *Blackrock, County Dublin*
Margaret Harte, *Dublin*
Richard Haworth, *Dublin*
Henry and Mary Heaney, *Glasgow*
Aidan Heavey, *Dublin*
Monica M. Henchy, *Dublin*
J. Heywood, *Dublin*
Norman Higham, *Bristol*
Francis M. Higman, *Nottingham*
Jean and Peter Hoare, *Nottingham*
Andrew and Monica Holmes-Siedle, *Oxford*
Catherine H. Horner, *Dublin*
Kenneth W. Humphries, *Birmingham*
F. John E. and Teresa A. Hurst, *Portrush, County Antrim*

Aideen Ireland, *Dublin*
The Earl of Iveagh, *Dublin*

Patricia S. Jennings, *Dublin*
P.E. FitzGerald Johnson, *London*
Myra A. Jordan, *Dublin*
Raymond Charles Jordan, *Dublin*

Conor Keane, *Dublin*
Marian Keaney, *Mullingar, County Westmeath*
Patrick Keatinge, *Dublin*
Tim Kelly, *Dublin*
Tony Kilroy, *San Francisco*
Vincent Kinane, *Dublin*

Eileen Laffan, *Dun Laoghaire, County Dublin*
Paul Larkin, *Dublin*
Rachel Kelley Laurgaard, *Oakland, California*
Ada K. Leask (née Longfield), *Fethard, County Tipperary*
T. C. Lee, *Dublin*
The Library Company of Philadelphia
William D. Linton, *Belfast*
Roger Little, *Dublin*
C. Salvadori Lonergan, *Dublin*
H.W. Love, *Armagh*
Alan D. Lowe, *Leeds*
John Victor Luce, *Dublin*
Jim Lydon, *Dublin*

Dermot McAleese, *Dublin*
E.J.W. McCann, *Belfast*
Muriel McCarthy, *Dublin*
A.J. McConnell, *Killiney, County Dublin*
David J. McConnell, *Dublin*
George S. A. McDonald, *Dublin*
R.B. McDowell, *London*
B.C. McGing, *Dublin*
Helen Watson McKelvie, *Dublin*
Alf Mac Lochlainn, *Galway*
Brian and Sara McMurry, *Dublin*
Elizabeth A. McNamara, *Dublin*
Gearóid Mac Niocaill, *Galway*
Eileen Ann Mangan, *Dublin*
Patrick Mangan, *Mullingar, County Westmeath*
June Manning, *Holyhead, Gwynedd*
James Mason, *Dublin*
Leonard and Rosemary Mathews, *Dublin*
Bernard Meehan, *Dublin*
Rosaleen Mills, *Dublin*
Annette Maria Minihane, *Dublin*
Frank Mitchell, *Dublin*
Brenda E. Moon, *Edinburgh*

Gerald and Janet Morgan, *Dublin*
Veronica Morrow, *Dublin*

Newberry Library, *Chicago*
Ciaran P. Nicholson, *Dublin*
Christine Nudds, *Dublin*

Ann O'Brien, *Dublin*
Nessa O'Connor, *Dublin*
Iosold Ó Deirg, *Dublin*
Raghnall Ó Floinn, *Dublin*
Dolores O'Higgins, *Dublin*
Felicity O'Mahony, *Dublin*
Tom O'Neill, *Melbourne*
John A. Oni, *London*
Breandán Ó Ríordáin, *Dublin*
W.N. Osborough, *Dublin*
Stuart Ó Seanóir, *Dublin*
Arabella Otway-Freeman, *Dublin*

H.W. Parke, *Redcar, Cleveland*
J.D. Trevor Peare, *Dublin*
John C. Pearson, *New Malden, Surrey*
Michael Pegg, *Manchester*
Sean Phillips, *Dublin*
M. Pollard, *Dublin*
Thelma Pope, *Dublin*
Ellen Power, *Dublin*
Mary J. Prendergast, *Dublin*

Queen's University, Main Library, *Belfast*

Frederick W. Ratcliffe, *Cambridge*
Valentine Rice, *Dublin*
Denis Roberts, *Edinburgh*
Ian N. Roberts, *Dublin*
Julian Roberts, *Oxford*
M.M. Robinson, *Dublin*
H.H. Robinson-Hammerstein, *Dublin*
Liz Roche, *Dublin*
Eamonn and Valerie Rodgers, *Dublin*
Geraldine Ryan, *Dublin*
Louden and Maudie Ryan, *Dublin*

Eda Sagarra, *Dublin*
Michael Schlosser, *Bad Windsheim*
Marcella Senior, *Dublin*
Robert Shackleton, *Oxford*
Sheffield University Library
Hugh Shields, *Dublin*
George O. Simms, *Dublin*
Tom Smail, *London*
Colin Smythe, *Gerrards Cross, Buckinghamshire*
Roger Stalley, *Dublin*
Roy Stanley, *Dublin*
M.D.M. Staunton, *London*
Stiftsbibliothek, *St Gallen*
Norbert Streb, *Frankfurt am Main*
Marie de Montfort Supple, *Dublin*
Frances Swaine, *London*
Phyl Swaine, *London*

John Tedeschi, *Madison, Wisconsin*
James Thompson, *Reading*
James Peery Williams Thompson, *Dublin*
Keith Tipton, *Dublin*
Brian Torode, *Dublin*
Patricia Trotter, *Monkstown, County Dublin*
Sue Tucker, *Bray, County Wicklow*

University College Library, *Dublin*
University College Library, *London*
University of East Anglia Library, *Norwich*

Paul S. Wagstaff, *Dublin*
Frederick Walker, *Dublin*
David Webb, *Dublin*
Anthony Werner, *Bellerive, Tasmania*
Edward N. West, *New York*
Kevin Whelan, *Dublin*
John and Jean Whyte, *Dublin*
Robert Brian Williamson, *London*
R.J.A. Wilson, *Dublin*
Franz Carl Winkelmann, *Dublin*
Barry Wintour, *Egham, Surrey*
James Woolley, *Easton, Pennsylvania*
Barbara Wright, *Dublin*

Barbara Young, *Dublin*

'THEY GLORY MUCH IN THEIR LIBRARY'

PETER FOX

The story of a library has two essential elements: the development of the institution and the growth of its collections. Later chapters of this book explore more fully aspects of the collections, in the form of either single masterpieces such as the Book of Kells or the Agostini Plutarch, or important collections of manuscripts or printed books such as those assembled by Ussher or Fagel. This chapter describes the growth of Trinity College Library as an institution and seeks to show the context in which the Library acquired the 'treasures' described in more detail elsewhere.

The Library of Trinity College Dublin came into being shortly after the foundation of the College itself in 1592. It is possible that the books belonging to Luke Challoner, the first Vice-Chancellor, served as the Library during the first decade of the College's existence, but early-seventeenth-century sources provide evidence that by 1601 the nucleus of a College Library proper had already been formed. This evidence appears in the Particular Book, the oldest extant volume recording the College's history, which contains a list dated 24 February 1601 of some thirty 'libri in Publica Collegii Bibliotheca' and ten 'libri manuscripti'[1] [1]. Most of the books in this list have been identified[2] and their current shelf-marks determined; a number are no longer in the Library, probably having been discarded when duplicates were acquired.

Receipts from London booksellers also exist, showing purchases made for the Library from June 1601 onwards. These receipts provide considerable information about the Library's early book-buying activities, giving the name of the bookseller, the date of the purchase, the name of the purchaser on behalf of the College, and a list of the books bought, together with their prices.[3] Typical of them is one dated 7 June 1601 for £58 worth of books bought by Luke Challoner from one Gregory Seton of Aldersgate.[4] During the early years of the seventeenth century substantial purchases were made, principally by Challoner and James Ussher, a Fellow of the College, a future Archbishop of Armagh and a man whose name is writ large in the history of the Library. These two Fellows were sent to England specifically to buy books for the Library, some of their purchases being made in Oxford and Cambridge, but most of them in London, where they met Sir Thomas Bodley, engaged upon a similar errand for his new library in Oxford.

The Particular Book provides information on the procedure involved in transporting the books from London to Dublin at a slightly later date, 1608:[5]

PURCHASE AND CARRIAGE OF BOOKS

July to September 1608.

For bookes bought of Adrian marins at London. See ye particulars in ye colledge chest 28^l^.16s.

Libri in publica Collegij Bibliotheca. 24° Febr. anno 1600.

· Euripides Graecolat. cum comentarijs Brodaei et aliorum. ex dono M. Henrici Lee.
· Platonis opera omnia graecolat.
· Aristotelis opera omnia graecolat.
· Ciceronis operum volumina duo in fol.
· Strabo Graecolat. fol.
· Dioscorides lat. fol.
· Ptolomei volumina duo. fol.
· Basilius. fol.
· Hieronymi index. fol
· Augustinus de consensu Evangelistarum.
· Stephanus de urbibus graece.
· Hermes.
· Livius. fol. in libros historicos fol.
· Albertus Magnus de physica.
· Aretinus in Ethica.
· Faber in Evangelia.
· Gesner de piscibus.
· Gesner de avibus.
· Fernelij opera fol.
· Munsteri Cosmographia.
· Tabulae geographicae Mercatoris.
· Sermones quidam papistica Anglice.
· Budaeus in Pandectas, et Landinus de vita contemplativa.
· Polyanthia Domini~~ci~~ Nani.
· Thomae prima secundae.
· Merula in Juvenalem, cum ~~Bembo~~ et adversus Domitium in ~~Juven~~ Martialem.
· Musculi loci communes. lent by Mr ~~W~~alsh.
· Tremelij Biblia novissima editio
· Marlorat in novum testamentum.
· Aristotelis Organon.
· Aben Ezra, David Kimchi, et Salomo Jarchi in Joëlem.
· Ursini Exercitationes.

For other bookes bought at London of Boile, at Camb. of Legate, at Oxford of Barnes	22s. 2d.
half a dosen calfe skinnes to lapp ye bookes, a dryfatt [box for dry goods] for them, cordes & canvas for mailinge, nailes & severall sortes of hanginge lockes [padlocks] att m^{r} Cutts of Cheapsyde	13s. 10d.
For cariage by carte from London to Chester	4^{l}.
To Tomlinson att Chester for receivinge & keepinge in his warehouse, to ye searchers att Chester & customers, carryinge to ye water syde from Tomlinsons, & thence by boate to the shippe, cariage by sea, & thence to ye colledge in toto	39s.

The source of funding for these early purchases is far from clear. Until the beginning of the present century it was generally believed that the Library had been founded with a subscription of £1800 made by the English army after its victory at the Battle of Kinsale in 1602. This story had appeared, in a number of slightly differing versions, in publications about the College and its Library and had gained wide acceptance. The legend is even commemorated in a painting of the battle which now hangs in the Conference Room of the Old Library. In 1903, however, J.P.Mahaffy, in an article in the University journal *Hermathena*, stated that he had failed to find any evidence to support the story. He argued convincingly that the whole episode was in fact a 'pious fraud' concocted in 1656 to encourage generosity on the part of Cromwellian troops.[6] Mahaffy's case rests on the absence of any contemporary evidence of a donation in support of the Library, on the appearance of conflicting versions of the story and on the existence of documents which show that, although soldiers *did* donate money to the College, the donation was made in the early 1590s, shortly after the foundation, and not specifically for the Library. It is likely that these benefactions were not actually realized until 1601 and that only then did the College decide to use the money for the purchase of books. Either the legend of Kinsale was a deliberate invention by Nicholas Bernard in his biography of Archbishop Ussher in 1656 or else Bernard's account reflects the distortions and inaccuracies that had crept into the story during the intervening half century.

The book-buying expeditions of the early 1600s seem to have been followed by a period of relatively slow growth for the next half century. Perhaps the new College was sufficiently satisified with its efforts to establish a library and felt that no more needed to be done. Certainly, Sir William Brereton, the Parliamentary general who visited Dublin in 1635, commented on the Fellows, 'they glory much in their library, whereof I took a full view'.[7] In Brereton's own opinion, however, the College had little to be proud of: 'This library is not large, well contrived, nor well furnished with books'. He dined with Ussher, who was by that time Primate, and who showed him his own collection of books: 'after dinner he took me into his closet, where although there be not many books, yet those that are, much used and employed... He also showed me his Articles of Religion, printed 1563; but I left mine with him, which was more ancient and orthodox than his'.

Ussher's personal library numbered at his death in 1656 some 10,000 volumes of books and manuscripts; it came to the College in 1661 as the first of the Library's great benefactions. Ussher had always intended to bequeath his library to the College, but straightened financial circumstances caused by the religious wars of the mid seventeenth century forced him to leave this his most valuable asset to his daughter. It was put up for sale in London by her husband and was purchased on the instructions of Cromwell, who

1. The Particular Book of Trinity College: the first Library catalogue, 24 February 1600/01.

Et iudicati sunt mortui ex hiis que scripta erant in libris secundum opera
ipsorum. Et dedit mare mortuos qui in eo erant. Et mors et
infernus dederunt mortuos qui in ipsis erant. Et iudicatum de singulis es
secundum opera ipsorum. Et infernus et mors missi sunt in stagnum ignis. Hec
mors secunda est stagnum ignis. Et qui non est inventus in libro vite
scriptus missus est in stagnum ignis.

LXX

intended it to form the library of a new college in Dublin. With the restoration of Charles II, however, these plans were abandoned and the library was presented to Trinity College. The collection contains important printed books, but its main strength lies in its extraordinary richness in medieval manuscripts.[8]

The acquisition of Ussher's collection marked a major development in the growth of the Library. At about the same time the College was presented with two of its most valuable possessions, the Book of Kells and the Book of Durrow.[9] Both of them are magnificently illustrated manuscript Gospel-books, the Book of Kells dating from the early ninth century, whereas the Book of Durrow is a century older. The Book of Kells [22-6, 28, 30] is named after the monastery in County Meath in which it was kept. After the dissolution of the monastery the manuscript passed into the possession of the diocese of Meath, but was moved to Dublin for safe keeping when Cromwell quartered his cavalry in Kells. In 1661 it was presented to the College by Henry Jones, the Bishop of Meath. The Book of Durrow [27, 31-3], associated with the Columban monastic settlement of Durrow in County Offaly, also came to the College as a gift from Bishop Jones.

In the original Elizabethan College buildings, which formed a small square known as the 'Quadrangle', the Library was housed above the Scholars' chambers. Records dealing with the running of the Library during the first hundred years or so of its existence are scanty, but the Particular Book offers us a few glimpses into contemporary activity. The books were placed on the shelves in the manner customary at the time, with the fore-edges, rather than the spines, facing outwards. A number of books acquired in the seventeenth century still have their original shelfmarks on the fore-edge [3] but unfortunately many others were trimmed when they were rebound and it is difficult to identify the volumes referred to by the somewhat sketchy entries in the early catalogues and binding records. The books were not chained individually, as can be seen from the fact that sufficient numbers exist in contemporary bindings with no marks of chains. The Particular Book records, however, that, in 1611, 'ye keeper of ye library' was paid '3d. for mending a chayne'; it is to be assumed that a chain was stretched across the front of each shelf to prevent the books being removed.[10]

The office of Library Keeper was first held, from 1601 to 1605, by Ambrose Ussher, brother of James. There are regular entries in the Particular Book for payments of 11s 3d a quarter to him and his successors 'for keeping ye library'. In 1627 it was resolved that 'ye custody of ye Library is devolved to one of ye Senior ffellowes in perpetuum: his stipend is six pounds per annum'. The stipend may have changed over the years but this in effect was the way in which the custody of the Library was exercised until the mid twentieth century, when the first full-time Librarian was appointed. Accession to the office of Librarian was not always regarded with enthusiasm by the appointed Fellow, as can be judged from a letter written by George Berkeley, the philosopher (Librarian 1709-10), in which he commented: 'I am lately enterd into my Citadell in a disconsolate Mood, after having passd the better part of a sharp & bitter day in the Damps & mustly [*sic*] solitudes of the Library without either Fire or any thing else to protect Me from the Injuries of the Snow that was constantly driving at the Windows & forceing it's Entrance into that wretched Mansion, to the keeping of which I was this day sennight elect'd under an inauspiciary Planet. What adds to my Vexation is that the Senior Fellows have this Evening naild up my Lord Pembroke's Books in Boxes; and so deprivd Me of the only Entertainment I could propose

2. The 'Dublin Apocalypse': the wicked are turned into hell (MS 64, fol. 34v).

to myself in that place...'[11]

In another letter, of 1722, he also remarked that the Library 'is at present so old and ruinous, and the books so out of order, that there is little attendance given'[12], though, as Anne Crookshank points out,[13] this comment was perhaps a little unfair, as a new library (now the Old Library) was almost finished by this date.

The generally unhealthy state of the Library had been brought about by both external and internal factors. In September 1689 the College was occupied by the Jacobite army and the Fellows and Scholars turned out; much of the College was wrecked by the troops and the Library was broken into, but fortunately the contents were saved from damage. In 1706 Narcissus Marsh, a former Provost but at that time Archbishop of Armagh, replied to the criticism of an Oxford correspondent about the state of the books by explaining that, during the rebuilding of the Hall the Library had provided an eating place for the students, with the books 'laid in heaps in some void rooms'.[14] Marsh continued: 'the Books not being chained cannot easily be secur'd, especially seeing they have no standing Library Keeper, But one of the Junior Fellows is chosen every year into that office, for which He only has six Pounds Salary'. He reported that, during his Provostship, after the election of each new Librarian, 'I carry'd Him into the Library, examined all the Books in his presence, and gave him a charge of them, & then at the end of the year w^{n} another Library Keeper was chosen, I carry'd both the old and new Library Keeper up, & run over all the Library, as before (which was not above two Hours' work), & what books were wanting I made the old Library Keeper restore or pay for to buy others of the same kind in their stead, & gave the New Librarian his charge; and doing this

3. J. Gobellinus, *Pii II pontificis commentarii rerum memorabilium* (1584), showing the original fore-edge shelfmark.

every year I kept the books entirely together, whilst I govern'd that Colledge.'

Marsh also complained that he found the College Statutes too restrictive in limiting the use of the Library to the Provost and Fellows and to others only in the company of one of them. However, even as Provost, he was unable to do anything to rectify this and he determined, therefore, to establish a library that would allow more general access. This library, which now bears his name, was sited not within the College but next to St Patrick's Cathedral and had as its purpose to admit 'all Graduats and Gentlemen'.[15]

The College had by this time accepted the need to house its own Library more adequately and on 1 June 1709 the Irish House of Commons petitioned the Queen for a sum of £5000 for the building of a new library. Further sums of the same amount had to be granted in 1717 and 1721 before it was completed. One episode not related in Anne Crookshank's chapter on the building of the Library is that recorded in the extraordinary entry in the College Register for 24 September 1717, which reports that the College offered the degree of LL.D. to any member of the Irish House of Commons who desired it, as a gesture of thanks for their address to the King for £5000 to complete the Library. Thirty-seven MPs took up the offer the following year![16]

By 1732 the College had a magnificent new Library [5]. Into it were moved the books purchased during the previous 130 years, together with the great benefactions, the donors of which are still commemorated in gold letters on the freize above the bookcases in the Long Room: Ussher; Charles II, to whom is given the credit for the Library's acquisition of Ussher's collection; William Palliser, Archbishop of Cashel, who, in 1726, bequeathed from his collection all the books that were not already in the Library; and Dr Claudius Gilbert, Vice-Provost and Professor of Divinity [10]. Gilbert's collection, of some 13,000 volumes, came to the Library in 1735, after the building was completed, and so the books are in their original position and order. Browsing through this section of the Long Room is, therefore, like being in an eighteenth-century library, with the books arranged according to the subdivisions of the time, including divinity (biblical criticism, Church Fathers, ecclesiastical history), law, natural philosophy (mathematics, geography, history), reference works, and literature.[17]

The opening of the new Library building seems to have had the effect of attracting further donations. In 1741 Dr John Stearne, Vice-Chancellor and Bishop of Clogher, bequeathed a collection of manuscripts relating to seventeenth-century Irish history and including the depositions of sufferers in the 1641 rebellion.[18] In 1786 the Library acquired from Sir John Sebright the collection of Irish manuscripts that had been bequeathed to him by Edward Lhuyd, the philologist. This collection contains many important items, including the Book of Leinster [40] and the Brehon law commentaries, a central monument of pre-Anglo-Norman law.[19]

In 1802 the size of the Library was increased by nearly fifty per cent at one fell swoop with the acquisition of the library of Hendrik Fagel, *Greffier* and chief minister of the Netherlands at the time of Napoleon's invasion. The Fagel collection contains a number of works of individual importance but it is significant also because of the fact that it consists mainly of continental works — Dutch, French, German, Italian — which had hitherto been poorly represented in the Library. It was placed in a separate room at the east end of the Long Room, where it still stands today [108]. The printed books in the collection are its major strength [105-15],[20] but it also contains important maps [119-22] and manuscripts.

Within a short space of time other smaller but notable additions were made to the Library. In 1805 Henry George Quin bequeathed a collection of 127 volumes, of great value both because Quin sought out the best editions available and because he either bought copies which were already in fine bindings or else had them rebound by the most accomplished binders of the time [127-36].[21] Thirty-two years later the Librarian, Franc Sadleir, gave the Library the fourteenth-century manuscript that has become known as the 'Dublin Apocalypse' [2]. The acquisition of this manuscript was the result of a strange deal made between Sadleir and the Board of the College, by which Sadleir presented the manuscript to the Library and received in return a series of uncatalogued yearbooks.[22]

In 1801 the status of the Library was fundamentally altered by the passing of the Copyright Act, which gave it the right to claim from publishers, without charge, a copy of every book, pamphlet, map and periodical published in the British Isles. Legal deposit in these islands had begun in 1610, when Sir Thomas Bodley concluded an agreement with the Stationers' Company granting the library of the University of Oxford the right to receive a free copy of every book printed by the Company, whose members included all the English printers except the university presses in Oxford and Cambridge. This was a voluntary agreement and it was not until the Press Licensing Act of 1662 that the deposit of books was made legally enforceable. This act required publishers to deposit copies of all new books with the Royal Library in London and the libraries of the two English universities. In 1709, following the Act of Union, legal deposit legislation was extended to Scotland and, a century later, the Irish Act of Union of 1801 and the Copyright Act of the same year extended the legislation to Ireland. A significant factor in this decision was an attempt to stop the constant piracy of English publications. Two legal deposit libraries were established in Ireland, Trinity College and the law library at the King's Inns; the latter retained the legal deposit privilege only until the Copyright Act of 1836, which largely established the pattern that exists today of legal deposit libraries covered by British legislation. Since Irish independence in 1922, the legislation of the United Kingdom and the Republic of Ireland has maintained the reciprocal rights of legal deposit, by which five British libraries (the British Library, the Bodleian Library Oxford, Cambridge University Library and the national libraries of Scotland and Wales) receive Irish publications as well as British ones and, similarly, Trinity receives both British and Irish books and periodicals. Under Irish legislation, the National Library of Ireland, the university colleges in Cork, Dublin and Galway, and St Patrick's College Maynooth are also entitled to claim legal deposit copies of items published in the Republic. British and Irish law has always included legal deposit legislation in the acts dealing with copyright (hence the rather misleading term 'copyright library'), but the publishers' duties of legal deposit have for long been separated from their rights of copyright protection.

Legal deposit legislation ensures that, in certain specified libraries, there is a collection of all the publications of a country, thus benefiting scholars who need access to as complete a collection as possible of the literature of their subjects. The privilege of receiving publications in this way does, however, impose obligations on the library; for example material received under legal deposit is not normally discarded. Out-of-date reference books, literature that is no longer in vogue, runs of magazines and journals, children's and school books — the type of material that is eventually thrown away by most libraries — are kept by a legal deposit library, so that, in a few places at least, these items are permanently available. Eventually they become the primary source material for the scholar of the future, in the same way as the nineteenth- and early-

4. The 'Brian Boru' Harp.

twentieth-century materials already are for the scholar of the present.

The storage of such a vast quantity of material does, however, become a major problem, and from the nineteenth century onwards the increasingly effective application of the Copyright Act has meant that the development of Trinity College Library has been dominated by the need for more and more storage space. In 1844 hinged bookcases were added to the gallery of the Long Room; in 1860 the gallery and ceiling of the Long Room were remodelled and the gallery shelved with new bookcases; and in 1892 the open colonnades below the Long Room were filled in to form bookstacks. By the end of the nineteenth century the Library's collection had risen to about a quarter of a million volumes.

After the First World War the shortage of storage space had again become critical and the College decided to build a new reading room separate from 'the Library'. In 1937 the Reading Room (now known as the 1937 Reading Room) was opened, with the Hall of Honour, a war memorial for members of the College who had died in the Great War, serving as the entrance hall. Books were delivered to the Reading Room by means of an underground conveyor from the Old Library.

The 1937 Reading Room relieved the Library's space problem for a time, chiefly by providing additional reading places for the expanding College, but within twenty years plans were under way for another library building. By 1960 the College was in a position to hold an international architectural competition for a new building to hold a million volumes and provide nearly five hundred reader places. This was considered to be adequate for many years of growth. The New Library (now the Berkeley Library), built to a design by Paul Koralek, was opened in 1967 but was full within a few years of its completion. It was decided that lesser-used material could be stored more cheaply away from the College campus, and so, in 1975, a book repository, shared with the National Library of Ireland and Dublin Public Libraries, was opened at Santry in the northern suburbs of Dublin. From time to time parts of the Library have been housed in various buildings on the campus. At present there are, in addition to the Old Library, the Berkeley Library and the 1937 Reading Room, the Lecky Library (1978) in the Arts and Social Sciences Building, and a temporary science library (1981) in the Luce Hall. The College also has a medical library at St James's Hospital. The total stock is now almost three million volumes, and the annual intake of 50,000 books and 80,000 periodical issues requires nearly a mile of additional shelving each year. As well as providing the normal university library services to staff and students of the College, the Library is also used by scholars from Ireland and abroad. Its collections are available to the wider public either through the inter-library loan service to a local library or to personal visitors who cannot obtain the material they need in any other library. It also provides an information service to government departments, semi-state bodies and private companies.

Providing for the needs of tourists also plays an important part in its activities. In 1881 exhibition cases were installed in the Long Room to display the Book of Kells and other treasures, and members of the public were admitted for the first time. But, both before this date and since, distinguished visitors to Dublin have been shown the Library and its collections, some of them subsequently describing their visit in print. Nineteenth-century 'tourists' included King George IV in 1821, Sir Walter Scott in 1825, and Mr Gladstone in 1877. In 1849, during the royal visit to Ireland, Queen Victoria and Prince Albert were shown the Book of Kells, and the Queen recorded in her journal: 'Dr Todd ... showed us some very interesting manuscripts and relics, including St Columba's Book (in which we wrote our names)'.[23] In fact the

5. The Old Library today.

page on which they wrote was a supernumerary leaf, which did not belong to the original volume and was removed for separate storage when the Book of Kells was rebound in 1953. The widespread myth that Queen Victoria signed the Book of Kells is not, therefore, strictly true.

The permanent display in the Long Room now consists of the books of Kells and Durrow, together with other early Christian manuscripts and various items not normally associated with a library. The most outstanding of these is the 'Brian Boru' Harp [4], which was presented to the College by William Conyngham in the eighteenth century. This elaborately carved harp, for long associated with Brian Boru, high king of Ireland who died in AD 1014, dates in fact from the fifteenth or sixteenth century. It is, nonetheless, the oldest known example of the medieval Irish harp still in existence. The soundbox consists of a hollow box of willow and it has metal strings which were plucked with long fingernails.[24]

Before concluding this brief survey of the Library's history a word needs to be said about the work being done to preserve the collections for the future. About 200,000 visitors a year pass through the Long Room, and much of the income that they generate is used to support the work of the Conservation Laboratory, which was set up in 1974. Large parts of

L731-3

~~14~~ 797

shiney new-moon maybe sinking on the hills. Wont it be great that time to have my two hands stretched around you and I squeezing kisses on your puckered lips till I'd feel a kind of pity for the Lord God does ~~bi~~ be sitting lonesome through the ages an his golden ~~###~~ chair.

Pegeen

Go on talking that way, Christy Mahon. I never heard till this day a man could talk at all.

Christy

Let you wait untill the spring time for to hear me talk, and we straying in the lonesome glens drinking a sup from a well, and making kisses maybe with our wetted ~~lips~~ mouths, or gaming in a gap of sunshine with yourself stretched back unto your neck ~~maybe~~ place in the flwowers of the earth.

Pegenn (in a low voice)

I'd be nice so is it?

Christy

If the mitred ~~bisph~~ bishops would see you that ~~tam~~ time they'd be the like of the holy prophets, I'm thinking, do be straining the bars of paradise to set their eyes on the Lady Helen abroad does be pacing all roads back and forward with a nosegay in her shawl.

(rhythm?) (on folder)

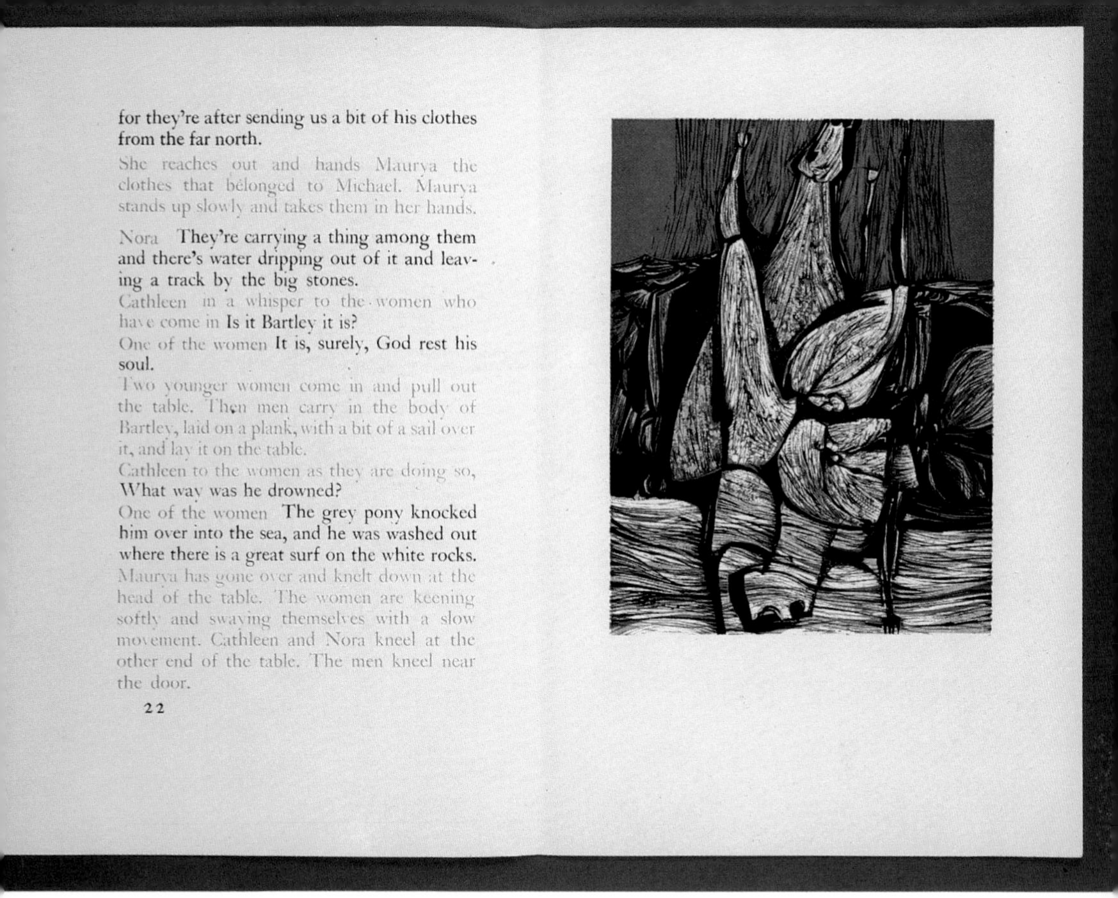

for they're after sending us a bit of his clothes from the far north.

She reaches out and hands Maurya the clothes that belonged to Michael. Maurya stands up slowly and takes them in her hands.

Nora They're carrying a thing among them and there's water dripping out of it and leaving a track by the big stones.

Cathleen in a whisper to the women who have come in Is it Bartley it is?

One of the women It is, surely, God rest his soul.

Two younger women come in and pull out the table. Then men carry in the body of Bartley, laid on a plank, with a bit of a sail over it, and lay it on the table.

Cathleen to the women as they are doing so, What way was he drowned?

One of the women The grey pony knocked him over into the sea, and he was washed out where there is a great surf on the white rocks.

Maurya has gone over and knelt down at the head of the table. The women are keening softly and swaying themselves with a slow movement. Cathleen and Nora kneel at the other end of the table. The men kneel near the door.

22

FAETH FIADHA: THE BREASTPLATE OF SAINT PATRICK
TRANSLATED BY THOMAS KINSELLA WITH DESIGNS BY GERRIT VAN GELDEREN

THE DOLMEN PRESS

6 (far left). J. M. Synge: late typescript draft of *The playboy of the western world,* with Synge's manuscript alterations.

7 (above). *Riders to the sea,* by J. M. Synge, edited by Robin Skelton; linocuts by Tate Adams. (Dolmen Edition VIII.) 1969. Trial setting printed in twenty-eight or twenty-nine proof copies in 1963.

8 (left). *Faeth fiadha: the breastplate of Saint Patrick,* translated by Thomas Kinsella; designs by Gerrit van Gelderen. Title page of one of ten handcoloured copies, printed on vellum.

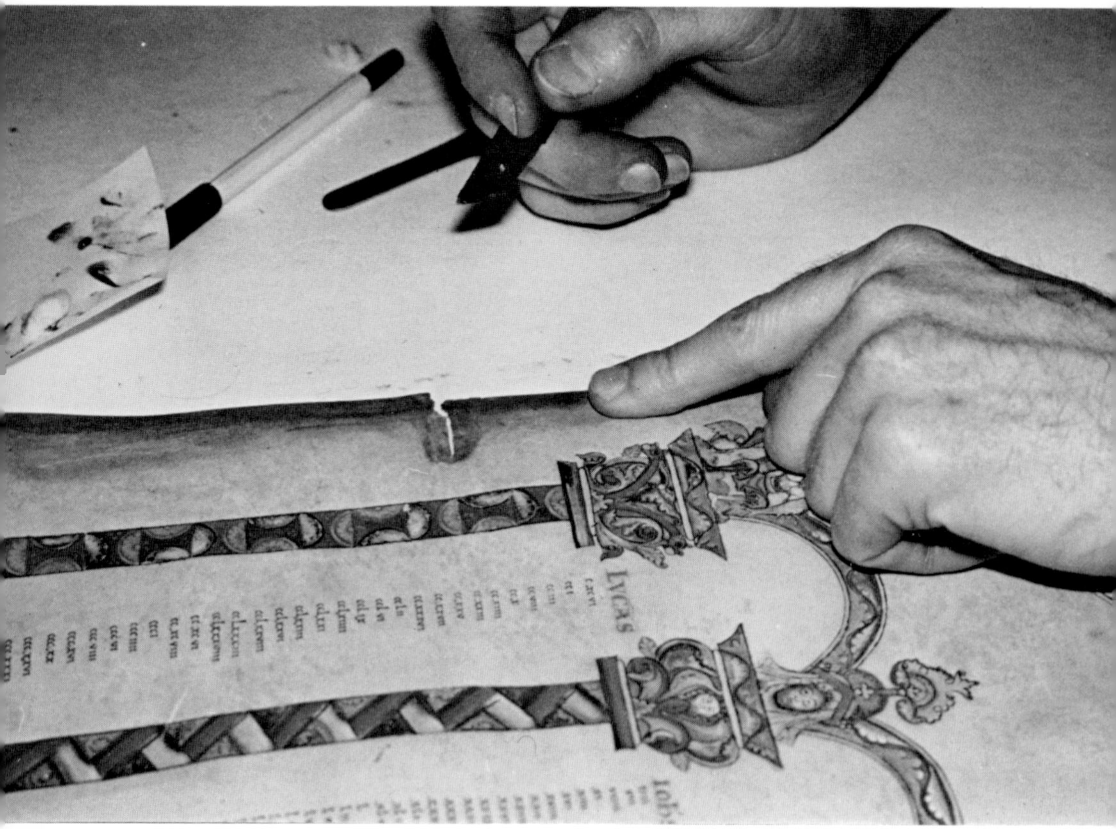

9. Conservation Laboratory: cleaning the old binding adhesive from a leaf of the Winchcombe Psalter.

the collections of most libraries are deteriorating — some because of excessive use or improper handling; some because they were (or are) stored in unsuitable conditions; others because they have self-destruction built into them. The paper that has been used to make books since the mid nineteenth century is made from wood pulp, which contains lignin and other substances that, over a period of years, cause the paper to become brittle. Major libraries are now having to face the fact that large parts of their collections are literally disintegrating on the shelves. Many library users are aware of the problem of 'brittle paper' in late-nineteenth- and early-twentieth-century books and periodicals, particularly newspapers. It is, however, now becoming apparent that this problem is more widespread than had been thought and that action will have to be taken if the books published in this century and the last are to be preserved for the future. The problem occurs on such a scale that international co-operation between the major libraries will be necessary to ensure that the techniques currently available — mass deacidification, microfilming and the use of digital optical discs — are used to maximum effect. Trinity College Library is playing a part in these discussions but at present the work of the Conservation Laboratory is concentrated on the collections of manuscripts and early printed books. Tasks recently undertaken include substantial preservation work on the Book of Mulling [35], the

Garland of Howth, the Winchcombe Psalter [9, 68, 70] and the Matthew Paris manuscript MS 177 [66].[25] The Laboratory is also carrying out refurbishing of the printed books in the Long Room and of the Library's collection of nineteenth-century Ordnance Survey maps of Ireland. The Conservation Laboratory is therefore playing a major role in preserving the Library's treasures for the benefit of future generations.

NOTES

1. TCD MUN/V/1/1r, fol.216v.
2. J.G. Smyly, 'The Old Library: extracts from the Particular Book', *Hermathena* 49 (1935) 166-83.
3. TCD MS 2160a.
4. William O'Sullivan, 'The Library before Kinsale', *Annual bulletin of the Friends of the Library of Trinity College Dublin* (1952) 10-14.
5. Smyly, 'The Old Library', pp 172-3.
6. J.P. Mahaffy, 'The Library of Trinity College Dublin: the growth of a legend', *Hermathena* 12 (1903) 68-78.
7. William Brereton, *Travels in Holland, the United Provinces, England, Scotland and Ireland, 1634-1635*, edited by E. Hawkins. Manchester: Chetham Society, 1844, p. 143.
8. See pages 97-110.
9. See pages 38-56.
10. Smyly, 'The Old Library', p. 170.
11. *The works of George Berkeley, Bishop of Cloyne*, edited by A.A. Luce and T.E. Jessop. London: Nelson, 1948-57, vol. 8, p. 24. The Earl of Pembroke gave £500 to the College for the purchase of books in 1698 and these may be the ones mentioned.
12. *The works of Berkeley*, vol. 8, p.126.
13. See page 16.
14. Letter from Marsh to Dr Thomas Smith, 19 January 1706, reprinted in *Christian examiner*, second series, 2 (1833) 762, and J.W. Stubbs, *The history of the University of Dublin from its foundation to the end of the eighteenth century*. Dublin: Hodges Figgis; London: Longmans Green, 1889, pp 172-3.
15. Muriel McCarthy, *All graduates and gentlemen: Marsh's Library*. Dublin: O'Brien Press, 1980, p. 36.
16. TCD MUN/V/5/2, pp 485 and 489, Board register 24 September 1717 and 10 March 1718.
17. F. M. Higman, 'Holdings and acquisitions in French, 1750-1850', *Hermathena* 121 (1976) 100-8.
18. See pages 111-12.
19. See pages 57-66.
20. See pages 159-169.
21. See pages 184-196.
22. B. Meehan, 'A note on the Dublin Apocalypse', *Scriptorium* 38 (1984) 82-3.
23. Queen Victoria, *Leaves from the journal of our life in the Highlands...tours in England and Ireland...*, edited by A. Helps. London: Smith Elder, 1868, p. 182.
24. R. Ó Floinn, 'Wooden harp — the "Brian Boru" harp', in *Treasures of Ireland: Irish art 3000 BC — 1500 AD*, ed. by Michael Ryan. Dublin: Royal Irish Academy, 1983, p. 180.
25. Anthony Cains, 'Repair treatments for vellum manuscripts', *The Paper Conservator* 7 (1982-3) 15-23.

10. Bust of Claudius Gilbert (1670-1743) by Simon Vierpyl.

THE LONG ROOM

ANNE CROOKSHANK

Despite the fact that practically every tourist to Dublin visits it, the Long Room of the Old Library of Trinity College Dublin has never been seriously studied [11]. All the chapters devoted to the Library in books on the history of the College concentrate on the books themselves and give only a very bare and inaccurate account of this remarkable room which, as it appears today, is the successful marriage of the ideas of the eighteenth-century architect Thomas Burgh and the mid-nineteenth-century partnership of Deane and Woodward. A very important component in its appearance is the collection of marble busts, which lines both sides of the room and is the only major collection of such historical and portrait busts in Ireland. Unfortunately there is very little documentation about them, but, for the building and later alterations of the room, extensive if incomplete contemporary evidence survives in the College archives and in the Board minutes.[1]

The decision to build a new library was taken in 1709, by which time the series of rooms in which the books had previously been housed had become totally inadequate. Complaints were being voiced with all the firmness that our seventeenth-century ancestors had at their command. Bishop Berkeley's remark made in a letter to Sir John Perceval in October 1722 that 'the library is at present so old and ruinous, and the books so out of order, that there is little attendance given'[2] is rather unfair, as by 1722 Burgh's library was nearly completed. The fitting out of the Long Room was started soon afterwards and must have taken up most of the Librarian's interests and time. But it indicates graphically the conditions that made the College authorities act.

The money for the building was obtained by successive applications for parliamentary grants in 1709, 1717 and 1721, when in each case £5000 was granted. There are virtually no Board minutes connected with the building of the Library, but one for 12 May 1712 says that 'the Foundation of the Library was laid, the Provost and Fellows being present'. Thomas Burgh, Surveyor General of Ireland, was the architect and indeed there really was no choice, as in 1712 no other architect of any standing was available in Dublin. Burgh had already shown his merits in a number of buildings in the city including the old Custom House and work in Dublin Castle, but the Library in Trinity was to become his undoubted masterpiece.

The prototype that was probably in the minds of the Provost and Fellows when they decided to build was the library of Trinity College Cambridge,[3] a work by Sir Christopher Wren, built between 1676 and 1699. The size of the Cambridge building had been determined by its site on one side of a courtyard, and the same consideration helped to determine the size and placing of the Library in Dublin, as at that date there were

11. The Long Room.

LITERARIA INSTRU
oo
nn
mm
ll
kk
ii
hh
gg
ff
ee
dd
cc
bb
aa

buildings forming three sides of a square, which was completed by the construction of the Library. Of these buildings only the Rubrics remain, so that the Library was virtually a free-standing block for over one hundred years, though since the building of the Berkeley Library and the Arts Building it has once again formed the side of a square. The actual building, though longer than Wren's, took many ideas from the Cambridge library; most obviously the main chamber was placed over open arcades, a precaution certainly in Cambridge, and probably in Dublin, to preserve the books from damp. Burgh's ground floor was divided longitudinally down the centre by a wall, so that it must have formed on the side of the Fellows' Garden a charmingly private walk, though on the other side the arcades were in more general use [12]. Since these arcades were filled in in 1892 to form book stacks, the outward appearance of the Library has been drastically changed for the worse, as the size of the building required the emphasis the arcades would have given it [5]. Unlike Cambridge, the building was terminated by pavilions, which projected slightly and abutted at both ends of the north side to existing ranges of buildings. The measurements of the Long Room compare with those of the Cambridge library, as it has an overall length of 209 feet 3 inches (63.78 m) and a width of 40 feet 3 inches (12.27 m); Cambridge is 191 feet 6 inches (58.37 m) by 38 feet (11.58 m). It was therefore conceived with great foresight and shows a remarkable faith in the future of Ireland and of the College by men who had lived through very violent and changing times. It is worth stressing that the size of the Library at that date was minimized because it consisted only of a first floor, except at the end pavilions. The accommodation included lecture rooms and offices as well as the Long Room, which was used as a book store and reading room. The Library was really the first building seriously designed in Trinity College for the specialist purpose of teaching.

The puzzling feature of the size of the Long Room is that it had from the beginning a gallery running the whole way round, thereby doubling its potential space in comparison with Trinity College Cambridge. This appears not to have been used for some years and it is very hard to imagine how the authorities envisaged needing so much room. Acquisitions to the Library were relatively few before the Copyright Act of 1801. After that date, when by law a copy of every book published in the British Isles had, if claimed, to be deposited in the Library, the accumulation soon filled up the space.

The Bursar's accounts give an excellent picture of the details of the building operation and the care that was taken to check the accuracy of bills. Professional measurers were employed throughout the building operation. They assessed, for instance, the amount of brickwork completed, or the square footage of ceiling painted or plastered, and on this basis worked out the bills. John Connell was the measurer throughout the main building operations, but towards the end other measurers were making up the accounts, including in 1733 and 1734 William Halfpenny, the English architect and author of a much-used builder's pattern book. He signed accounts for painting in the Library on 14 April 1733, and for 'the plane ceiling in the MS room' in 1734. These measurers' accounts are among the most informative as they tend to be the most detailed. One can check from them the progress made in the building. For instance, on 3 September 1722 the College paid the mason Moses Darley's bill, which had been measured by John Connell, who mentions that it includes carved ornaments on the exterior and chimneys. This bill was checked and corrected by Thomas Burgh. The building was clearly almost finished and by 6 November 1723 John Connell was measuring the glazing in 'the Philosophy School' and 'the other rooms at the East end of library'.

One may imagine therefore that any carpentry or joinery paid for from about this date would be for the Long Room itself. This is important, as few of the joiners' bills are measured and very rarely state where precisely the work was done.

As with the measurers, the same principal craftsmen were employed throughout the work. Isaac Wills, the carpenter, was probably not only a carpenter, but the architect's man on the site, a job he did on other occasions. Mr Henry Darley and Mr Moses Darley were the principal masons and members of a family associated for about a hundred and fifty years with the buildings of Trinity College. The joiner was John Sisson. He was sometimes paid for actual work but more often he was the contractor for the joinery work and, like the other main craftsmen, employed other men. Despite the fact that the Library was such an enormous job, other buildings were being put up or repaired in College throughout the period. The same craftsmen's names appear on these accounts as well, giving the impression that they were virtually College employees. They first appeared in 1711, before the Library was started, also working for Thomas Burgh on a new laboratory. The fact that so much other work was being done to the College buildings and the same men were employed accounts for the slow progress, especially in finishing the interiors, for if the shell of the building was finished by late 1723 it seems strange that the Long Room was not ready for more than a decade afterwards.

John Sisson was paid large sums throughout the 1720s and it is evident that a great deal of joinery work in the interior was being undertaken. He was paid £300 in June, August and October 1722, but only £100 in December, for materials and joinery work. Though fewer slips survive for the later years, he continued to be paid considerable sums, usually £200 at a time, throughout 1723, 1724 and 1725. Assuming that there was an even

12. The Old Library about 1820, showing the Fellows' Garden and the open colonnades (J.A. O'Connor, oil on canvas).

more pressing need for lecture rooms, which would of course all have been panelled (a joiner's job), he may have worked on them first, but much of the work would have been for the Long Room, an enormous task for a joiner. In his bills he mentions the woods used; they were nearly always oak but from different sources, including Danzig, England and Ireland.

Interior work, some of which was only removed as late as the 1960s, started in the east pavilion with the two rooms on the ground floor described as the Philosophy School. These were accessible only from the colonnades, as the present east door did not exist and there was no staircase up to the first floor where the manuscripts room was situated. The east pavilion had been glazed by February 1722, and George Spike was paid on 11 November 1723 for work measured in June, for painting the Philosophy School. This included 'guilding with Leafe Gould and painting the Rose in the Scool'. This sounds as though these rooms had elaborate interiors. They were probably the rooms for which John Kelly, the carver who had earlier been employed on the laboratory, was paid in part on 19 December 1722 'for carveing the Imposte Moulding of two Roomes, one Room contains 113 ft. the other 69 ft. in all 102 ft. [his addition appears to be wrong] att 1^{s} 6^{d} a ft. = £15. 3. 0.' He got the final part on 27 May 1723 when Thomas Burgh cut his bill from £19 16s 7½d to £18. Various additional items were included, such as '4 Corinthian Pillastor Heads for a chaire in ye largest room att 10/10^{d} each 2. 3. 4 ... and for a large flower in ye Middle of ye bigg Room — 1-10-0'. However there is no absolute proof that these rooms were in the Library as that word is not included in the bill. Moses Darley's black Kilkenny marble mantelpieces, paid for in July 1723, were probably for these rooms. Spike was also paid in November 1723 for painting the 'Roposetory' where he painted the ceiling black and the 'inside of presses' blue. It is not clear whether this room was in the east or west pavilion, though it was probably on the ground floor of the latter.

The staircase, which must have been built before serious work began on the first floor and was under construction as 'Oak timber sawed for ye stares of ye New Library since ye 30th October 1721', is mentioned in one of Nathan Hill's bills, and Spike was paid 'for painting Ye stays case in ye New Library' in January 1723. Though this staircase was replaced for an unknown reason by Richard Castle's in 1750 [13], many features of the carved detail of Castle's staircase link up with work in the Library and rather indicate that at least some of the woodwork is original. The Library floor was being put in in September 1723, when Isaac Wills annotates an account saying that he has 'cutt up in plank to make an End of the library flower'.

The first of Sisson's accounts definitely associated with the Long Room is dated in November 1728. He had clearly worked from the ground upwards, making bookcases and the panelling, and by November 1728 he was putting in bills for the 'reales and bannistors'. These prove, from an account signed by Thomas Burgh for 3 December 1729, to be 'for the Ballustrade'. He was therefore working on the gallery from 1728. The rails and bannisters are not for the staircases to the gallery, as a separate account exists for them. Isaac Wills, the carpenter, was paid, on 11 December 1732, £115 1s 3d for work in the College, which included 'Gallery staircases 503 ft. in ye stairs and halfe pares of 1½ inch seasoned Irish oak at 5½ a ft. — £11. 10. 6½'. He was also paid for handrails and for 'oak woanscoat up both staircases' and '46 ft. of carving in the freezs' which is annotated in the margin 'to carver Turner'. This is a particularly important account, as the two staircases to the gallery at the west end of the Long Room have been said to come from the seventeenth-century library buildings. Stylistically the story seems unlikely, but the discovery of Wills's accounts proves quite certainly that these beautiful staircases were designed and built for the Long Room [14]. One unfortunate omission in the Bursar's accounts is the bill for the carved capitals supporting the gallery. These are not likely to have been the work of Sisson as they were a 'carver's' job, though he certainly made the pilasters for which he charged, on 3 December 1729, '96 Pallasters with raised pannels and breaks above and below at 8^{s} and 6^{d} each = £40. 16. 0'.

The building work in the Long Room was finished in 1732. On 24 January Sisson was paid for 'deall wainscot' in the gallery, four benches and forty-two window boards. He moved on to the manuscripts room and was paid for Danzig oak. The manuscripts room could be reached only through the Long Room as it was on the first floor of the east pavilion. The back stairs, which were built behind the main staircase, went up to the second storey of the west pavilion, but there were no stairs in the east pavilion. The room above the manuscripts room was approached along the gallery of the Long Room.

Few of the plastering and painting accounts are precisely stated to be for the Long Room, but throughout the building this work was done by George Spike and what appears to be a final account for the painting work was measured by Halfpenny on 14 April 1733,[4] and included work outside and inside the Library, on the stairs and rooms, etc. It is useful in naming the uses put to the rooms in the Library building. The 'Library Keeper's room' was, presumably, that used for the Librarian until 1967 on the first floor of the pavilion and the 'bookbinder's room' was no doubt on the second floor, but it is not easy to decide where the 'observatory' was. It was mentioned earlier, on 28 January 1723, when payments were made to the smith for work on the 'stairs to the Observatory room'. This indicated that it was on the top floor of the west pavilion.

On 20 November 1733, Mr Hudson was paid £60 for placing the books in the Library.[5] This date fits with the building accounts, so that the Long Room must have been ready for use by the end of 1733. It looked very different from now. It had a flat plaster ceiling much lower than that of the nineteenth century, about level with the top of the present bookcases in the gallery. Only some of the bays on the ground floor level were in use for books, though they all appear to have been made. The present low bookcases with scroll ends are an adaptation of the seats seen in the Malton drawing [15]. These are no doubt all part of Sisson's work. Another alteration is the staircase in the centre of the room which is a modern addition. Access to the Library was limited and so security was no problem, nonetheless great care was taken and the manuscripts were isolated in the east pavilion. This undoubtedly explains their remarkable state of preservation.

13. Staircase by Richard Castle in the West Pavilion of the Old Library (1750).

Though the College had spent some money on books from its foundation, the real reason for the Library's size was a series of very generous donations. These were kept together and the names of the donors written, as they still are, in letters of gold above the bay in question [cover]. The two great donors before 1733 were Archbishop Ussher, whose books came to the Library about 1661, and Dr Palliser, Archbishop of Cashel, whose bequest was in 1726. Dr Gilbert, who was Vice-Provost and Professor of Divinity and one of the leading figures in the College, gave his very large collection of books to the Library in his lifetime. Presumably with Trinity College Cambridge in mind, he also left in his will, on his death in 1743, the sum of £500 'for the purchase of busts of men eminent for learning to adorn the library'. The Cambridge library was the first college library in the British Isles to adopt the scheme of displaying such busts, and in 1743 was still the only one to do so, though series of busts became a popular form of decoration in the eighteenth century. The choice of subjects in Cambridge is wide and includes more Roman notables than Greek, and also has a wide range of English literary and scientific figures.[6] The choice for the fourteen busts bought with Gilbert's money must have been decided on by the College and, though nine are the same as examples in Cambridge, five are original subjects. The nine with corresponding busts in Cambridge are Homer, Demosthenes, Socrates, Plato, Cicero, Shakespeare, Milton, Newton and Locke. The five additions in Dublin are Aristotle (a

14. Staircase at the west end of the Long Room (*c.*1730).

strange omission in Cambridge), Bacon (who is included in a later series in Trinity College Cambridge),[7] Robert Boyle the scientist, who was the son of the great Earl of Cork and was born in Ireland, James Ussher the archbishop and benefactor of the Library, and Thomas, eighth Earl of Pembroke who gave the Library £500 for books in 1698. It is surprising that a bust of Archbishop Palliser was not included. All those busts were of dead persons and cannot be regarded as necessarily accurate portraits, though they are frequently considered in this light. The Librarian in the late nineteenth century, the Rev. T. K. Abbott, was so worried that the Demosthenes was not an authentic likeness that he removed it, though it has since been replaced.[8]

The College commissoned the set from Peter Scheemakers, a sculptor of Flemish parentage who settled in London. Only the Shakespeare is fully signed P. Scheemakers, but seven others (Ussher, Locke, Homer, Cicero, Milton, Demosthenes and Pembroke) are signed P.S. We have no notion when these works reached the Library, neither do we know why Scheemakers was selected nor what he was paid, but the English writer Vertue gives us some clues in his *Note-books.* For instance, he reports Scheemakers as 'having been very assiduous in his studies in Rome etc. after the best antique Statues, makeing of most exact and correct Moddels in Clay'. These models included busts as well as statues of 'Fauns, Bacchus, Venus etc.'[9] He also made the monument to Shakespeare in Westminster Abbey, which brought him great popular fame. Vertue adds that Scheemakers was 'also allwayes underworking the others price' and goes on to compare his prices with those of Rysbrack: 'As Mr Rysbrake for a Marble Bust moddel and carving his lowest price was 35 guineas, the other [Scheemakers] woud and dos do it for near ten guineas less'.[10] Assuming that Vertue was accurate, the College must have paid about £27 per bust, making £378 in all. One wonders what the balance went on — transport, etc., or did they, years later, pay for Dr Gilbert's own bust out of the change? Rumour started by a sentence in Horace Walpole's *Anecdotes of painting*[11] attributed these fourteen busts to Roubilliac until W.G. Strickland in his 1916 *Catalogue* of the pictures and busts in the College put the matter right.[12] Walpole had said that Roubilliac 'had little business till Sir Edward Walpole recommended him to execute half the busts at Trinity College, Dublin'. This was probably a misprint for Trinity College Cambridge, as their second set of busts includes seven by Roubilliac.[13] Certainly the only one by him in Trinity College Dublin is the bust of Swift [16] which is fully documented in Faulkner's *Dublin Journal* of 21 March 1749, where it is recorded: 'There is arrived from London a marble bust of the late Rev. Dr. Swift, D.D., D.S.P.D., the workmanship of Mr Ruvilliac. It is done with exquisite skill and delicacy, and is looked upon by persons of taste as a masterpiece. It deserves to be mentioned that the class of Senior Sophisters who, according to academical custom, formed themselves into a senate in the year 1738, applied the money usually laid out in an enter tainment to the purchase of this busto, which they have given to be placed in the College Library, among the heads of other men eminent for genius and learning — an instance of public spirit in young persons worthy of praise and imitation.'

The Swift was the first bust commissioned for the Library, as the students raised the money in 1738, five years before Gilbert's death. However, the Gilbert-bequest busts may have arrived before the Swift, so that Faulkner can say that it is to be placed 'among the heads of other men eminent for genius'. It is inscribed '*Ex dono quartae classis an: 1745 Procurante Digbaeo French*'. A plaster model for it was sold in the sale after Roubilliac's death.[14] The portrait cannot have been taken from life as Swift was not in London after 1738. It was presumably modelled from a painting by Jervas.

After those fifteen busts, others were added at regular intervals until there are now too many for the available sites at the end of the bookcases or in the niches. The next acquired was by Simon Vierpyl, the sculptor who made antique copies for Lord Charlemont in Rome, and later worked on the Casino at Marino, Charlemont House and the City Hall. It is appropriately of Claudius Gilbert [10], and it seems likely that the £34 2s 6d it cost was defrayed from his own bequest. The *Gentleman's Magazine* on 4 February 1758 states that it was done in that year and 'for expression and elegance, does great honour to the taste and skill of the statuary'.[15] Later, in 1835, the College was left another bust by Vierpyl, that of Robert Clayton, Bishop of Clogher. As Clayton died in 1758 this bust may have been made from life. The bust of John Lawson, the Librarian in 1745 and Professor of Divinity from 1753, was commissioned in the year of his death, 1759, from Patrick Cunningham, an interesting Irish sculptor who was a pupil of John Van Nost the younger and one of the first students of the Dublin Societies Schools. He is famous for his bust of Swift in St Patrick's Cathedral. Provost Baldwin, in whose term of office the Library was completed, was also carved by Vierpyl, and this again is a posthumous work as it was done in 1761, three years after the sitter's death. Vierpyl was paid £34 2s 6d for it.

The bust of Dean Delaney by John Van Nost [17] was much admired by the anonymous writer on Delaney in the *Dublin University Magazine* for November 1858, who regarded it as 'the most singular bust in the room'.[16] It was probably done from life as the Dean and his famous wife admired Van Nost's work very much. Mrs Delaney wrote after they visited the sculptor on 14 March 1752: 'If our lawsuits end well, the Dean, I hope, will sit to him. He bought four busts, and bespoke two more for his library'.[17] He is said to be

15. The Long Room in the eighteenth century. Detail from the drawing by James Malton showing seats and reading desks in each bay.

eighty-four on the inscription, and if so must have been sculpted in the year of his death. He does not look this age and it is possible that the inscription is a later addition. The only other eighteenth-century busts are by Edward Smyth, the famous Irish sculptor. The Thomas Parnell is a posthumous work, as Parnell had died in 1718. He was a friend of Pope and Swift and a poet in his own right. His great grandson was the politician Parnell. The second bust by Smyth is of William Clement, who was an MP, a Fellow and professor [18]. He was Vice-Provost of the College from 1743. Provost Baldwin's old age made him responsible to a considerable extent for the building programme in the College in the mid century, including the building of the West Front.

A number of interesting busts were acquired in the early nineteenth century, though the sitters often did not rise to Gilbert's dictum of 'men eminent for learning'. The two royal busts — those of Ernest August, Duke of Cumberland and later King of Hanover, who was appointed Chancellor in 1805, and of George III — are by Peter Turnerelli, the Belfast-born sculptor, who made an international reputation for himself. A more interesting sitter was Edward Sexton, Viscount Pery, who was Speaker of the Irish House of Commons from 1771 to 1785 and an important landowner in Limerick, on whose property new and carefully-planned town developments took place. His bust, done in 1807, is by J.C.F. Rossi, an English sculptor.

The fine bust of Oliver Goldsmith was done in 1827. The College paid the sum of £84 15s 5d for it. It is by an Englishman, William Behnes, who was something of a rival of the Irish sculptor Foley, whose statue of Goldsmith stands outside the West Front. The bust of Burke, by an unknown hand, was also a later acquisition and is not a contemporary likeness.

In the first half of the nineteenth century the College was unusually interested in commemorating its staff, and a great many portraits both in paint and in marble were commissioned, usually at rather low prices, and sometimes the results achieved are less than the highest quality. However, Thomas Kirk served the College well with his busts of Matthew Young (dated 1827), William Magee (1840), Samuel Kyle (1842), Thomas Elrington (undated), Bartholomew Lloyd (during the 1830s), Charles W. Wall (1840) and George Millar (undated). All were distinguished Trinity men, the first four becoming bishops or archbishops and three, Elrington, Kyle and Lloyd, provosts.

Thomas Kirk was probably the most popular sculptor of his generation resident in Ireland, and his son Joseph Robinson Kirk inherited his business, though he was never as good an artist. However, as the sculptor of the four allegorical figures on the campanile, his work has become part of the daily Trinity scene. The Long Room contains a bust by him of Professor Rudolph Thomas Siegfried (1864).

Christopher Moore, an Irish sculptor who was particularly successful making portrait busts of Regency notabilities during his long residence in London, is represented in the Library's collection by three examples of his work: one is unidentified, the others are of Thomas Langlois Lefroy (1839) who became Lord Chief Justice in 1852, and William Conyngham, Lord Plunket (1846), who had been appointed Lord Chancellor of Ireland in 1830. Two busts by two great Irish Victorian sculptors are the James Whiteside, who was a chief justice, by Patrick MacDowell, and Sir William Rowan Hamilton by John Henry Foley. It is a posthumous bust as Hamilton died in 1865, and Foley made the bust in 1867, but it is based on an earlier plaster by Thomas Kirk. Hamilton was the great mathematician, and should be the patron professor of every student as he must be unique in having been appointed a professor while still a student. Two great political Irishmen represented in

16. Bust of Jonathan Swift by Louis François Roubilliac, commissioned in 1745.

the collection are the Duke of Wellington by Sir Francis Chantrey, the English sculptor, and Wolfe Tone, a bust by the Irish artist Thomas Farrell, made in 1852 but only added to the collection in the 1920s.

An Irish sculptor whose work is little known nowadays is Joseph Watkins, who sculpted William Connor Magee in 1869, a graduate who became Archbishop of York. Another mid-nineteenth-century bust in plaster, which was signed by J.E. Jones in 1862, is of a Librarian, John Adam Malet. Provost Humphrey Lloyd is represented by a posthumous bust by Albert Bruce Joy done in 1888 which was, however, regarded as a good likeness by his widow. The only bust by a woman sculptor is the posthumous portrait of Bishop James Thomas O'Brien, done in 1905 by Blanche Stack, and in view of the august surroundings in which it lives, it has a somewhat inappropriately pretty leafy base.

Taken together, the busts in the Long Room form a unique example of the contribution of Irish artists to this form of sculpture, for practically every artist of any importance, except Hogan,[18] is represented. The changing styles of the artists and the attitudes of our ancestors in their choice of subject matter are also most fascinatingly displayed.

Few alterations were made to the appearance of the Long Room till the mid nineteenth century and few references to it exist in the century after it was completed. But, from a Board minute of 22 July 1777, it appears that the ceiling shown in the Malton drawing may not be the one put up about 1730 though it may be a replica of the original as it has the heavy geometrical divisions typical of the 1730s. The minute says that 'the new ceiling of the library shall be in compartments and not coloured; and that it shall be proceeded on, as soon as the plan and Estimate shall be approved of by the Board'. Another hint as to the original appearance of the room comes in an account of 6 December 1753 where Hu Darley is paid for various items of work including 'painting 7 new ladders green for the library'. The overall brown is clearly a nineteenth-century colour scheme. A splendid description of the room, giving an idea of how it was used, is included in the article on Dean Delaney in the *Dublin University Magazine* of November 1858[19] which mentions the catalogues on the centre tables, a feature which remained until the 1960s, and the marble busts 'at each division of the oaken recesses'. Originally they had been placed on the balcony where they can be seen in the Malton drawing, but no doubt as more were acquired, and as the balcony was more used, it was easier to place them as they are now.

By the 1850s, the balconies were already needed for books and, in his report to the Board on 19 November 1858, the Librarian said that 'there are now about 2000 vols for which no room can be found in the Library'. Intake of books had increased fantastically as a result of the Copyright Act of 1801. In the two years between November 1856 and November 1858 the increase was 4935 books, and in those honest days losses were very small, usually only one or two. In the 1856 report 'only one volume was found to be missing' and the one missing from 1855 was 'recovered it having been accidentally misplaced'.

But from the Board minutes it does not seem as if book storage was the primary reason for the alterations which resulted in 1860. It appears that the roof was in bad enough repair for an examination to be ordered on 15 November 1856 and that, as a result of the ensuing report, the Bursar was instructed 'to get the opinion of Sir Thomas Deane upon the same and also to procure from Mr McCurdy a plan and estimate of an open work roof'. The Board must have been well aware of the provocative nature of their instructions. Mr McCurdy and Sir Thomas Deane were old rivals in College architectural affairs. McCurdy had won the competition for the Museum Building which is in fact built on his ground plan, though the work was carried out under the firm of Deane and Woodward and to the designs of Benjamin Woodward. Naturally, McCurdy was much offended and it was deliberate bravado to invite the same pair to advise on the Library roof. Both parties gave opposing advice and led the College authorities a pretty dance in further examinations, reports, etc. which were really unnecessary. The unfortunate Mr Cockburn, whose building firm eventually carried out the work to Deane and Woodward's specifications, appears as a reluctant buffer between the two parties.

Because of all the endless vacillation which ensued, the Library roof practically collapsed in October 1858, and the ceiling had to be shored up as an emergency measure. The points of argument were the extent of the rotting of the timbers in the roof, where Mr McCurdy's gloomy view appears to have been justified, and the state of the floor, where Deane and Woodward had actually to admit that they were wrong. As a firm, they were clearly not very good at assessing the condition of old buildings. Their solution to the problem was also more radical than McCurdy's and it is impossible to decide if the right decision was taken as none of the drawings survives. McCurdy proposed to keep the old ceiling and prop up the roof with iron trusses. He was naturally supported in this scheme by Mr Mallett, a manufacturer of iron work, though he advocated 'a construction different from that suggested by Mr McCurdy'. Mallett thought the job 'could be done without touching the slates or lead of the roof, and without injuring the ceiling'.[20] He also intended to convert 'the space between the ceiling and the roof into a large chamber for books'.[21] What is more, he thought he could do it all for £2459.

There is evidence in the minutes of a fierce controversy, and even after the contract for the rebuilding had been signed with Cockburn on 17 September 1859 (using Deane and Woodward plans), efforts were made in the Board to have the plans reconsidered. But 'the Board saw no reason to alter their former decision at present, and no vote was come to'.[22] In fact all of Deane and Woodward's suggestions appear to have been accepted as far back as January 1858, and despite arguments these plans were clearly substantially carried out in 1860. The reasons given on 2 January 1858 for favouring Messrs Deane and Woodward's plans instead of Mr McCurdy's included the following points: 'that it did throw the whole weight on the ground, and entirely relieve the walls, which have already in one place been found to be out of plumb; that it will double the accommodation for books . . . That there is danger to the walls of the Library from the contraction and expansion of iron trusses, and that the ceiling if held to such trusses, must necessarily from the same cause be soon shaken and cracked'. Despite proof that the floor was sound, Deane and Woodward insisted (certainly correctly) on underpinning it with stone columns which still exist, now hidden in the book stacks. Originally they must have appeared very unsightly in the open colonnades. Deane and Woodward apparently raised the roof line only slightly, their great wooden barrel vault was fitted into a considerable void between the original ceiling and the roof. The possible change of roof line and the desecration of a hallowed interior called forth much public criticism which is summed up by an anonymous writer in the *Dublin Builder.*[23] He, and no doubt others of his day, was under the impression that the Long Room was opened in about 1593 'having occupied two years in building'. But nonetheless he does not agree with 'some personal correspondence in the daily Journals wherein the architects are accused of vandalism'. He says: 'The alterations now progressing comprise the removal of that ceiling, the substitution of a new cylindrical vault formed of semi-circular oaken ribs, and sheeted with planking of the same material following the curve; the construction of an entirely new roof, *exactly the same outline as before* — though alleged *not* to be so — and the adding of granite columns inside the ambularium central on the arcade piers . . . The Library will be materially improved . . . the architects have . . . surmounted a difficulty most nobly . . . The expenditure will be £7,250.'

17. Bust of Dean Delaney (1684?-1768) by John Van Nost.

Certainly it was a bold decision by the Board and no doubt reflected their admiration for the great Museum Building of Woodward. The Library alterations were Woodward's last work and the Deanes would seem to have supervised the construction, as they were the members of the firm who attended the Board meetings. Woodward died in June 1861 after a long illness. It was Deane too who dealt with the controversy over the wood to be used.[24] He was fully justified in his choice of Canadian white oak, despite the letter Matthew Good, shipwright surveyor to the Board of Trade, wrote to John McCurdy on 15 June 1860 where he says 'I have almost in all instances found it entirely defective after five years'. After over a hundred and thirty years it is still in very good order. But there is nonetheless some doubt as to it being Canadian white oak as the sample sent to Professor Samuel Haughton in June 1860 proved to be British! His scholarly letters on the immense variety of Canadian white oak, and indeed British oak, cannot have been any practical help to Deane, who certainly thought he was using a Canadian white variety. The College was now insuring its property, and concern was shown over various practical points such as the danger of fire from the temporary canvas roof which was coated with a mixture of tar, sand and alum to diminish the risk of fire. When the work was near completion, the Board was worrying over whether 'to clean the old work and leave the new oak unstained'.[25] They clearly decided on staining. The Library was closed on 4 May 1861 'for the purpose of having the books cleaned and arranged'. The work was completed.

Since 1861 no great outward changes have occurred in the appearance of the Old Library. The spiral staircase up to the gallery at the east end of the Long Room was inserted early in 1870. William James Mulhall, a builder, was paid on 22 January 1870 for various alterations and for 'a story of cast iron spiral stairs, and handrail complete, £30-0-0'. More recent restorations have attempted to be invisible — with considerable success. Though it is still a working library, the Long Room is also a showpiece and something of a museum, for it houses changing exhibitions of rare items in the College collection, and such relics as the coat of arms from the first chapel and, above all, the great early Irish manuscripts, the Book of Durrow, the Book of Dimma, the Book of Armagh and the Book of Kells. To them it owes its popularity and its fame but the Long Room is, in its own right, a great Irish work of art.

NOTES

1. Revised version of *The Long Room*, published 1976 in the series 'Gatherum', Dublin: Gifford and Craven. Unless otherwise stated, the information from the College archives comes from the Bursar's Accounts, series TCD MUN/P/2. The Board minutes, series TCD MUN/V/5, are usually dated in the text and are footnoted only where they are not.

2. *The works of George Berkeley, Bishop of Cloyne* edited by A.A. Luce and T.E. Jessop. London: Nelson, 1948-57, vol. 8, p. 126.

3. The facts concerning the library in Trinity College Cambridge are all taken from *An inventory of the historical monuments in the city of Cambridge.* London: Royal Commission on Historical Monuments, 1959, part II, pp 236-41.

4. TCD MUN/P/2/59/14.

5. J.W. Stubbs, *The history of the University of Dublin from its foundation to the end of the eighteenth century.* Dublin: Hodges Figgis; London: Longmans Green, 1889, p. 174.

6. *City of Cambridge*, pp 240-1.

7. *City of Cambridge*, p. 241.

8. T.K. Abbott, 'On the bas-relief of Demosthenes in Trinity College', *Hermathena* 36 (1910) 1-10.

9. *The note-books of George Vertue, relating to artists and collections in England* edited and published by the Walpole Society. Oxford: Walpole Society, 1930-47, vol. 22, Vertue III, p. 44.

10. Vertue, *Note-books*, p. 116.

11. Horace Walpole, *Anecdotes of painting in England.* Strawberry Hill: 1765-71, vol. 4, p. 99.

12. W.G. Strickland, *A descriptive catalogue of the pictures, busts and statues in Trinity College Dublin and in the Provost's House.* Dublin: University Press, 1916. The catalogue contains much additional information on the busts in the Library.

13. *City of Cambridge*, p. 241.

14. Katharine A. Esdaile, *The life and works of L.F. Roubilliac.* London: Oxford University Press, 1928, p. 186.

15. *The Gentleman's Magazine* 28 (1758) 91.

16. *Dublin University Magazine* 52 (1858) 378-9.

17. *Autobiography and correspondence of Mary Granville, Mrs Delaney* edited by Lady Llanover. London: Richard Bentley, 1861, vol. 3, p. 96.

18. There is a memorial by John Hogan to Bishop Brinkley in the hall of the staircase in the west pavilion of the Old Library.

19. *Dublin University Magazine* 52 (1858) 378-9.

20. Board minute, 11 January 1858.

21. Board minute, 24 April 1858.

22. Board minute, 21 January 1860.

23. *The Dublin Builder* 2 (1860) 196.

24. TCD MUN/P/2/363-75 (College buildings papers, April-August 1860).

25. Board minute, 23 March 1861.

18. Bust of William Clement (1707-82) by Edward Smyth.

PAPYRI

B.C. McGING AND H.W. PARKE

The papyrus was a very versatile plant in antiquity, just as other types of sedge still are today. You could eat it, burn it as incense or firewood, and make a whole range of useful goods from it — baskets, ropes, sails, mats, furniture, sandals, boats (even large ones, as Thor Heyerdahl demonstrated with his *Ra* vessels).[1] Its best known and most common use, however, was in the production of writing paper, a use attested in Egypt as early as 3000 BC. Egypt in fact was virtually the only place where the plant grew (there was some in Syria and Babylonia), and almost certainly was the only commercial centre for paper in the Mediterranean world. This resulted in the growth of what was evidently a huge industry, centred on the lower Nile and its Delta and producing enormous quantities of paper both for the extensive home market and for export abroad.[2] If the damp marshlands of Egypt were the main producer of paper in the first place, the dry sands of that same country have proved its best preserver.[3] By far the largest quantities of pieces of papyrus writing paper, papyri as they are called, have been found in Egypt, although the Judaean desert has yielded an interesting store, and there have been freak survivals in the wetter lands of the northern Mediterranean: in the eighteenth century, for instance, 800 rolls of carbonized papyrus were discovered at Herculaneum in Italy, buried in ash from the famous eruption of Mount Vesuvius in AD 79.[4]

After the unrivalled resources of Oxford, Trinity College probably has the next most important collection of Greek papyri among the universities of these islands. Furthermore, it is historically important as one of the earliest collections to be exploited for the purposes of classical scholarship. Around 1885 Trinity acquired some papyri collected by Charles Graves at Luxor in 1882, but most of the several thousand fragments in the Library's possession came from the excavations of Sir W. Flinders Petrie during the 1880s in the Fayyûm district of Egypt. Petrie was, for the time, a comparatively advanced archaeological thinker, in that he appreciated that all finds were of importance and that, to reconstruct the life of the past, the excavator should not set his sights solely on great monuments or gold treasures. He found papyri at Tunis in 1883-4 and at Hawara in 1889, but most interesting was the discovery at Gurob in 1890 of numbers of unspectacular mummies of the Ptolemaic period.[5] When carefully unwrapped, they were found to be cased in a sort of *papier mâché* made from torn scraps of papyrus (called 'cartonnage') – functionally fulfilling the purpose of waste-paper wadding in modern parcels (you could also wrap your purchases from the fish market and elsewhere in used papyrus: Catullus and other Roman poets amusingly complain that this is the fate awaiting their written poetry).[6] Petrie showed his papyrus finds to the Oxford scholar, A.H. Sayce, who persuaded him that J.P. Mahaffy of Trinity College Dublin would be the best man to edit them.[7] Hence their presence in Dublin, although not all of them are there: Petrie also distributed his finds to the British Museum and the Bodleian Library, Oxford.

At that time papyrology was very much in its infancy. In the late 1870s the volume of papyri found in Egypt began to increase dramatically, as a result of a corresponding increase in the demand for the particularly fertile soil found in ancient sites: as the soil was removed in ever increasing quantities, so a greater number of papyri began to turn up.[8] Not many classical scholars would have been immediately interested in these scruffy bits of papyrus containing scarcely legible writing in Greek, which was often of a quite illiterate kind. In the British Isles scholarly attention was focused almost exclusively on the philological study of authors from the golden periods of Greek and Latin literature. But Mahaffy was not altogether in the traditional mould of contemporary scholars: his interest in social history, for instance, was rare in the nineteenth century. The material that Sayce showed him proved to be of the most miscellaneous kind: fragments of private letters, all sorts of official documents, and occasionally even examples of high literature. Mahaffy was excited, and recognized at once that, besides the rare possibility of finding lost literary masterpieces, careful study of the papyri would cast much light on the ordinary life and social organization of Ptolemaic Egypt. He proceeded to publish the results of his work in three splendid volumes, the first two edited by himself, the third with the help of J.G. Smyly, a future Regius Professor of Greek and Librarian at Trinity, who in fact did most of the work.[9] Volume one was published in 1891 and coincided with the appearance of Frederic Kenyon's first publications of the exciting British Museum papyri.[10] Papyrology was suddenly a sensation, and Mahaffy was at the centre of it. There had been doubts beforehand about his true scholarly ability, but for the most part these doubts were now dispelled by his fine treatment of the Flinders Petrie papyri.[11] Mahaffy was one of the handful of scholars responsible for setting papyrology on its way to becoming a recognized and valued branch of classical scholarship.

In 1895 the Egypt Exploration Fund sent Hogarth, Grenfell and Hunt specifically to search for papyri, which until this time had merely turned up by accident in excavations looking for other things.[12] In the following years their searches resulted in the recovery of huge numbers of fragments. As a subscriber to the Fund, Trinity received a share of the finds, most notably from the rubbish dumps of Oxyrhynchus, which have proved over the years the richest and most spectacular source of all.

Finally there is in the Library a small number of texts of the Roman and Byzantine periods, whose provenance is unknown.

These, then, are the Greek papyri. It should also be noted that the collection includes some Egyptian papyri in the hieroglyphic, hieratic and demotic scripts.[13] They were, in fact, the very first pieces of all to come to the Library; their arrival in 1840 thus marks the beginning of the collection [19 and 21].

It would be difficult to define what Trinity's 'best' papyri are, and different people would have different opinions. The following selection is arbitrary, but should give some idea of the variety and interest of the material in the Library's possession.

COPIES OF KNOWN WORKS

Homer, *Iliad* 19.291-315 (PAP. Sel. Box inv. 128).[14] Second century AD.

Plato, *Laches* 189 D-E (PAP. F 8A. Pack² 1409). Third century BC. This is over a thousand years older than our earliest parchment authority.

19. Papyrus: Egyptian Book of the Dead in hieroglyphs (nineteenth dynasty: thirteenth century BC).

Xenophon, *Cyropaedia* 1.6.11 and 2.1.30 (PAP. E 9; P. Oxy 4.697: Pack[2] 1546). Third century AD.

Theophrastus, *Characters* 25-26 (PAP. F 11a; P. Oxy. 4.699). Third century AD.

These need little comment. It might be observed, however, that the discovery of literary papyri added a whole new dimension to the editing of classical texts: very often a papyrus fragment gives us the text of an ancient work that is many centuries older than our oldest surviving parchment evidence for the work. For instance, the earliest parchment

20. Papyrus of the third century BC reporting Ptolemy's advances during the Third Syrian War (246 BC).

of Homer goes back to the fifth century AD; the oldest Homeric papyri date from the third century BC, bringing us some six or seven hundred years nearer the original text of Homer. Such a link in the transmission of ancient texts is clearly of the greatest importance.

NEW LITERARY TEXTS

Epigram on the daughters of Lycambes (PAP. F 90; Pack² 1752).[15] Third century BC.

This is an interesting piece in the style of Archilochus of Paros, the seventh-century BC lyric poet. It refers to the famous story of Archilochus' attempt to marry Neobule, the daughter of Lycambes. She was promised to him, but then Lycambes changed his mind, and Archilochus attacked the family in his poetry with such ferocity that the daughters hanged themselves. In this poem the daughters themselves tell their sad tale. The text is very fragmentary, but the first editor suggested the following translation (the square brackets indicating suggested restorations):

[Behold the maidens who died] by violence chattering: approaching wayfarer, we are the daughters of Lycambes. A fellow-citizen had the heart of a stone; [he hurled] immeasurable insults [against us] in . . . iambics, [and] we put our necks [in nooses. Do not bring up false tales] against us. Earth and . . . [will testify that we are pure].

Local Egyptian calendar (PAP. F 99-103; C 18; D 29; E 49; P.Hib 27).[16] Third century BC.

This famous papyrus contains a detailed and highly technical calendar of a year in the Saite nome (a nome was an administrative district in Ptolemaic Egypt). There is an introductory passage in which the writer says he received instruction on astronomy from a certain wise man, now usually assumed to be an Egyptian astronomer, who showed him an impressive water-clock. The first three months of the calendar are missing, but the details thereafter concern the changes of the season; the movement of the sun; the rising and setting of certain stars; weather forecasts; stages in the rising of the Nile; certain festivals; the length of day and night.

Ritual of the Orphic (?) mysteries (PAP. Sel. Box 1; P. Gurob 1; Pack² 2464). Third century BC.

The piece of papyrus on which this is written was torn down the middle, leaving only the second half of thirty lines of text. It is in prose, although there are snippets of verse included. The sacrifice of a ram and a goat is described as well as some mystic symbols, and there is a list of the contents of a basket: a spinning-top, a special instrument whirled around on the end of a string, dice, a rattle and a mirror. It is not altogether clear to which particular mystery the ritual should be attributed, but the weight of evidence seems to point to Orphism. At any rate, this papyrus is an unusually important document for the history of the Greek mysteries.[17]

OFFICIAL DOCUMENTS AND LETTERS

Thousands of the papyri coming out of Egypt have richly illustrated the elaborate bureaucratic system of the Ptolemies, and later of Roman Egypt: tax receipts, accounts, contracts, leases, valuations and so on have created a fascinating dossier of social documents. The Library has plenty of examples of these informative pieces, but more immediately spectacular are the following three items.

21 (overleaf). Papyrus: Egyptian Book of the Dead in hieroglyphs (nineteenth dynasty: thirteenth century BC).

Report on the Third Syrian War (PAP. C 16; P. Petrie 2.45 and 3.144; Pack² 2206).[18] About 246 BC.

This is an extensive, but puzzling and much discussed papyrus of major importance [20]. After the death of Alexander the Great in 323 BC, his enormous empire was broken up into what became the three major monarchies of the Hellenistic east: the Antigonids in Macedonia, the Seleucids in Syria and the Ptolemies in Egypt. Hostility between the Seleucids and Ptolemies was strong and constant: there were four wars between them in the course of the third century. The Third Syrian War (also called the Laodicean War) broke out in 246 BC when the Seleucid king Antiochus II died. His former wife, Laodice, whom he had set aside in order to marry the Egyptian princess Berenice, claimed the throne for her son (the future Seleucus II). Berenice of course did the same for hers and called in her brother Ptolemy III to help. Ptolemy advanced into Seleucid territory and was given a friendly reception at Seleucia and Antioch, no doubt as the champion of Berenice and her son. Ptolemy made good progress, but then his sister and nephew were murdered, and anyway very soon he was forced to return to Egypt to deal with an uprising. The war took on a new life and continued in other theatres until 241, but the report recorded on this papyrus deals with the early stages of the war only, during Ptolemy's invasion. The writer appears to be Ptolemy himself. He describes the capture of 1500 talents of silver, and the death of the Seleucid governor of Cilicia, and then goes on to record the reception he received at Seleucia and Antioch. One of the puzzles of the piece is that Ptolemy says Berenice was at Antioch when he arrived: our other sources indicate that she and her son had already been murdered at this stage. If she was still alive, it is curious that there is no mention in the report of her taking part in the welcoming of her brother. In fact she may well have been dead, and Ptolemy was trying to hide this from his readers.

Report on an insurrection in Egypt. Second century BC.[19]

The Library has several papyri from Lycopolis which had long been completely forgotten about until 1973, when W. Clarysse examined them. The most important records the results of an uprising caused by a troublesome Egyptian pretender named Chaonnophris. Many people have been killed and the irrigation system apparently destroyed. Survivors have taken possession of more land than they were entitled to, and are not paying all the taxes due. The Ptolemaic administration is now trying to restore order.

Death of Claudius and accession of Nero (PAP. F 18; P. Oxy 7.1021). 17 November AD 54.

This seems to be the rough draft of a public proclamation or official circular. It reads as follows:

'The Caesar who had to pay his debt to his ancestors, god manifest, has joined them, and the expectation and hope of the world has been declared emperor, the good genius of the world and source of all good things, Nero, has been declared Caesar. Therefore ought we all wearing garlands and with sacrifices of oxen to give thanks to all the gods. The first year of the Emperor Nero Claudius Caesar Augustus Germanicus, the 21st of the month Neos Sebastos.'

The date is only thirty-five days after the death of Claudius, a very short time for the news to have travelled from Rome to the town of Oxyrhynchus.

PRIVATE DOCUMENTS AND LETTERS

Wills feature prominently. A good example is provided by the wills of three soldiers (dated to 236-235 BC) from the Petrie papyri re-edited by W. Clarysse.[20] Here is some of the text:

'Kalas, Macedonian . . . about 70 years old,

small, white skinned . . . being sane and sensible [has made the following will]:

May I enjoy good health [and manage my own affairs, but if] I suffer the lot of man, I leave [all my possessions] and the billet I received from the crown . . . to my wife and to Demetria my daughter . . . and I leave nothing to anyone else.'

King Ptolemy and Queen Berenice and their children are appointed executors, and then the witnesses are listed and described. Herakleides, for instance, was 'about 35 years old, tall . . . and having a scar above the left eyebrow'. Kephalon was 'about 70 years old, of ruddy complexion, square-faced. . . .'

Notice of credit (PAP. F 96).[21] 26 May AD 155.

The bank of Ptolemaeus at Arsinoe informs Arius, son of Heron, age about 25 years, scar under his forehead to the right under the hair of his eyebrow, that his account has been credited with a loan from Gaius Sextus Priscus.

Letter of Sempronius (PAP. D 28).[22] Third century AD.

Sempronius writes to a priest named Cephalon, who is too free and easy with money, especially that of other people, for Sempronius' taste. 'You're not like your father', he says, 'you can't look after things honestly for someone who is away.' At one point in this fast-moving, castigatory letter, Sempronius introduces an interesting proverb, or what seems to be a proverb: 'you should not eat porridge on my signature'. It is not clear exactly what this means, but it is probably, as the editor suggests, something like 'don't pamper yourself on my authority'.

The care and preservation of the collection has advanced considerably since Mahaffy and Smyly's early work of sorting and cataloguing. However there is much still unpublished, and even the published material could be re-edited with profit. The scholarly resources of the papyri in Trinity College's splendid collection are by no means yet exhausted.

NOTES

*The authors wish to thank Stuart Ó Seanóir of the Library's Manuscripts Department for his help.

1. N. Lewis, *Papyrus in classical antiquity.* Oxford, 1974, pp 21-32.
2. Lewis, *Papyrus,* part 3.
3. E.G. Turner, *Greek papyri: an introduction.* Oxford, 1980, chapters 2-3.
4. D. Comparetti, G. de Petra, *La Villa Ercolanese dei Pisoni.* Torino, 1883.
5. Turner, *Greek papyri,* p. 24.
6. Catullus 95.7-8. See also Horace, *Epistles* 2.1.269-70; Juvenal 13.116-7.
7. W.B. Stanford and R.B. McDowell, *Mahaffy: a biography of an Anglo-Irishman.* London, 1971, p. 183.
8. Turner, *Greek papyri,* p. 21.
9. *The Flinders Petrie papyri,* edited by J. P. Mahaffy and J.G. Smyly. Dublin, 1891-1905.
10. F.G. Kenyon, *Classical texts from the British Museum.* London, 1891.
11. Stanford and McDowell, *Mahaffy,* pp 185-7.
12. Turner, *Greek papyri,* p. 26.
13. E. Hincks, *Catalogue of the Egyptian manuscripts in the Library of Trinity College Dublin.* Dublin, 1843.
14. A. Wouters, 'Two papyri of the *Iliad* Book T', *Ancient Society* 2 (1971) 52-65.
15. G.W. Bond, 'Archilochus and the Lycambides: a new literary fragment', *Hermathena* 80 (1952) 3-11.
16. See S. West, 'Cultural interchange over a water-clock', *Classical Quarterly* 23 (1973) 61-4.
17. For the most recent discussion and a translation see M.L. West, *The Orphic poems,* Oxford, 1983, pp 170-1.
18. Translated in *Greek historical documents: the hellenistic period,* edited by R.S. Bagnall and P. Derow. Ann Arbor, 1981, pp 50-2.
19. See W. Clarysse, 'Ptolemaic papyri from Lycopolis', *Actes du XVe congrès international de papyrologie.* Bruxelles, 1979, pp 163-4.
20. W. Clarysse, 'Three soldiers' wills in the Petrie collection: a re-edition', *Ancient Society* 2 (1971) 7-20.
21. See P. Parsons, 'Three documents from Trinity College Dublin', *Chronique d'Égypte* 44 (1969) 313-14.
22. Parsons, 'Three documents', pp 318-24.

EARLY CHRISTIAN MANUSCRIPTS

GEORGE OTTO SIMMS

Seven biblical manuscripts, dating from Ireland's 'golden age' of faith and culture, between the sixth and ninth centuries AD, form a famous family among the treasures of Trinity College Library.

Through these early centuries, a spirit of discipline and reverence marked the pages of all the books in this collection; yet each one has its distinctive features. Some in the group are world-famous; some are *de-luxe* Gospel-books, famed for their beauty and colourful dignity; some are large, others are pocket-size; some are plainer than others; a few are fragmentary. Yet all share a great tradition of fine writing and dedicated copying. Their 'house-style' script, nurtured variously in the monastic foundations of Iona, Ireland and Northumbria as well as on the European con-

22. Book of Kells: the words of St Matthew's Gospel, 'Tunc crucifixerant' ('They crucified Christ and with him two thieves') in the shape of a cross (fol. 124r).

23 (below). Book of Kells: symbols of the evangelists (fol. 27v).

24 (right). Book of Kells: canon-table with the 'four creatures' symbolizing the evangelists (fol. 5r).

tinent, is quickly recognizable. High standards for these scribes were set by St Colum Cille (St Columba, AD 521-97); his biographer urged them 'after careful copying, to compare what they had written with the exemplar and to emend with the utmost care'.[1]

The name of James Ussher (1583-1656) frequently crops up in the history of these manuscripts. The debt owed by the College Library to Ussher is indeed great. He was an avid collector of antiquities; he never thought a good book too dear. He studied and collated the Book of Kells and the Book of Durrow; writing in Latin about these two special treasures he breaks into Greek (κειμηλια) to emphasize their rare worth.[2] Ussher's pupil, Henry Jones, Vice-Chancellor of the University of Dublin and later Bishop of Meath from 1661 to 1682, assisted with this collating, and then donated both these books to the Library. The so-called 'Ussher Gospel-books' (*Codex Usserianus I* and *Codex Usserianus II* or 'The Garland of Howth') received these names from T.K. Abbott (Librarian 1887-1913), although there is no evidence to show that Ussher owned them. When Ussher became Archbishop of Armagh in 1625 he had the added opportunity of studying the Book of Armagh with the goodwill of its guardian (the *Mac Moyre* or 'maor') from whom he received it on loan for a period.[3]

The Books of Dimma and Mulling were added to the Library much later, in the nineteenth century, and were not connected with Ussher's name.

These seven surviving samples from the libraries and writing rooms (*scriptoria*) of Irish monastic foundations either in this island or in neighbouring islands or in the 'greater Ireland' of Europe, where books (*libri scottice scripti*) written in an 'Irish hand' still abound, help to illustrate the way of life in these ancient places of prayer and learning. The regular display of these manuscripts in the exhibition-cases of the Long Room points to a tradition which has done much to shape the history of this country and College.

Gerald Plunket in 1568 wrote ecstatically on a page of the Book of Kells (fol. 4v), 'this work doth pass all mens conyng that now doth live in any place'. Many in our day still express their amazement at what they see and what, even at minute detail, the naked eye cannot adequately capture. Sir Gerald Kelly (former President of the Royal Academy) on his visit to the Book of Kells exclaimed to this writer, 'why Picasso!', at the sight of folio 130r. The 'page of the day' lying open for James Joyce (fol. 124r [22]) set him musing upon the 'tenebrous *Tunc*' which introduced the account of the Crucifixion; he, like others, marvelled at the 'penelopean patience' of the scribe.[4]

THE BOOK OF KELLS (CODEX CENANNENSIS)

The Book of Kells,[5] in Peter Brown's words, is 'the most sumptuous of the books to have survived from Europe's early Middle Ages'.[6]

On all but two of the six hundred and more surviving pages there is colour and design of some sort. Each page becomes a picture; there is something to attract the interest and taste of young and old in this splendid, weirdly eccentric Gospel-book.

Yet the planning of the book was basically traditional. The great pages include colourful portraits: the Christ (fol. 32v), and two evangelists, Matthew (fol. 28v) and John (fol. 291v), are imposing figures; their presence is solemn and majestic, their style oriental. Full-page illustrations treat decisive moments in the life of Christ: the Nativity, portrayed with an ikon-like presentation of the Virgin and child flanked by adoring angels (fol. 7v); the Temptation scene, with a young, scarcely bearded Christ confronting the sinister, dark figure of the devil from the roof-top of the

25. Book of Kells: St Mark's narration of the Passion, 'Erat autem hora tertia' ('It was the third hour').

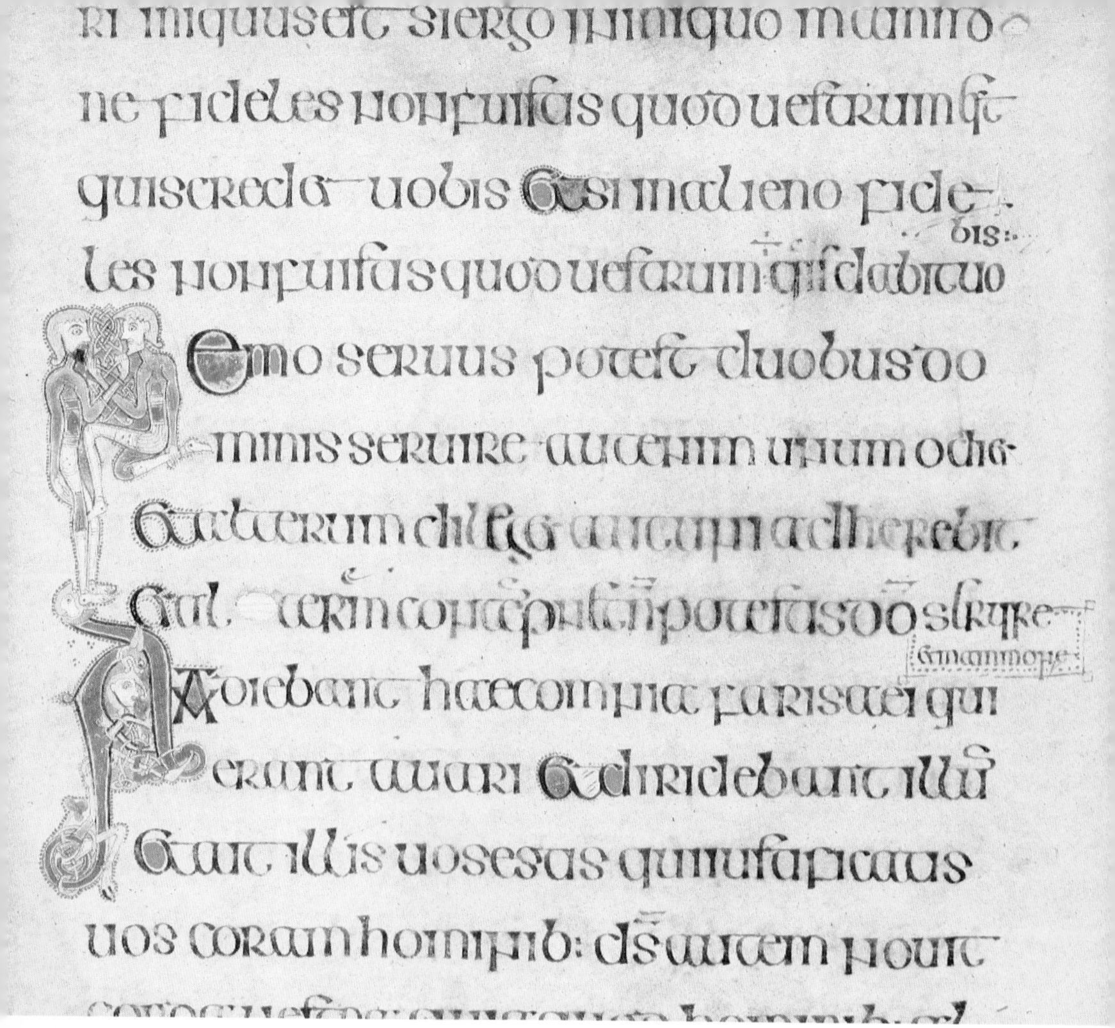

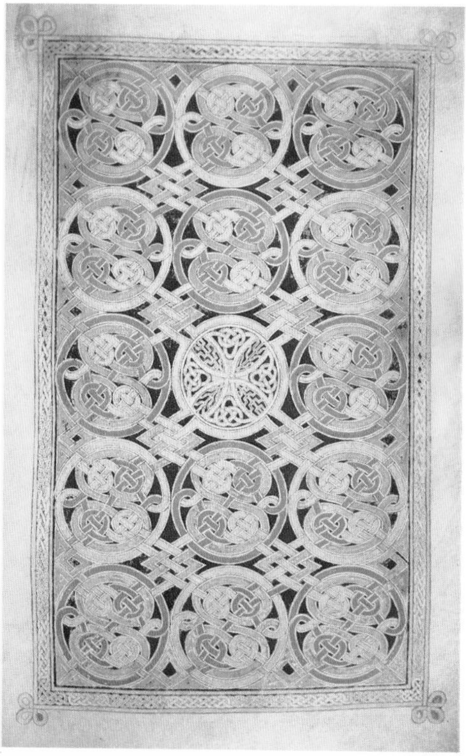

26 (above). Book of Kells: letter *N* of *Nemo* ('No man can serve two masters') formed by two men fighting (fol. 253v, detail).

27 (left). Book of Durrow: carpet page, 'roundels' (fol. 85v).

28 (right). Book of Kells: the Chi-Rho page, representing the birth of Christ, using the Greek letters *χρι*, the abbreviation for 'Christ' (fol. 34r).

h generatio

temple, an Irish-style oratory (fol. 202v).

Traditional also are the symbols of the four evangelists. Yet the treatment in *Kells* of these 'living creatures' (the man, the lion, the ox or calf, and the eagle) is both original and ingenious. There are three fully decorated pages of these 'evangelical' symbols (fols 27v [23], 129v, 290v) and a fourth one (fol. 187v) partially decorated; they preface in turn each Gospel narrative and emphasize the unity of the four separate Gospel records. This unity is further illustrated by the elaborate presentation of the 'four creatures' on the ten canon-table pages (fols 1v-6r [24]) in a series of architectural frameworks of intricate, Byzantine-like arcading, and of the section numbers of each Gospel, set out between columns. Gospel symbols, rather than names of Gospel writers, head the relevant columns and pillars, with over-arching tympana within which the 'creatures' preside, enclose and order the neatly penned lists of numbers. Sometimes at the topmost pinnacle of these colourful façades the head of the Almighty (*Pantocrator*) looks down with authority upon the handiwork.

The so-called *Tunc* page [22], which records 'they crucified Christ and with him two thieves' (fol. 124r), is written with dramatic touch, not in straight lines but in the shape of a saltire, diagonal cross. This page is tense with lions roaring and people witnessing; its message is tragically eloquent.

On the Marcan page of the Passion (fol. 183r [25]), only a few words fill the pale white vellum with 'It was the third hour' (Mark 15.25). The restraint and solemnity are deeply expressive; yet even here the artist is moved to inject one of those quirks, typical of *Kells,* which adds a helplessly human touch when all around are awe-struck; a tiny head surveys the scene from the top right-hand corner of the page's frame and wears a lost, almost quizzical look; the feet of this hidden figure emerge at the bottom left-hand corner and seem to tell a despairing story of dismay and collapse.

The life which is constantly stirring through the pages of *Kells* accounts for much of the book's popularity. Scholars continue to differ about the origins of the manuscript. Several hands appear to have been responsible for the writing; a few of the early pages have a more flexible, less formal script than is found in the rest of the book; a variety of coloured inks is used in these preliminaries; mauves and reds are added to the regular black or brownish lettering of the 'insular' semi-uncials (e.g. fol. 22v). The wide range of pigments includes red lead, kermes (carmine), yellow orpiment, emerald verdigris, ultramarine lapis lazuli, varying shades of purple folium and white lead. St John's Gospel, which lacks the last four chapters, is written in smaller letters than those of the first three evangelists, with eighteen long lines to the page rather than the more regular seventeen or sixteen lines.

There are signs that the artist and the scribe were separate persons; on folio 253v, for example, a decorated capital *A* becomes redundant at a point where a plain *A* has already been penned. Those fascinating capitals which begin as letters and spring to life, sprouting human heads or writhing animal bodies, sometimes indicate the mood of the sentence they decorate; tails, paws and ears in riotous confusion can spell doom or joy. On the same page (fol. 253v [26]) two little men can be seen confronting each other in considerable tension clutching beards and in this posture they shape the outline of a capital *N*. Their bodies are deftly twisted to provide the first letter of *Nemo* 'no man' in the passage which reads 'no man can serve two masters' (Luke, 16. 13). The two men are two masters.

Unparalleled in the other manuscripts of this Irish family are the writhing, chasing, struggling, frolicking creatures, now hiding, now scampering between the lines, filling the gaps at the ends of paragraphs, serving as brackets to protect portions of words which have run over the margin's edge, marking the places where a jump in reading (and a u-turn later) must be made, helping the hang-over syllables to find a haven above or below the text. Dogs, cats, mice, hares, fish, lizards, spotted scorpions, birds of bright plumage, farmyard fowl [30] sometimes seem to illuminate the words they beautify; more often these *jeux d'esprit* may reflect happy, relaxed moments snatched from the long hours of concentrated copying.

Many influences have shaped *Kells*. The text is a mixture of two versions, the Old Latin and Jerome's Vulgate. This accounts for the sprinkling of 'doublet readings' not found to any great extent in other texts. For example, in the passage which refers to the ostentatious fasting of the hypocrites who disfigure their faces, *Kells* includes two words for 'disfigure', the old 'exterminate' and the new 'demolish'. In folio 45v the Latin words *demuliuntur exterminant* appear side by side on the written line as a 'doublet'; *exterminant* was rejected by Jerome as an exaggeration of the Greek word which he was translating (Matthew 6.16).

One of the great pages, the Chi-Rho (fol. 34r [28]), represents the 'birth of Christ' (Matthew 1.18). The golden yellow of the orpiment pigment sheds a glory over the $\chi\rho\iota$, the historic and reverent abbreviation of *Christi* ('of Christ'). Ribbon interlacement, fret-work patterning, spirals and trumpet designs bring movement to the page with a revelry of curves and colours, and add mystery

29. Silver shrine of the Book of Dimma: detail showing metal interlacing.

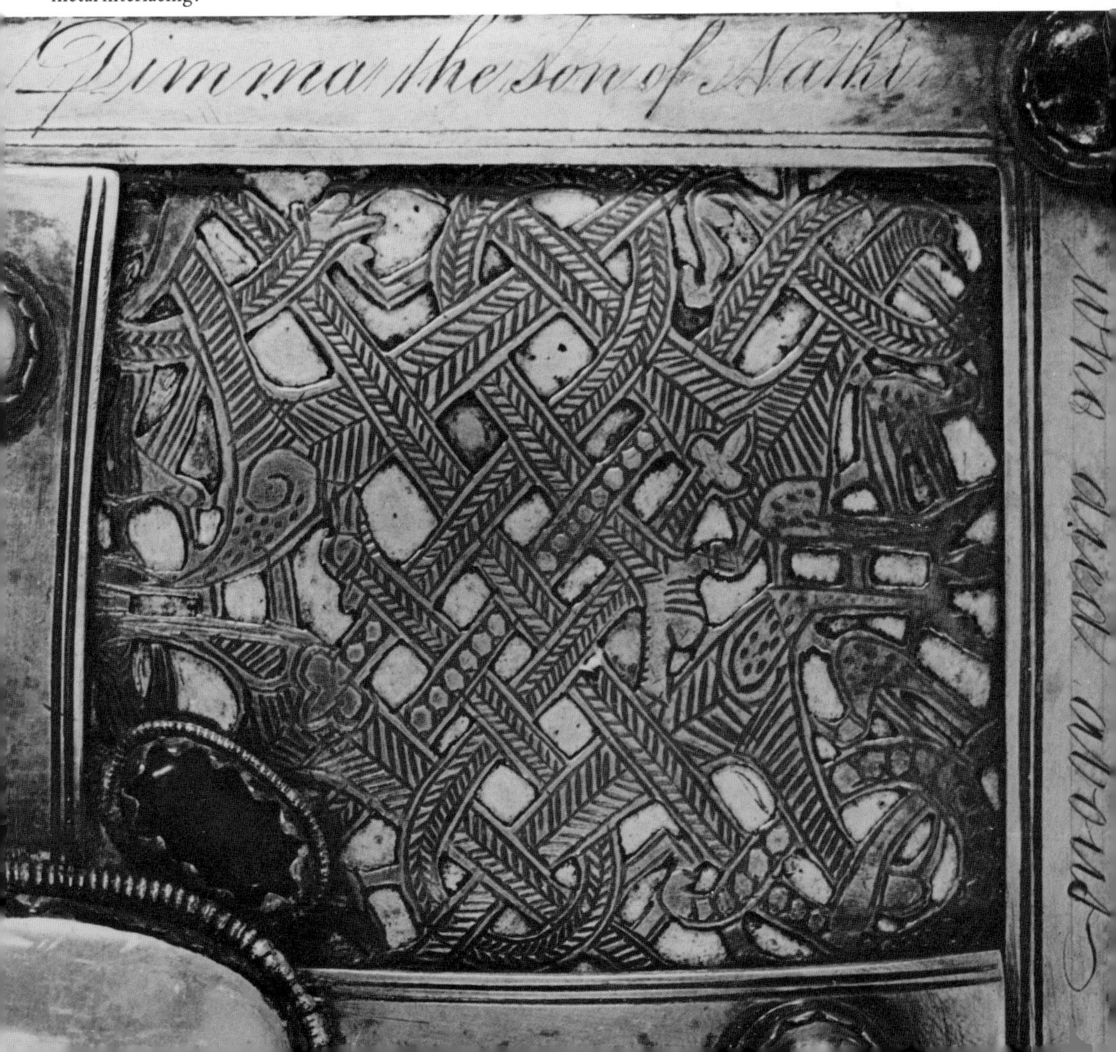

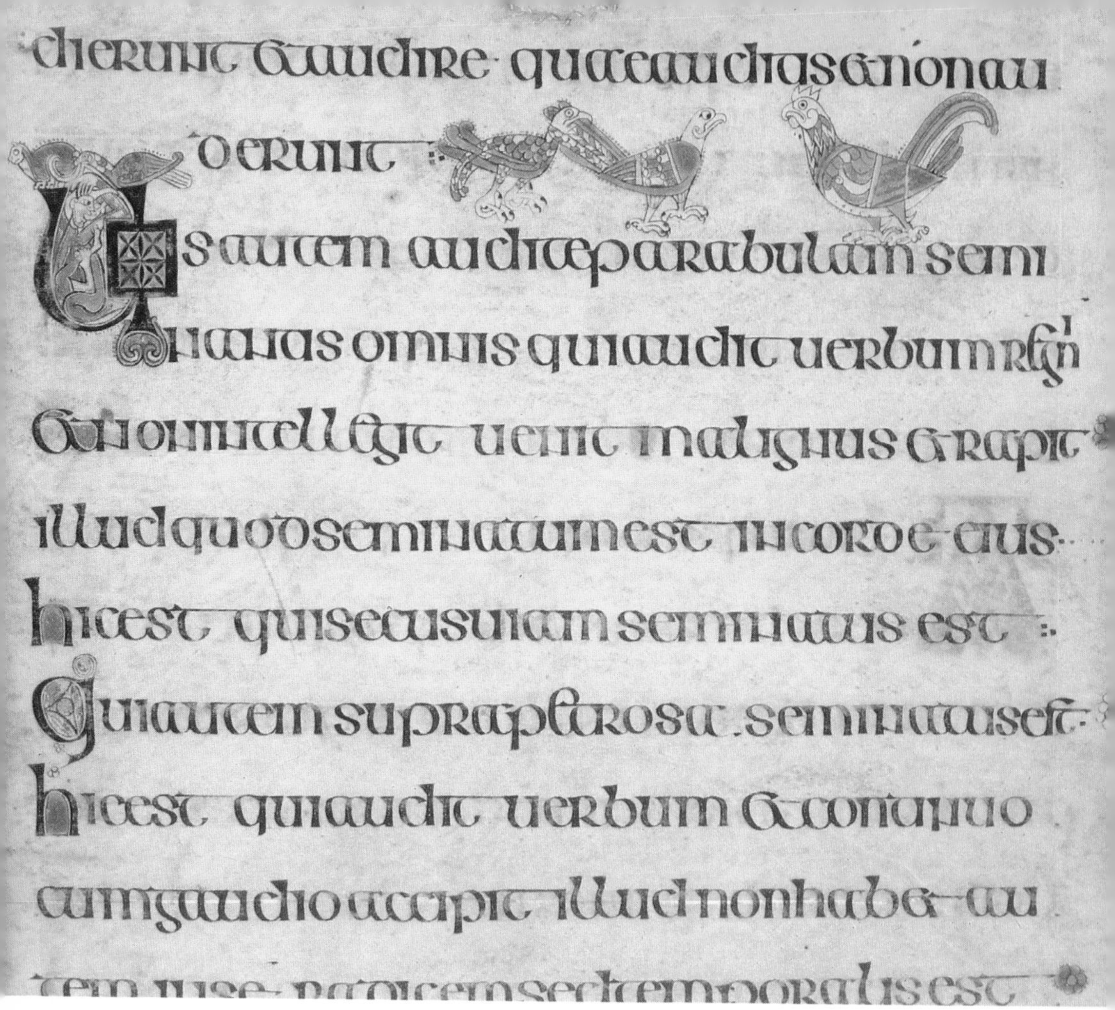
dierunt et audire quae audistis et non au
dierunt
Uos autem audite parabulam semi
nantis omnis qui audit uerbum regni
et non intellegit uenit malignus et rapit
illud quod seminatum est in corde eius
hic est qui secus uiam seminatus est
Qui autem supra petrosa seminatus est
hic est qui audit uerbum et continuo
cum gaudio accipit illud non habet au
tem in se radicem sed temporalis est

30 (above). Book of Kells: farmyard fowl (fol. 67r, detail).

31 (right). Book of Durrow: carpet page, 'biting animals' (fol. 192v).

32 (far right). Book of Durrow: the beginning of St Mark's Gospel ('Initium evangelii Ihu χρι') (fol. 86r).

incipit euangelium
secundum marcum

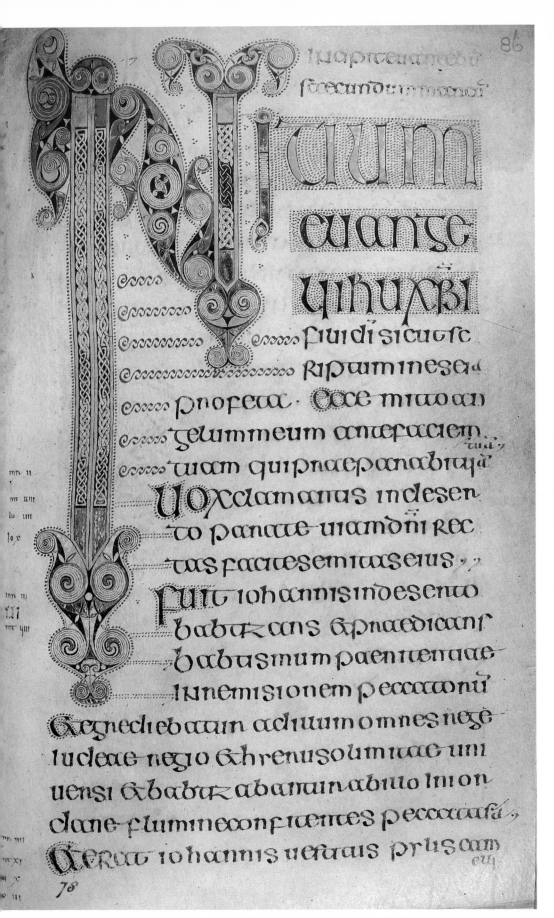

INITIUM
EUANGE
LII IHU XPI
filii di sicut sc
riptum in esseia
profeta. Ecce mitto an
gelum meum ante faciem tuam
uiam qui praeparabit uiam
mr ii Uox clamantis in deser
mt iiii to parate uiam dni rec
lu iiii tas facite semitas eius.
io x Fuit iohannis in deserto
mr iii babtizans et praedicans
mt viii babtismum paenitentiae
in remisionem peccatorum
Et egrediebatur ad illum omnes rege
iudeae regio et hirusolimitae uni
uersi et babtizabantur ab illo in ior
dane flumine confitentes peccata sua.
mr iii Et erat iohannis uestitus pilis cam
mt xi ei
lu x

to the theme of nativity; the circles and rhythms recall the La Tène style of metal engraving; the Anglo-Saxon patterns characteristic of the Book of Durrow are also included in the many shapes and forms. Hidden animal life and branching foliage suggest creation's growth and ordering; an otter with fish in mouth, cats among their kittens, a pair of moths, human figures half-concealed, all are given a place in the spaces left by the mighty monogram which sweeps across a most remarkable page.

The leaves of *Kells* were enshrined in a *cumdach* (shrine), plated with gold, as recorded at the year AD 1007, in the Annals of Ulster. The theft of the precious cover and the rescue of the calf-skin leaves of 'the Great Gospel of Colum Cille' made history.[7] The beginning and ending of the manuscript are missing. There is thus no extant colophon-sentence to provide a clue to authorship or origin. Iona, Northumbria and Kells (County Meath) shared a great tradition of biblical learning; all three centres of Columban influence have been considered as possible places of the book's beginnings.[8] There was a specially close link between Iona and Kells; this was strengthened when Iona was pillaged and the survivors of the community escaped to Kells. The monastery of Kells received gifts of land from benefactors in the neighbourhood; details of some twelfth-century grants were recorded in the Irish language on folio 27r, which had originally been left blank. The book remained in Kells until the seventeenth century. It was donated to the Library by Henry Jones, Bishop of Meath, in the early 1660s.

THE BOOK OF DURROW

The calligraphy of the Book of Durrow[9] wins wide praise from the experts. With letters written close and yet clear, the long lines of script, sparsely punctuated and with few ligatures, display an evenness and a precision of great dignity and beauty. Paragraphs are introduced with letters subtly decreasing in height; this *diminuendo* device recalls the style of the earlier Cathach psalter.[10] The letters *l* and *b* in *Durrow*, together with other 'ascenders', are short and, at times, squat; similarly, the 'descenders' such as *g*, *p*, and *q* are curtailed below the line. The opening page of each Gospel has a large initial letter of impressive beauty (e.g. fol. 86r [32]); the rhythms and proportions are enhanced by a setting of red-ribbon horizontal lines of scroll-work and a framework of finely pointed red dots.

There are eleven fully decorated pages in the manuscript. The colours used are red, yellow, green, and occasionally brown. The names given to the grand, full-page, colourful designs which frequently recall the curving lines and circular tracery of Celtic (La Tène) metal work, hint at their decorative splendour: trumpets and spirals (fol. 3v), roundels (fol. 85v [27]), panels (fol. 125v), biting animals (fol. 192v [31]), and yellow trellis (fol. 248r).

Full-page illustrations are also assigned to the symbols of the four Gospel writers. The human figure (fol. 21v) is stiffly, formally portrayed; the only other instance of a human form in *Durrow* appears on the 'four symbols of the evangelists' page (fol. 2r). The Matthew figure, nevertheless, is of particular interest for the hair-style, reminiscent of the Celtic tonsure and pointing to an early date.

The order of these four separate 'symbolic living creatures' is also significant. After the 'man', appears the 'eagle' (fol. 84v [33]), followed by the 'calf' or 'ox' (fol. 124v) and the 'lion' (fol. 191v). This is the Old Latin order — Matthew, John, Luke and Mark. Although the text of *Durrow* is Vulgate with a mixture of Old Latin readings, the pictorial framework preserves the earlier order before Jerome's work of revision began. While Jerome's letter to Damasus in AD 383 appears on folio 4r with the colourful and shapely opening words *Nouum opus*, the flavour of the old version lingers on.

Henry Jones, Bishop of Meath, presented the Book of Durrow to the Library. In the catalogue of 1688 mention is also made of its silver-plated cover (*operimentum*); this was apparently the shrine (*cumdach*) made for Flann, king of Ireland in AD 916. This shrine disappeared during the Williamite wars, but the words of the inscription engraved upon the cross on the face of the cover were happily copied before its loss by the historian Roderick O'Flaherty and are bound with the manuscript (fol. 11v). This reference to Flann (tenth century) and the Irish charter concerning transference of land in the eleventh century to the monastery (fol. 248v) have linked the manuscript for many centuries to Durrow, County Offaly, where to this day a stone cross and a well mark the site of the monastic settlement founded by St Colum Cille in the sixth century before he left for Iona (AD 563). The presence of two colophons (fol. 247v) at the end of the book marks a connection with Colum Cille; one colophon is the scribe's genuine request for a colleague's prayer; the other is a copy of the tail-piece to an earlier 'little book' which asks for a favour 'remember me Columba the writer who wrote this Gospel in twelve days by the grace of our Lord'. This is 'the scribe's *Finis*', to quote A.A. Luce in his introduction to the work.[11]

THE BOOK OF DIMMA

This small, portable Gospel-book[12] was apparently used for pastoral needs among the sick as well as for study. There are picture pages; three portraits of the evangelists, Matthew, Mark and Luke, while St John's Gospel is introduced with a handsome eagle [34] set in a framework decorated with panels of ribbon interlace and fret-work patterns. Blues, yellows and browns colour this symbol of the fourth Gospel-writer; the design of this page and of the initial at the opening of the Gospel (IN PRINCIPIO 'in the beginning', John 1.1) is similar to corresponding pages in the Book of St Gall.

The script of the Book of Dimma varies; at the beginning it is closely written, in a cramped style, with numerous abbreviations to keep the book small and light. St John's Gospel is written in a more formal manner than is found 'in the everyday running hand of the first scribe'.[13] The name 'Dimma' appears three times through the manuscript but the fact that two or perhaps three scribes worked on this manuscript makes clear that the names of the writers are unknown; nor is it possible to be precise about the date.

'Dimma' probably symbolizes a tradition rather than an individual scribe. The book belonged to Roscrea in County Tipperary, where indeed a Dimma had made his name. St Cronan founded a monastery there on a desert promontory of a nearby lake. Before his death, he founded a second monastery, on a site more convenient for travellers and the poor; to this second foundation the book belonged.

The book and its silver shrine (partly twelfth century and partly fourteenth to fifteenth century) were purchased by the College from Sir William Betham in 1836 for £150. Through the years, the book had remained in Roscrea. The *cumdach* (shrine) of silver-plated bronze was made at the order of Tatheus O'Carroll, chieftain of Ely O'Carroll. The Latin inscription written in Lombardic script is translated 'Thadeus Ua Cearbaill, King of Éile, had me gilt; the lord Domnall Ua Cuanain, coarb, was the last to restore me; Tomas the craftsman fashioned this shrine'. Its measurements show that the book would have fitted closely inside with no room to spare. A detailed account of the shrine by Raghnall Ó Floinn describes the four openwork plaques of differing patterns cut from sheets of silver, ornamented with interlaced quatrefoils [29].[14] There were later additions including the crucifix on the cover; the jewels on the back were added when Monck Mason, from whom Betham had acquired the shrine,

33 (above). Book of Durrow: the eagle. symbol of St John (fol. 84v).

34 (top right). Book of Dimma: the eagle, symbol of St John (p. 104).

35 (right). Book of Mulling: 'Portrait' of St John.

heavily restored the surface.

THE BOOK OF MULLING (MOLING)

This pocket Gospel-book and the fragment of another Gospel-book[15] came to light enshrined together in one *cumdach* (shrine). The folios were preserved, and previously bound in an incorrect order. The re-numbering of the folios, followed by rebinding in the Library's Conservation Laboratory, was carried out in 1977 by William O'Sullivan, at that time Keeper of Manuscripts. There are three full-page 'portraits' of Matthew, Mark, and John [35]; elaborate and finely drawn initial letters introduce the Gospels e.g. *Liber* (Matthew 1.1), *Initium* (Mark 1.1), *Quoniam* (Luke 1.1), and *In principio* (John 1.1) as well as $\chi\rho\iota$ (Matthew 1.18). The colours range from blue to green, yellow ochre, mauve, purple and cherry red, but all are damaged by chemical change and decay.

The text is 'mixed', with both Old Latin and Vulgate versions of words and phrases. As in the Book of Dimma, prayers for the sick have been included. A colophon at the end of St John's Gospel gives the name of the scribe as Moling, but it is not thought that the Moling of the monastery at St Mullins in County Carlow can be the scribe (St Moling died in AD 698). The colophon or tail-piece writes *finit* with a Greek letter for f (ϕ), a habit found several times in the book. A map or circular plan plots the lay-out of a monastery (possibly Teach-Moling, Moling's house) with crosses at the cardinal points and the four evangelists ranged to match their Old Testament counterparts, the prophets: Matthew and Daniel, Mark and Jeremiah, Luke and Isaiah, John and Ezekiel. It has been surmised that the three circles drawn on this page enclosing these features may represent the rath of St Mullins. This ground plan links the book with the charming spot among the hills in the Barrow valley, where a figured high cross, the stump of a round tower, a well and the ruins of some churches and other buildings (but no rath) survive.

The evangelist St John [35] lends a special atmosphere to the book; the archaic smile, the fixed gaze which engages the reader's attention with a compelling fascination, and the robes, decking his figure with folds and flaps in Book of Kells style, point to a development in the tradition of an art soon to flower on a grander scale.

The Book of Mulling was in the custody of the royal McMurrough Kavanagh family of Leinster for generations; it was presented to Trinity College in the eighteenth century. For a time the shrine was also in Trinity College but it was later returned to the family; it is inscribed with the name of Art McMurrough Kavanagh (1402).

The 'Mulling fragment' contains a portion of St Matthew's Passion narrative and the opening chapters of St Mark's Gospel. A decorated INI introduces the *Initium* of Mark, shaped by dog-like creatures intertwined; the purple and black, framed by red dots, make an impressive introduction to this Gospel, written in minuscule lines stretching right across the page. The text of the Book of Mulling is written on two-columned pages. The Book and the 'Fragment' are apparently of similar date.

THE BOOK OF ARMAGH (CANÓIN PHÁDRAIG)

The Book of Armagh is a prestigious manuscript.[16] Despite its 'pocket' size, this small squarish codex is remarkably rich in content. It is the earliest surviving Latin New Testament on Irish soil; the biblical portion is prefaced by documents dealing with St Patrick's life and work, described by Ludwig Bieler as the Saint's 'dossier'; a life of St Martin is appended at the end of the book. A record of Brian Boru's inspection of the book in the year AD 1004 indicates the importance of Armagh and its book at that period; Brian's

IN PRINCIPIO
erat
uerbum
et uerbum er
at apud
deum et deus
erat uer
bum hoc er
at in prin
cipio apud deum omnia per ipsum
facta sunt et sine ipso factum est nihil
quod factum est in ipso uita est et uita
erat lux hominum et lux
lucet in tenebris et tenebrae
eam non conprehenderunt nomen
fuit homo missus a deo cui
erat iohannis hic uenit in tes
timonium ut testimonium per
hiberet de lumine ut omnes cre
derent per illum non erat ille
lux uera sed ut testimonium perhiberet de lu
mine erat lux uera quae inluminat omnem
hominem uenientem in hunc mundum in mun
do erat et mundus per ipsum factus est et mundus
eum non cognouit in propria uenit et sui eum
non receperunt quotquot autem receperunt eum dedit
eis potestatem filios dei fieri his qui credunt
in nomine eius qui
non ex sanguinibus
neque ex uoluntate carnis
neque ex uoluntate uiri
sed ex deo nati sunt

Et uerbum caro factum est et habitauit in no
bis et uidimus gloriam eius gloriam quasi u
nigeniti a patre plenum gratiae et ueritatis
iohannis testimonium perhibet de ipso et cla
mat dicens hic erat quem dixi qui post me uen
turus est ante me factus est quia prior me erat et de
plenitudine eius nos omnes accepimus et gratiam
pro gratia quia lex per moysen data est gratia autem
et ueritas per iesum christum facta est deum nemo uidit
umquam nisi unigenitus filius qui est in sinu
patris ipse enarrauit et hoc est testimo
nium iohannis quando miserunt iudaei ab hierusolimis
sacerdotes et leuitas ad eum ut interro
garent eum tu quis es et confessus est et
non negauit et confessus est quia non sum ego christus et inter
rogauerunt eum quid ergo helias
es tu et dicit non sum propheta es tu et respondit non
dixerunt ergo ei quis es ut
responsum demus his qui miserunt nos
quid dicis de te ipso ait ego uox claman
tis in deserto dirigite uiam domini sicut
dixit esaias propheta et qui missi fuerant ex pha
risaeis et interrogauerunt eum et dixerunt ei
quid ergo baptizas si tu non es christus neque
helias neque propheta respondit eis iohannes dicens
ego quidem baptizo in aqua medius autem
uestrum stetit quem uos nescitis ipse est qui
post me uenturus est qui ante me factus est cuius
non sum dignus ut soluam corrigiam
calciamenti eius haec in bethania facta
sunt trans iordanen ubi erat iohannis bab
tizans altera die uidit iohannis ihesum
uenientem ad se et ait ecce agnus dei

name and his title 'emperor of the Irish' are to be found in Latin on folio 16v b.

Bound in two volumes by Roger Powell in 1957 after extensive repairs, this manuscript was written by one Ferdomnach at the request of his patron in Armagh, the abbot Torbach who held office for one year only in AD 807. Ferdomnach is described in the Annals of Ulster (AD 845) as 'the wise and very best scribe';[17] he may have been helped in his task by one or two pupils, for there is a change to be observed in the handwriting.[18] A delighted footnote scribbled in the lower margin of folio 73r at Luke 10.10ff perhaps points to an enthusiastic pupil, whose remark in Irish might be translated: 'the last page was written with three dippings of the pen'. However, J. Gwynn, R.I. Best and L. Bieler were of the opinion that one hand worked throughout the pages with signs of change in style due to Ferdomnach's advancing years.[19]

The documents on St Patrick include: the life by Muirchú (fols 3-16); the memoirs of Tírechán, mingling Irish with Latin and tracing the place-names of the Saint's travels (fols 17-30); the Book of the Angel, establishing the prerogatives and supremacy of Armagh; and an abridged text of St Patrick's Confession omitting some but not all of the unhappy self-critical passages concerning the Saint's early life.

The New Testament (known to scholars as text D, for Dublin) is counted as an important version in the group of manuscripts which have an 'Irish' family likeness (D, E, Ept, L, Q, R are the symbols for the Book of Armagh, the Egerton manuscript, the Echternach Gospels, the Lichfield Gospels, the Book of Kells and the Rushworth (Birr) Gospels). The text is a mixture of Old Latin and the Vulgate. The Lord's Prayer, although Latin, is written in Greek capitals and is thus accorded special honour (fol. 36r a). The Acts of the Apostles are placed last, after Revelation, as in the Clermont manuscript, but rarely found elsewhere. A strange Laodicean letter of Paul is included on folio 139r; this was explicitly rejected by Jerome as quite spurious. An impressive ground-plan of the heavenly city (Revelation 21.16) lies four-square on folio 171r; the twelve gates are skilfully inserted with attractive pen-work. The only colour ornament in the book is to be found in the decorated capitals introducing the Pauline Epistles and Revelation. Graceful penmanship, however, outlines initial letters of the Gospels; symbols of the four evangelists (e.g. fol. 91r [36]) and a small Chi Rho (fol. 33v [37]) are among the charming, sensitively drawn black and brown decoration.

36. Book of Armagh: the Eagle, symbol of St John (fol. 91r).

USSERIANUS PRIMUS

Although fragmentary, extensively damaged and discoloured, this Gospel manuscript[20] has retained its dignity. Its original home may have been at Bobbio in northern Italy, where the name of Columbanus, who died around AD 615, is honoured to this day. The bold, somewhat angular script has an Irish flavour; the influence of neighbouring European texts, found in such centres as St Gall in Switzerland, was widespread, strengthened by the missionary zeal of those 'travellers and pilgrims' who were ever on the move and brought their writing skills and the style that went with them to monasteries on the continent, the origins of the famous *Schottenklöster*.

The central portions of the 180 folios survive and are mounted in paper. The lettering has a distinctive elegance, yet, at this early date (seventh century?), the ornament is sparse, introduced to decorate the half-capitals which mark the sections and paragraphs.

One page, however, (fol. 149v [38] depicts a shapely cross of reddish-brown, set in a wide frame; three rows of alternating red dots and hatched brown lines, while a crescent neatly surmounts each of the four corners of

1 XPI autem
generatio sic
erat
cum esset
desponsata mater eius Ma
ria Ioseph antequam con
venirent inventa est in
utero habens de spiritu sancto.
Ioseph autem vir eius cum esset homo iustus
et nollet eam traducere voluit oc
culte dimittere illam. Haec autem eo cogitan
te ecce angelus domini in somnis appa
ruit ei dicens Ioseph fili David noli ti
mere accipere Mariam coniugem tu
am quod enim in ea natum est de spiritu sancto est.
Pariet autem filium et vocabis nomen eius Iesum
ipse enim salvum faciet populum suum
a peccatis eorum. Hoc autem totum factum est ut impleretur
quod dictum est a domino per prophetam
dicentem ecce virgo in utero ha
bebit et pariet filium et vocabunt no
men eius Emmanuel quod est interpretatum nobiscum deus.
Exsurgens autem Ioseph a somno fecit sic
ut praecepit ei angelus domini et accepit co
niugem suam et non cognoscebat eam donec
peperit filium suum primogenitum et vo
cavit nomen eius Iesum.
2 Cum ergo natus esset Iesus in Bethlem Iudae
in diebus Herodis regis ecce magi ab ori
ente venerunt Hierusolimam dicen
tes ubi est qui natus est rex Iudaeorum
vidimus enim stellam eius in oriente
et venimus adorare eum.
Audiens autem Herodes rex turbatus est et om
nis Hierusolima cum illo. Et con
gregans omnes principes sacerdo
tum et scribas populi sciscitabatur
ab eis ubi Christus nasceretur. At illi
dixerunt ei in Bethlem Iudaeae sic enim
scriptum est per prophetam dicentem Et tu
Bethlem terra Iuda nequaquam minima
es in principibus Iuda ex te enim exiet dux
qui regat populum meum Israhel.
Tunc Herodes clam vocatis magis dili
genter didicit ab eis tempus stellae quae ap
paruit eis et mittens eos in Bethlem dix
it Ite interrogate diligenter de puero et
cum inveneritis renuntiate mi
hi ut et ego veniens adorem eum. Qui cum au
dissent regem abierunt et ecce
stella quam viderant in oriente
antecedebat eos usque dum veniens sta
ret supra ubi erat puer.
Videntes autem stellam gavisi sunt ga
udio magno valde et intrantes
domum invenerunt puerum cum
Maria matre eius et procidentes ado
raverunt eum et apertis thesauris suis
obtulerunt ei munera aurum tus
et murram et responso accepto
in somnis ne redirent ad Herodem
per aliam viam reversi sunt in regi
onem suam. Qui cum recessissent
ecce angelus domini apparuit in som
nis Ioseph dicens surge et accipe
puerum et matrem eius et fuge in Aegyptum

the squares. The handle of this monogram cross (crux ansata) suggests the Greek ρ which follows the *Ch* (Greek χ) of Christ's name. Below the ends of the horizontal bar of the cross are inscribed an Alpha and an Omega, the first and the last letters in the Greek alphabet; they deliver in pictorial style the message that the cross is 'the centre of eternity'. This decoration of early date is a foretaste of much more elaborate developments in Irish art to follow.

THE GARLAND OF HOWTH— USSERIANUS SECUNDUS

'Garland' is said to reproduce phonetically the sound of the Irish words for 'four books' *ceírthe leabhair*), allowing for some im-

37 (left). Book of Armagh: the Chi-Rho page, the Greek letters $\chi\rho\iota$, the abbreviation for 'Christ' (fol. 33).

38 (below). *Usserianus primus*: cross, with the Greek letters alpha and omega (fol. 149v).

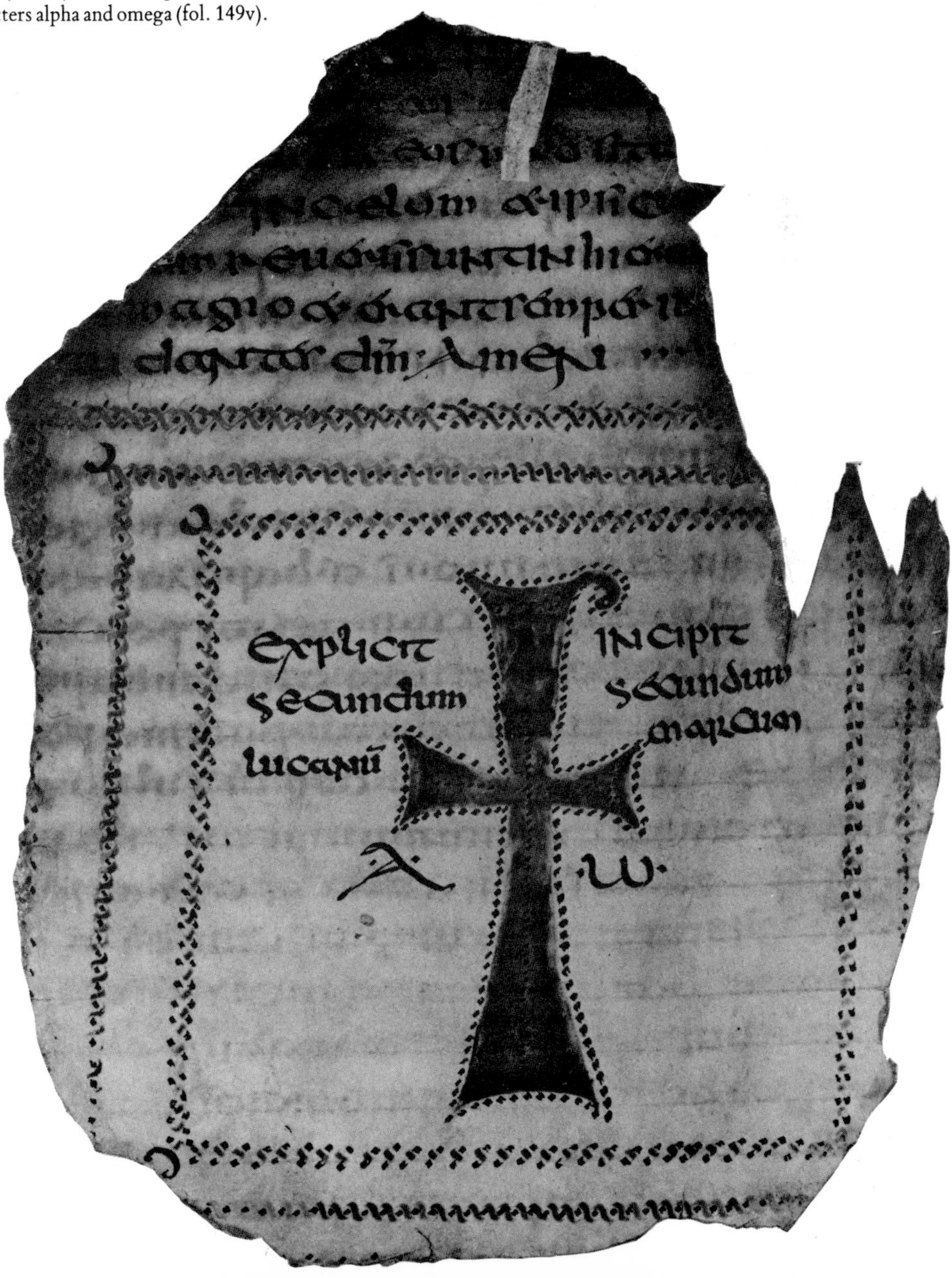

aginative slurring of syllables. These 'four books' (the New Testament Gospels) are in the Old Latin order — Matthew, John, Luke and Mark. The more familiar order of the Vulgate version of Jerome (*c*. AD 383) was accepted rather slowly in Ireland. Hence, some of the Old Latin readings, found in the two 'Ussher' manuscripts, have had considerable importance in textual studies. The 'Garland'[21] has a venerable background; it was associated in its earliest days with St Nessan's monastery on Ireland's Eye off the coast at Howth. Ussher examined the book and noticed some silver 'tongues' attached to it with the name of one St Talman inscribed on them.[22] These labels have since disappeared.

The vellum of the book is heavy, almost 'horny'. In places the pages are like boards. The texture of the calfskin is often 'rough and grainy with a wild mottled look', to quote the words of Anthony Cains, Technical Director of the Library's Conservation Laboratory, where an impressive work of rehabilitation and rebinding of the 'Garland' was carried out in 1977. The two extant decorated pages have been expertly conserved; they are somewhat primitive in design and have been drained of much of their colour; nevertheless they exhibit the characteristic genius and artistry of the period. The colours are red, white, yellow and a light blue (fols 1 and 22). The first picture (fol. 1) shows two frontal figures, seated and holding books in their left hands; the figure on the left raises his right hand, the figure on the right is carrying what is apparently a sword in his right hand; above each figure is an angel in a square compartment.[23]

The second decorated page (fol. 22) shows St Mark between the two uprights of a large IN, capitals which introduce the word *initium* (Mark 1.1 'The beginning ...'). Above the evangelist a lion is depicted as St Mark's symbol. The cable-interlace ends in animal heads as in other manuscripts of the 'family'. Thus the page comes alive. The tubular folds of the evangelist's robes are similar to those in the portraits of the St Gall Gospels and the Book of Dimma.

NOTES

1. *Adomnan's Life of Columba* edited by A.O. Anderson and M.O. Anderson. London: Nelson, 1961.
2. James Ussher, *The whole works* edited by C.R. Elrington. Dublin: Hodges Smith, 1847-64, vol.6, p.232.
3. James Ussher, *Works*, vol.4, pp 318, 330. See also *Liber Ardmachanus: the Book of Armagh* edited by J. Gwynn. Dublin: Royal Irish Academy, 1913.
4. James Joyce, *Finnegans wake*. London: Faber, 1939, p.122.
5. TCD MS 58. 340 folios, eighth-ninth century.
6. *The Book of Kells* selected and introduced by Peter Brown. London: Thames & Hudson, 1980, p.7.
7. *The Annals of Ulster* edited by S. Mac Airt and G. Mac Niocaill. Dublin: Dublin Institute for Advanced Studies, 1983, pt 1, pp 436-7.
8. *The Book of Kells* with a study of the manuscript by Françoise Henry. London: Thames & Hudson, 1974.
9. TCD MS 57. 248 folios, seventh century.
10. Royal Irish Academy manuscript. Sixth-seventh century.
11. *Evangeliorum quattuor codex Durmachensis*. Olten: Urs Graf, 1960, vol.2, p.18.
12. TCD MS 59. 74 folios, eighth century.
13. Timothy O'Neill, *The Irish hand*. Mountrath: Dolmen Press, 1984, p.66.
14. Raghnall Ó Floinn, 'The shrine of the Book of Dimma', *Éile, Journal of the Roscrea Heritage Society* 1 (1982) 25-39.
15. TCD MS 60. 84 folios, seventh century? Also 'Mulling fragment', 4 folios, seventh century?
16. TCD MS 52. 215 folios, *c*. AD 807.
17. *Annals of Ulster*, pt 1, pp 304-5.
18. Timothy O'Neill, *The Irish hand*, p.8.
19. *Liber Ardmachanus* ed. by J. Gwynn; R.I. Best, 'The Book of Armagh (palaeographical notes)', *Ériu* 18 (1958) 102-7; *The Patrician texts in the Book of Armagh*, edited by L. Bieler. Dublin: Dublin Institute for advanced Studies, 1979, p.3.
20. TCD MS 55. 180 folios, seventh century.
21. TCD MS 56. 86 folios, eighth-ninth century.
22. James Ussher, *Works*, vol.6, p.551.
23. J.J.G. Alexander, *Insular manuscripts from the sixth to the ninth century*. London: Harvey Miller, 1978, p.80.

THE IRISH-LANGUAGE MANUSCRIPTS

GEARÓID MAC NIOCAILL

Trinity College Library possesses something over two hundred Irish-language manuscripts. The figure is imprecise, since some of the more important Latin manuscripts, such as the Book of Armagh and the Book of Kells, contain material in Irish, and other manuscripts, such as MS 1318, almost entirely in Irish, are in reality several manuscripts under a single number. Over the generations some volumes have been broken up and parts recombined, often in a rather arbitrary fashion; and more recently, some composite manuscripts have, in the interests of conservation, been taken apart and the components bound separately.

The collection ranks as one of the half-dozen most important in the world in its range and in the quantity of unique items in it, and this despite some losses. In the seventeenth century, it included two great medieval manuscripts, the Book of Lecan and the Book of Ballymote, but these passed out of the College's possession at the end of the seventeenth and beginning of the eighteenth century, in obscure circumstances, and are now in the library of the Royal Irish Academy; by something of a freak, however, nine detached leaves of the Book of Lecan came later into Trinity's possession and are now part of a composite manuscript, MS 1319. For the most part, the collection consists of scholars' manuscripts, intended primarily for use, and hence little decorated, though ornamented initials are not uncommon in the medieval codices; and it ranges from manuscripts of the kind described below to such items as MS 1380, the Oxford Almanack for 1703, which is interleaved with notes on Irish grammar and prosody, and to the papers and transcripts of nineteenth- and twentieth-century scholars.

The collection grew from very modest beginnings: a handful of manuscripts presented by Sir George Carew, President of Munster, who died in 1629. More came from the library of James Ussher, Archbishop of Armagh, antiquarian and Biblical scholar, and were presented to the College in 1661; others were presented by John Stearne, Bishop of Clogher, in 1741. Yet others are the fruits of the activity of Dr Francis Stoughton Sullivan, Fellow of the College, who almost until his death in 1766 was not only a collector of Irish manuscripts but also employed a scribe, Hugh O Daly, to copy those that he could not acquire.[1] A number of important manuscripts came from the collection of the Dublin physician, John Fergus, and a handful from that of General Charles Vallancey, the amateur antiquarian, who died in 1812. The most important bulk acquisition of all, however, was that presented to the College in 1786 by Sir John Sebright, who had inherited them from Sir Thomas Sebright, who himself had bought the manuscripts from the collection of the Welsh antiquary, Edward Lhuyd: it includes many of those discussed below.[2]

The earliest manuscript in the Library containing a substantial amount of Irish is MS

[illegible]

Audiat me scs michel diebus ac noctibus
horis atque punctis in bonorum scorum consortiis
Scs michel intercedat ad meam probabilis
pro me quia sum peccator uerax atq; fragilis
Scs michel me defendat semper scs in uiribus
anima egrediente cum scorum milibus
Scs gabriel scs raphiel atq; omnes angeli
intercedant pro me semper simul cum archangeli
Ut ima possim pstare regis regni caelestia
ne possideam cum xpo paradisi gaudia
Gloria sit semper do patri atque filio
simul cum spu sco uno consilio
Dominus nos archangelus per michel dignissimus
[illegible]

[illegible]

Martine te deprecor pro me rogaris patrem
xpm ac spm scm habentem mariam matrem
Martinus mirus more ore laudauit dm
puro corde cantauit atq; amauit eum
Electus di uiui signa sibi salutis
donauit ds patris magnae atq; uirtutis
Uerbum di locutus secutus in mandatis
uirtutib; impletis mortuis suscitatis
Amen

1441, the *Liber hymnorum,* of the eleventh century [39]: it is a collection of hymns in both Latin and Irish that were used in the services of the early Irish church. The texts themselves, in a large script, have been embellished with a quantity of glosses and commentaries, explaining, in the traditional and typical Irish fashion, when, where and why the text was composed, and such other useful information as the virtues attached to it.[3] So, of the hymn *Altus prosator* attributed to the sixth-century Irish saint Columba, founder of Iona, the commentator notes: 'This hymn . . . has many graces: e.g. angels are present during its recitation; no demon shall know the path of anyone who shall recite it every day, and foes shall not put him to shame on the day he shall recite it; and there shall be no strife in the house where it is customary to recite it; and indeed it protects against every death except death in bed; nor shall there be famine or nakedness in the place where it shall be frequently recited; and there are many others'. The texts themselves are attributed to a wide variety of authors of the fifth to eighth centuries, including Secundinus, Ultán, Cuimmíne the Long, and Columba; the latest is probably Mael Ísu ua Brolcháin, who died in 1086.

The earliest manuscript wholly in Irish is the Book of Leinster (MS 1339), a large manuscript in every way, both physically, with leaves averaging 33cm by 23cm, and in its contents, which are in effect a summation of the native learning of Ireland down to the twelfth century. It was written over a period of years in the middle of the twelfth century, by six scribes, of whom only one is known by name, a certain Aed mac Crimthainn, probably ecclesiastical superior of Clonenagh in Laois, to whom Bishop Find of Kildare wrote a letter enquiring about a poem-book; the letter was copied into the book itself. If there is a single theme running through it, it is historical, with the proviso that it is history as understood by the men of the twelfth century. It opens with a copy of the *Lebor gabála,* 'The book of invasions', that imaginative account of the various invasions that were believed to have swept over Ireland in pre-historic times; it includes a version of the *Táin bó Cuailnge,* 'The driving of the bull of Cooley', the central tale in the heroic cycle of stories centring on Ulster and on the hero Cúchulainn, and this is flanked by texts of a number of the subsidiary tales; there are lists of rulers both of Ireland and of provinces and kingdoms within Ireland, down to the twelfth century, and a list of the successors of St Patrick in Armagh. All this is buttressed by swathes of versified history or pseudo-history [40] and miscellaneous anecdotes; by texts of the *Dindsenchas,* the origin-legends of places within Ireland; by the tale of the *Bóroma Laigen,* the cattle-tribute levied on the Leinstermen; by the tale of the 'War of the Gaeil with the Gaill', which is a propaganda account of the Norse invasions of Ireland and the part played by Brian Boroimhe (Boru) in repelling them; and the whole is

39 (far left). Liber hymnorum: a hymn by Colman in praise of St Michael, and a hymn by Oengus in praise of St Martin (MS 1441 fol. 8v).

40. Book of Leinster: a poem by Mac Cosse, and a poem by Gilla Mo Dutu ua Casaide (MS 1339 facs p. 136).

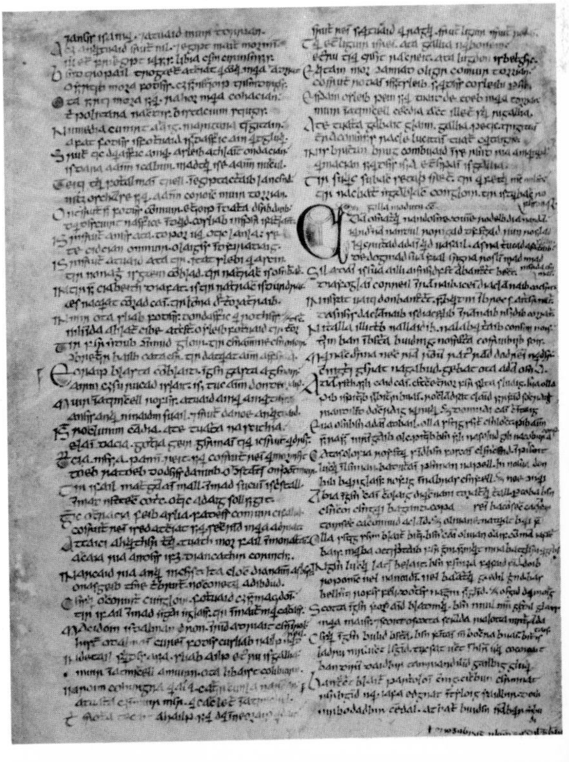

rounded off with a mass of genealogies, both secular and ecclesiastical, the essential background and articulation of early Irish politics, the end result of a process of recording, elaboration, interpolation and pure invention that had been in train since the seventh century. No summary can do justice to so monumental a collection of material, which in the modern diplomatic edition runs to over 1700 printed pages; but the Book of Leinster is in itself a monument to the twelfth-century Irish view of the country's past, and a library of sources for many different aspects of that past.[4]

The Book of Leinster has some unity of composition; much more typical however in Trinity's collection is MS 1318, known as the Yellow Book of Lecan, which comprises seventeen distinct sections of various lengths, themes and dates, spatchcocked together by the accidents of history and the whims of previous owners. The 'real' Yellow Book of Lecan is represented by only one section of the manuscript, columns 370-400; other fragments are now to be found in the library of the Royal Irish Academy and the Bodleian Library, Oxford. Three sections (cols 437-99) contain medical tracts, another (cols 500-72) is largely grammatical and aphoristic, and a fifth (cols 3-122) is mainly the glossary attributed to Cormac mac Cuilennáin (d. 908), copied in 1572. Much closer to the kind of material favoured by the Book of Leinster is an incomplete section (cols 401-36) giving part of the *Dindsenchas,* and a large section of 99 leaves (cols 573-958) with the texts of such early tales as the *Táin bó Cuailnge* and its subordinate tales, the 'Storming of Da Derga's hostel', and miscellaneous prose and verse tales, historical and pseudo-historical, on secular and ecclesiastical themes. This part is the work of Giolla Íosa son of Donnchadh Mór Mac Firbhisigh, in 1380. Other sections of the same kind are columns 217-80, written by Donnchadh Ó Duinnín in 1475, and columns 281-344, written by Murchadh Ó Cuindlis in the last decade of the fourteenth and the opening years of the fifteenth century.[5]

41. Yellow Book of Lecan: poems of Tadhg Óg Ó hUiginn: Da bhraighid uaim a n-Inis; Dúthaidh deorudh Magh Maine (MS 1318 cols 185-6).

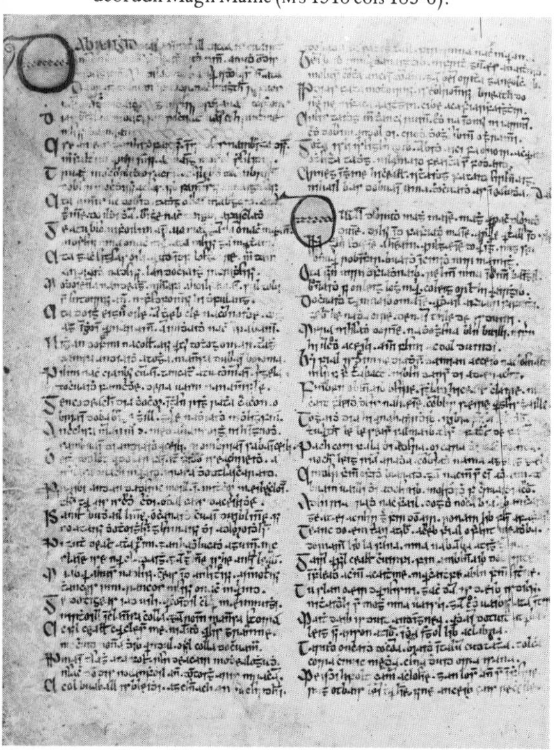

Apart from these rather variegated sections, what mention of the Yellow Book of Lecan most readily calls to the mind of the specialist is that characteristic product of the late Middle Ages, the *duanaire* or poem-book, much like the *cancioneros* of Spain:[6] columns 129-216 contain fifty-six poems by three prominent poets of the midfifteenth century, Tadhg Óg Ó hUiginn (d. 1448) [41], Tuathal Ó hUiginn (d. 1450), and Cormac Ruadh Ó hUiginn, copied by Seanchán son of Maelmhuire Ó Maoilchonaire in 1473. They are addressed to patrons in this world and the next; it was an amiable habit of the medieval Irish poet not only to expect substantial reward for poems addressed to secular patrons — Tadhg Óg boasts of having received twenty cows from Tadhg son of Cathal Ó Conchubhair for a poem — but also to expect God to reward him with paradise for poems on pious and moral subjects.

Linked to this collection of poems in the Yellow Book of Lecan is another important collection, in MS 1340, which contains four of the poems by Tadhg Óg and one by Tuathal Ó hUiginn found in the Yellow Book. It is known as the 'Tinnakill duanaire', since it was compiled for Aodh Buidhe MacDonnell of Tinnakill in County Laois, who died in 1619. It is written almost entirely on parchment, rather than the more usual vellum, and is one of the most important sources known for late medieval religious verse, containing poems attributed to Pilib Bocht Ó hUiginn (d. 1487), Donnchadh Mór Ó Dalaigh (d. 1244), on whom much later religious verse was fathered, Maoileachlainn Ó hUiginn and Cormac Ó Dalaigh, as well as numerous anonymous poems. In large measure it reflects the wave of religious enthusiasm associated with the Observantine reform of the Franciscans, to which Pilib Bocht Ó hUiginn belonged, and which reacted against the corruption and sloth of the church in fifteenth-century Ireland. Why this collection should have been commissioned, a century later, by a secular, indeed warlike, patron is unclear.

Another aspect of the religious revival of the fifteenth century that figures in the Library's manuscripts is the wave of pious translations. An excellent example of this type of material is MS 1434, a vellum manuscript of perhaps the sixteenth century, which preserves texts of the *Meditations on the life of Christ* attributed, wrongly, to St Bonaventure, translated into Irish in the mid fifteenth century by Tomás Gruamdha ('the gloomy') Ó Bruacháin, canon of Killala, and the Irish translation of a Latin life of the Virgin, by an unknown translator. Both satisfied the late-medieval passion for minute and concrete detail, and the reader who ploughed through the long-windedness of the *Meditations* could learn such notable detail as the exact number of lashes inflicted on Christ in the scourging at the pillar, and many other matters on which the New Testament is silent. Both were popular texts and answered the need felt by the pious for material to stimulate an emotional relationship to Christ and the saints, as did other tracts such as the *Dialogue on Christ's Passion* which was translated by a certain Seán Ó Conchubhair at the beginning of the fifteenth century. These texts, in medieval terms, were bestsellers, and one of the more prolific copyists of such material, Tadhg Ó Rígbhardáin in the 1470s, is represented in the Library by three manuscripts, MSS 1303, 1304 and 1309.

This passion for translations was equally prominent in another field, that of medicine, and several versions of such translations are to be found in Trinity. A fairly typical example is the fifteenth-century MS 1343, which contains a tract on materia medica translated, according to the colophon, by one Tadhg Ó Cuinn, bachelor of physic, from the antidotaries and herbals of the schools of Salerno and Montpellier, in the year 1415; another text of it, in MS 1323, copied by Maghnus son of Gillananaomh Mac an Leagha towards the end of the century, names a certain Aonghus Ó Callanáin as Ó Cuinn's collaborator in the work. In MS 1343 it was copied by the scribe Aodh Buidhe Ó Leighin, and it is accompanied by tracts on anthrax and on infections

42. Irish treatise on Materia Medica: Aronbarba, Accacia, Absinthium (MS 1343 p. 47).

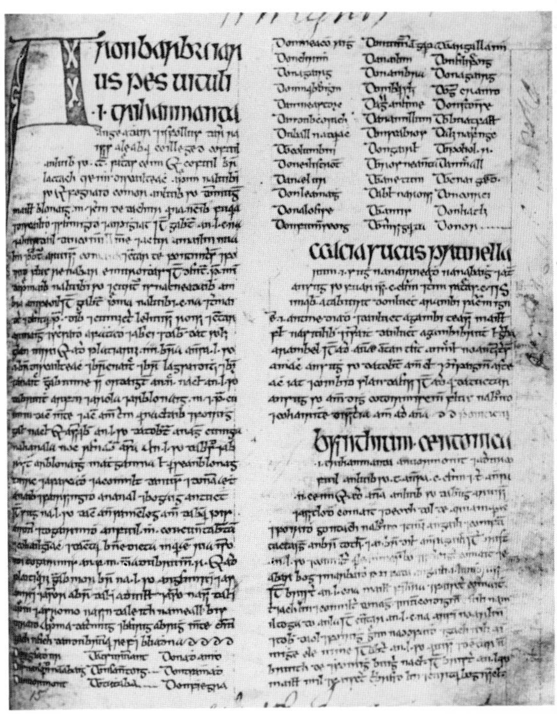

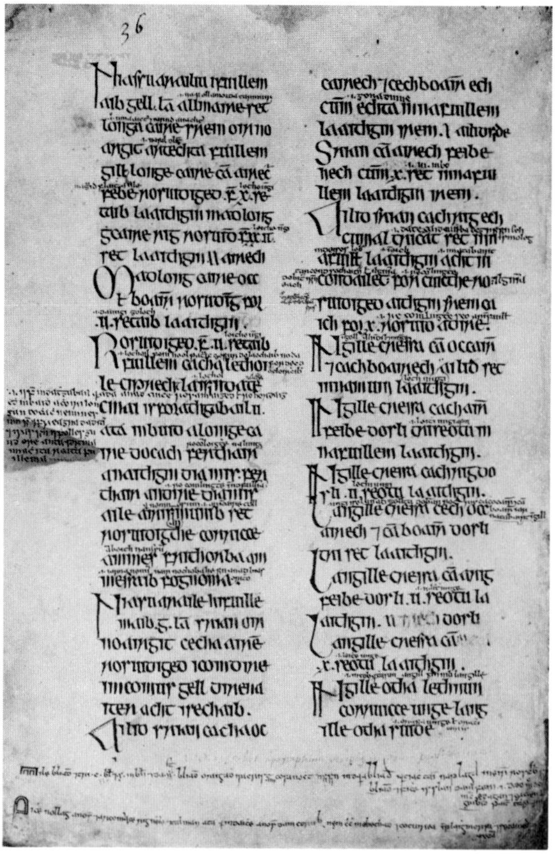

43. Senchas Már, with a marginal note of Mac Aodhagáin school of law at Dun Daighre (MS 1316/2 p. 36).

44 (right). Law (heptads): disqualified churches (MS 1336 col. 355-6).

of the lungs, copied by Uilliam Ó Finnghaine [42].

This outburst of translating activity, of such internationally standard texts as Bernard of Gordon's *Lily of medicine,* John of Gaddesden's *Rosa Anglica* and Magninus of Milan's *Rule of health,* with many others, may in fact have benefited the invalids treated under their auspices very little, since the efficacy of their prescriptions is frequently in inverse proportion to their picturesqueness: thus, to cure a fever, one such text recommends the application to the patient's feet of the hot and bloody halves of a freshly bisected chicken, to 'draw' the fever. Nevertheless, the very choice of medical texts to translate and the wide circulation given them are just as important in the intellectual history of the late Middle Ages in Ireland as those of pious texts.

What we may term the native tradition of intellectual activity found scope mainly in three fields: in the transmission of the early tales and of the type of material preserved in the twelfth century by parts of the Yellow Book of Lecan; in the field of Irish law; and in the cultivation of history.

The Library possesses several of the prime witnesses to the native Irish legal tradition, in MSS 1316, 1336 [44], 1337, 1363, 1387 and 1433. As manuscripts they are something of a *mixum-gatherum*: with the exception of MS 1387, they were owned by Edward Lhuyd, a poor man who could ill afford to have each fragment he acquired bound separately. Most of the mini-manuscripts thus brought together within a single binding, with little heed to differences of size, bear the signs of use. A large number of them were copied in the fifteenth and sixteenth centuries by or for members of the Mac Aodhagáin family, the leading dynasty of jurists in the country. The texts they transmit are not of this late date, but to a great extent belong to the seventh, eighth and ninth centuries, with abundant glosses and commentaries from succeeding centuries, so that the original text accumulated over the generations an onion-like series of layers of interpretation (or misinterpretation) around it. Perhaps the handsomest example of this is afforded by the earliest part of MS 1316, containing part of the great seventh- to eighth-century collection of law tracts, the *Senchas már*;[8] it was copied in 1350, 'the second year after the plague' (i.e. the Black Death), by a Mac Aodhagáin, Aodh son of Conchobhar, who was then aged twenty-one [43]. Another manuscript, MS 1337, preserves a kind of student's handbook of Irish law compiled by the same Aodh's grandfather, Giolla na

nat oingnois alegra . ise
madeoin de argain tuad
aib anedaig tuinest de
nagba soimmine dooingni
each de nabi unfuill
doine ualuicet nobia
Atait .iiii. nanfot forlur
inmomun arodeng
cortal atabt acorbche
ban los peccha doden
um dib atabuir dob
nus ins acon fadhaisi

Une atabt nanou
air fit ghenuic a
cinta aneic fadher
anfine natacona
fine pollaib inta
donegat nahinnraro
Ca amoinsetren
actuaich anur
cuisle coin nuain
acma toich anuaic
amma uaotaib alan
amnitr insolless

Naomh son of Donnsléibhe, who got himself killed in battle in 1309.

The third field of native intellectual activity, history, is to some extent represented by the historical material preserved in the Yellow Book of Lecan and the Book of Leinster; but it is represented also by the compilation of annals, giving an account of the principal events of a series of years as seen, or heard of, or read of by the compiler. Perhaps the most important of these is MS 1282, known as the Annals of Ulster: most important for its range, from the coming of St Patrick down to the beginning of the sixteenth century, and for the precision, whether deliberate or mechanical, with which the compiler preserved, for the most part, even the linguistic peculiarities of his original sources — for, like the Book of Leinster, it was put together 'from many books'.

45. (below). Annals of Ulster: in AD 1498 the death of Cathal Mac Maghnusa, described as a gem of purity . . . turtle-dove of chastity (MS 1282 fol. 139v).

46 (far right). Book of the De Burgos: Riocard mór son of William Conqueror Burke (MS 1440 fol. 19).

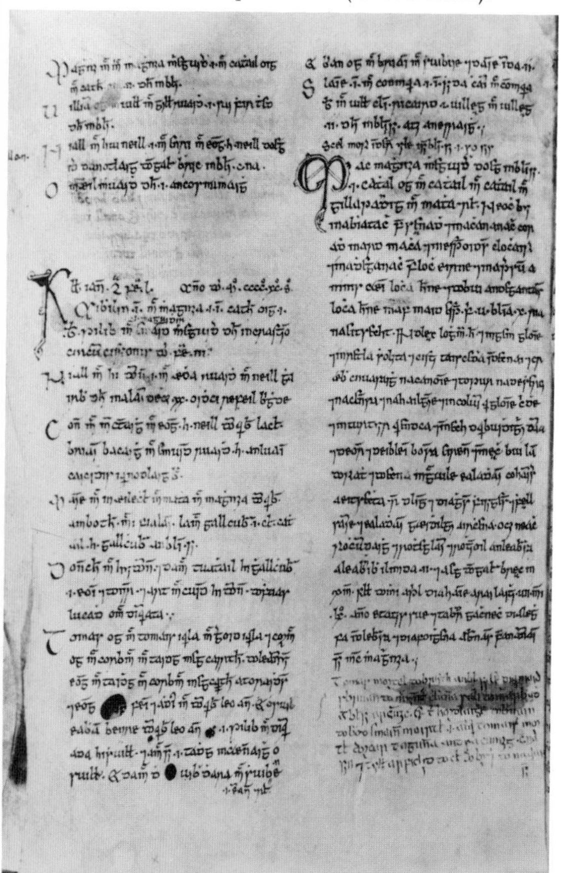

Who precisely should have the honour of fathering it is a moot point. The actual work was done by one Ruaidhrí Ó Luinín, who died in 1528; but it was done for, and perhaps under the direction of, one Cathal Mac Maghnusa, and his obituary, entered in the annals, credits him with it. He was vicar general of the diocese of Clogher for fifteen years, canon choral of Armagh and Clogher, Dean of Lough Erne and parson of Iniskeen; and he represented much of what the reformers of the Irish church in the fifteenth century would have liked to eliminate. Although his obituary [45], recording his death at the age of sixty, from smallpox, on 23 March 1498, laments him as 'the turtle-dove of chastity' — by which the reformers would have understood clerical celibacy — this reputation is a little marred by the record, in this his manuscript, of the birth of various offspring: of Catherine in 1475, Cathal Óg in 1476, Éamonn in 1479, Cormac in 1482, Cú Chonnacht in 1485 and Maghnus in 1486. Nonetheless, he has deserved well of historians for ensuring the preservation, though in composite form, of a series of annals that constitute one of the principal primary sources for early and medieval Irish history.

Of lesser importance, but still indispensable, is MS 1293, known as the Annals of Loch Cé, compiled in the later sixteenth century by Pilib Ballach ('the spotty') Ó Duibhgeannáin for his patron Brian Mac Diarmada and showing some inclination to magnify Brian's accomplishments and those of his ancestors [47]. It is narrower in range than the Annals of Ulster — it begins with the battle of Clontarf in 1014 — and has larger gaps, but it usefully supplements and corroborates them, and provides evidence for events in the sixteenth century that is not independently found elsewhere.

A third set of annals, MS 1292, the *Chronicum Scotorum,* survives as a transcript by

the great seventeenth-century scholar An Dubhaltach Mac Firbhisigh: other copies exist, but all can be shown to derive from MS 1292. The manuscript that Mac Firbhisigh copied is lost, but this conscientious transcript — leaving blanks where the original was damaged — preserves a set of annals for the period from the fifth to the twelfth century, which at some stage of their existence were worked over in Clonmacnois. Again, it is less important than the Annals of Ulster, but in some periods equally indispensable.

In the field of family history, finally, MS 1440 deserves mention. Genealogical tracts are not rare in collections of Gaelic manuscripts, but MS 1440 is that uncommon thing, an attempt at a family history, of the Burkes, compiled in the later sixteenth century and containing in its early stages some measure of fiction, since it claims Baldwin, King of Jerusalem, as a Burke. It also contains an account of the lands and dues of the Burkes, and — rarest of all — fourteen illustrations; four are of Christ, and nine are full-length portraits of various Burkes in full armour [46]; and these are rounded out by the family's coat of arms.

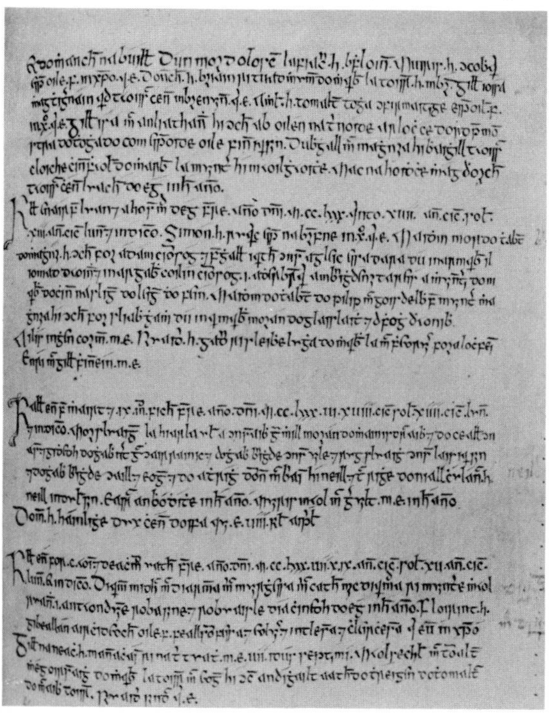

47. Annals of Loch Cé: in AD 1286 the Earl of Ulster invades Connacht, subjects Cenél Conaill and Cenél Eoghain and replaces the Ó Néill (MS 1293 fol. 71r).

NOTES

1. W. O'Sullivan, 'The Irish manuscripts in Case H in Trinity College Dublin catalogued by Matthew Young in 1781', *Celtica* 9 (1976) 229-50.

2. A. O'Sullivan and W. O'Sullivan, 'Edward Lhuyd's collection of Irish MSS', *Cymmrodorion Society Transactions* (1962) 57-76.

3. J.H. Bernard and R. Atkinson, *The Irish Liber hymnorum.* London, 1898 (Henry Bradshaw Society, vols 13-14); L. Bieler, 'The Irish Book of hymns: a palaeographical study', *Scriptorium* 2 (1948) 177-94.

4. W. O'Sullivan, 'Notes on the scripts and make-up of the Book of Leinster', *Celtica* 7 (1966) 1-31; *The Book of Leinster formerly Lebar na Núachongbála,* ed. by R.I. Best *et al.* Dublin, 1954-83.

5. R.I. Best, 'The Yellow Book of Lecan', *Journal of Celtic Studies* 1 (1950) 190-2; H.P.A. Oskamp, 'The Yellow Book of Lecan proper', *Ériu* 26 (1975) 102-21.

6. B. Ó Cuív, *The Irish bardic duanaire or 'poem-book'.* Dublin, 1973.

7. A. O'Sullivan, 'The Tinnakill duanaire', *Celtica* 9 (1976) 214-28.

8. *The oldest fragments of the Senchas már,* ed. by R.I. Best and R. Thurneysen. Dublin, 1931.

A 'QUEER STORY': THE INQUISITORIAL MANUSCRIPTS

JOHN TEDESCHI

The collection of inquisitorial records owned by Trinity College Library is one of the largest gatherings of documents of this type in any European or American repository. It is also one of the most precious sources available to historians intent on studying early criminal jurisprudence, the spread of Reformation currents in Italy, the censorship practices of post-Tridentine Rome, witchcraft and magic, and a broad array of other subjects. In fact, increasingly, it is becoming recognized that inquisitorial records constitute one of the few available channels that we have at our disposal to reconstruct many aspects of popular culture in the early modern period.

How the documents, after many travails, finally found their resting place among Trinity's collections is a story that almost defies belief.[1] It begins early in the nineteenth century when, to fulfil Napoleon I's dream of a central archive for the empire and of a supranational centre of learning in Paris, valuable books and manuscripts were removed from the libraries and archives of conquered Europe, including the Holy See. From Rome, more than three thousand crates were scattered over several convoys, the first setting out in the dead of winter, February 1810. In their long and laborious journey over the Alps they were accompanied by Church archivists, whose feelings we can imagine when they watched two wagons disappear into the rushing waters of a torrent at Borgo San Donnino, near Parma, or when eight cases fell into a canal on the road between Turin and Susa.

An inventory of the foreign material that had ended up in Paris from the four corners of the empire was compiled in 1813 by Pierre Claude Daunou, Napoleon's archivist. It is an incredible list: Roman depositories, for example, had been stripped of the contents of the nunciatures, Dataria, Propaganda Fide, Penitenzieria, the entire series of acts and registers pertaining to the Council of Trent, and, of course, the trials, sentences, decrees, correspondence, dispensations, petitions and doctrinal pronouncements that made up the archive of the Roman Inquisition.

Immediately after Napoleon's fall, Marino Marini, the archivist and papal commissioner who had accompanied these collections to Paris, began to organize their return to Rome. He was hampered by the lack of funds to pay for their transport. 'We are not a spending ministry', he was virtuously informed by the French Minister of the Interior who repeatedly refused financial assistance and eventually disbursed a sum sufficient to cover only a fraction of the total expenses. Napoleon's brief return to power for the famous Hundred Days brought Marini's efforts to a standstill, and he obtained permission from his superiors to return to Rome. On 23 March 1816, Ercole Consalvi, the Cardinal Secretary of State, wrote to Count Giulio Ginnasi in Paris to resume Marini's work. To reduce the expenses of the transport as much as possible, Consalvi instructed him to forgo the shipment of certain useless papers (*'alcune carte che sono inutili'*). And to assist the Count in separating the valuable from the useless he included a list prepared by a Roman abbot, Domenico Sala. On 9 June the Secretariat of State circulated a memorandum to the various Congregations requesting them to specify what material formerly in their custody might be abandoned in Paris and, presumably, destroyed.

The archivists of the Inquisition replied to Consalvi on 12 July and explained that, although a large quantity of material had been recovered, the large volume that was the index to the Holy Office decrees on doctrine was still missing. Many other volumes that comprised this series were also still in Paris. These had to be returned at all costs. As for the rest, the trials and related papers, which in their estimation made up roughly two-thirds of the transported material, these could be disposed of as His Holiness saw fit. Despite the guidelines that had been provided for him, Count Ginnasi's efforts left much to be desired. Although his sale of inquisitorial trials to the delicatessen shops of the city may have fallen within the purview of his instructions, his failure to tear them up first proved to be a cause for embarrassment when a number of volumes fell into hostile hands; and his sale of hundreds of registers of papal bulls belonging to the Papal Chancery, the Dataria, clearly was contrary to Consalvi's intentions. By the spring of 1817, roughly one year from Ginnasi's assumption of his duties, two convoys of archival materials reached Rome. As their contents gradually came to light, great cries went up on all sides from the archivists of the Congregations. They complained, in the words of Consalvi's written rebuke to Ginnasi (18 May 1817), 'that they had received the useless papers, and not those which were useful and necessary'.

There was nothing for the Cardinal Secretary of State to do but replace the hapless Count. Marini was dispatched to Paris to organize the shipment of the remaining material. He succeeded in reclaiming a considerable portion of the archive of the Dataria alienated by Ginnasi, but he also sold another 2600 volumes of inquisitorial trials as scrap to paper manufacturers. As a precaution against the kind of embarrassment suffered by Ginnasi, he had them shredded before they left their depository. From Rome, Consalvi expressed his enthusiastic approval. Later Marini would inform him that his travel and maintenance were costing nothing to the Holy See. The sale of the Holy Office records more than covered the expenses. Among the untold treasures that perished in Paris were the youthful writings of Tommaso Campanella and the defence testimony in the trials before the Inquisition of Giordano Bruno.

Somehow, by ways that no one has as yet succeeded in explaining, a portion of this material became separated and was saved. Thirty-seven volumes containing trial proceedings found their way into the hands of a group of French bankers who promptly offered them back for sale to the Church, threatening otherwise to turn them over to the liberal newspaper, the *Mercure de France.* Rome had little choice, made the purchase in 1819 and immediately eliminated the manuscripts from public view.

Roughly forty years after the dispersal of the documents in Paris, another sizeable group, originally belonging to the Congregation of the Holy Office and the Dataria, made their way to Trinity College in Dublin. It has not been possible to reconstruct every stage in this final journey. Our best and virtually only source is an account[2] dated 7 March 1855, left by the Rev. Richard Gibbings, a graduate of the University and Rector and Vicar of Killcleagh in the diocese of Meath, who would one day sit as Regius Professor of Divinity at his old college from 1863 to 1878. It was Gibbings who engineered the final acquisition of the documents for Trinity. According to his written account, while the wholesale destruction of precious historical records was being perpetrated with official sanction in the streets of Paris the documents in question came into the possession of a French officer and remained in the hands of Roman Catholic families in France who, at one point, offered them for sale to the British Museum for £1200, a price thought too dear by the Trustees. About the year 1840, George Montagu, Viscount Mandeville (Duke of Manchester after 1843), while residing in Rome, first heard of these records through a Mr Somerville, described by Gibbings as an eminent scientific writer.[3] Mandeville, who had served as a commander in the Royal Navy and as an MP and who is described in the *Complete peerage* as a 'zealous Protestant' and an author of religious pamphlets, pursued the matter. A Rev. Robert McGhee was commissioned by Mandeville to proceed to Paris, and in 1841 obtained possession of the manuscripts for him at a price of £600.

After these materials were transported to Mandeville's residence at Kimbolton Castle, they came to Gibbings's attention, and in 1850 he wrote to the Duke asking whether he would consider either selling them or making them available for publication. The response was favourable and Gibbings was invited to examine the documents personally in March 1851. It was agreed that the clergyman could offer them to the Board of Trinity College for £300. When the proposal was declined, Gibbings purchased the materials, then numbering some fifty volumes, for himself. Suspecting that the collection was not complete, after some intensive searching he succeeded in locating another twenty in the London storeroom of the shippers who had transported the documents from the continent some eight years before. In July 1854 Gibbings, who had determined to place his newly acquired possessions in the Bodleian Library, Oxford, made one more attempt to interest the Trinity authorities. Just as it appeared that he would fail again, the Vice-Provost, the Rev. Charles William Wall, generously agreed to purchase the collection and make a gift of it to the College.

Later, in a letter written by Gibbings to 'My dear George', he described his triumphant journey to Dublin in the company of his precious Roman documents: 'How I proceeded, and ultimately succeeded, it is not necessary now to state, but it is a queer story. In 1854 the Mss. were brought on the roof of the coach from Strabane to Dublin, and this was a marvellous adventure, but I would not lose sight of my treasures.'[4] In the same letter Gibbings went on to say that he had written an account of the whole matter at the request of the Librarian, James Henthorn Todd, which was placed in the first volume of the collection, 'but as he [Todd] brought in Jesuits and others to examine the records, my narrative soon vanished from its place'.

The dispersed Roman manuscripts in the Library consist of three main groups of materials.[5] The first is made up of thirteen volumes of Lateran Registers, most probably originating from the Dataria, containing letters and bulls from Boniface IX (1389) to Pius VI (1787).[6] The second group is made up of nineteen volumes of sentences, with accompanying abjurations, issued by the supreme Congregation of the Holy Office in Rome or by provincial Italian tribunals under its jurisdiction between 1564 and 1659.[7] Only four volumes deal with the sixteenth century, spanning the years 1564-8 and 1580-2 and containing roughly five hundred sentences for this period. Sentences do more than declare a defendant's guilt or innocence; they summarize in detail the charges against him and sometimes even his responses to them. They frequently run to many pages and, consequently, are often satisfactory substitutes for the records of the complete trials, which, for the most part, perished in Paris. The third series, consisting of thirty-five volumes, contains progress reports on litigation before provincial tribunals — denunciations, examinations of witnesses, results of preliminary inquests — which had been sent to the Holy Office in Rome for its information or decision.[8] They range in date from 1625 to 1789, with the exception of the depositions of witnesses in the trial against the Bishop of Policastro in 1565 contained in volume 1. In the course of the sixteenth century it increasingly became the practice for the Roman Congregation of the Inquisition to be kept minutely informed about developments in the outlying courts. The quest for uniformity in procedure resulted in a series of measures that assigned to Rome the final disposition of all but the most ordinary cases. By the end of the century, for example, interrogations under torture, hedged in by many restrictions and precautions even in earlier periods, rarely were conducted without the prior authorization of the central tribunal. And this authorization was not granted until the cardinal inquisitors, assisted by their staff of canon lawyers and theologians, felt that they were in full possession of all the facts in a given case.

The Trinity documents reveal how the pursuit of Italian evangelicals had given way by

48. Inquisition manuscripts: beginning of the case of Edward Bullock of Limerick.

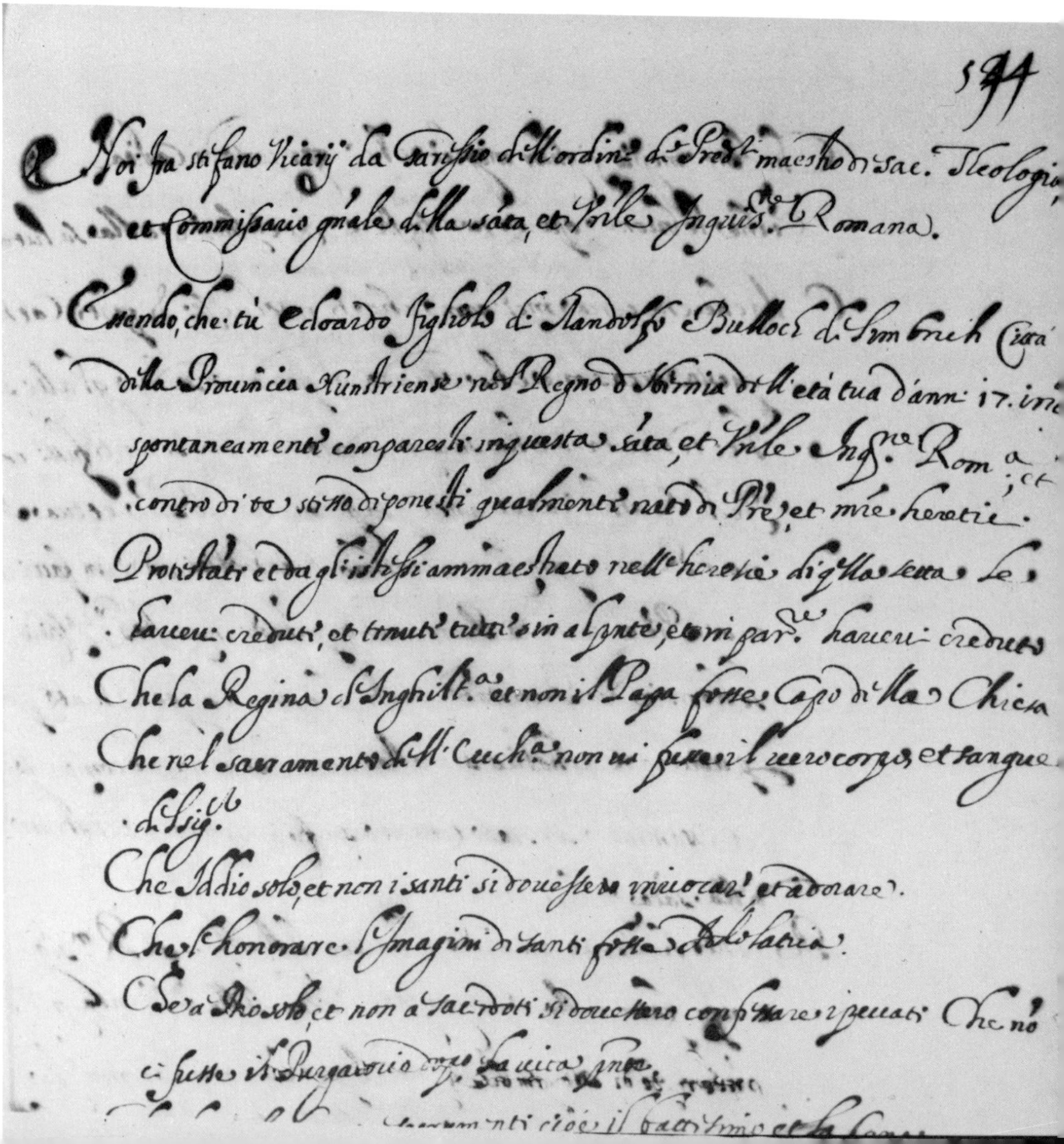
Noi fra Stefano Vicarij da Garessio dell'ordine de Pred.ri maestro di sac. Theologia
et Commissario gn.ale della s.ta, et V.le Inquis.ne Romana.
Essendo, che tu Edoardo figliolo di Randolfo Bulloch di Limbrich Città
della Provincia Munstriense nel Regno d'Ibernia dell'età tua d'anni 17. in c
spontaneamente comparesti in questa s.ta, et V.le Inq.ne Romana
contro di te stesso diponesti qualmente nato di P.re et m.re heretici
Protestanti et da gli istessi ammaestrato nelle heresie di quella setta, le
haver creduto, et tenuto tutte sin al p.nte, et in par.re haver creduto
Che la Regina d'Inghilt.a et non il Papa fosse Capo della Chiesa
Che nel sacramento dell'Euch.a non vi fusse il vero corpo, et sangue
di Ssig.re
Che Iddio solo, et non i santi si dovessero invocare et adorare.
Che l'honorare l'Imagini di Santi fosse idolatria.
Che a Dio solo, et non a sacerdoti si dovessero confessare i peccati. Che no
ci fusse il Purgatorio dopo la vita pnte.

the closing years of the sixteenth century to vigilance against blasphemy, magic arts, the relapse of converts from Judaism, and the circulation of suspended or prohibited books. These materials have been studied exclusively for the light they shed on Italian religious and historical concerns. Gibbings himself, as early as 1852, two years before the collection found its final home in Dublin, began to fire off a series of anti-Roman salvos, publishing three of the most famous sentences it contained.[9] He was followed in the 1860s and 1870s by such students of the Italian Reformation as the Frenchman, H. Gaidoz,[10] the distinguished German historian, Karl Benrath,[11] who was the first foreign scholar to make critical use of the materials, or antiquarians such as Lorenzo Salazar,[12] the Italian Consul-General in Dublin, who combed through them for the sentences and abjurations of citizens of Naples and its territory. On the contrary, we know now that the Library's records are invaluable to historians working in such broader and diverse fields as the English Reformation and Ottoman history.

Turkish expansion northward in eastern Europe, lightning-like raids by Barbary corsairs on the coasts of southern Italy, the endemic piracy of the Mediterranean, all resulted in the enslavement of thousands of Christians during the late sixteenth century. Many of these unfortunates eventually returned to their homes. Some were ransomed, while others escaped or were rescued when the Muslim galleys on which they served were defeated in combat with Christian vessels. It was customary for the Inquisition to examine these re-entrants to Christendom who washed ashore in Italy. An analysis of the Trinity sentences dating from 1580 to 1582 and 1603 indicates that the investigation of apostasy to Islam was now an important item of inquisitorial business.

Suspects who confessed having fallen away from Catholicism invariably claimed that they had been reduced to this extremity to escape the beatings of their masters who desired their conversion (claims that the Inquisition was cautious in accepting), and they insisted that their adherence to the law of Mohammed had been purely external, that in their hearts they had never separated from the teachings of the Roman Church. The Inquisition generally dealt lightly with these apostates, and a simple abjuration, the performance of salutary penances, and a brief refresher course on Catholic fundamentals sufficed for their reconciliation.

The question became more complicated in the case of many renegade Christians captured on Barbary corsairs, who were not serving as rowers chained to the benches of the galleys but in positions of responsibility, as gunners, navigators and even, on occasion, as masters of vessels. The Inquisition handled these men with circumspection and did not accept unreservedly their statements that they had apostatized so that they could sign aboard the pirate craft and hopefully find an opportunity to escape. Too many complaints had been received from the Knights of Malta that renegades who had been absolved and released were returning voluntarily to the lucrative life of piracy. Unfortunately, the records of all these important inquisitorial proceedings remain neglected sources for the study of Mediterranean culture and of European relations with North Africa and the Ottoman Empire in the last quarter of the sixteenth century.

By the end of the century, the Inquisition in Rome was occupied with the reconciliation of still another class of religious deviant, not apostates or suspected apostates, as was the case of the Christians who had bowed to Islam, but foreign heretics who travelled to the Holy See to re-embrace the faith that they or their forefathers had abandoned. They came, a few dozen each year, from every corner of Europe, Arians from Transylvania and Calvinists from Scotland, by devious and dangerous routes to be received as prodigal children of the Catholic Church [48]. Many of them attributed their change of heart to the effectiveness and purity of Jesuit preaching. A certain Thomas Busbridge, for example, a man of twenty-seven from the diocese of Canterbury, who abjured in Rome on 20 April 1582, claimed that the impulse to conversion had been provided by the eloquence and fortitude in martyrdom displayed by Edmund Campion during his clandestine mission to England in 1581[13] [49]. The English College in Rome, over which Cardinal William Allen presided for many years, assisted the Inquisition in its work of reconciliation. The names of its priests and seminarians appear in the trial records as interpreters, and among the salutary penances imposed on the English converts a period of instruction in the College is occasionally encountered. How many of these conversions were sincere? It is difficult to give a definite answer because a majority of the names encountered in the Trinity sentences belong to obscure individuals of modest birth, and to trace their steps is probably next to impossible. It is legitimate to entertain doubts, however, because travel in Italy by citizens of Protestant countries was an enterprise filled with uncertainties and dangers; it seemed natural to assume that a foreigner who had aroused suspicion might try to explain that he was there for the good of his soul.

Thousands of Italians, for a variety of political, commercial or religious motives, travelled to and frequently settled permanently in Protestant lands in the sixteenth century. Other Italians, their ears filled with rumours about the religious revolution in the north, ventured forth briefly to observe it with their own eyes. Geneva was the object of special curiosity. Many of the inquisitorial trials of individuals returning to Italy after visits to the north record that travel to the birthplace of Calvinism had been undertaken simply to observe how the 'Lutherans' were living. The interrogations or trials to which the Holy Office subjected these returning travellers, suspected of harbouring heretical leanings, are sources that have been ignored by students of the Protestant Reformation in the north of Europe. The importance of the information that these sources furnish naturally varies depending on the powers of observation of the individual and the length of his sojourn abroad. It could be as trifling as the peep at Geneva's blue laws provided by one disenchanted visitor who lamented that the inns of the city refused to serve food and drink during the hours of religious services (Geneva, as everyone knew, was the city that boasted that the Word of God was preached many times a day and ten times on Sunday), or it could be as substantial as that provided by a Genoese merchant who had resided in Lyons for much of his adult life. His descriptions of events under the short-lived Huguenot regime (May 1562-June 1563) are as valuable for the historian as are his insights into the unwitting erosion worked on his Catholic beliefs and practices by the many years he spent in a milieu where Catholicism and Calvinism enjoyed an uneasy coexistence. His statements attest that he increasingly ignored fast days, that social concerns might occasionally cause him to hear the sermons of heretical preachers, and that his Scriptural readings came to be based on readily available vernacular texts rather than on the prescribed Vulgate. The inquisitorial records in Trinity College Library can contribute significantly to areas of historical investigation that are European in scope. I hope that these few examples may stimulate the serious studies that this incomparable collection of manuscripts deserves.

49. Inquisition manuscripts: the case of Thomas Busbridge of Canterbury.

Nos fr Thomas Zobbius ordinis predicator, sacre Theologie Magister, ac
Officij Sancte Romane, et Universalis Inquisitionis Commissarius generalis

Cum tu Thomas anglus filius alterius Thome Busbridg de loco Temne Can-
tuarien. Dioecesis aetatis tue annorum Vigintiseptem, uel circa sponte
comparueris in hoc S.to officio, atq3 confessus fueris quod a parentibus haereticis natus, atqs a magistris haereticis imbutus didiceris
Cathechismum Caluini, et alium haereticum Cathechismum Nouelli Decani
londinen., quodqs alias protestantium haereses, que in Anglia circum-
feruntur, et praesertim, credideris et praesertim

Quod Christi anima ad inferos non descenderit, quodqs Simboli locus
descendit ad Inferos exponendus esset de Christi corpore in
sepultura posito

Quod Ecclia Romana non esset illa de qua dicitur in Simbolo Sanctam
Ecclesiam catholicam

Quod asserit Regina Anglie Ecclesie Anglicane etiam in spiritualibus
caput esset

Quod Papa non esset Christi Vicarius, nec caput Universalis Ecclie
sed tantum Ecclesie Romane

Quod tantum duo essent sacramenta Baptisma scilicet, Cenaqs
Dominica

Quod sacramentum Baptismatis conficeretur, ex omnibus alijs praeter
quam ex aqua

Quod Hostia consecrata signum tantum esset aut memoria tantum
Dnice Passionis, et quod propterea illius adoratio esset Idolatria

Quod non ex operibus sed ex sola fide iustificaretur homo

Quod bona opera nullius essent meriti

NOTES

1. For the documentation of the following account, see J. Tedeschi, 'La dispersione degli archivi della inquisizione romana', *Rivista di storia e letteratura religiosa* 9 (1973) 298-312.
2. TCD MS 3216.
3. Perhaps to be identified with the physician William Somerville, a Fellow of the Royal Society, who resided principally on the continent after 1838 and died in Florence in 1860. See *Dictionary of national biography*, vol. 18, p. 666.
4. TCD MS 3791.
5. They are partially calendared in T.K. Abbott, *Catalogue of the manuscripts in the Library of Trinity College, Dublin*, Dublin and London, 1900, pp 241-84.
6. TCD MS 1223.
7. TCD MSS 1224-42.
8. TCD MSS 1243-77.
9. *Were 'Heretics' ever burned alive in Rome? A report of the proceedings in the Roman Inquisition against Fulgentio Manfredi; taken from the original manuscript brought from Italy by a French officer, and edited, with a parallel English version, and illustrative additions* (London, 1852); *Records of the Roman Inquisition; case of a Minorite friar, who was sentenced by St Charles Borromeo to be walled up, and who having escaped was burned in effigy, edited with an English translation and notes* (Dublin, 1853); *Report of the trial and martyrdom of Pietro Carnesecchi, sometime secretary to Pope Clement VII and Apostolic Protonotary, transcribed from the original manuscript* (London, 1856).
10. H. Gaidoz, 'De quelques registres de l'Inquisition soustraites aux Archives romaines', *Revue de l'Instruction publique*, nos 16 & 23 (May 1867) 102-4, 114-17.
11. Karl Benrath, 'Akten aus roemischen Archiven in Trinity College Library, Dublin', *Historische Zeitschrift* 41 (1879) 249-62. Karl Benrath, 'Atti dagli Archivi romani della biblioteca del Collegio della Trinità di Dublino', *La rivista cristiana* 7 (1879) 457-72, 497-505; 8 (1880) 10-13, 55-8, 94-7, 137-43.
12. L. Salazar, 'Documenti del Santo Officio nella Biblioteca del Trinity College', *Archivio storico per le province napoletane* 33 (1908) 466-73.
13. TCD MS 1227, fol. 57.

WORD AND IMAGE IN EARLY MODERN GERMAN PRINT

H. ROBINSON-HAMMERSTEIN

An extensive collection of early printed German books and pamphlets such as Trinity College Library possesses must be counted among its treasures.* The value of the collection lies not so much in any outstanding individual masterpieces (which are, however, contained in it) as in the composite nature of the whole. Every known category or classification of early modern German book is represented: Bibles, breviaries, hymn books, catechisms, travelogues, advice on good housekeeping, astronomical and other scientific works, chronicles, social satires, grammars, devotional, theological and polemical pamphlets, proclamations, etc. In all their diversity they share and proclaim a common conviction: they are testimonies to a firm belief in the power of print. They clearly reveal their authors' and/or publishers' keen appreciation of the potential of a relatively new medium, which they seek to utilize for different ends. It is the purpose of this brief survey to draw attention to some of the aims pursued by publicizing messages in print. Three major classifications have been singled out for closer scrutiny: Bibles, chronicles and Reformation pamphlets.

In the later fifteenth century the Catholic Church was in the vanguard of users and sponsors of books in print. The switch to print apparently did not involve any radical rethinking of its mission: on the contrary, clarity and efficiency, the advantages of printing, were most highly valued. Throughout the Middle Ages the Catholic Church, with its need for a large number of eminently learned men to guard and define its teaching, had produced manuscript books, heavy, unwieldy tomes, which preserved the canon of scholastic knowledge. The Bible — the sacred page — had occupied pride of place among the manuscript books, elaborately illuminated to the greater glory of God. The scribes and artists working on biblical manuscripts were deemed to perform an act of worship. The result of their labours could be venerated and displayed like precious relics. It is therefore true to say that the Catholic religion had always been the religion of books, and that printing was welcomed as an efficient assistant in reinforcing the traditional bookishness of the scholarly ecclesiastical elite. That the use of printing presses did not signal a sudden change in the role of books and in attitudes to them is also indicated in the way in which the conventions of manuscript copying were followed. This is evident in the hand-illuminated initials and especially in the numerous abbreviations. However, a high standard of typography — with clear, aesthetically pleasing lettering — had been set by the pioneering work of the Gutenberg Bible (completed in 1455) and was generally maintained. The Biblia Sacra, the Vulgate, printed by Anton Koberger of Nuremberg in 1480 is an excellent example of early Bible printing.[1]

Large Bibles as comprehensive works of

printed art were, however, not exclusively used in the service of ecclesiastical ritual and scholarly study. Among the wealthy merchants and other leading burghers of south German cities there was a strong demand for vernacular Bibles to which enterprising printers responded. The first vernacular printed Bible was produced by Johann Mentelin of Strassburg in 1466. Although his aim in printing such a work on a massive scale was to supply a marketable product and to make a considerable profit, it might seem reasonable to assume that this process would also facilitate a more direct communication of the message of the biblical texts. This translation was so antiquated as to be almost incomprehensible; nevertheless between 1466 and 1518 there were no fewer than fourteen editions of this Bible, all of which were produced in southern Germany, nine in Augsburg alone.[2] The Bible printed by Heinrich Eggestein[3] about four years after Mentelin's coup already shows significant emendations of the text. It would, however, be utterly anachronistic to argue that the improvements were due to pressure by laymen wishing to instruct themselves in the Word of God. In the case of the printed vernacular Bibles the attraction seems to have been to own a relatively novel, expensive luxury item: a relic for the home, not for private study. This may also explain why, as far as is known, the enterprise went unchecked by Church authorities, who certainly never considered the sacred page suitable for untutored lay reading.

The power of print to promote critical reading among a scholarly elite was, however, the fervent conviction of the most eminent humanist scholar and reforming thinker of the age, Erasmus of Rotterdam (1469-1536). He sought to stimulate reform of the dominant institution of society, the Church, by a scholarly search for scriptural truth on the basis of the most authentic sources. His Greek New Testament with a new Latin translation, published as a dual language text by his printer friend, Johann Froben of Basel, in 1516, was dedicated to Pope Leo X.[4] In the preface Erasmus denied any intention of superseding the established Vulgate text — on which indeed the whole power-structure of the Church rested — but pointed to the urgent need for scholars to check this Vulgate text against the better authorities. He charged constructive biblical scholarship with a task totally different from that of scholasticism, the dominant intellectual tradition of the day, which used traditional glosses to arrive at the acceptable meaning of words. The proper study of this New Testament was bound to lead to criticism of the Church and its doctrines. Erasmus himself was a cautious man; but he pleaded with his learned peers to use the New Testament as an instrument of a 'reform-from-within', which would not affect institutional structures. It was indeed not a book set aside but one avidly studied. The first full impact of this work could be gauged at the general chapters of the religious orders in Germany in the two years after 1516. Young members of the orders greeted the publication with warm enthusiasm, as something that truly satisfied their spiritual needs. Involuntarily, however, this New Testament provided a sharp offensive weapon against the existing ecclesiastical institutions, which could be used by equally learned, reform-conscious scholars, who had come up against the impossibility of a 'reform-from-within'. The power of print had become dangerous to the Church.

Erasmus never believed in giving the Bible to the layman: he considered that an act of rabble-rousing. It was Martin Luther who finally prised the Bible out of the canon of scholastic erudition and made it available to the people at large. Having adopted Scripture as the sole basis of his own theological studies,

50. Lucas Cranach's polemical representation of the great dragon of the Apocalypse wearing the papal triple crown. From Luther's translation of the New Testament, September 1522 (Revelation 14).

and having by the means of humanist textual analysis discovered that justification by faith alone depended on a new way of listening to the Word (*fides ex auditu*), he considered it absolutely vital to give the Word of Life to all Christian men and women. Since his faith in the power of the Word was supreme, he saw in the printing press the gracious gift of God, which could serve the more extensive and effective proclamation of that Word. Luther's translation of the New Testament was accomplished in a remarkably short time in late 1521 and early 1522. It was printed as a clarified text, from which the misleading accretions of tradition had been removed: the message could now speak for itself. Luther was confident that the printed Word would make its revolutionary spiritual impact, despite his knowledge that up to ninety per cent of the population were illiterate.

Several considerations informed Luther's faith in the power of the printed Word even against such odds. The sermons of academically, but non-scholastically, trained ministers were an indispensable part of enlightening the darkened souls. The printed translation of the Word in the vernacular was in clear simple prose, which followed the cadences of spoken language and could therefore be read out with ease. It relied on familiar verbal imagery and its message was highlighted by apt woodcut illustrations. In the so-called September Testament[5] only the Apocalypse was illustrated, as had been the custom in the past. This was the obscurest text of the whole Bible, whose own verbal depiction of graphic scenes seemed, however, to call forth illustrations that would suggest and fix its meaning in the mind of the user. Lucas Cranach's workshop in Wittenberg went well beyond convention by providing illustrations for Luther's New Testament with a strongly anti-papal polemical edge: e.g. the whore of Babylon was represented wearing the papal triple crown [50]. The first, only partial, publication of the Old Testament in 1523, printed, like the New Testament, by Luther's printer friend Melchior Lotter the Younger of Wittenberg, was also illustrated by the Cranach workshop.[6] In some of the copies woodcuts were hand-coloured [53 and 54]. A special arrangement could be negotiated by the purchaser who was prepared to pay more. The complete Bible of 1534 was lavishly illustrated and variously hand-coloured. Whenever possible, the scenes were transposed into a German landscape and the people given contemporary dress, so as to make the message immediately relevant to Germans in the early sixteenth century. For Luther it was a 'new kind of listening to the Word', which involved reading, hearing, decoding of illustrations that constituted the power of the Word in print. He expected the mere publicizing of the Word — which was after all the creative force that had made the whole world — to promote the right understanding and to destroy what was evil. Man need not use violence, 'the Word will accomplish everything'. Even when after some years of promoting the Word, the world was no brighter place and Christians were no better than when they had been shrouded in darkness, Luther did not waver in his faith in the power of the Word, printed or otherwise. To him this situation was a measure of the power of the Devil — the anti-Christian force — who was stung into action the more clearly and fervently Christ's Word was proclaimed.[7]

For the compiler of chronicles, the belief in the power of print encompassed a very direct appreciation of the technical possibilities of the presses. The production of a beautiful, sumptuous book would enhance the reputation of a city or an eminent personage among an intellectual, political elite worth impressing. This was the motive behind the two major chronicling ventures of the period. Hartmann Schedel's chronicle, which places the city of Nuremberg in the context of world history, and Emperor Maximilian's imaginary autobiographical chronicle, *Theuerdank*.

Hartmann Schedel's *World chronicle* is the product of a most impressive printing cooperative [51]. Schedel sponsored the Nuremberg printer Anton Koberger, a number of famous artists (among them Michael Wolgemut, Wilhelm Pleydenwurff and the young Albrecht Dürer) and more than one hundred highly skilled printer's journeymen, who operated twenty-four presses to accomplish this work in 1493. The various contracts and detailed lists of expenses have been preserved.[8] The Library possesses an intriguing pirated reprint of 1497.[9]

The extraordinarily lavish production of the *Theuerdank* was worked out — as was everything else that was printed for the imperial court — in close consultation with the emperor himself.[10] Whereas other rulers would seek self-glorification through sponsoring a massive building programme, Maximilian seems to have believed in the greater efficacy of the power of print to glorify his person by projecting a programmatic hero image of himself for the benefit of contemporary and future political elites. The preservation of the memory of a good ruler — even if this was obviously imaginary or idealized — was taken for an essential aspect of the reality of good government.

As part of a projected thirty-seven-title publishing venture (of which only three items eventually appeared), the *Theuerdank* was finished in 1517. It was printed on vellum with a type-face that simulated the fine tracery of Gothic cursive lettering. It consisted of 118 very delicate woodcuts by such leading artists as Leonhard Beck, Hans Schäufelein and Hans Burgkmair, with a matching number of rhymed prose pieces, which chronicled individual adventures of Maximilian's journey to the Low Countries to win his bride in 1477. The favourable marriage is celebrated here as a sound basis for reform policies.

In 1494 there had been published in Basel an altogether different kind of chronicle: a conspectus of the whole of society mirrored in its follies — Sebastian Brant's *Narrenschiff* (*The ship of fools*). A Latin version had followed three years later.[11] As is evident from the preface, the author printed the book with the aim of encouraging moral reformation by confronting vices and abuses. In line with this purpose Brant did not appeal to an intellectual elite, but addressed himself to a wider, popular audience. It became indeed the most widespread enunciation of the reform theme. Jacob Wimpheling, the Strassburg humanist, recommended it as the most suitable book in German to be read in schools. The popular Strassburg preacher, Johann Geiler von Kaisersberg, preached a cycle of over one hundred sermons in the Strassburg Minster in 1498-9, using the individual follies as the texts for his exegesis. Brant's book consists of 112 separate woodcuts, each with a three-line motto and a rhymed exposition of a particular vice. The 'follies' might very well have been issued as individual broadsheets. The framework for this subject-matter is the ship peopled with fools and steered by them to a fools' paradise. It is a publication as yet insufficiently evaluated for the careful matching of the pictorial and verbal sketches with which it attempted to impress the popular mind. The mirror that Brant held up to society may be considered very conventional, but it reflects more than merely stereotype abuses, weaknesses and vices. His characterization allows for individuality; and this is in no small measure due to the woodcuts commissioned in part from the young Albrecht Dürer.[12] It is safe to assume that these woodcuts inspired the iconography of the entire range of polemical illustrations of the era of the Lutheran Reformation, at least in so far as they established and fixed symbols that were readily assimilable by everybody: the fool motif runs through the whole period in many permutations of purpose.

An interesting insight is communicated by

the fact that Brant makes the 'Book Fool' the first occupant of his ship. This fool is surrounded by many books, which 'he neither reads carefully nor understands'. He cherishes them by swatting the flies that threaten to settle on them, but he does not permit the books to teach him anything [52]. While pursuing the didactic purpose of unmasking human folly in print, Brant is only too keenly aware of the limitations of the power of print. A book can only exercise its power if man possesses and cultivates the right attitude to it. However, on the whole this reservation did not discourage the urge to influence contemporaries through the medium of printing.

The introduction of censorship is another testimony to the belief in the efficacy of print to influence people's convictions and actions. Even before the end of the fifteenth century the authorities felt the need to curb the printing output. Even before Emperor Maximilian appointed a general superintendent of books for the whole of Germany in 1496, ecclesiastical princes had made efforts to control the printing of 'reprehensible' books in their territories.[13] However, the censorship issue only came to a head with the early activities of Martin Luther. An 'act concerning printing' was encapsulated in the Edict of Worms of May 1521.[14] In this act Luther's writings were condemned and all authorities charged with vigilance in the interests of protecting German society against this corrosive heresy. In addition, any publications by other authors must be confiscated or their printing prevented if they contained slanderous views. It was urged that this type of printing output did damage to the Church as well as causing confusion and turmoil in the secular realm. What was suddenly considered so dangerous was precisely what Cardinal Joannes Andrea de Bussi had stressed as the advantage of printing in a letter to Pope Paul II in 1468: 'In our time God gave Christendom a gift which enables even the pauper to acquire books'.[15] The statement had been over-optimistic at the time, but it had become true by 1521: not Bibles nor heavy books of secular literature, but a profusion of Reformation pamphlets were indeed within the reach of people who had little cash.

51. Frontispiece to Hartmann Schedel's *World chronicle*; pirated reprint Augsburg 1497.

Luther did not stand alone as a popular writer: a substantial number of his educated followers and opponents of various shades of conviction developed skills — hitherto frowned upon in scholars and preachers — to present their views concisely and persuasively in pamphlets of frequently no more than four leaves. Individual tracts might deal with a self-contained theme, but they were also part of an intricate network in the art of persuasion, challenge and refutation. These writers did not publish for profit. However, the sales figures and the numerous authorized and unauthorized reprintings of pamphlets attest the printers' ability to make money by responding to a demand. They often pestered writers, especially Luther, to write more rapidly: Luther had some harsh words to say about the excessive greed of printers and publishers.

Most of what Luther produced was non-polemical, devotional, didactic in content and amounted to a conscious attempt to transform popular piety in all its aspects and to rescind the traditional sacraments to those with a scriptural basis. All this was either written in response to requests from friends who wished to be better instructed or arose from the requirement to adhere in sermons to the canonically prescribed texts for a particular day. The themes were marriage, monastic vows, death, confession, processions, penance, the Lord's Prayer, the Ten Commandments, etc. The same topics were worked over by other authors: many more people than ever before were encouraged to express their views in printed pamphlets. The popularity of these pamphlets seems to have been linked to the infinite variations on the

52. Sebastian Brant identified the 'book fool' as the first occupant of his *Ship of fools.*

same themes, which were in any case close to ordinary people's spiritual concerns. Luther's famous pamphlets of 1520, his *Address to the German nobility,* his *Prelude to the Babylonian captivity* and his *Freedom of the Christian man*[16] cannot, however, be said to publish simple verifiable truths. Yet in all this Luther decided to take even ordinary Christians into his confidence. When he was accused of 'innovation' (the worst accusation that could be levelled at a preacher) and of revealing too much of the mysteries of God in people's own common language, he was prepared to take that risk.

All pamphleteers were naturally very keen to have their texts accompanied by interpretative woodcuts, to assist the assimilation of the message by the illiterate. However, many tracts had to restrict themselves, obviously for reasons of economy of production, to merely ornamental, re-usable title borders. But there is also a striking number of specifically created negative images on the title-pages of pamphlets. This may be connected with the pamphleteers' endeavour to desanctify existing images, which they considered an obstacle to true faith. The pamphleteers and the artists were not above stimulating a campaign of iconoclastic defacing so as to remove more effectively the graphic hold traditional beliefs and practices might still have over people who were otherwise quite willing to be impressed with new simple ideas. There is no doubt that Reformation artists were engaged in a difficult struggle to give to the essentially verbal, abstract message of salvation by faith alone a simple visual expression, while avoiding the dangers of creating new images for veneration. In one respect, in the case of Luther himself, they took the easy way out by suggesting an immediately plausible identification of the validity of the teaching with the reputation of the person who taught. Thus the portraits of Martin Luther by Lucas Cranach[17] and Hans Baldung Grien[18] sought to represent him as a man of God whose faith in the Word lent him strength; but it was almost inevitable that Luther should be cast in the role of a substitute saint. The belief in the power of the Word in print to confront people with the will of God and to make them respond to it settled down to a glorification in text and woodcut of the man who had rediscovered and brought to the light of day the treasure of the pure Word. In many pamphlets the reputation of Luther became the touchstone of his Reformation.[19]

Conversely, vilification of the enemies of the Reformation — the tarnishing of their reputation — through text and illustrations in print played an essential role in the promulgation of the Word. Opponents were either given animal characteristics because, it was asserted, in their refusal to accept the truth they were behaving savagely and inhumanly;[20] or they were shown conspiring with the devil.[21] Such sentiments were, of course, mutual between promoters of, and objectors to the Lutheran Reformation, as is evidenced in a whole series of verbal and pictorial denunciations, which form much more than the irrelevant sub-plot of the Reformation endeavours.[22] The shockingly gross texts and the unsubtle woodcuts make it difficult for the later reader to penetrate to the genuine convictions of their originators. The belief in the power of print seems to manifest itself here in an expectation of some exorcising qualities of word and image.

Despite their fervent and imaginative use of the power of the printing press to transmit spoken words in printed texts and woodcuts as part of a multimedial communications exercise, the Lutheran pamphleteers were the first to realize their failure to initiate a lasting change in the attitude of the layman, to prompt him to organize his life in accordance with the living Word. As in the case of the vernacular Bible they readily acknowledged that no substantial improvement could be discerned in society.[23] Very few of the pamphleteers were open to the suggestion that the failure of their Reformation attempts might be directly related to their static view of society and their refusal to be drawn into any kind of movement for social change. Apart from Thomas Müntzer, one of the very few who believed in the power of print to create preconditions for a total transformation of society was Hans Hergot, printer of Nuremberg and wandering bookseller, who was executed for his beliefs in Leipzig in 1527. Only three copies of the pamphlet for which he died, *Von der newen wandlung,* were not burnt with him. One of these is in the College Library.[24] This tract, which envisaged a new age where social relations were completely transformed, was probably not even written by Hergot.[25] This authorship question may never be solved; but there is no doubt that the authorities saw the tract as a serious challenge to their power of social control — in fact an incitement to the kind of revolutionary agitation recently encountered in the Peasant War. In the context of the progress of the Lutheran Reformation towards respectability, even the simple motto of the pamphlet, 'For the honour of God and the furtherance of the commonweal against selfishness', was highly suspect. Contemporary official comments reveal the great fear of the authorities, which resulted in the staging of the public execution of the culprit as a deterrent to all those who might have allowed themselves to be influenced by revolutionary ideas in print.

NOTES

*This article is a revised and shortened version of the exhibition catalogue *Reformation and society in Germany, 1500-1530.* Dublin: The Friends of the Library, Trinity College, 1980.

1. [Biblia Sacra Latina]. (Nuremberg: A. Koberger, 1480) 2°. TCD, D.cc.33.

2. Hans Volz, *Bibel und Bibeldruck in Deutschland im 15. und 16. Jahrhundert.* Mainz: Verlag der Gutenberg-Gesellschaft, 1961, pp 30-4.

3. [Biblia Sacra Germanice]. [Strassburg: H. Eggestein, *c.* 1466] 2°. TCD, D.cc.30.

4. *Novum Instrumentum omne, diligenter ab Erasmo Roterodamo recognitum et emendatum* ... . (Basel: J. Froben, 1516) 2°. TCD, BB.b.23.

5. *Das Newe Testament Deutzsch.* [Wittenberg: M. Lotter the Younger, 1522] 2°. TCD, D.dd.25.

6. *Das Allte Testament deutsch.* M. Luther. Wittenberg. [Wittenberg: M. Lotter the Younger, 1523] 2°. TCD, D.dd.24.

7. Heiko A. Oberman, *Luther: Mensch zwischen Gott und Teufel.* Berlin: Severin und Siedler, 1981, pp 223ff.

8. Adrian Wilson, *The making of the Nuremberg chronicle.* Amsterdam: Nico Israel, 1976, p. 191.

9. [Hartmann Schedel], *Liber cronicarum cum figuris et ymaginibus ab inicio mundi usque nunc temporis.* (Augsburg: J. Schönsperger, 1497) 2°. TCD, M.aa.37.

10. [Theuerdank] *Die geverlicheiten ... des loblichen streytbaren und hoch berimpten helds und ritters herz Tewrdannckhs.* [Nuremberg: A. Koberger] 1517. 2°. TCD, Quin. No. 88. Cf. Gerhard Benecke, *Maximilian I (1459-1519), an analytical biography.* London: Routledge & Kegan Paul, 1982, pp 16ff.

11. [Sebastian Brant], [*navis stultifera*]. [Augsburg: J. Schönsperger, 1497] 8°. TCD, Press A.44.

12. Sebastian Brant, *Das Narrenschiff,* edited with a postscript by Hans-Joachim Mähl. Stuttgart: Philipp Reclam Jun., 1975, pp 512ff.

13. Ulrich Eisenhardt, *Die kaiserliche Aufsicht über Buchdruck, Buchhandel und Presse im Heiligen Römischen Reich Deutscher Nation (1496-1806).* Karlsruhe: C. F. Müller, 1970, pp 5-6.

14. *Der romischen Kaiserlichn̄ maiestat edict wider M. Luther bůcher vnd lere* .... [Worms: H. von Erfurt, 1521] 4°. TCD, C.tt.1/4.

15. Rudolf Hirsch, *Printing, selling and reading, 1450-1550.* Wiesbaden: Otto Harrassowitz, 1967, p. 1.
16. Martin Luther, *Von der Babylonischen gefenknuß der Kirchen.* [Strassburg: J. Schott, 1520] 4°. TCD, Gall. Z.1.47. Martin Luther, *Von der Freyhait Aines Christenmenschen.* [Augsburg: M. Ramminger, 1520] 4°. TCD, C.tt.1/7.
17. In: *Serenissime domine Imperator* .... [Latin version of Luther's address to the Diet of Worms]. [Augsburg: S. Grimm & M. Wirsung, 1521] 4°. TCD, Gall. Z.1.82/8.
18. In: Michael Stifel, *Von der Christförmigen, rechtgegründten leer Doctoris Martini Luthers.* [Strassburg: J. Schott, 1522 ?] 4°. TCD, DD.nn.51/13.
19. Michael Stifel, *Von der Christförmigen, rechtgegründten leer Doctoris Martini Luthers.* [Strassburg: J. Schott, 1522 ?] 4°. TCD, DD.nn.51/13.
Joannes Marcellus, *Passio Martini Lutheri.* [Strassburg: J. Prüss ? 1522] 8°. TCD, Gall. H.7.50.
20. [Johannes Agricola], *Eyn kurtze anred zu allen mißgūstigen Doctor Luthters vund der Christenlichen freyheit.* [Erfurt: M. Maler, 1522] 4°. TCD, C.tt.4/1. See also my facsimile edition with English translation and introduction, Dublin: The Friends of the Library, Trinity College, 1983.
21. *Ain grosser Preiß so der Fürst der hellen* ... . [Augsburg: M. Ramminger, 1521] 4°. TCD, C.tt.1/1.
22. Johannes Schwitalla, *Deutsche Flugschriften, 1460-1525. Textsorten-geschichtliche Studien.* Tübingen: Max Niemeyer, 1983, p. 83.
Michael A. Pegg, *A catalogue of German Reformation pamphlets (1516-1546) in libraries of Great Britain and Ireland.* Baden-Baden: Valentin Koerner, 1973. Nos 1690A, 1753, 3674, 3675.
23. Hans Greiffenberger, *Die Weltt sagt sy sehe kain besserung* ... . [Augsburg: M. Ramminger, 1523] 4°. TCD, E.s.38/3.
24. [Hans Hergot ?], *Von der newen wandlung eynes Christlichen lebens.* [Leipzig: M. Blum, 1526 ?] 8°. TCD, C.pp 40/3.
25. *Hans Hergot und die Flugschrift 'Von der newen wandlung eynes christlichen lebens'.* Faksimilewiedergabe mit Umschrift. Mit einem Vorwort von Max Steinmetz und einem Anhang von Helmut Claus. Leipzig: Veb Fachbuchverlag, 1977, pp 5ff.

53 (far left). Cranach workshop: Jacob's ladder set in a German landscape. From Luther's translation of parts of the Old Testament, 1523 (Genesis 28).

54 (above). Cranach workshop: Aaron, the model priest as described in Exodus, chapter 29. From Luther's translation of parts of the Old Testament, 1523.

THE AGOSTINI PLUTARCH: AN ILLUMINATED VENETIAN INCUNABLE

LILIAN ARMSTRONG

Among the treasures of the Fagel Collection is a masterpiece of Italian printing and illumination, a two-volume edition of Plutarch's *Lives* in Latin.[1] Printed in Venice on fine parchment by the most brilliant of early printers, Nicolaus Jenson, and illuminated by a refined miniaturist, the Master of the London Pliny, the work provides a magnificent example of early book production. Additionally, coats of arms on the frontispieces reveal that the book was decorated for a Venetian family, the Agostini. When considered along with other books known to have belonged to the Agostini, a picture emerges of the literary and artistic tastes of this little known family of Venetian merchants.

Plutarch's most famous work is the *Lives* in which the life of a famous Greek is paralleled with that of a famous Roman. Little known in Western Europe in the Middle Ages, the fifty surviving lives (twenty-three pairs and four single biographies) were first translated from Greek into Latin in the fifteenth century in Italy.[2] The *editio princeps* in Latin was edited by Giovanni Antonio Campano and printed in Rome by Ulrich Han about 1470, to be immediately followed by an edition in Strassburg. The Jenson Plutarch, dated 2 January 1478, is the third Latin edition, also based directly on that of Campano. The text is set in the beautiful Roman type for which the printer was famed. Each of the lives is preceded by a title in capital letters naming the subject and the translator. Eight to twelve lines of type are indented at the beginning of each life to provide space for a large capital to be added by hand after the printing. The stately layout of this large folio edition makes it one of the most handsome of all Venetian incunables.

In the Library's copy of the Jenson Plutarch the wide margins of the first folio in each volume have been painted in gold and brilliant colours to provide a sumptuous frontispiece [56 and 61]. Nearly every life has also received a large decorative initial either painted in tempera like the frontispieces [63], or drawn in brown ink and modelled with delicate watercolour wash [60 and 55]. Surprisingly, these major examples of Venetian book illumination have not previously been discussed in the scholarly literature.

The attribution of the Plutarch illuminations is most easily established in the second volume. The frontispiece [61] is the work of one of the finest Venetian Renaissance miniaturists, the Master of the London Pliny. This artist was active in Venice from 1472 to 1480 when he seems to have left for Rome or Naples in the employ of Cardinal Giovanni d'Aragona.[3] His painting reveals a classicizing style, using architectural and decorative motifs *all'antica* with miniatures elegantly populated by slender mythical creatures. This use of the antique and the mastery of illusionism derive ultimately from paintings of the 1450s by the great Paduan artist, Andrea Mantegna. In addition, the love of vibrant colours shows a Venetian training and the influence of two famous contemporaries, Giovanni Bellini and Antonello da Messina. Far from being a derivative artist, however, the work of the London Pliny Master has an important position in the development of Renaissance art in Venice, and his exquisite classical compositions helped to shape the taste of the Venetian aristocracy for the new style.

The frontispiece of Volume II of the Library's Plutarch consists of an illusionistically painted architectural monument apparently set in front of a brick wall [61]. Beyond the wall a fragile tree is silhouetted against the blue sky. Tall bronze candelabra and a pair of centaurs with golden brown bodies contrast with the purple porphyry of the monument. On a green entablature pairs of bronze sea-creatures flank a roundel, while at the bottom the centaurs hold green palms and a wreath around the arms of the Agostini family.

This elaborate composition relates to those appearing in several other incunables decorated by the London Pliny Master. For example, the rich colours and classical busts recall a similar composition in a Pliny of 1476 in Cambridge University Library [58].[4] The prancing centaurs were used in another book with Agostini arms, a Sallust of 1474 in the John Rylands University Library of Manchester.[5] Closest of all is a heretofore unpublished frontispiece in a Virgil of 1476 in the British Library, also executed for the Agostini [59].[6] In its handsome frontispiece bulging columns on tall cylindrical bases support an entablature on whose frieze appear similar winged sea-creatures, urns and cornucopias. To the right of the monument a brick wall punctuated with a roundel again blocks a view into depth and a bare tree is outlined against the sky. The architectural frontispiece of both the Sallust and the Virgil is drawn in brown ink and tinted with watercolour wash, a favourite technique of the London Pliny Master.

Admiration for antique art was also a primary characteristic of the London Pliny Master. This can be particularly well appreciated in the British Library Virgil. In the lower margin four winged cherubs or *putti* playfully attack a fallen faun in a composition virtually identical to one painted by the artist in a *Breviary* of about the same date in the Bodleian Library, Oxford.[7] For both compositions the artist draws on images of Pan from two types of Bacchic sarcophagi known in the fifteenth century.[8] The antique models are not slavishly imitated, but are freshly interpreted to recall the classical era.

Typical of the initials in Volume II of the Agostini Plutarch is the one painted in gold and brilliant colours that opens the *Life of Lucullus* [63]. The strokes of the *L* resemble polished green cylinders with gold joints and finials. The three dimensional letter gives the illusion of resting on a blue plaque to which is affixed a roundel. This contains profile busts of a man and a woman divided by a palm tree, which is encircled by winged snakes to form a caduceus. Similarly paired busts and a jewel-like capital are also found in the Cambridge Pliny of 1476 [58].

In contrast, two of the initials in the second volume are drawn in dark ink with touches of coloured wash. Initiating the *Life of Plato* is a vivaciously rendered putto-triton carrying a lyre [60], a typical image in the decorative vocabulary of the artist and his colleague, the Putti Master [59].[9] In such images there is no specific allusion to the text, but instead the artist evokes the world of antiquity suitable to the book as a whole. Reference to the text is doubtless intended, however, in the initial for the *Life of Aristotle* [55]. In this miniature two satyrs support a medallion on which is a bust of Aristotle.

The decoration of Volume I raises broader issues regarding miniaturists active in Venice in the later 1470s. The frontispiece is also the work of the London Pliny Master, but in contrast to Volume II the design shows the mark-

ARISTOTILIS VIRI
PER GVARINVM VI
ARISTO
fuit noĩe S
claritate ref
pfessorẽ ar
cõtinuata c
comachus :
& medici &
regno potu
ut quidam
quoq; habi
tiles autem prima ætate in Macedonia edu
gra missus cum cæteris operã disciplinis h
academiam mira discipulorum celebritate in
ætatis anno fuisse phibent cum Platonẽ a

55 (above). Two satyrs holding a medallion on which is a portrait of Aristotle. From Plutarch's *Vitae virorum illustrium,* Venice 1478.

56 (far right). Frontispiece, with mythological scenes, from volume 1 of Plutarch's *Vitae virorum illustrium,* Venice 1478 (London Pliny Master).

ed influence of another superb miniaturist who worked for the Agostini, Girolamo da Cremona [56 and 62]. The borders of the frontispiece consist of wide bands of brilliant blue edged by bronze mouldings and filled with decorative motifs also in bronze with gold highlights. At the corners, ovals made of green cylinders and bronze joints surround mythological scenes painted in *grisaille*: Hercules and the Nemean Lion, the Rape of Europa, the Birth of Aesculapius, and Apollo and Daphne. Male and female busts *all'antica* fill roundels, and the Agostini arms gleam among the pearls and jewels of the right-hand margin. While the busts and mythological scenes are characteristic of the London Pliny Master and may be found, for example, in the border decorating the *Letters* of St Jerome now in the Kupferstichkabinett, Berlin,[10] other elements show the influence of Girolamo da Cremona. In particular, the large cluster of jewels and the scene of deer in a landscape are not typical of the earlier works by the London Pliny Master.

Girolamo da Cremona's early career in Mantua and Siena is well documented, as is his presence in Venice in 1475-6.[11] Subsequently a series of incunables painted in his style attest to his continued activity in Venice from 1475 to 1483.[12] Scenes of animals in delicate landscapes and huge conglomerations of gems and pearls are frequently found in his Venetian works [62] and the presence of these motifs in the Trinity College Plutarch frontispiece suggests that the London Pliny Master knew and imitated them.

That Girolamo da Cremona was in turn affected by the London Pliny Master can be seen in a commission which must have been intimately related to the Trinity College Plutarch. Girolamo painted the frontispieces and initials in another two-volume copy of the Jenson Plutarch, now divided between Paris and New York, which also belonged to the Agostini.[13] The animals, satyrs and enormous jewels in the frontispiece of Volume I of this copy [62] are typical of Girolamo's style. On the other hand the cramped mythological scenes in roundels and the image of Plutarch in his study painted in the first initial of this work are most characteristic of the London Pliny Master and suggest that Girolamo was imitating the classicizing compositions for which his contemporary was better known.

An intriguing feature of the mythological scenes and classical busts in the Trinity College Plutarch is the use of identifying labels. Usually these are the names of the characters and they are written in Roman epigraphic capitals. For example, scenes in the corners of the Volume I frontispiece [56] are inscribed DAP/HNES and PHE/BVS, and EVROPA and JVPITER. The letters by the profile bust of a soldier in the roundel prominently set in the centre of the upper border are, by contrast, Greek capitals [57]. Arranged vertically

THESEI VITA PER LAPVM FLORENTINVM EX PLVTARCO GRAECO IN LATINVM VERSA.

QVEMADMODVM IN ORBIS TERRAE SItu describendo historici solent: ut ad quæ ipsi cognitione aspirare non possunt: extremis tabularũ partibus supprimentes quibusdam adiiciunt locos esse uastos arenosos & cælo terraq; penuriam aquarum: aut limum insuperabilem: aut mõtem sciticum: aut astrictum frigore pontum: ita & nobis in hac uirorum collatione perpetua rerũ historia quantũ probabili oratione assequi potuimus: de his quos supra memorauimus uiris tempora percurrẽtibus uere licuit affirmare. Quæ uero antiquiora ac uetustiora sunt: tragica & monstruosa poetæ & fabulosi rerum scriptores occupant: nec ultra fidem ullam nec certitudinem præ se ferunt. Cum igitur Lycurgi legũ latoris & Numę regis res gestas litteris mandauerimus: haud ab re fuerit ad Romulum orationem conuertere: quando historia ipsa ad eius tempora q̃ prope accessimus. Sed mihi diu cogitãti huic uiro (ut inquit Aeschilus) quis conueniret: quem illi opponerem: quis dignus secum in comparatione cõiungi: uisum est tandem faciendum esse: ut a quo celebrata Atheniensium ciuitas amplificata est: eum cum gloriosissimæ atq; inuictissimæ urbis Romæ parente conferrem & compararem. Licet autem nobis reiectis fabulis ad ipsam claram historiæ lucem & ueritatem accedere. Quod sicubi necessitas coget nos ab hac parumper digressos: ad id quod uerisimile sit conferre: a quo fortasse historia abhorreat: nec admittat ullum cũ probabilitate cõmertium: æquis auditoribus opus erit: quiq; benigne & humane initium orationis exaudiant atq; approbent. Videtur igitur Theseus multis de causis Romulo q̃simillimus extitisse. Ambo.n.cum spurii & obscuri forent: existimati sunt a Diis ĩmortalibus procreati esse. Ambo ẽt belicosi ac manu strenui: hoc quidem omnes scimus: & quanta maxime fieri potuit prudẽtia præstiterunt. ex duabus quoq; clarissimis ciuitatibus Roma & Athenis: alteram hic condidit: alteram ille nouis colonis compleuit. Fœminarum præterea raptus de utroq; feruntur: nec eorum quisq̃ domesticam cladem & crimina suorum effugit: sed ad postremum ambo dicuntur in inuidiam & offensionem ciuium incidisse. Siquid igitur ex his quæ minus tragice dici uidentur ad ueritatem conducit: Thesei quidem paternum genus in erechtheum ac primos indigenas referebatur: maternum uero in Pelopem. Pelops enim non opibus magis & copiis q̃ natorum sobole cæterorum Pelopõnesi regum potentissimus fuit: cũ filias permultas optimatibus in matrimonio locasset: multosq; in rebusp. passim pricipes dispersisset: e quibus unus Pittheus extitit Thesei maternus auus: qui urbem nõ magnam trœzeniorum incoluit: is qui per id temporis omnibus sapientia & eloquentia plurimum præstare putabatur. Fuit eius sapientiæ ut uidetur talis quædam uis ac forma: qualem complexus Hesiodus cum sua scripta sententiis plurimis refersisset: sapiens imprimis est habitus: atq; eam unam ex Pitthei sententiis fuisse memorant: Esto satis comiti merces promissa laboris. Cuius rei Aristoteles philosophus ẽ auctor. Euripides etiam cum Hippolytum casti Pitthei disciplinam appellet: hanc eandẽ de Pittheo opinionem perspicue attestari uidetur. Aegeo uero cum filiis indigeret: uulgatum illud oraculum Pythiam uatem cecinisse ferũt: quo iussit ne cum muliere coiret: priusq̃ Athenas accederet. quod cum non satis aperte dixisse uideretur: in Trœzenem profectus: de Dei responso cum Pittheo communicauit: quod huiusmodi fuit: Neue

they are

·Ƥ·
A
Ɯ
Y
Z·

on the left and

MƬ
·Γ
Z
P
Θ·

on the right.

57. Greek letters from roundel of frontispiece (vol. 1).

Although these await decoding, a clue to their meaning may be found in the bust in the frontispiece of a Jenson *Bible* of 1476 again decorated for the Agostini.[14] The Augustan profile bust is labelled straightforwardly DIV [V] S/AVGVS/P/.P., but it seems to be inappropriate iconographically for the opening of Genesis. It may therefore be intended as a flattering play on the name Agostini, as I think the Plutarch label will also prove to be.

58. Architectural frontispiece from Pliny's *Historia naturalis,* Venice 1476 (London Pliny Master). (Camb. Univ. Libr.)

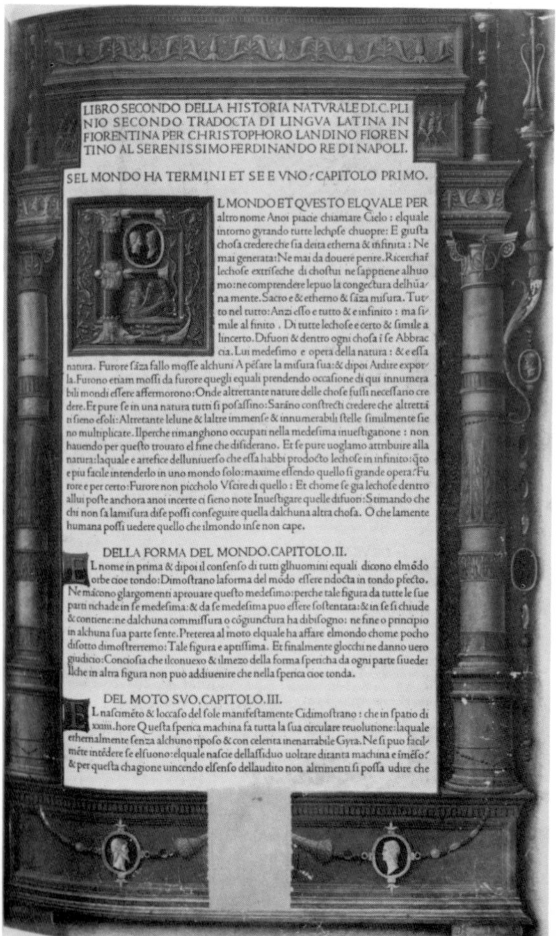

The importance of the Trinity College Plutarch cannot be fully appreciated without further details about the printer, Nicolaus Jenson, and the patrons, the Agostini. Nicolaus Jenson came from Sommevoire, near Troyes in eastern France.[15] He began to print in Venice in 1470, the year after Johannes de Spira had opened the first press there. Jenson was the most successful printer in Venice in the 1470s judged both by the number of his editions and by the beauty of the typography. In the early 1470s he established his reputation with handsome folio editions of the Latin classics presumably destined for readers interested in the burgeoning humanist movement. Many of his early books were also decorated by hand after the printing. Following a financial setback in 1473, Jenson was forced to reorganize the firm. The production of classics was drastically curtailed and the emphasis shifted to the printing of legal and religious texts with more traditional appeal. The Latin Plutarch of 1478 was the last of the splendid classical editions to be printed before Jenson's death in 1480, and a number of copies are known with decoration added after the printing.

Printing a luxury folio edition such as the Jenson Plutarch required special financial backing, and various arrangements are known to have been developed for this purpose.[16] The extravagant custom of printing a few copies on parchment may have been a way of making particularly fine copies available to the backers. For example, the two Florentine families, the Strozzi and the Ridolfi, who financed Jenson's 1476 edition of Pliny in Italian, each had a decorated parchment copy complete with miniatures and their arms.[17] Additionally, Jenson's documented business associate, the German merchant Petrus Ugelheimer, owned at least twelve incunables on parchment each magnificently decorated and bearing his coat of arms, including yet another copy of the 1478 Plutarch, which is now in Wolfenbüttel. Might not the Agostini also owe their collection of illuminated incunables to similar business arrangements with printers, especially Jenson?

Little is known about the Agostini. In earlier centuries a noble family with this surname but with another coat of arms existed in Venice, but the two lines of this family became extinct in 1221 and in 1423 respectively.[18] The coat of arms now familiar from the Trinity College Plutarch appears in fifteen incunables decorated in Venice in the 1470s, and later Venetian heraldic manuscripts always indicate that this family had the non-noble status of *cittadini* of Venice.[19] At the end of the 1490s the family is the Agostini dal Banco and it is known that the Agostini bank had business dealings with booksellers.[20] More important, however, are the specific links that can be established between the Agostini and Nicolaus Jenson. Documents show that the family sold paper to the Florentine merchants who commissioned Jenson in Venice to print the 1476 Pliny mentioned above.[21] In his will of 1480, Jenson named Pietro and Alvise Agostini 'brothers from Fabriano living in Venice' as executors.[22] Fabriano had since the twelfth century been one of the great centres of paper manufacture, and it is thus likely that the Agostini of Venice maintained commercial contacts with their city of origin. The relationship between the Agostini and Nicolaus Jenson may well have originated in the commerce of paper, the single most expensive element in the manufacture of incunables, and developed into one of considerable personal friendship and trust. What remains unknown, however, are the details of the business arrangements that resulted in the Agostini acquisition of beautifully decorated incunables.

Books that belonged to the Agostini can be identified in two ways. Until recently they were recognized only if the decoration of the volume included the Agostini coat of arms.[23] Now in addition several volumes printed on

59. Architectural frontispiece with the tormenting of Pan from Virgil's *Opera*, Venice 1476 (London Pliny Master). (Brit. Libr.)

parchment have been found in which the name *B agustini,* or in one case *Bart* (?) *agustini,* has been written in the lower margin of one or more folios well into the body of a given copy on parchment.[24] These signatures do not appear to be a normal *ex-libris.* Instead they may be a means of indicating that certain lots of parchment were to be reserved for the Agostini copy of an edition. The name was probably meant to be cut off when the margins of the folios were trimmed. The Agostini may thus have been providers of parchment as well as paper, receiving part of their payment in kind.

Generalizations about the contents of the Agostini 'library' are impeded by several factors. We do not know if members of the family chose books because of their subject matter, or if they received books from printers as par-

PLATONIS VIRI ILLVSTRIS
SEM EDITA.

VLTVM
uir doctiſſ
quibus eff
rerũ cognit
cellas. Eiu
Homerus
dicus prec
ſi carus ad
principi ſu
optimo: C
& ſapiẽtia inter mortales antecedit: Tu
ſe tibi ſum teſtis non infimus: quẽ ſingu
conſuetudine colloquiis intimis tuenda
ſitudine tibi deuinctum tenes. Cuius qu

60 (above). Initial letter *M* of Plutarch's *Life* of Plato (1478), with putto-triton holding a lyre.

61 (far right). Architectural frontispiece, with centaurs, from volume 2 of Plutarch's *Vitae virorum illustrium*, Venice 1478 (London Pliny Master).

tial payment for parchment or paper. Additionally, more than one member of the family probably owned the books that carry their arms. Pietro and Alvise are the brothers named in Jenson's will, and Bartolommeo may be the name of the *B agustini* who signed several volumes. The fact that two copies of the 1478 Latin Plutarch, the Trinity College volumes and the Paris/New York set, are both elaborately decorated and both bear the Agostini arms must mean that they were destined for two different persons. Furthermore, while the Paris copy of a 1474 Jenson edition of Clemens V *Constitutiones* clearly has the Agostini arms,[25] another copy on parchment from which the decoration has been excised, in the Biblioteca Marciana, Venice, is signed *B. agustini* but is also inscribed *De la Carita.*[26] The Marciana copy may thus have been commissioned by 'B. agustini' for the church or the school of Santa Maria della Carità of Venice, and may not have been destined for private ownership at all.

Any conclusions about the literary tastes of the Agostini will necessarily be conditioned by subsequent finds and by answers to the problems of acquisition that have just been raised. Despite these restrictions, a few observations about the contents of the 'library' may be made. Only two of the texts are in Italian rather than Latin, a romance of *Guerino il Meschino* and a translation of Pliny's *Historia naturalis,* which had earlier been acquired in Latin as well.[27] The romance and a collection of ancient and humanist antiquarian texts[28] are the only manuscripts, and both are on paper. Among the incunables, nine of the texts are by ancient authors. Four are by writers on history (Herodotus, Plutarch, Sallust and Valerius Maximus) and three are on science (Pliny, Solinus and the *Scriptores rei rusticae*). The serious tone of the collection is continued with Virgil, Cicero, Gratian, Clement V, Tortellius and a Latin *Bible.* Absent are works of philosophy and theology, poetry other than Virgil, vernacular saints' lives, and the writings of the great Florentines, Dante, Petrarch and Boccaccio, which might equally well have been acquired from Venetian printers in the 1470s.

More certain than the literary tastes are the artistic tastes of the Agostini. The London Pliny Master was their favourite artist. Ten of the twenty-one volumes owned by the family were decorated by him, and four more were done by his associate, the Putti Master. In the early and mid 1470s the works were usually drawn in pen and ink, and tinted with watercolour wash, the technique for which the workshop was well known. The architectural frontispieces [59] and initials incorporating mythical creatures are masterfully drawn in the classical style so suited to Jenson's majestic opening folios. By contrast, in the later 1470s the London Pliny Master shifted to painting miniatures whose subtle effects of light and colour reveal both Venetian and Flemish tendencies. The frontispieces of the Trinity College Plutarch combine the antiquarian in-

CIMONIS VIRI ILLVSTRIS VITA EX PLVTARCHO GRAECO IN LATINVM PER LEONARDVM IVSTINIANVM VERSA.

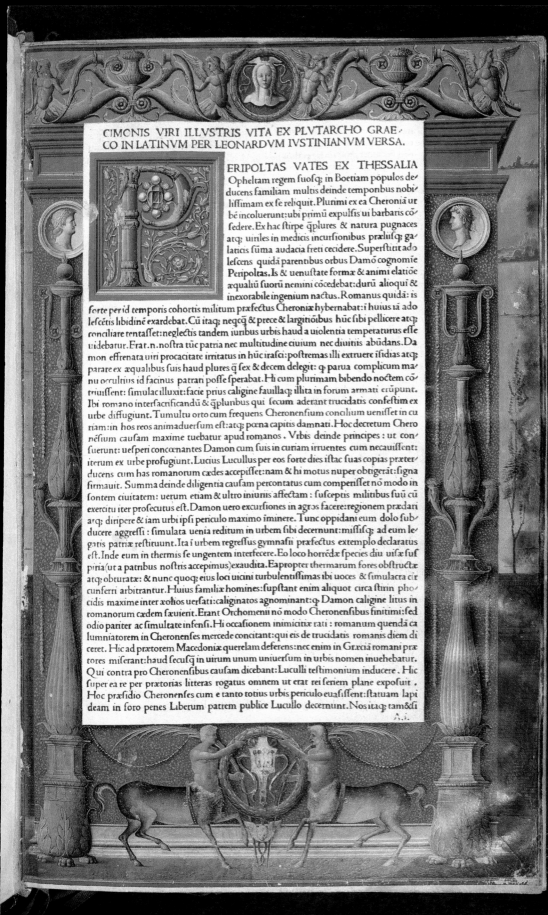

PERIPOLTAS VATES EX THESSALIA Opheltam regem suosq; in Boetiam populos deducens familiam multis deinde temporibus nobilissimam ex se reliquit. Plurimi ex ea Cheroniã urbẽ incoluerunt: ubi primũ expulsis ui barbaris cõsedere. Ex hac stirpe q̃plures & natura pugnaces atq; uiriles in medicis incursionibus præliisq; galaticis sũma audacia freti cecidere. Superstitit adolescens quidã parentibus orbus Damõ cognomĩe Peripoltas. Is & uenustate formæ & animi elatiõe æqualiũ suorũ nemini cõcedebat: durũ alioquĩ & inexorabile ingenium nactus. Romanus quidã: is forte per id temporis cohortis militum præfectus Cheroniæ hybernabat: ĩ huius iã adolescẽtis libidinẽ exardebat. Cũ itaq; neq̃c̃q̃ & prece & largitiõibus hũc sibi pellicere atq; conciliare tentasset: neglectis tandem iuribus urbis haud a uiolentia temperaturus esse uidebatur. Erat.n. nostra tũc patria nec multitudine ciuium nec diuitiis abũdans. Damon effrenata uiri procacitate irritatus in hũc irasci: postremas illi extruere ĩsidias atq; parare ex æqualibus suis haud plures q̃ sex & decem delegit: q̃ parua complicum manu occultius id facinus patrari posse sperabat. Hi cum plurimam bibendo noctem cõtriuissent: simulac illuxit: facie prius caligine fauillaq; illita in forum armati erũpunt. Ibi romano inter sacrificandũ & q̃pluribus qui secum aderant trucidatis confestim ex urbe diffugiunt. Tumultu orto cum frequens Cheronensium concilium uenisset in curiam: in hos reos animaduersum est: atq; pœna capitis damnati. Hoc decretum Cheronẽsium causam maxime tuebatur apud romanos. Vrbis deinde principes: ut consuerunt: uesperi concœnantes Damon cum suis in curiam irruentes cum necauissent: iterum ex urbe profugiunt. Lucius Lucullus per eos forte dies istac suas copias præterducens cum has romanorum cædes accepisset: nam & hi motus nuper obtigerãt: signa firmauit. Summa deinde diligentia causam percontatus cum comperisset nõ modo insontem ciuitatem: uerum etiam & ultro iniuriis affectam: susceptis militibus suũ cũ exercitu iter prosecutus est. Damon uero excursiones in agros facere: regionem prædari atq; diripere & iam urbi ipsi periculo maximo ĩminere. Tunc oppidani eum dolo subducere aggressi: simulata uenia reditum in urbem sibi decernunt: missisq; ad eum legatis patriæ restituunt. Ita ĩ urbem regressus gymnasii præfectus extemplo declaratus est. Inde eum in thermis se ungentem interfecere. Eo loco horrẽdæ species diu uisæ suspiria (ut a patribus nostris accepimus) exaudita. Eapropter thermarum fores obstructæ atq; obturatæ: & nunc quoq; eius loci uicini turbulentissimas ibi uoces & simulacra circunferri arbitrantur. Huius familiæ homines: supstant enim aliquot circa stirin phocidis maxime inter æolios uersati: caliginatos agnominant: q̃ Damon caligine litus in romanorum cædem sæuierit. Erant Orchomenii nõ modo Cheronensibus finitimi: sed odio pariter ac simultate infensi. Hi occasionem inimicitiæ rati: romanum quendã calumniatorem in Cheronenses mercede concitant: qui eis de trucidatis romanis diem diceret. Hic ad prætorem Macedoniæ querelam deferens: nec enim in Græciã romani prætores miserant: haud secusq̃ in uirum unum uniuersum in urbis nomen inuehebatur. Qui contra pro Cheronensibus causam dicebant: Luculli testimonium inducere. Hic super ea re per prætorias litteras rogatus omnem ut erat rei seriem plane exposuit. Hoc præsidio Cheronenses cum e tanto totius urbis periculo euasissent: statuam lapideam in foro penes Liberum patrem publice Lucullo decernunt. Nos itaq; tam & si terests of the earlier works with the rich pictorial effects of the artist's later style.

At least one member of the Agostini family must also have favoured Girolamo da Cremona, a second artist in the *avant-garde* of the 1470s. In addition to decorating two incunables for the Agostini in the middle of the decade,[29] he painted the frontispieces of the second copy of the Jenson Plutarch of 1478, which bears their arms [62]. His distinctive style is seen in their opening pages, which are almost overwhelmed with bejewelled monuments set in landscapes inhabited by melancholic satyrs and animals.

Printing and the classical style were both new in Venice in the 1470s. Each opening of the Trinity College Plutarch proves that the printer intended the creation of beautifully designed pages. A painter who had mastered the new style further enhanced the folios with exquisite paintings. Encouraging both printer and painter was a patron who welcomed both the new technology and its artistic compliment. The sublime conjunction of word and image in this incunable makes it a major monument in the history of the Renaissance book.

NOTES

1. Fag. GG.2.1, 2. Plutarchus, *Vitae virorum illustrium,* Venice, Nicolaus Jenson, 2 January 1478. 2 vols. On parchment. Hain 13127. S. Peterson, *Bibliotheca Fageliana.* Part I, March 1, 1802, p. 109, No. 2394. J. van Praet, *Catalogue des livres sur vélin de la bibliothèque du roi,* Vol. V. Paris, 1822, p. 49. T. K. Abbott, *Catalogue of fifteenth-century books in the Library of Trinity College, Dublin.* London: Longmans Green and Co., 1905, p. 147, No. 434.

Both frontispieces bear the coat of arms of the Agostini family of Venice *(per fess dancetty or and azure each point terminating in a roundel counter-changed).* On fol. 70^r are the faint remains of what was probably the word *agustini.*

2. V.R. Giustiniani, 'Sulle traduzioni delle "Vite" di Plutarco nel Quattrocento', *Rinascimento,* 2nd ser., 1 (1961) 3-59.

3. L. Armstrong, *Renaissance miniature painters and classical imagery: the Master of the Putti and his Venetian workshop.* London: Harvey Miller Publishers, 1981, pp 30-49 (hereafter Armstrong). A. C. de la Mare, 'The Florentine scribes of Cardinal Giovanni of Aragon', in *Il libro e il testo.* Urbino: Università degli Studi di Urbino, 1984, pp 245-93.

4. Cambridge University Library, Inc. I, B.3.2 (1360). Plinius, *Historia naturalis* (in Ital.). Venice, Jenson, 1476 (Armstrong, p. 130) possibly originally belonging to the Agostini.

5. John Rylands Library, No. 10547 (Armstrong, pp 126-7 and ill. 89).

6. British Library, C.19.e.14. Vergilius Maro, *Opera.* Venice, Antonio di Bartolommeo, Miscomini, 14[7]6.

7. Bodleian Library, MS Canon. Lit. 410 (19476), fol. 234^v (Armstrong, pp 127-9 and colour pl. II).

8. Armstrong, p. 58. R. O. Rubinstein, 'A Bacchic sarcophagus in the Renaissance', *British Museum Yearbook* 1 (1976) 103-56.

9. Armstrong, ills 2, 48, 89, 97.

10. Berlin, Kupferstichkabinett, MS 78 D 13. Armstrong, p. 131 and ill. 117.

11. M. Levi d'Ancona, 'Postille a Girolamo da Cremona', in *Studi di bibliographia e di storia in onore di Tammaro de Marinis.* Verona, 1964, Vol. III, pp 45-104. M.G. Ciardi Dupré, *I corali del duomo di Siena.* Milan: Electa Editrice, 1972, pp 11-12, 253-6. G. Mariani Canova, 'Girolamo da Cremona nel Veneto', in *Studi di storia dell'arte in memoria di Mario Rotili.* Naples: Banca Sannitica, 1984, pp 331-46.

12. G. Mariani Canova, *La miniatura veneta del rinascimento.* Venice: Alfieri, 1969, pp 58-66, 117-21.

13. Vol. I: Paris, Bibliothèque Nationale, Vélins 700 (J.J.G. Alexander, 'Notes on some Veneto-Paduan illuminated books of the Renaissance', *Arte veneta* 23 [1969] 10). Vol. II: New York, Pierpont Morgan Library, ChL ff 767a, No. 77565 (New York, Sotheby Parke Bernet, *Fine printed books,* 25 June 1982, Lot 113, colour pl. on cover). On fol. 20^r is written *B. agustini,* and on fol. 71^r *bart* (?) *augustini.*

14. Ravenna, Classense, Inc. No. 31 (*Ravenna, La Biblioteca Classense,* Vol. I. Bologna: Grafis, 1982. pp 98, 125). On sig. R2^r in the lower margin is written *B. agustini.*

15. L.V. Gerulaitis, *Printing and publishing in fifteenth century Venice.* Chicago: American Library Association, 1976, pp 20-30.

16. A. Colla, 'Tipografi, editori e libri a Padova, Treviso, Vicenza, Verona, Trento', in *La stampa degli incunaboli nel veneto.* Verona: Neri Pozza, 1984, pp 37-54.

62. Architectural frontispiece with satyrs and animals from Plutarch's *Vitae virorum illustrium,* Venice 1478 (Girolamo da Cremona). (Bibl. nat. Paris)

THSEI VITA PER LAPVM FLORENTINVM EX PLVTARC GRAEC IN LATINVM VERSA

VEMADMODVM IN ORBIS TERRAE SI
tu describendo historici solent: ut ad quæ ipsi cognitione aspirare non possunt: extremis tabularũ
partibus supprimentes quibusdam adiiciunt lo
cos esse uastos arenosos & cælo terraq; penuriam
aquarum: aut limum insuperabilem: aut mõtem
stiticum: aut astrictum frigore pontum: ita & no
bis in hac uirorum collatione perpetua rerũ histo
ria quantũ probabili oratione assequi potuimus:
de his quos supra memorauimus uiris tempora
percurrẽtibus uere licuit affirmare. Quæ uero antiquiora ac uetustiora sunt: tragica & monstruosa
poetæ & fabulosi rerum scriptores occupant: nec ultra fidem ullam nec certitudinem
præse ferunt. Cum igitur Lycurgi legũ latoris & Nume regis res gestas litteris mandauerimus: haud ab re fuerit ad Romulum orationem conuertere: quando historia ipsa
ad eius tempora q̃ prope accessimus. Sed mihi diu cogitãti huic uiro (ut inquit Aeschilus) quis conueniret: quem illi opponerem: quis dignus secum in comparatione cõiun
gi: uisum est tandem faciendum esse: ut a quo celebrata Atheniensium ciuitas amplificata est: eum cum gloriosissimæ atq; inuictissimæ urbis Romæ parente conferrem &
compararem. Licet autem nobis reiectis fabulis ad ipsam claram historiæ lucem & ue
ritatem accedere. Quod sicubi necessitas coget nos ab hac parumper digressos: ad id
quod uerisimile sit conferre: a quo fortasse historia abhorreat: nec admittat ullum cũ
probabilitate cõmertium: æquis auditoribus opus erit: quiq; benigne & humane initium orationis exaudiant atq; approbent. Videtur igitur Theseus multis de causis Ro
mulo q̃ simillimus extitisse. Ambo.n.cum spurii & obscuri forent: existimati sunt
a Diis ĩmortalibus procreati esse. Ambo ẽt belicosi ac manu strenui: hoc quidem omnes scimus: & quanta maxime fieri potuit prudẽtia præstiterunt. ex duabus quoq; cla
rissimis ciuitatibus Roma & Athenis: alteram hic condidit: alteram ille nouis colonis
compleuit. Fœminarum præterea raptus de utroq; feruntur: nec eorum quisq̃ domesticam cladem & crimina suorum effugit: sed ad postremum ambo dicuntur in inuidiam & offensionem ciuium incidisse. Siquid igitur ex his quæ minus tragice dici uidentur ad ueritatem conducit: Thesei quidem paternum genus in erechtheum ac primos indigenas referebatur: maternum uero in Pelopem. Pelops enim non opibus ma
gis & copiis q̃ natorum sobole cæterorum Pelopõnesi regum potentissimus fuit: cũ
filias permultas optimatibus in matrimonio locasset: multosq; in rebusp. passim prĩ
cipes dispersisset: e quibus unus Pittheus extitit Thesei maternus auus: qui urbem nõ
magnam trœzeniorum incoluit: is qui per id temporis omnibus sapientia & eloquentia plurimum præstare putabatur. Fuit eius sapientiæ ut uidetur talis quædam uis ac
forma: qualem complexus Hesiodus cum sua scripta sententiis plurimis refersisset:
sapiens imprimis est habitus: atq; eam unam ex Pitthei sententiis fuisse memorant:
Esto satis comiti merces promissa laboris. Cuius rei Aristoteles philosophus ẽ auctor.
Euripides etiam cum Hippolytum casti Pitthei disciplinam appellet: hanc eandẽ de
Pittheo opinionem perspicue attestari uidetur. Aegeo uero cum filiis indigeret: uulga
tum illud oraculum Pythiam uatem cecinisse ferũt: quo iussit ne cum muliere coiret:
priusq̃ Athenas accederet. quod cum non satis aperte dixisse uideretur: in Trœzenem
profectus: de Dei responso cum Pittheo communicauit: quod huiusmodi fuit: Neue

63. Initial letter *L* of Plutarch's *Life* of Lucullus (1478) with roundel and profile busts.

17. L. Armstrong, 'The illustration of Pliny's *Historia naturalis* in Venetian manuscripts and early printed books', in *Manuscripts in the fifty years after the invention of printing,* ed. J. B. Trapp. London: The Warburg Institute, 1983, p. 99.

18. Venice, Biblioteca Marciana, MS Ital. VII, 15 (8304), G. A. Cappellari, *Campidoglio veneto,* Vol. I, fol. 28^{r}.

19. Venice, Biblioteca Correr, MS Cicogna 3627 (2673), fol. 187^{v}. Venice, Biblioteca Marciana, MS Ital. VII, 2437 (10593), G. de Pellegrini, *Amerista dei cittadini veneziani.* See note 23 for the incunables.

20. M. Lowry, *The world of Aldus Manutius.* Ithaca, New York: Cornell University Press, 1979, pp 98, 129.

21. F. Edler de Roover, 'Come furono stampati a Venezia tre dei primi libri in volgare', *Bibliofilia* 55 (1953) 110.

22. Dr Martin Lowry kindly showed me this reference. C. Castellani, *La stampa in Venezia dalla sua origine alla morte di Aldo Manuzio seniore.* Venice: Ferdinando Ongania, 1889, pp 85 ff.

23. In addition to the volumes identified by Alexander (pp 10, 19) and Armstrong (pp 112-13, 116, 123-5, 126-7, 130-1) see above, notes 1, 6, 13, 14. The Agostini arms also appear in: Manchester, John Rylands, No. 3260, Cicero, *De oratore,* 1470; Venice, Marciana, MS Lat. X, 231 (3731), *Descriptio originis mundi et urbis Romae, etc.* (S. Marcon, *Calcografia monumentale: miniature della Biblioteca di San Marco.* Padua: Università di Padova, Scuola per bibliotecari, 1984-5, pp 66-7); and Andrea da Barbarino, *Guerino il Meschino* (H. P. Kraus, *Catalogue 153, Bibliotheca Phillippica: the final selection.* New York, 1979, p. 73 and ill. p. 149).

24. For the full name see notes 13, 14, 26, and Venice, Marciana, Membr. 6, Bonifacius VIII, *Liber sextus decretalium,* Venice, Jenson, 1476, fols 27, 42, 78, 126, 138, 140. Fragments of the name are visible in London, Brit. Libr., IC 19678, Gratianus, *Decretum,* Venice, Jenson, 1474, fols 34, 36, 43-5, 53-4, 164, 167, 207; and in the Dublin Plutarch (note 1).

25. Armstrong, pp 130-1.

26. Membr. 5. On fols 41^{r} and 66^{r} is the name *.B. agustini,* and in the fold of some bi-folios is written *De la Carita.*

27. Notes 4, 23.

28. Note 23.

29. London, Brit. Libr., IC 19678 (note 24), and Ravenna, Inc. No. 31 (note 14).

THE MANUSCRIPT COLLECTION OF JAMES USSHER

BERNARD MEEHAN

Writing to his father-in-law Luke Challoner in 1613, Ussher warned him, 'you may do well to have a care that the English popish books be kept in a place by themselves and not placed among the rest in the library, for they may prove dangerous'.[1] Ussher was referring to the Library of Trinity College, which he had helped Challoner to build up, and his letter indicates several of his lifelong preoccupations: not only his interest in Trinity, where he had been one of the first students on entering in 1594 and where his library came to rest in extraordinary circumstances after his death, but also his intense concern for books and libraries, as well as the confessional base which profoundly informed his scholarship.

It was, too, in Challoner's company that he had first made the acquaintance of the circle of collectors and scholars who were to dominate his intellectual friendships: men such as Sir Thomas Bodley, then forming his library at Oxford; Sir Robert Cotton, whose collection, now in the British Library, he greatly exploited; Henry Savile of Banke in Yorkshire; William Camden, the author of the great antiquarian work *Britannia*; John Selden, the jurist and orientalist; and the astronomer Henry Briggs. Ussher maintained a steady cor-

64. Matthew Paris, *Vie de Seint Auban*: battle between Christians and pagans (MS 177 fol. 48r).

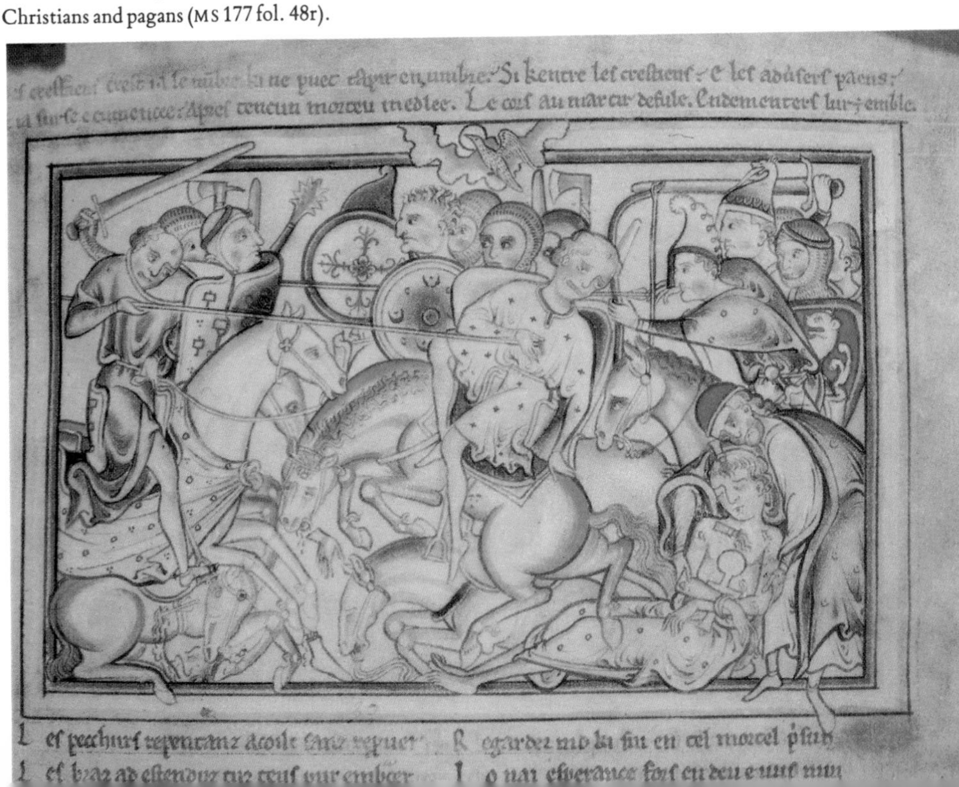

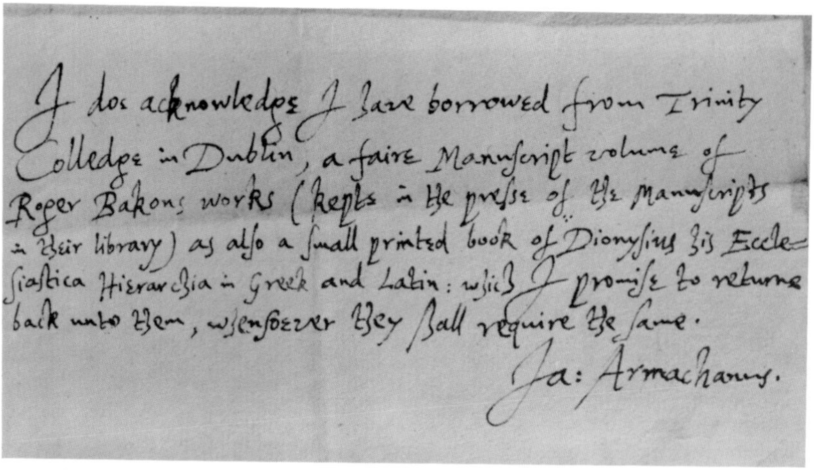
I doe acknowledge I have borrowed from Trinity
Colledge in Dublin, a faire Manuscript volume of
Roger Bakons works (kept in the presse of the Manuscripts
in their library) as also a small printed book of Dionysius his Eccle-
siastica Hierarchia in Greek and Latin: which I promise to returne
back unto them, whensoever they shall require the same.
Ja: Armachanus.

65. Ussher's receipt for books borrowed from the Library (MUN/LIB/10/8).

respondence throughout his life with these and other scholars both at home and in Europe, and held a high place in their esteem. Delivering the eulogy at his funeral in Westminster Abbey, his chaplain Nicholas Bernard itemized tributes to Ussher published during his lifetime. Among others, Alexander Morus had described him as 'the Athanasius of our age, his breast a breathing Library'; Selden had announced him to be 'a man of great piety, singular judgement, learned to a miracle, and born to the promoting of the more severe studies'; while John Prideaux, Bishop of Worcester, had called him simply the 'most rich magazine of solid learning, and of all antiquity'.[2]

Richard Parr, whose biography of Ussher occasionally bears a strong resemblance to medieval hagiography, contrasted Ussher's devotion to study with his lack of interest in the normal bodily comforts: 'A little sleep served his turn . . . he would feed heartily on plain, wholesome meat, without sauce . . . he liked not tedious meals, it was a weariness to him, to sit long at table'.[3] The surgeon who performed a post-mortem on him attributed Ussher's great energy to constitutional peculiarities of a type that in a lesser person would have been worth preserving in a jar.[4]

Today, Ussher is best remembered for his calculation that the world began in 4004 BC, accepting the Bible as a literal source. Among his contemporaries, his reputation was founded on his biblical and historical studies, his biblical scholarship having been nurtured from his earliest days by two blind aunts who had developed prodigious memories and were able to teach him to read from scripture, which they knew by heart. Biblical and historical studies came together for Ussher in a natural way. His first published treatise, the *De ecclesiarum christianarum successione et statu* (1613), attempted to show that before the sixteenth century there had always been 'a visible church of true christians . . . who had not been tainted with the errors and corruptions of the Romish church: and that even in the midst of the darkest and most ignorant times: and that these islands owe not their first Christianity to Rome'.[5] It was in pursuit of evidence for such propositions that Ussher's historical researches were primarily directed. His methodology, according to Parr, was superior to that of his religious adversaries. The Irish Jesuit William Malone, who engaged Ussher in public controversy, used, Parr says, false quotations from the Fathers and 'divers suppositious authors'. His intention was 'to blind the eyes of ordinary readers, who are not able to distinguish gold from dross'.[6] For Ussher, historical gold in the form of reliable texts was to be found in the study of the best manuscript sources. He considered familiarity with manuscripts to be the *sine qua non* of a true scholar, and on one occasion went so far as to write scathingly to Sir Robert Cotton that his messenger 'was altogether unfit, having never read a manuscript in his life'.[7]

Ussher employed every means at his disposal to ensure that he gained access to the best sources, printed as well as manuscript. Purchase, on a large scale, was his chief means. Many of his medieval texts were bought at the sale, after 1617, of the library of Henry Savile of Banke. This included several manuscripts from northern English monasteries, one of which was once bound with a manuscript that passed into Cotton's collection.[8] One of his most spectacular purchases, at a sale in about 1626, was of manuscripts belonging to the scientist and astrologer John Dee, including a volume of St Albans hagiography by the great thirteenth-century historian and artist Matthew Paris, now TCD MS 177, arguably the most accomplished of Matthew's artistic productions [64, 66, 67].

To obtain oriental copies of biblical texts, Ussher used agents resident in the east, such as Dr Christian Ravius at Constantinople and Thomas Davies at Aleppo. The former's efforts were not always to Ussher's satisfaction; in 1640 he wrote to Samuel Hartlib: 'I gave order unto Mr Ravius to procure for me a copy of Ignatius his Epistles in the Syriac language, to which he hath returned me no full answer. I am sure there is a Syriac copy of them in Rome.'[9] But Davies was one of Ussher's most assiduous though frequently frustrated helpers. In 1625 he complained to Ussher that Aramaic copies of texts were 'very rare and valued as jewels, though the possessors are able to make little use of them'. The only extant copy he could find of the Aramaic Old Testament was 'in the custody of the patriarch of the sect of Maronites, who hath his residence in Mount Libanus, which he may not part with upon any terms'.[10] The patriarch did however consent to the making of a transcript and Davies commissioned one, a task which he hoped would be completed in four or five months. Transcripts were also made for Ussher of many manuscripts in European libraries: Parr cites the Vatican, the Escorial, the Imperial Library at Vienna, the French Royal Library, the libraries of de Thou at Paris and Thomas van Erpe in Holland.[11]

Ussher examined manuscripts *in situ*, spending months at a stretch in the private and public libraries of Oxford, Cambridge and London. It was however not always necessary for him to travel. He had access even at a distance to the riches of other libraries, as books tended to move from one scholar to another on request. While resident at Much Haddam near Oxford, where he spent the years 1623-6 comfortably engrossed in study, Ussher was told by Samuel Ward, Master of Caius College Cambridge, that he had obtained for him ' the manuscripts of Bede's Ecclesiastical history which I have of Sir R. Cotton's, and have sent it unto you by this bearer Walter Mark: I will expect the book from you, when you have done with it, for that I would keep it till Sir Robert restore a book of mine, which he had of Mr Patrick Young'.[12]

The anxiety of scholars that volumes once borrowed would not be returned was on occasion fully justified. An example was of the preacher William Crawshaw, who appealed to Ussher to recover for him a book he had seen, to his distress, on the shelves of a London shop. He wrote plaintively: 'I lent you Josseline de Vitis Archiep. Cant. in fol which you said you lent Dr Mocket and I believe it, yet I could never get it; and now I find my book at Mr Edwards his shop, near Duke-Lane, and he saith he bought it with Dr Mocket's library, but I cannot have it. Happily you might by your testimony prevail to get it me, for I charged him not to sell it: I pray

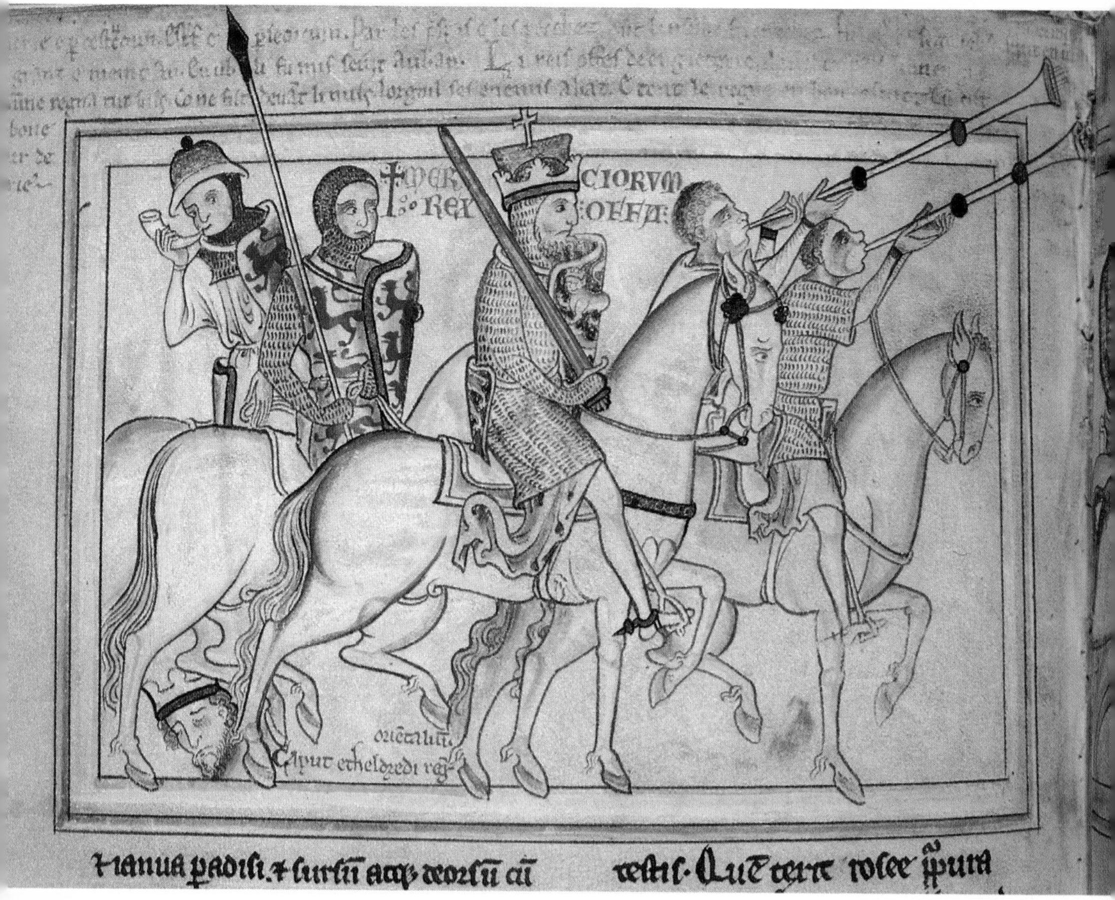

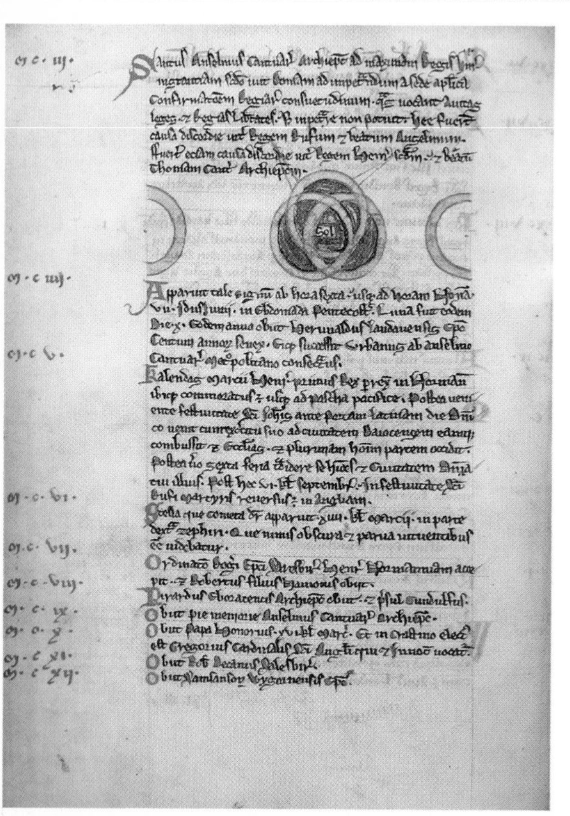

66 (above). Matthew Paris's account of the invention and translation of St Alban's relics, and the foundation of the abbey in his honour by King Offa of Mercia. The illustration depicts Offa setting out on his expedition (MS 177 fol. 55v).

67 (left). Thirteenth-century annals from the Cistercian abbey of Margam (Glamorgan), acquired by Ussher from the library of John Dee. The diagram depicts false suns claimed by the annalist to have appeared in 1104 (MS 507 fol. 3v).

68 (right). Winchcombe psalter: portrait of St Matthew, with initial *L* depicting twenty-eight of Christ's ancestors. (MS 53 fol. 7v).

think of it as you go that way.'[13]

Ussher continually apologised to correspondents for holding on to books too long. Even Cotton, whose generosity was considerable, had occasion in 1622 to send Ussher a gentle but pointed reminder: 'I have received eight of the manuscripts you had; the rest are not returned: if I might know what my study would afford to your content, I would always send you; and that you may the better direct me, I will, as soon as it is perfected, send your honour a catalogue of my books.'[14]

In addition to such private sources, Ussher was often able to borrow from college and university libraries. The same, incidentally, was not normally true for European scholars in search of material in English libraries. During his time as Archbishop of Armagh, Ussher borrowed from Trinity College 'a fair Manuscript volume of Roger Bakons works (kepte in the presse of the Manuscripts in their library) as also a small printed book of Dionysius, his Ecclesiastica Hierarchia in Greek and Latin', which he promised to return on demand. His receipt survives among the College muniments [65]. The supposed Bacon manuscript was one of the most prized possessions of the College in its early days and had been shown proudly to Sir William Brereton in 1635.[15] It was evidently returned by Ussher and survives as MS 381, though the Library does not now appear to possess a copy of Dionysius such as Ussher describes.

Towards the end of his life, Ussher received a reminder from the Oxford University Archivist Gerard Langbaine of two items he had apparently borrowed some time previously from Corpus Christi College — one of them the 'Chronicon Wigorniense'[16] and the other a manuscript of the epistles of St Ignatius of Antioch. Ussher returned these via Patrick Young only to be told by Langbaine that he had decided on investigation that the Ignatius belonged not to Corpus but to Baliol.[17] In 1624 Ussher could ask Samuel Ward to borrow for him a manuscript of Symeon of Durham's history of the church of Durham from Cambridge University Library.[18] It is not clear whether Ussher succeeded in borrowing the manuscript, though the object of his request is probably extant as CUL MS Ff.1.27.

On some occasions Ussher suffered disappointments. Samuel Ward, having been asked by Ussher to look in the library of his own college for a particular copy of the epistles of Ignatius, was forced to report sadly that 'the worst thing is, the book cannot be lent out of the College'.[19] Once, when told in Magdalen College Library, Oxford, that a book he was looking for was not available because it had been 'conveyed away', Ussher commented bitterly to Ward that this 'did not a little offend me'.[20] With books so often in transit among scholars, Ussher had little reason to complain.

Nor was it surprising that manuscripts could move permanently from the collections into which they had first passed after the dispersal of the monastic libraries in the previous century. Ussher's library both gained and lost by this movement of books. From Cotton's collection he gained a fourteenth-century volume of Wycliffite tracts,[21] an early twelfth-century collection of English saints' lives,[22] and a late-fourteenth-century English historical collection which had been presented to Cotton by William Camden.[23] In 1630 Ussher reciprocated by giving Cotton his oldest and most valuable copy of the Samaritan Pentateuch, now in the British Library.[24] One of the most visually splendid manuscripts in Ussher's collection, a twelfth-century New Testament and psalter from the benedictine abbey of Winchcombe, had previously been in

69. Twelfth-century copy of letters of Ivo of Chartres (died 1116) owned by Ussher after passing through the hands of St Peter's Abbey, Gloucester, whose fourteenth-century *ex libris (liber monasterii sancti Petri Gloucestrie)* is at the top of the page; then Thomas Cranmer (died 1556: *'Thomas Cantuariensis'*); then Lord Lumley, whose signature also appears (MS 184 fol. 2r).

Thomas Cantuariensis
Lib monast. sci petri et monasterio

suo ɔsecrat' ab eo car' ep̄s.

ōmdat' a sūmo pontifice. clero ℸ poplo
ōmdat' ab eod' ℸ metropolitano suo seno
dicnū q̄d dat pontifex ep̄o q̄ ɔsecr. q' neusi.
on lic' cuilibet abbi monachū recipe q̄
semel alā monastio in abbem ascesserit.
d' q̄ adultia agit in eis ɔsencientes digni s̄t
d' oēs abdecandis. scli remotiores ex pe
tende sint ℸ exoptande a religiosis ī in
fluctib; scłariū positis negociorū s̄ morte.
d' auctores gałe erroneos ℸ famosa sua
debeat familiaritate ppellē.
d' heretici ēē ɔstat q̄ romane ecclē n̄ ɔcor
dat. aq̄ nusq̄ prius appellari debē sacri
canones sanxerūt. debeat ēuitari.
d' n̄ debeat ep̄e regie potestatis timore
t gr̄a aut iusticie timite declinare. sario inuie.
uo dscē sc̄imonales iuxta pposituī suum
on p desidio ī āne q̄eas. prium curā deserē.
d' sac' legiū sit altario n̄ seruire ℸ de al
alle debe quē pr̄a ep̄m n̄ ēē q̄ pusillū gre
gē di. legis puaricacioē scandalizare.
ℸ ep̄i canes muti n̄ sint. latre n̄ ualentes.
d' salomon p mulierū ɔcupiscenciā adeo
apostatauit. ℸ multi seducti sunt.
ūrū q̄s habe possit eā mulierē ī coniugem.
q̄ prī habuit pelicē. ualeat penitēre.
porte platos l'e sororū nocte sub posite licet
lippe tā diu tolerare. donec expleto sena
rio ope. ad āplex' speciose rachel di gr̄a
d' ab anathematis uinculo nequeat absol
ui. q̄ eq; in eodē p q̄ excōmunicat' ē. crimine
pseuerat. cadit s̄r nos.
idelēs adūsa pati debē p iusticiā. ut cōpa
cientes ℸ ɔregnat. ℸ q̄d dicē sit pec̄s monacū
n adūsitate ecclē dō supplicandū oroīb;
in sistendū. n̄ sanguinis effusioī. n̄ incendus.
n̄ deuastacionib; paupū.
d' fidelib; orōnib; dn̄s in naui dormiens
suscitat'. ℸ nubilosa sedat' adūsitatū tēpestā
d' meliora s̄r uulnia diligentis. q̄ fraudulenta oscłā blandientis. ℸ q̄d de ecclā

stieis in ecclā. de curialib; nego
cus respondendū sic in curia.
e pace regis ℸ ep̄i carnot' inē in
ucē cōponenda. exempl' cōmdata.
x hortacio ad lugdunensē ārep̄m.
ne legacionē aplicā refutet inlos
inltū psuasibilib; scōr patrū ex
burbano papa petit uirga cui
ferrea q̄ carnot' ep̄s uasa lutea
ɔterat fitq; lamtabil' equest' q̄d
p rachel nocte l' sit subposita lia.
d' abbas oīi l' impositū n̄ deponat. n̄.
si aliq̄b; in regimine p dēē poxit.
s; bonos ūbo ℸ exēplo ad melio
ra puocet. malos corrigendo
toleret. ōs cōmunicantet. q̄ ibi
eq̄minuit portandi s̄r mali ubi
aliq̄ repiunt boni. peniret.
d' inuasor ℸ simoniacus ep̄e n̄ ē.
d' regi. x magis obedire oporteat.
q̄ regi philippo. oīb; peccatie
ut p relat' quisq; n̄ solū nullū
flagiciū ppetret. s; ne salt' de
se p babilit' cōfingi possit. modis
undanā supbiā n̄ armis mun
dane milicie. s; armis xane mi
licie ep̄m supare debē.
litteras suas absens corpore. p sens
spū deponit ī manu beluacensis
ep̄i placionē ecclē sci q̄ntin
carnot' ep̄s. gē n̄ differat.
cā ℸ salubris exhortatio carnot'
ep̄i ad filios suos beluacenses ca
nonicos. ut dignū sibi p latū eli
ℸ impiculi suis fideles clamant
ad dn̄m cū mare ℸ uenti obe
dunt. ut p cellā uitat iniurā.
q̄ suos tēptari n̄ patit' supra q̄
possunt. se ipsū retineat s.
d' q̄ recte offert. recte aut' n̄ diuid. n̄
peccat: ut q̄ sua dō tribuit. n̄ n̄
ℸ q̄s cū uis uolit ēē ɔsētaneus ī
culpa. cū n̄ uult ēē ɔsors ī pena.

Lumley

Incipit Regalis prosapia ...

ADAM . c . xxx . annorum genuit Seth . ADAM . et postea octingentis annis

Seth . c . v . annorum genuit Enos . SETH . et postea uixit octingentis septem annis

Enos . xc . annorum genuit Cainan . ENOS . et postea uixit octingentis . xv . annis

Cainan annorum lxx . genuit Malaleel . CAINAN . et postea uixit annis

Malaleel . lxv . annorum genuit Iared . MALALEEL . et postea uixit annis

Iared annorum . clx . duorum genuit Enoch . IARED . et postea uixit annis octingentis reductus.

Enoch annorum . lxv . genuit Matusale . ENOCH . et postea uixit . ccc . annis . uiuusque in paradisum est

Matusale . a . clxxxvii . genuit Lamech . MATUSALE . et postea uixit septingentis . lxxx . duobus annis ,

Lamech . a . clxxx . duorum genuit Noe . LAMECH . et postea uixit annis quingentis . xc . quinque

Noe annorum genuit Sem . Cham . et Iaphet . NOE . et Seth .

Adam primus Homo genuit filium nomine Seth:

. ex libro domini Willelmi Lambarde

SEM . CHAM . IAPHET .

Elam . A quo Helamite .
Assur . A quo Assirii .
Arphaxat . A quo Chaldei . Madis unde
Sale Ludi . A quo Lidi . fuit Iob .
Heber . A quo Hebrei . Aram a quo Syri .
Iectan . A quo Indi . Phalech . Chus . Traco .
Elmodad . Salec . Reu . Vl a quo Armenii .
Aselmoth . Iare . Sarug . Gether a quo Carme . nii .
Adura . Vzal . Nachor . Mesa a quo Meones .
Doda . Hebal . Thare .
Abimael . Saba .
Ophir . Euila .
Iobab . Nachor . Abraham . Sara . Aran .
Laban . Bathuel . Rebecca . Loth . Moab a quo Moabite .
Lia . Rachel . Amon a quo Amonite .
Ismael . Isaac .
Nabaioth . Iacob . Esau .
Cedar . Ruben . Eliphaz . Rauel .
Abdeel . Simeon . Theman . Naath .
Mapsa . Leui . Omar . Zara .
Masma . Iudas . Sephue . Sema .
Duma . Isachar . Gatham . Meza .
Massa . Zabulon . Cenez .
Adad . Neptalim . Chore .
Thema . Dan . Amalech .
Iaur . Gad .
Naphis . Aser .
Cedma . Ioseph . Beniamin .
Manasse . Ephraim .

SETH
BEADUUI
WALA
HATHRA
ITERMOD
HEREMOD
CEAWALA
BEAU
CETUUA
GODUULF
FINN
FRITHEUULF
FRELAF
FRITHEUUALD
WODEN .

Chus . A quo Ethiopes . Gomer . A quo Galathe i. Galli .
Saba . A quo Sabathei . Magog . A quo Gothi et Scithi
Euila . A quo Getuli . Madai . A quo Medi .
Sabatha . A quo Sabatheni . Iauan . A quo Ioni .
Regma . Dadan a quo Occi . Tubal . A quo Hiberi i. Hispani .
Sabacta . dentales Ethiopes . Mosoch . A quo Cappadoces .
Mesraim . A quo Egiptii . Thiras . A quo Traces .
Ludim . Ascanez . A quo Sarmate .
Ananim . Riphat . A quo Paflagones .
Laabim . A quo Libii . Thogorma . A quo Friges .
Nephtuim . Tharsis . A quo Cilices .
Phetrusim . Cethim . A quo Cethii i. Cipri .
Cesluim . A quo Philistii . Dodanim . A quo Rodii .
Furth . A quo Furthei .
Chanaan . A quo Affri .
Sidon . A quo Sidonii .
Hethe . A quo Hethei .
Iebuse . A quo Iebusei .
Amorre . A quo Amorrei .
Gergese . A quo Gergesei .
Eue . A quo Euei i. Gabaonite .
Arache . A quo Aracades .
Asene . A quo Asenei .
Aradi . A quo Aradii .
Amare . A quo Coelis Siria .
Amache .

WEHTA . CASERE . WEAGDEIG . BEALDEAIG . WILGELS . WIHTA .

Ab hoc regum Uectorum genealogia .

Ab hoc regum West Saxonum et Bernicorum prosapia .

Ab hoc olim Cantuariorum prosapia .

71. Winchcombe psalter: *Beatus* initial with King David and his choir (MS 53 fol. 151r).

70(left). Worcester chronicle: genealogies of the English kings, beginning with Adam (MS 502 fol. 10r).

the Royal Library [68, 70]. From the library formed by Sir George Carew, Lord President of Munster, Ussher obtained at least four manuscripts, though by what means remains a mystery.[25]

Another important collector, Lord Lumley, like Cotton and Camden a member of the Elizabethan Society of Antiquaries, is now represented in Ussher's library by at least three manuscripts, including a twelfth-century copy of letters of Ivo of Chartres which had previously belonged to Archbishop Cranmer of Canterbury and before him to St Peter's Abbey, Gloucester. The *ex libris* of these three owners can be seen on the opening page [69]. Ussher borrowed frequently from the library of Lord William Howard of Naworth in Cumbria, sharing with Howard an interest in the twelfth-century chronicle attributed to John and Florence of Worcester. Howard's 1592 edition of the work was based on two manuscripts that passed into Ussher's collection and are now MSS 502 and 503 [71].

In the years after 1640 Ussher's library went through a series of travails. That year he set out for England on what he intended to be a routine study trip, but in 1641 rebellion broke out in Ireland and Ussher never returned, spending the remaining years of his life in England. With the revenues from his see at Armagh cut off, he was forced to sell or pawn his plate and jewels. His palace at Drogheda

72. Ussher's initials (before his consecration as Bishop of Meath in 1621) on either side of a stem of pinks. Back board of MS 123, fifteenth-century manuscript from the Cistercian house of St Mary's Dublin. Perhaps one of the earliest surviving Dublin bindings.

was destroyed by the rebels, with his library being saved only through the protection of Nicholas Bernard. His books were sent the following summer to Chester, and subsequently in 1647 followed him to Lincoln's Inn. Ussher's movements during his years in England were such that he seldom had full access again to his books.

In 1643 further misfortune befell him when his travelling library was confiscated by Parliament as punishment for a sermon by Ussher which it interpreted as favourable to royal authority. His library was restored to him through the intervention of his old friend Selden and his former chaplain John Featley, but some volumes were lost from it. Two years later, on his way to St Donat's in Wales, his party was attacked by an irregular force of parliamentarians and his chests of books and working papers broken open and plundered. Sir James Ware commented that 'the loss of his papers broke his patience more than all the sufferings he had ever undergone',[26] but the bulk of what had been taken was recovered for him within a few months by local gentry and clergymen. Two manuscripts remained lost, one of which he prized especially and had intended to use in a sequel to his *De ecclesiarum christianarum successione*; it was a history of the Waldenses, a persecuted medieval sect whom Ussher greatly admired for their resistance to Rome.[27]

Such adventures, and advancing years, took a natural toll of Ussher's health. His eyes deteriorated, the result, it was thought, of 'constant studying',[28] and his terminal illness began with a recurrence of sciatica of the hip 'which about 35 years ago, he had by sitting up late in the Colledge Library of Dublyn'.[29]

At his death in 1656, Ussher left his library to his daughter Elizabeth, the wife of Sir Timothy Tyrrell. The King of Denmark and Cardinal Mazarin both expressed an interest in buying it but the government would not allow the library to go abroad. The Bodleian Library and Sion College in London were also thwarted, and Ussher's collection was purchased for Ireland on the orders of Cromwell and the Council of State. The purchase price of £2500 was raised by the army in Ireland. In doing so, the army was influenced by Bernard's misleading account of the generosity of the army of 1603 towards Trinity College Library. Late in 1657 Ussher's library reached Dublin and was housed in the Castle. The intention of the government was that the collection should form the library of a projected new college under the patronage of Cromwell's son Henry, but the restoration of Charles II put an end to such notions and the new King bestowed the library on Trinity.[30]

The library which the College acquired in this way, and which now forms the core of the medieval manuscript collection, numbered in all around ten thousand volumes, as well as some contemporary papers such as those of Luke Challoner and the Oxford mathematician John Bainbridge, and was especially rich in manuscripts from English monasteries. There were few Irish-language manuscripts, and this aspect of the collection was weakened further within a few decades by the loss of the books of Lecan and Ballymote, subsequently acquired by the Royal Irish Academy. Other losses occurred, including the catalogue of Ussher's manuscripts (a great frustration for librarians), and a twelfth-century Greek Gospel-book which was reported missing from the Library in 1742 and is now, after several changes of ownership, in the hands of the New York dealer H.P. Kraus. This was one of the manuscripts in Ussher's collection which, like the Winchcombe or the Ricemarch psalters [73], was extensively decorated, though for Ussher's scholarly purposes the value of a manuscript always lay primarily in the text.

NOTES

1. *The whole works of the Most Rev. James Ussher, D.D.*, edited by C. R. Elrington. Dublin, 1847-64

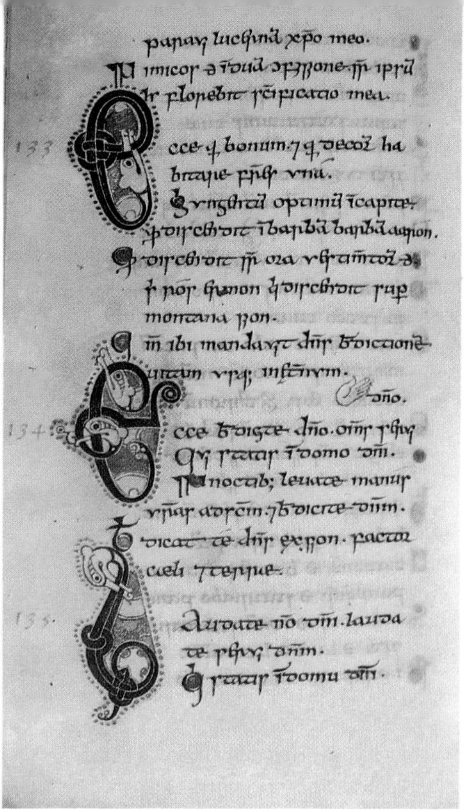

73 (left). Ricemarch (Rhygyfarch) psalter: written in late-eleventh-century Wales by a scribe trained in the Irish style of script and decoration (MS 50 fol. 147v).

74 (bottom left). Late-twelfth-century Bible from Ussher's collection: portrait of St Paul. Notes by Ussher on this and other pages show that he compared prologues in the Pauline epistles with those of the Book of Armagh (MS 51 fol. 173v).

75 (right). Detail from twelfth-century copy of sermons of St Augustine from Ussher's collection. The *ex libris* shows that it belonged to the Tironensian abbey of Kelso in Scotland (MS 226 fol. 93r).

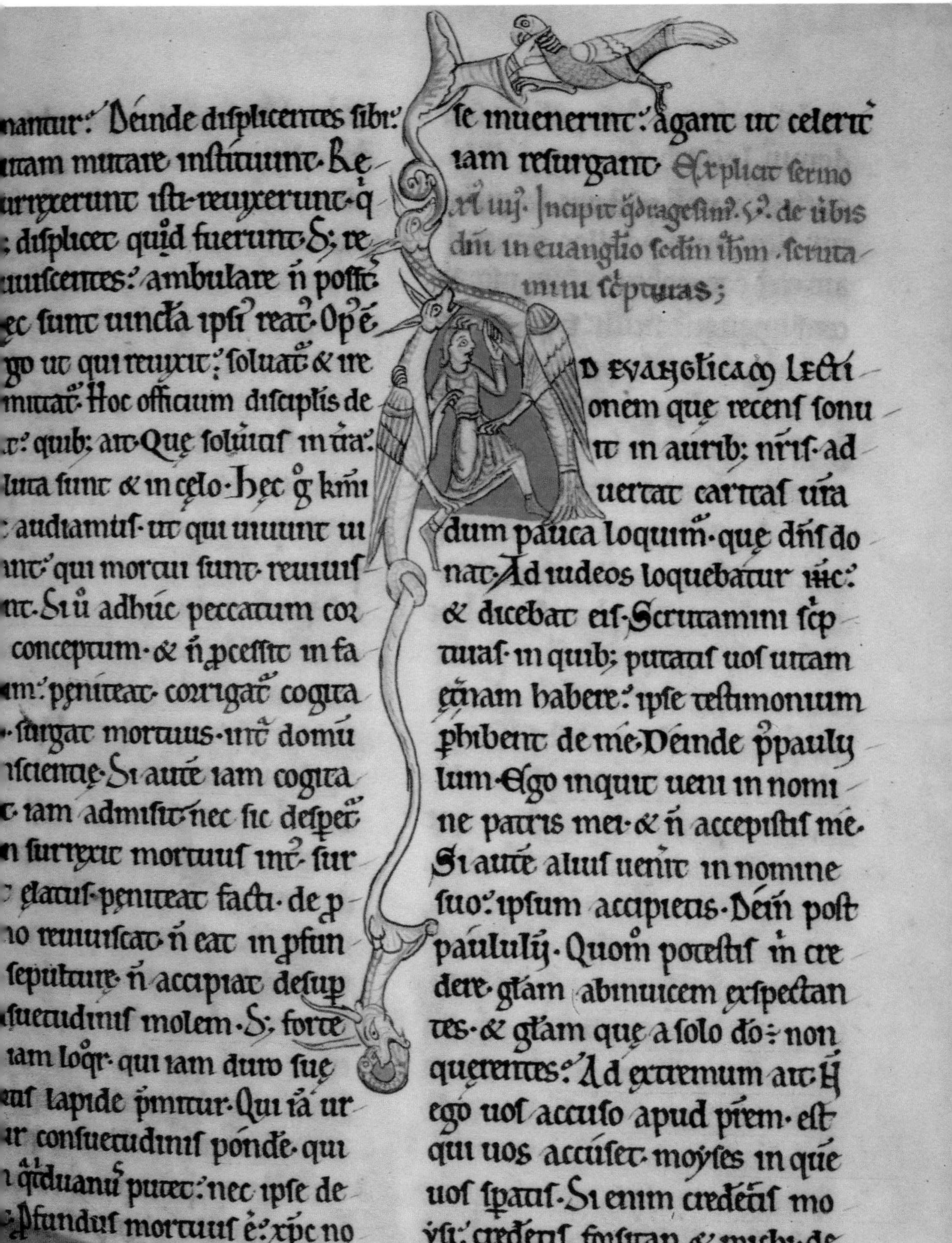

hereafter cited as *UW*, vol. 15, p. 74.

2. Nicholas Bernard, *The life and death of the Most Reverend and learned father of our Church Dr James Ussher*. London, 1656, pp 8-9.

3. Richard Parr, *The life of the Most Reverend and learned father in God, James Ussher, late Lord Archbishop of Armagh.* London, 1686, p.79.

4. Parr, pp 79-80.

5. Parr, p. 14.

6. Parr, pp 25-6.

7. *UW* vol.15, p. 276.

8. TCD MS 114. The Cotton MS is now British Library Cotton Faustina A.v.

9. *UW* vol.16, p. 64.

10. *UW* vol. 15, p. 285.

11. Parr, p. 99. Some of these transcripts survive as TCD MSS 197, 225, 234, 236-40, and 265-6.

12. *UW* vol.15, p. 229. Young was Librarian of the Royal Library.

13. *UW* vol. 15, p. 116.

14. *UW* vol.15, p. 171.

76. Engraving of Ussher by William Faithorne, 1653.

15. Sir William Brereton, *Travels in Holland, the United Provinces, England, Scotland and Ireland*, ed. by Edward Hawkins. Manchester: Chetham Society, 1844, p.143.

16. Probably now Corpus Christi College Oxford MS 157.

17. *UW* vol. 16, pp 570-3.

18. *UW* vol.15, p. 230.

19. *UW* vol.15, p. 504.

20. *UW* vol.15, p. 349.

21. Now TCD MS 244. This aspect of Ussher's career is covered in detail by William O' Sullivan, 'Ussher as a collector of manuscripts', *Hermathena* 88 (1956) 34-58, to whose work I am heavily indebted.

22. Now TCD MS 176.

23. Now TCD MS 497.

24. British Library Cotton Claudius B. viii.

25. Now TCD MSS 195, 1432, 1435, 1436. The bulk of Carew's collection is now divided between the Bodleian Library Oxford and Lambeth Palace Library.

26. *The whole works of Sir James Ware concerning Ireland*, ed. by Walter Harris. Dublin, 1764, vol. 1, p. 111.

27. Other Waldensian MSS from Ussher's collection survive in the Library as MSS 258-67. See J. H. Todd, *The books of the Vaudois.* London & Cambridge, 1865.

28. Parr, p. 76.

29. Bernard, p. 108.

30. There is a detailed account in T. C. Barnard, 'The purchase of Archbishop Ussher's library in 1657', *Long Room* 4 (1971) 9-14.

THE 1641 DEPOSITIONS

AIDAN CLARKE

From the moment that rebellion broke out in the north of Ireland on 22 October 1641 there has been passionate disagreement about what really happened. On the same evening an informer alleged that a general massacre of Protestant settlers was intended,[1] and the first of many pamphlet accounts of atrocities was on sale in London little more than a week later.[2] Precise information was hard to come by but in August 1642 a Tyrone clergyman who had been in captivity among the rebels reported that 154,000 Protestants had been killed.[3] That figure gained wide currency when it was incorporated in a declaration on the rebellion, which the English House of Commons ordered to be read in all churches in the following year.[4] Agents sent by the Dublin government to King Charles in 1644 raised the total to 250,000;[5] Sir John Temple's influential history of the rebellion increased it to 300,000 in 1646;[6] and John Milton, noticing that the original estimate of 154,000 referred only to Ulster, multiplied it by four to produce a countrywide figure of 600,000.[7] Thereafter, the estimates decreased, as it began to be realized that the contemporary calculations were out of all proportion to the likely size of the Protestant population, and David Hume's widely read and often reprinted *History of England,* published in 1754, settled for a total of about 40,000 'by the most moderate, and probably the most reasonable account'.[8] More than two hundred years later the historian of Irish Presbyterianism accepted that figure.[9]

From the outset, however, the very fact that a massacre had taken place at all was strenuously denied. It was both philosophically observed that war always engendered such rumours and bitterly asserted that the allegations had been concocted to elicit money and support for the suppression of the rebellion.[10] That point of view was also assimilated into the historiography of the rebellion, where it assumed the characteristic form of denying the authenticity and credibility of the evidence.[11] That evidence largely consists of the collection of material in Trinity College Library commonly known as 'the 1641 depositions' and the value of these papers has been a central issue in the protracted historical debate on the massacres. A striking aspect of the controversy, however, has been the virtually ritual status of this evidence. The Trinity collection has been continuously evoked, but more often in terms of its size than with reference to what it actually contains. Every so often in the past, the thirty-three volumes have been thrown as so much bulk weight into the scales of historical judgement by one side, and thrown out again by the other: but they were rarely opened in the process. Thus both David Hume's careful estimate and his celebrated dictum that Irish Catholics who questioned the massacres were 'men beyond the reach of argument or reason, and must be left to their prejudices'[12] rested on his confidence in the sufficiency of evidence that he had never seen. Those who did look at the deposition books were prone to ransack them for ammunition rather than to examine them systematically. The purpose of this essay is to provide an overdue archival description of these controversial materials.

The deposition books came into the possession of the College in 1741, when Bishop Stearne of Clogher marked the centenary of the 'bloody massacre' by presenting what were, in effect, the papers of his predecessor in that see (and in the Vice-Chancellorship of the University), Dr Henry Jones. The collection was already famous, for a good many items from it had been published in the past to illustrate the character of the massacre, most notably by Jones himself in 1642[13] and by Temple in 1646. From the inference that what had been printed was representative there had arisen, and there was to survive, the belief that every page in the collection told similar tales of horror – compelling or fanciful, according to entrenched prejudices. How the materials were ordered when they were received is unknown, but the College authorities at once arranged to have them bound,[14] using the simple principle of grouping the various papers according to the county to which they referred. The result was thirty-one uniform volumes, neatly embossed with the words 'Depositions: 1641' on the spine, ranging between 154 and 457 sheets each, and totalling more than 19,000 pages. Some of these volumes covered a single county, some contained more than one, while some counties occupied more than one volume.[15] Later in the same year, two additional volumes of related material were added,[16] and the collection has remained in that form to this day.

These arrangements have proved a great disservice to scholarship. The assumption that this was a single coherent collection on which an order of convenience might reasonably be imposed was incorrect. A large number of distinct numerical sequences, criss-crossing the various volumes and involving both folio and serial numbers, discloses earlier systems of orderly arrangement of the material, which were destroyed in the binding, if not before. Their reconstitution indicates that Jones's papers were actually an amalgam of five discrete units, each with its own principles of association and its own distinct organization, and most with separately numbered subdivisions.

The first of these five categories of material is the core element, the depositions from which the collection takes its name, of which it is commonly thought to be entirely composed, and from which Jones and Temple drew in their publications. It consists of the sworn statements of Protestant refugees taken by a group of eight clergymen, headed by Henry Jones, acting on the authority of three successive commissions issued by the Dublin government: the first, dated 23 December 1641, required the collection of information about robberies and spoils committed against the Protestant English; the second, dated 18 January 1642, extended the scope of the inquiry to include murders and massacres; and the third, dated 9 June 1642, replaced a deceased member and altered the legal status of the Commissioners.[17] Each of the depositions was made before at least two Commissioners, almost invariably in Dublin, though one session was held in Athy in April 1642. They range in time from 28 December 1641 to the autumn of 1647. In general, they are most numerous for the early years, but their incidence fluctuates observably with the military situation, so that, for instance, the relief of a besieged garrison or the opening up of communications with an outlying region normally produced a spate of deponents. At some stage after the Commissioners had completed their business, the original depositions were assembled into five groups — Ulster, Munster, Connacht and two Leinster groups – in each of which they were sub-divided by county and arranged in the alphabetical order of surnames. When they were bound in 1741, no principle whatever, either of chronology, alphabet or district, was employed. The proportions, as between counties and regions, are uneven, but the variations are not connected with the distribution of alleged massacres. They naturally bear some relation to the distribution of Protestants in Ireland, but they are chiefly influenced by wartime lines of communication between the country and Dublin. Thus Leinster depositions greatly outnumber the others: they occupy 2659 sheets. Ulster is second, with 1411 sheets, and the geographical distribution of these confirms the general point, for it is the border counties — Cavan, Fermanagh, Monaghan and Armagh, in that order — that are most numerously represented, while County Antrim, from which escape to Scotland was so much easier than escape to Dublin, is not represented at all. Depositions from Connacht and Munster amount to only 347 and 209 sheets respectively. In the aggregate, these depositions comprise a little less than half of the materials in the collection.

Their form is fairly standardized. Typically, they begin with the name, address and social status or occupation of the deponent; they briefly state the circumstances in which the deponent was robbed and spoiled; they list the value of the goods and chattels lost; they name those responsible; they furnish information about the identity of others in arms; and they conclude by recounting what disloyal and traitorous words they have heard the rebels utter and what miscellaneous information they possess. These six uniform divisions correspond to the terms of the first commission, and the evidence of phraseology indicates that they represent the answers to a set of standard questions to which two were added after 18 January 1642, when murder was added to the Commissioners' brief and they were required to discover what Protestants had turned Papist. A significant proportion of the depositions, however, differs from this format: they are simply inventories of losses, submitted in advance by the deponents and crudely converted into depositions by the clerk of the Commission who wrote in the set introductory formula, erratically substituted the third for the first person, and appended what additional information the hearing yielded [77]. The contrast between these holograph submissions, which dealt solely with losses – and with those in meticulous detail – and the depositions drawn up by the Commissioners, in which property was described in rough general categories and prime attention was paid to the words and deeds of rebels, reflects the dual purposes of the Commission. Its formal function was to register claims and to issue certificates of loss to the deponents. Its informal function was to act as an information gathering system. The collection of information about killings arose naturally from these activities. The depositions do indeed contain plenty of examples of atrocities, many at first hand and many more on hearsay, but the vast majority deal only with property. Though the balance is significantly different in the depositions from the Ulster counties, the greater number are similar to those made by refugees from other areas: at a rough estimate, three out of five made no reference to deaths; one out of five reported death through privation; and one out of five told of death by violence. Almost all recorded their property losses, many of them in the familiar prepared inventories.

A small number of the depositions are very different in character. They arose from an attempt made in the second commission to set up a procedure for reporting, through clergymen, robberies that had been committed against those who were now dead. Many of the better known and most widely quoted depositions — the rambling, disjointed compilations of local rumour that excited the anger of Protestant historians and the contempt of Catholics — were in fact the efforts of clergy to fulfil this obligation.

The second component of the Trinity collection consists of a set of fair copies of these originals. These were made at some stage in the late 1640s by the clerk of the Commission, Thomas Waring. The circumstances are suggested by a pamphlet on the rebellion, which Waring published in 1650 and which he described as a 'fore-runner' to the publication of 'a large volume' of the depositions themselves:[18] this work was already in hand, but had become so 'swoln' that he had been forced to delay publication. The copies were made, mostly by Waring himself, on a county-by-county basis: each county set was separately foliated, and each was authenticated at beginning and end by two of the Commissioners [78]. Within the county sets, no discernible order was observed: the sequence seems to have been simply the one in which they came to hand, which suggests that the alphabetical arrangement of the originals was later still. Waring's intention seems to have been to copy all the originals, but transcripts for only eighteen counties survive: not all the sets are complete, and even where they are correlation is imperfect: the collection contains originals that were not copied, and there are copies for which no originals are extant. Part of the explanation for this may be provided by the occasional marginal notes and endorsements, which make it clear that the depositions were from time to time made available to the courts as evidence in the 1640s and that there was considerable difficulty in recovering them. When the collection was bound, the copies were included with the other material relating to the county to which they referred, usually as an integrated group, but sometimes not.

The third part of the collection elucidates the shortage of Munster material in the depositions collected by the Dublin Commissioners. It consists of a body of similar statements from English Protestants taken under the authority of a special commission issued on 5 March 1642 to Philip Bysse, an English cleric recently appointed Archdeacon of Cloyne. The commission itself seems not to have survived, but occasional formal rehearsals of its terms in the introductory formula to depositions suggest that it was modelled on the original commission of 23 December rather than on the revised commission of 18 January: that is to say, it was confined to robberies and spoil. The reasons why it was issued are easily reconstructed. On 16 March 1642, Jones personally presented a report to the English House of Commons, which was subsequently published by order of the House together with an appendix containing eighty-five depositions — about one in seven of those already collected. The preparations for his journey included a tabulation of the results to date, which revealed that 'out of the whole province of Munster . . . no one hath yet appeared'.[19] Special arrangements were at once made to counter the difficulties of access to Dublin and the natural tendency of Munster refugees fleeing to England to travel direct. Bysse was dispatched, with Oliver Davorin as his clerk, to collect statements in Munster similar to those being taken in Dublin and to issue similar certificates of loss.[20] The materials he produced related mostly to Munster, of course, but the deponents included refugees from other areas as well. He seems not to have been authorized to act alone, but was left free to appoint *ad hoc* Commissioners to work with him, and the fifteen hundred or so depositions that he amassed bear a wide variety of counter-signatures, almost all of laymen. The history of these materials is in-

77. 'The humble petition of Thomas Johnson' cursorily converted into a deposition. The deleted ending read: 'Your suppliant doth most humbly beseech your worships to examine your petitioner upon oath touching these his great losses and that the same may be recorded and certificate made thereof under your hands, whereby your suppliant may receive such present and future relief from his sacred Majesty as others in his case do or shall receive. And he shall pray etc.' In fact, the subjoined information was derived from the examination of Hugh Johnson, who evidently submitted the petition on behalf of Thomas (MS 816, fol. 117).

~~[illegible]~~

~~The humble Petition of Thomas Johnson~~

Thomas Johnson of Browne Rath in the County of Meath deposeth that in the beginning of November 1641 he was Robbed stripped and despoiled of all that ever he had in the world att Browne Rath in the County of Meath by certen Rebells ~~[illegible]~~ in those parts to the utter ruine of this dept his wife familie & three small Children; the particulars of which losse are as followeth: first in Cattall as Cowes horses and the like fowerteene pounds in household stuff & apparrell to the value of Tenn pounds ster; in Hay to the value of Twelve pounds ster; in all manner of Corne and graine in the Haggard, to the value of ffifteene pounds ster; in Corne in the ground to the value of fortie pounds ster; in Butter and Cheese to the value of Tenn pounds ster; in all amounting to the summe of one hundred and one pounds ~~[illegible]~~

Jurat 9 ffebr 1641
Roger Puttocke
John Sterne

Thomas Johnson

~~The supt therefore humbly beseecheth your Lordships to examine him the supt upon oath touching this his losse and that the same may be Recorded and Certificate thereof made under your hands, whereby your supt may receive such present and future Releife from the [illegible] as shall [illegible] And he shall pray &c~~

The deponent Hughe Johnson of Browne Rath aforesaid also deposeth that Thomas Colgan of Colmestowne was one of the Rebells that committed the foresaid Robbery, and [illegible] sixty persons of men & women from Blackhall in the County of Meath and some 5 or 6 young men from Colmestowne aforesaid but knowne by name to this deponent [illegible] about the tyme aforesaid [illegible] Stood of Staffords towne [illegible] George Goodman of the same, George Lea of Kiltrone [illegible] were robbed and despoyled by their neighbours of the [illegible]

Hughe Johnson

Jur 9 ffebr 1641
John Sterne
Roger Puttocke

distinct. The last Munster deposition seems to have been taken on 13 August 1643. Bysse was killed sometime before 28 October 1643. His papers were taken to Oxford by Lord Inchiquin early in 1644 and passed subsequently through the hands of a number of custodians, all of them Munster office and property holders.[21] Their existence was not forgotten. Davorin provided extracts of a few of them to the Dublin Commissioners in July 1645,[22] and Temple, who was an adherent of the English parliament when he published his account in 1646, referred to them obliquely as 'most unhappily carried another way'.[23] In October 1652, a search for them was instituted in Dublin and they had been found by 1 December 1653, when some of them were introduced in evidence to support charges against Viscount Muskerry.[24]

On the evidence of numerical series, it is clear that these Bysse depositions were at some stage divided into three parts: one comprising the material relating to Cork, one consisting of the material relating to the other Munster counties and one that brought together the statements made by deponents from outside the province. When the collection was bound, or perhaps earlier, these groupings were broken up and the depositions dispersed among the county volumes.

In the course of the review undertaken in March 1642, it was also observed that no deponents had come forward from Antrim, Donegal or Down, and a second special commission was issued on 6 April 1642 to a group of Ulster clergy requiring them to collect depositions in the province, or part of it. There is no evidence to indicate that they ever did so: all that survives of their work is contained in a pamphlet published by one of them, Daniel Harcourt, in July 1643, which retailed what had been discovered about the fate of Protestant clergy in the province.[25]

The fourth category of papers in the collection consists of sworn statements made by individuals, captured Irish and Old English as well as refugee Protestants, by coercion as well as by choice, before an officer of state: most frequently, a judge; occasionally, a Privy Councillor; sometimes, a local garrison commander. They range in date from the beginning of the rebellion to its end, and they were concerned almost exclusively with public affairs: that is, they supplied information about the activities of the rebels, about their governmental and financial arrangements and the condition and disposition of their armies, or they informed on particular individuals who had joined or associated with the rebels. There are multiple systems of foliation among this group of 'informations', as they were often called, and it is clear that at some stage innumerable sub-groups were brought together into one or more larger groups before they were sorted into the county volumes, a principle of organization that was often extremely unhappy in its application to these statements, since many of them have regional rather than local reference.

The history of the fifth and last group of documents may be traced to April 1652, when the English parliamentary nominees who ruled Ireland were presented by Henry Jones with a set of skeletal abstracts from the Dublin depositions. They expressed themselves both shocked and grateful, and dispatched the submission to the English parliament with a recommendation that judicial machinery should be set up to find and deal with the culprits. In response, parliament ordered the publication of the abstracts and approved the proposal.[26] As a result, special High Courts of Justice were established in Ireland later in the same year. Their function was to 'hear and determine all murders and massacres of any protestant English or other person . . . done or committed by any person or persons' since 23 October 1641. About sixty Commissioners, Henry Jones among them, were appointed, any twelve of whom were to constitute a court: they were not only empowered to try cases and impose punishment, but also to ex-

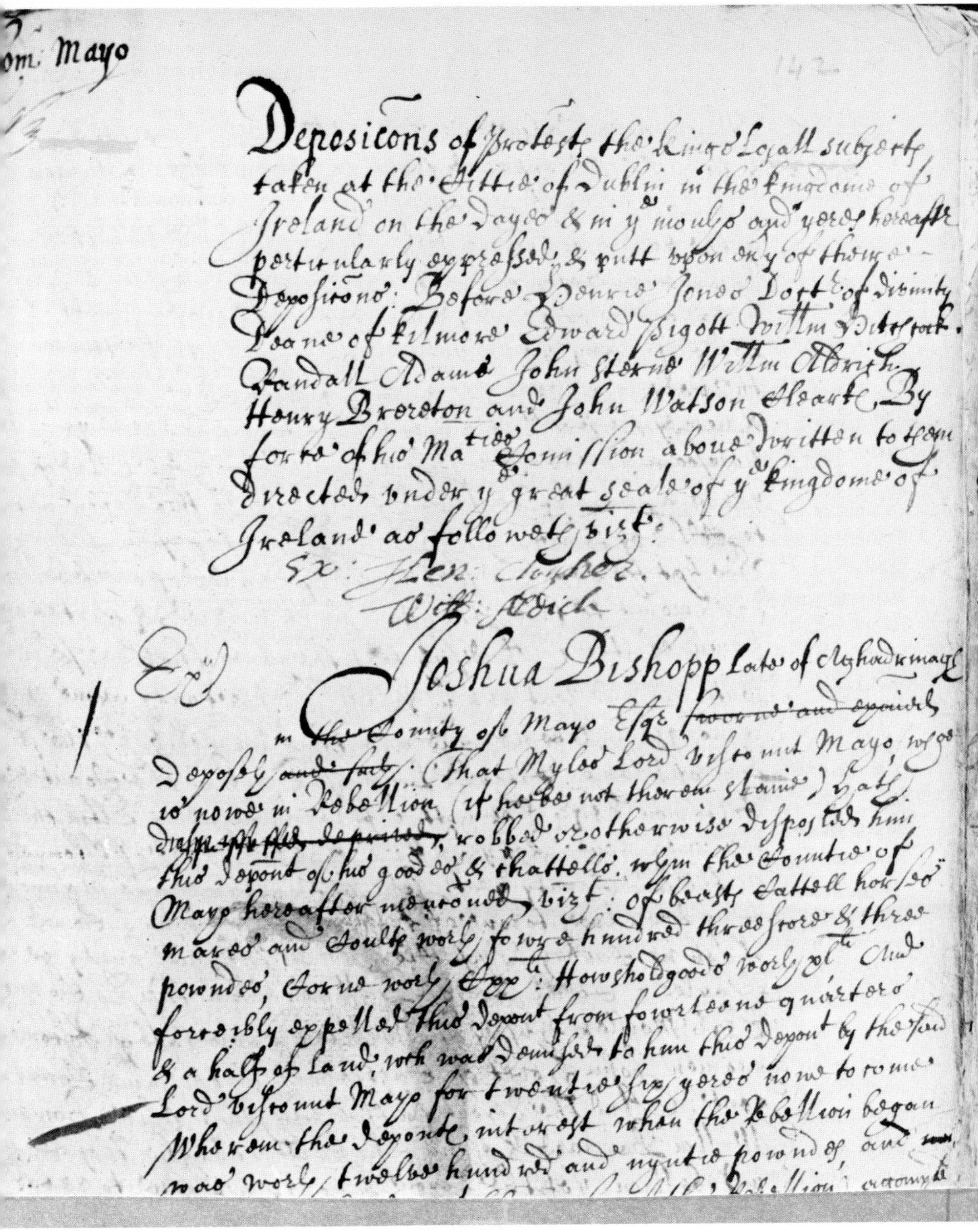
Com: Mayo

142

Deposicons of Protest the Kings Legall subjects taken at the Cittie of Dublin in the kingdome of Ireland on the dayes & in ye monthes and yeres hereafter perticularly expressed, & putt upon oath of them Deposicons: Before Henrie Jones Doctr of divinity Deane of Kilmore Edward Pigott Willm Hitchcock Randall Adams John Sterne Willm Aldrich Henry Brereton and John Watson Clearks By force of his Maties Commission above written to them directed under ye great seale of ye kingdome of Ireland as followeth vizt.

Ex: Hen: Clogher.
Will: Aldrich

Exd

Joshua Bishopp late of Aghadromaye in the County of Mayo Esqe ~~sworne and examined~~

1. Deposeth ~~and saith~~: That Myles Lord Viscount Mayo, who is nowe in Rebellion (if he be not thereunto starved) hath ~~dispossessed deprived~~, robbed or otherwise dispossed him this depont of his goodes & chattells within the Countie of Mayo hereafter mencioned, vizt: of beasts cattell horses mares and coults worth fower hundred three score & three poundes, Corne worth £xx: Howsholdgoods worth xl li And forcibly expelled this depont from fowrteene quarters & a half of land wch was demised to him this depont by the said Lord Viscount Mayo for twentie six yeres nowe to come Whereon the deponte ... when the Rebellion began was worth twelve hundred and nyntie poundes, and ...

78. The first page of the Mayo set of Waring copies, certified by Henry Jones (who became Bishop of Clogher in 1645) and William Aldrich. The deposition has been lightly edited by the removal of redundancies, including the words 'sworn and examined'. The hand denotes special interest, and the reference to Lord Mayo, who was allegedly responsible for a massacre at Shrule, has been marked for easy reference (MS 831, fol. 142).

amine witnesses upon oath 'for taking any evidence concerning the same'.[27] The fifth component consists of examinations taken in the context of these proceedings. They were taken in many places throughout Ireland, some at the scenes of alleged massacres, some in open court, most at fairly formal sessions in some local centre, from a variety of people, some of whom were complainants, some of whom were local residents suspected of having material knowledge, and some of whom were the accused. They were taken in relation to the murder of Catholics as well as to the murder of Protestants. Elsewhere among the manuscripts presented by Stearne are notes of the actual proceedings of the courts.[28] The foliation suggests that they were not originally part of the collection of examinations, which consisted of three sub-groups: two small ones, confined to materials dealing with happenings in Cork and Wexford, and one large one comprising the remainder. They were ordered in clusters according to the particular cases to which they related: the order of the cases, however, discloses no obvious principle of arrangement. Like all the other material, these documents were disarranged and re-grouped by county in the bound volumes, where the case-clusters were sometimes preserved, but more usually not.

There are obvious connections between these five categories of material. Logically, as well as by virtue of the way in which the judicial proceedings were initiated, the earlier depositions constituted the primordial body of evidence upon which prosecutions could be founded in the 1650s. They were admissible as evidence in themselves, being duly sworn on the Bible, and they were a point of departure for further inquiries. The most convenient form in which they existed, however, was not in the variegated and often patchwork originals, but in the set of transcripts that Waring had prepared some years before. That, presumably, is why it was that in August 1652 Jones and the fellow Commissioner with whom he had worked most closely, Henry Brereton, appeared before the Lord Mayor of Dublin and procured a certificate authenticating the accuracy of the Waring copies.[29] That, presumably, is why elaborate indexes were prepared, listing in parallel columns the names of rebels, the offences alleged against them by deponents, and the serial or folio number of the Waring copy in which the details were to be found. It is certain that it was at this stage that the hunt for the Bysse depositions began and very likely that it was in the course of these preparations that the 'bundles of originals', as Waring called them, were arranged in alphabetical order and foliated, that the informations were gathered together for combing and the Bysse depositions given their distinctive order.

It may be concluded that the archive consists of five separate groups of papers brought together as a working collection to service judicial proceedings during and after 1652, and subsequently shuffled, in or before 1741, to conform to a simple county arrangement. The result may be expressed in the words that Thomas Carlyle applied to the history of Ireland in the 1640s: it is both confused and confusing. There are four contributory reasons for this. Firstly, it is due to the internal scrambling produced by the failure to preserve the integrity and order of the different materials within the county arrangement. Secondly, it is to some extent created by the physical appearance of the collection. The term 'books' is in itself misleading. The reality consists of so many pieces of paper, of all shapes and sizes, in varying states of preservation, and in innumerable handwritings, bound together with, for good measure, many errors: documents have been split up, bound in upside-down, entered in the wrong books and so on, and every so often stray pieces, or chunks, of wholly irrelevant material have been included, most of it connected with local administration in the 1650s. The total effect is kaleidoscopic and baffling.

Thirdly, confusion derives from the fact that the distribution of different kinds of material among the counties is extremely uneven: thus some counties have a high proportion of examinations taken in the 1650s, while others have hardly any; some county volumes are largely composed of Bysse depositions, others have a sprinkling of them, and some have none at all; some counties, particularly those close to Dublin, have many informations, while others have few or none; some counties have Waring copies, others do not; one county has no depositions whatever. In short, no two books have a similar make-up, and this has defeated both sampling and generalization.

The fourth source of confusion bears very directly on the evidential value of the collection and was central to the debate on the massacres for more than a century after an Anglican clergyman, Ferdinand Warner, reported on his inspection of the manuscripts in the 1760s. He was already familiar with the work of the Dublin Commissioners through his discovery of an unpublished sequel to Jones's original *Remonstrance,* which had been prepared in similar style with an appendix of 208 depositions in the autumn of 1643,[30] and he was unimpressed by the originals. He observed that 'in infinitely the greater number of them the words "being duly sworn" have the pen drawn across them' and that in these and other cases 'many parts of the examination are struck out'. He drew two conclusions: that the 'bulk of this immense collection is parole evidence', and therefore worthless, and that the parts that had been deleted had been 'intentionally invalidated'.[31] His findings gave considerable comfort to Catholic controversialists, the more so since, having discounted most of the evidence, Warner concluded that the number killed could be precisely estimated as 4028. Though he convinced only those who wished to be convinced, his work posed problems until 1884, when Mrs Mary Hickson refuted it by pointing out that the removal of 'being duly sworn' was immaterial, since the attesting formula '*jurat coram nobis*' invariably remained, and that the matter 'struck out' of the text consisted uniformly of itemized property losses for which a concise statement of total value was substituted. The deletions, she argued, were marks of contraction for the guidance of a copyist, and she went on to deduce that the copyist involved was the one who had transcribed the pieces appended to the 1643 report.[32] It is easy to show that her deduction was wrong: the transcriptions were confined to depositions made in Dublin between March 1642 and October 1643; the deletions do not occur in the original Dublin depositions at all. They are to be found only in some of the Waring copies and in the Bysse depositions, which Waring himself testified in court to having 'abbreviated'.[33] This pattern of distribution suggests two possible explanations. The first is that since these were the two categories of material mainly used in court, they may have been contracted for that purpose: the objection is that, after contraction, many of the depositions amount to a simple statement that so-and-so of such a place had been despoiled by unknown rebels of goods valued at so many pounds [79]. It is difficult to see that this served any useful judicial end. It seems more likely that Waring abridged his transcripts for publication and subsequently decided, when his already 'swoln' manuscript was enlarged by the addition of the Bysse material, to skip the transcription stage and merely edit the originals, which were neater and more uniform than his own, for the printer. The historiography, however, is instructive: Warner must have confined himself to sampling the Munster books, which alone fit his description; Hickson's extensive study of the confused materials did not save her from confusion.

Superficially, the views that have been taken of those who compiled these materials have been widely divergent. From one side they have been represented as busily finding 'pretexts for indicting and outlawing the Catholic landholders throughout Ireland', dredging up and encouraging the wildest stories of horror and maltreatment in a crude propaganda exercise designed 'to give not merely "the rebels" but the Irish nation and the Catholic religion a bad name':[34] from the other, they have appeared as labouring manfully to record the terrors of the time, to preserve the memory of the dead, and to note the names of their murderers. In reality, of course, these views converge: both present the purpose of the Commissioners as being 'to take evidence upon oath to keep up the memory of the outrages of the Irish to posterity'.[35] Although this is actually an enduring misunderstanding of the original intention, it was a not unreasonable conclusion from the evidence of what was published, as well as being a logical inference from the use which the Commissioners themselves made of the depositions. Their first report, published in Jones's name, was openly designed to elicit relief funds from England, and may very well have been intended, as it was certainly used, to promote investment in the reconquest of Ireland under the Adventurers' Act of February 1642. Their second report, presented to the Irish Council in November 1643, was clearly designed to subvert the recently concluded truce between the King and the confederate Catholics and to influence the ensuing negotiations by reviving memories of massacre. Thomas Waring's pamphlet was both a triumphalist celebration of Cromwell, Drogheda and Wexford and a cry for further vengeance, and Jones's *Abstract* of 1652 was simply a short county-by-county collection of horror stories. Those associated with the Commission acted, in short, as if their business was to preserve 'the memory of the outrages of the Irish'.

There is no doubt that the evidence that they collected in the course of their official duty of registering the losses of despoiled Protestants convinced the Commissioners that massacres had taken place, and the evidence itself confirms that some large scale, indiscriminate killings and quite a few small scale atrocities did happen at various times and places. But none took place as early as October 1641. Placed side by side, the pamphlet literature and the depositions disclose a revealing paradox. The massacre was an accepted fact before any of the verifiable incidents that might be supposed to constitute its parts had actually occurred. The myth preceded the events, but it was sustained by them as they happened.[36] Thus the depositions do not prove the authenticity of the general massacre that was thought to have accompanied the outbreak of rebellion: they do provide evidence that Protestant settlers were killed in considerable numbers in the north of Ireland and a few other places throughout its first year.

NOTES

1. M. Hickson, *Ireland in the seventeenth century, or The Irish massacres of 1641-2: their causes and results.* London, 1884, vol. 2, pp 367-8.
2. *The last newes from Ireland, being a relation of the bloudy proceedings of the rebellious Papists there.* London, 1641.
3. TCD MS 809, fols 5-12.
4. *A declaration of the Commons assembled in Parliament concerning the rebellion in Ireland, 25 July 1643.* London, 1643.
5. *Historical Manuscripts Commission: Egmont MSS.* London, 1905, vol. 1, part II, p. 229.
6. Sir John Temple, *The Irish rebellion.* London, 1646.
7. John Milton, *Eikonoklastes,* in *The works of John Milton.* New York, 1931-8, vol. 5, p. 188.
8. David Hume, *The history of Great Britain, Volume I, containing the reigns of James I and Charles I.* Edinburgh, 1754, p. 100.
9. J.M. Barkley, *A short history of the Presbyterian Church in Ireland.* Belfast, 1959, p. 10.
10. A. Clarke (ed.), 'A discourse between two councillors of state', *Analecta Hibernica* 26 (1970) 72.
11. Most influentially, by John Curry: *A brief account from the most authentic Protestant writers of the causes, motives and mischiefs of the Irish rebellion.* Dublin, 1752. *Historical memoirs of the Irish rebellion.* London, 1758. *An historical review of the civil wars in Ireland.* Dublin, 1775.
12. David Hume, *History of England.* London, 1773, vol. 5, p. 504.

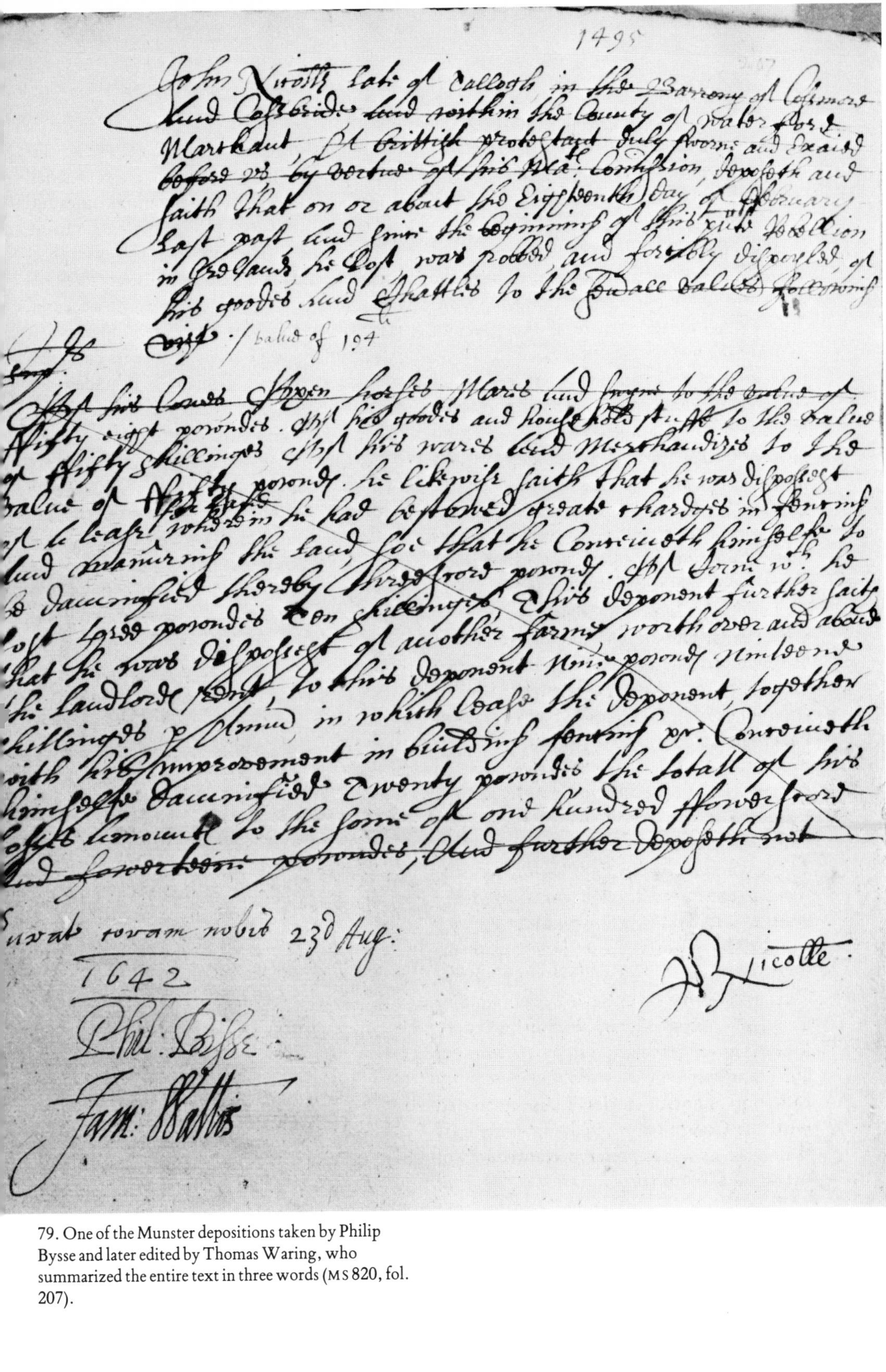
1495

207

John Wrott late of Callogh in the Barrony of Lismore and Cosbride and within the County of Waterford Marchant, A Brittish protestant duly sworne and examined before us by vertue of his Ma:tie Commission deposeth and saith that on or about the Eighteenth day of February last past and since the beginning of this p'nte rebellion in Ireland he lost was robbed and forcibly dispoyled of his goods and chattles to the totall value followinge viz / valud of 194 li

Inprimis that his cowes Sheepe horses Mares and swyne to the value of fifty eight poundes. Itm his goods and household stuffe to the value of fifty shillings Itm his wares and Merchandizes to the value of fifty poundes. he likewise saith that he was dispossest of a lease wherein he had bestowed greate chardges in fencing and manuring the land soe that he conceiveth himselfe to be damnified thereby threescore poundes. Itm corne w:ch he lost three poundes ten shillings. This deponent further saith that he was dispossest of another farme worth over and above the landlords rent, to this deponent Nine poundes Nineteene shillings p Annu, in which lease this deponent, together with his improvement in building fencing &c. conceiveth himselfe damnified twenty poundes the totall of his losse amounteth to the some of one hundred fowerscore and fowerteen poundes, And further deposeth not

Jurat coram nobis 23d Aug: 1642

Phil: Bisse

Tam: Wallis

J. Nicolle

79. One of the Munster depositions taken by Philip Bysse and later edited by Thomas Waring, who summarized the entire text in three words (MS 820, fol. 207).

13. Henry Jones, *A remonstrance of divers remarkable passages concerning the church and kingdome of Ireland.* London, 1642.

14. W. O'Sullivan, 'The eighteenth century rebinding of the manuscripts', *Long Room* 1 (1970) 21, 28.

15. TCD MSS 809-839. The books are made up as follows: 809, 810 Dublin; 811 Wicklow; 812 Carlow, Kilkenny; 813 Kildare; 814 King's County; 815 Queen's County; 816 Meath; 817 Longford, Westmeath; 818, 819 Wexford; 820 Waterford; 821 Tipperary; 822-7 Cork; 828 Cork, Kerry; 829 Clare, Limerick; 830 Galway, Roscommon; 831 Mayo, Sligo, Leitrim; 832, 833 Cavan; 834 Louth, Monaghan; 835 Fermanagh; 836 Armagh; 837 Down; 838 Antrim; 839 Donegal, Londonderry, Tyrone.

16. TCD MSS 840, 841.

17. TCD MS 815, fols 1-6.

18. Thomas Waring, *A brief narration of the plotting, beginning and carrying on of that execrable rebellion and butcherie in Ireland.* London, 1650.

19. Jones, *Remonstrance,* p. 80.

20. Public Record Office, London: State Papers, Ireland 63/265; 289, 290.

21. TCD MS 826, fol. 171; *HMC: Egmont MSS,* i, part I, 192, 201.

22. TCD MS 821, fols 1-3.

23. Temple, *Irish rebellion,* p. 111.

24. Hickson, *Ireland in the seventeenth century,* vol. 2, pp 199-200.

25. Daniel Harcourt, *A new remonstrance from Ireland.* London, 1643.

26. *An abstract of some few of the barbarous, cruell, massacres and murthers, of the Protestants and English in some parts of Ireland, committed since the 23 of October 1641.* London, 1652. R. Dunlop, *Ireland under the Commonwealth.* Manchester, 1913, vol. 1, p. 179.

27. Dunlop, *Ireland,* vol. 2, pp 285-6, 295-6. The Commission was dated 8 September 1652: TCD MS 847.

28. TCD MS 866.

29. TCD MS 812, fol. 29.

30. British Library, Harleian MS 5999, 'A treatise giving a representation of the grand rebellion in Ireland'.

31. F. Warner, *The history of the rebellion and civil-war in Ireland.* London, 1767, pp 294-7.

32. Hickson, *Ireland in the seventeenth century,* vol. 1, pp 128-33.

33. Hickson, *Ireland in the seventeenth century,* vol. 2, p. 199.

34. Thomas Fitzpatrick, *The bloody bridge and other papers relating to the insurrection of 1641.* Dublin, 1903, pp 224, 164.

35. J.P. Prendergast, *The Cromwellian settlement of Ireland.* 3rd ed. Dublin, 1922, p. 60.

36. Walter D. Love, 'Civil war in Ireland: appearances in three centuries of historical writing', *The Emory University Quarterly* 22 (1966) 57-72. The late Dr Love is the only scholar who has undertaken research on the massacres in recent years: his research materials have been deposited in the Library (TCD MSS 7227-41). Valuable use has lately been made of the depositions as sources of social and economic information: N.P. Canny, 'Emigration and opportunity: Britain, Ireland and the new world in the seventeenth century', *Irish Social and Economic History* 12 (1985); Mary O'Dowd, 'Landownership in the Sligo area, 1585-1641' (PhD thesis, NUI, 1980); Brian MacCuarta, 'Newcomers in the Irish midlands, 1540-1641' (MA thesis, NUI, 1980); Ciarán Ó Murchada, 'Land and society in seventeenth century Clare' (PhD thesis, NUI, 1982).

THE FIRST AMERICAN EDITION OF 'THE VICAR OF WAKEFIELD'

M. POLLARD

For a number of years Trinity College Library has been attempting to build up its collection of the works of Oliver Goldsmith, one of the College's more distinguished graduates. Recently the first, second and third editions of *The Vicar of Wakefield* have been added, together with early Irish printings and the so-called first American edition, that of Philadelphia, printed for William Mentz in 1772. Some of these copies the Library owes to the good offices of the firm of antiquarian booksellers, Falkner Greirson, and in particular to the discerning eye of its chairman. Some time ago Noel Jameson returned from a visit to the United States with an interesting addition to the collection, a fourth edition bearing the imprint 'Dublin: printed in the Year MDCCLXVII' [81]. This edition was quite unknown to him and to me, but, in spite of the imprint, we were convinced it was printed in America. Apart from the provenance of the book, which is entirely American, there was no reason for this conviction other than the general impression conveyed by the contemporary binding, by the paper and, particularly, by the distinctive type face used. Certainly, this was not a product of the Dublin book trade and it was very unlikely to have come from a London press, but the possibility of a Scottish origin had to be considered. Unfortunately Trinity College Library is not well supplied with American printings of the 1760s and any Scottish printings that could be found bore no resemblance to the new *Vicar*. Further research, however, led to John Alden's work on the Boston bookseller and printer, John Mein, and on Scots type used in America.[1]

To summarize John Alden's account, Mein arrived in Boston from Scotland late in 1764 and at once set up shop. His early business association with a Robert Sandeman soon broke up and his next venture, a circulating library, was announced by the publication in October 1765 of a catalogue of its contents. Other publications followed. At first Mein's printing was done by William McAlpine in association with another Scot, John Fleeming, but in 1766 partners were changed and Mein and Fleeming set up their own printing shop with plant bought for that purpose in Scotland. In this partnership Fleeming was the working printer while Mein acted as bookseller-publisher, and over the next three years a number of books were issued from the partners' shop, some with and some without the imprint of Mein and Fleeming. Mein also exercised his literary talents as editor of his newspaper, the *Boston Chronicle*. This paper seems to have been popular enough at first, but politics took over and when, in 1769, he supported the British administration, opposing the Boston Non-Importation movement against British goods, he 'incurred the displeasure and the resentment of the whigs, who were warm advocates for American liberty'. Mein was eventually chased out of Boston; he 'became extremely odious, and to avoid the effects of popular resentment, he secreted himself until an opportunity was presented for a passage to England'.[2]

As a publisher Mein suffered from modesty where some of his titles were concerned and this fact was sufficiently well known to be noted by Isaiah Thomas, who states that some of his books 'had false imprints, and were palmed upon the public for London editions, because Mein apprehended that books printed in London, however executed, sold better than those which were printed in America; and, at that time, many purchasers sanctioned his opinion'.[3] The chief means by which Mein's unacknowledged publications have been identified include the type faces used in his books in conjunction with his newspaper advertisements. John Alden found, in particular, that from 1767 Fleeming used the distinctive bold or strong faced roman, presumably acquired in Scotland in 1766 on the visit recorded by Isaiah Thomas,[4] and he has shown, with 'no more than a perfunctory doubt', that it came from the Edinburgh foundry of John Baine. In 1767 or 1768 the partners issued a specimen,[5] without date or name of founder, illustrating six text types including the Long Primer in which the text of *The Vicar* is set [82]. Although the Long Primer is not shown in the only extant Baine specimen book of twenty years later, *A specimen of John Baine & Grandson & Co.*, Edinburgh, 1787, it does include three of Mein and Fleeming's types, the Great Primer, English and Pica.[6] James Mosley has also pointed out to me that, though the 'Small Pica Roman strong face' of the 1787 specimen differs in detail from the Small Pica at the head of the second column of Mein's sheet, the capitals are the same. He sees a similar relationship between Baine's 'Small Pica Roman no. 1' of 1787 and 'Baine's Small Pica' appearing in the 1768 specimen of the Edinburgh printer John Reid.[7] It therefore seems that some of Baine's types underwent modifications in the twenty years between the only known specimens, and that Mein's Small Pica of 1767 was a forerunner of the 'strong face' of the specimen book. In view of these relationships and the similarity in design of the Long Primer to the Small Pica it seems logical to conclude that the Long Primer also came from Baine's foundry.

Although the Long Primer is not included in John Reid's specimen of 1768, one would have expected its first use to have been at Edinburgh but, as yet, no example has been identified earlier than 1770,[8] and the London appearance in 1767 in Tissot's *Advice to the people in general with regard to their health*, cited by Lawrence Wroth,[9] turns out to be printed by Mein and Fleeming under one of their false imprints.[10] It has been suggested that *The Vicar* may have been printed for Mein at Edinburgh by Kincaid and Bell. Mein certainly bought books from them which they had bound on his behalf, but I can find no positive evidence of any printing work done for him in

80. Oliver Goldsmith 1730?-74: etching by James Bretherton after Henry William Bunbury. (Portrait without subscript: 15.6 × 12.3 cm).

the firm's letter book; this gives no details of customers' orders or their replies, and the letters to Mein consist chiefly of attempts to get him to settle his account. A summary of Mein's debts and payments sent to him on 15 September 1767 shows that he had placed no order since June 1766,[11] some weeks before the publication in London on 28 August of the third authorized edition of *The Vicar* used by Mein as his copy text. Any reprinting order from Mein must therefore have been made late in 1767, a full year after the copy text was issued. I find it difficult to accept the possibility that Kincaid and Bell printed Goldsmith's novel and perhaps other works for Mein in Baine's strong-faced Long Primer while Mein and Fleeming at the same time were using the same type face in, for instance, the *Boston Chronicle*.

Having shown that Mein and Fleeming possessed and used a fount of the type in which *The Vicar* is set, Mein's own advertisements prove that he was indeed selling an edition of the novel. The earliest advertisement of this fact in his own newspaper appears to be that of 8 August 1768,[12] unexpectedly late in the year for a book dated 1767. As we have seen, the copy text was published in London in August 1766 and, considering the speed with which Mein issued other reprints, three at least appearing in Boston in the same year as the London edition, there should have been ample time for him to have acquired the third London edition and printed and published his reprint in the year shown in the imprint. If the advertisement of 8 August is indeed the first there was obviously considerable delay in publication and unless there was some unusual difficulty in binding up copies I cannot account for this. Apparently binders in the colonies were both scarce and expensive as is shown by the booksellers' anxiety to import their foreign books bound rather than in sheets.[13] But binding troubles do not seem seriously to have afflicted Mein's more recent publications in 1768, though *Sermons to asses*, first announced on 15 August, is advertised as 'sewed' rather than bound.

On 15 August 1768 *The Vicar of Wakefield*, described as 'Moral, Entertaining and Pathetic', is included with twenty-two other titles in a partial stock-list headed 'John Mein hath just imported a very Large Assortment of all the New Novels and Books of Entertainment'.[14] But in the following year, after the Boston Non-Importation movement had been in operation for some time and in spite of Mein's public opposition to it, a 'patriotic' list of books 'Printed in America, and to be sold by John Mein' appeared in the *Chronicle* of 2 October 1769. Now these two lists have many titles in common and include not only works to which Mein put his own name but also others with anonymous imprints, some of which were said to be printed in London. Mein must have had a very high opinion of his customers' gullibility if they were supposed to accept this odd mixture as wholly imported in 1768 but all printed at home a year later.

Working from the patriotic list of 1769 John Alden identified nine of the nineteen titles as acknowledged Boston editions, seven of them certainly and the remaining two probably issued by Mein. Four of the titles were of children's books which he was then unable to locate.[15] Of the remaining six, copies of five were found that could be identified through the type face used as printed for Mein, despite the fact that all were without printer's name, two showing the date alone and three giving London as the place of printing. The sixth work listed was, of course, *The Vicar of Wakefield.* With its title-page statement 'Dublin: printed in the year 1767' another variation can be added to Mein's tally of false and anonymous imprints. Using Mein's advertisements and type analysis John Alden located and identified two further editions. All eight disguised imprints occur in the 1768 list of 'imported' books, the disguises consisting of the date only in two cases, with North America added once, London three times and Dublin once.

The chief reason for this practice was doubtless that suggested by Isaiah Thomas: fashionable American readers tended to prefer a book originating in London to one of the home grown variety. Mein, therefore, obligingly catered for his customers' snobbery and labelled some of his reprints as London products; after all, his shop was called 'The London'[16] and this might even have served as his tongue-in-cheek excuse if he were ever to be accused of falsity. But he was caught in an uncomfortable predicament when his patrons about-turned and demanded American goods, refusing to buy the London imports. It must have hurt to have been forced to acknowledge

81. *The Vicar of Wakefield,* fourth edition, Dublin [i.e. Boston] 1767. TCD copy: title-page, vol. I (page: 17.1 × 10.1 cm) with Sever signatures and book plate.

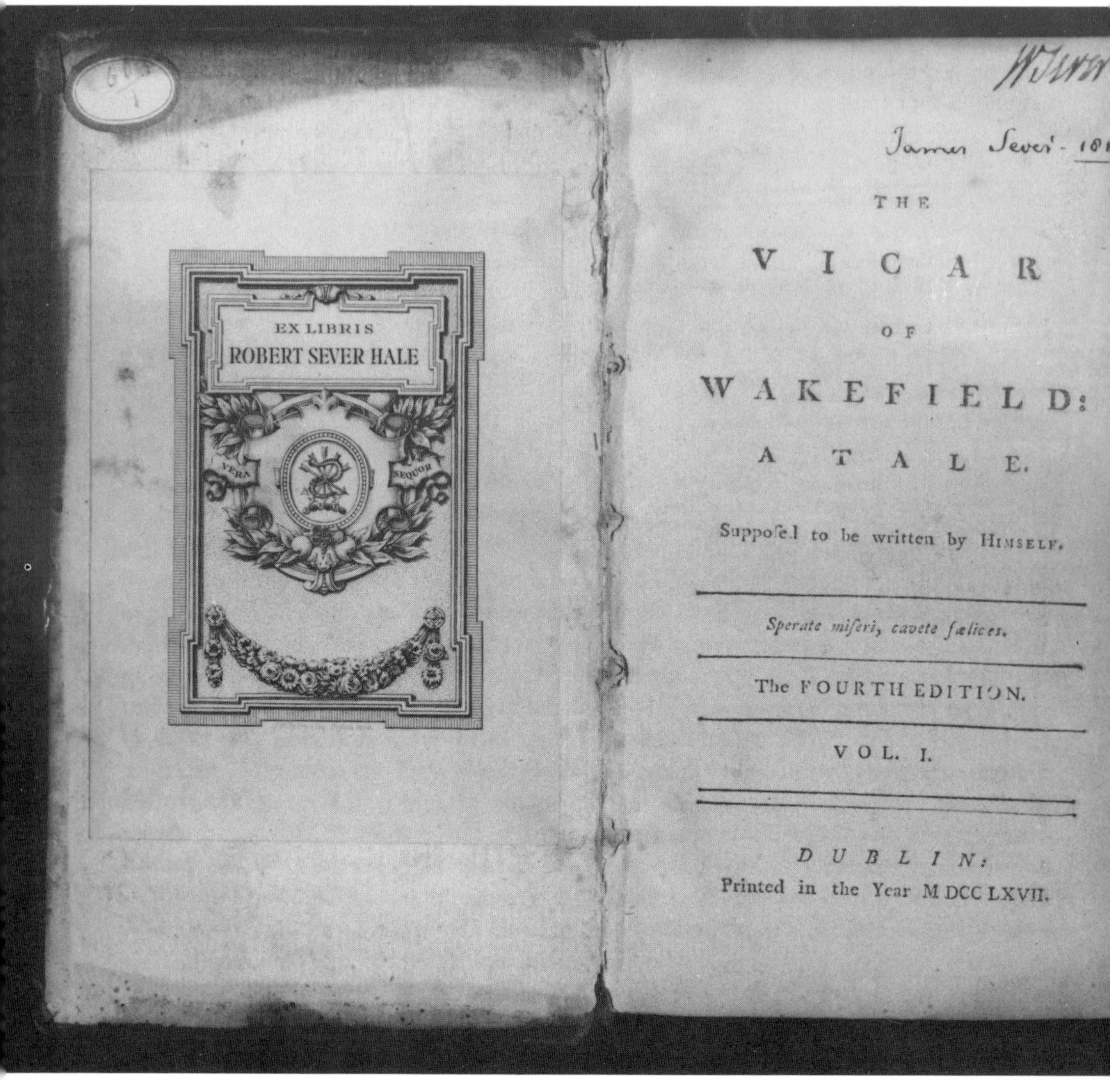

the truth in his advertisement list of books printed in America; did his customers query the London and Dublin imprints? And how did he explain them away in the face of his vociferous and publicized opposition to the movement?

Though three of the eight anonymous editions now identified as Mein's were disguised as London printings on the grounds of customer preference, Thomas's explanation does not account as convincingly for the three showing the date alone and the single instances of North America and Dublin. It seems possible that Mein, as an emigrant Scot, may have had more respect for the power of the London book trade and the problems caused by infringing a London bookseller's copyright than an American or an Irishman would have had. In reprinting for the home market a work whose copyright was the property of a London bookseller an Irish printer had no hesitation in putting his name and address in his imprint, while a Scot would more often use a false imprint or other disguise. This is illustrated in the various pirated editions of *The deserted village*; four of the Scottish reprints carry the imprint of W. Griffin, the London copyright owner, while the two Dublin editions bear the Dublin booksellers' names. When a Dublin printer used a false London imprint we suspect that the copies were designed to be illegally imported into Great Britain, or illegally exported to America. But Scotland was subject to British copyright law and from the late 1750s to 1774, when the London booksellers' claim to perpetual copyright was finally disallowed, the London trade waged continual war against Scottish reprints. British copyright law did not run either in America or in Ireland, but as a good Scot Mein may have felt unable, when helping himself to other men's copy, to cast off the shackles of British law and expose his moral piracy to the light of day, especially as he had an establishment reputation to keep in repair. That the question of the right to use copy owned by the London trade was not entirely ignored in America is shown by the echoes of a debate in 1770 emanating from Philadelphia. In the 'Address to the subscribers' in his edition of Robertson's *History of Charles the Fifth*, the bookseller, Robert Bell, sets out the proof, quoting Blackstone, that he had the legal right to reprint the London copy, and he goes to this trouble because 'some inimical incendiaries, exotics to the native rights of American Freedom, have insinuated, that this Edition is an infraction on the monopoly of literary property in Great-Britain'.[17] This is not to say that Mein was over conscientious in his delicate treatment of pirated material. Though his disguised imprints include six reprints of new works first and recently issued in London and two originating in America, he put his name to other books that might be considered in the same category, such as John Ogilvie's poem, *Providence*,[18] and he seems to have had no hesitation in claiming as his the children's stories and the odd school book.

In considering the reasons for Mein's imprint in the case of *The Vicar of Wakefield*, Dublin as the place of origin would have made a poor selling-point in comparison with London, unless the author's Irish nationality was sufficiently well known in Boston to have lent it verisimilitude, and this seems a doubtful attraction considering the thoroughly English setting of the novel. If, on the other hand, Mein was disguising his moral 'piracy', Dublin was a particularly clever piece of mystification. The Irish reprint trade was notorious, and cheap, and Dublin editions cannot have been entirely absent from the booksellers' shelves in Boston even though Irish trade with America was illegal until 1779, when the commercial restraints imposed by Britain on Ireland were lifted. There had already been two Dublin printings of *The Vicar* in 1766, the year of its first appearance, and one in 1767; no one, therefore, would have questioned the origin of yet another edition from Dublin, though the modesty of the bookseller in omitting his name might have occasioned some surprise. It is unlikely, however, that the imprint was suggested by the use of a Dublin edition as printer's copy since Mein has correctly, if such a term can be used in this situation, called his edition the 'fourth'. The third authorized edition was issued in London by 28 August 1766 and it is this text that is reprinted by Mein,[19] while the Dublin editions of 1766 and 1767 follow the text of the first Salisbury-London edition.

However inconclusive speculations on the reason for a Dublin imprint may be, at least we can with some certainty identify this particular Dublin edition of *The Vicar of Wakefield* as printed at Boston by Mein and Fleeming. The proof rests on a positive result from a comparison of the text type used, Baine's Long Primer bold or strong faced roman, with Mein and Fleeming's specimen and other acknowledged printings of the firm. Inclusion of the title in advertisements of books sold by Mein confirms the identification. This reprint of the text of the third authorized edition can thus claim to be the first American edition of *The Vicar*, antedating William Mentz's Philadelphia edition of 1772[20] by five years.

THE LIBRARY'S COPY OF 'THE VICAR OF WAKEFIELD'

Oliver Goldsmith, *The Vicar of Wakefield.* 4th edition. Dublin [i.e. Boston]: printed [by John Mein and John Fleeming] in the year 1767. 2v. in 1.

THE / VICAR / OF / WAKEFIELD: /A TALE./ Supposed to be written by HIMSELF. / [rule] /*Sperate miseri, cavete fælices.*/ [rule] /The FOURTH EDITION. / [rule] / VOL. I. [VOL. II.]/[double rule] /*DUBLIN:* /Printed in the Year M DCC LXVII.

Collation: 12°.
Vol. 1: *A*⁴ B-M⁶, 70 leaves, pp [*8*], 129 [*3*]; $3 (-B3) signed, misprinting G2 as G3.
Vol. 2: *A*² B-L⁶ M⁴, 66 leaves, pp [*4*], 124, [*4*]; $3 (-B2, C2,3, F2, 3, M2) signed, $1 (-L) also signed Vol. II.
Those pages on which a new chapter starts are without headline throughout.

Contents:
Vol. 1: *A*1ʳ title-page; *A*1ᵛ blank; *A*2ʳ advertisement; *A*2ᵛ blank; *A*3ʳ contents of the first volume; *A*4ᵛ blank; B1ʳ text, without drophead title; on M5ʳ End of Vol. I; M5ᵛ – M6ᵛ blank.
Vol. 2: *A*1ʳ title-page; *A*1ᵛ blank; *A*2ʳ contents of the second volume; B1ʳ text, without drophead title; M2ᵛ text ends, without 'finis'; M3ʳ – M4ᵛ blank.
Note: The text is set from the third authorized edition, London, 1766.

Running title: The VICAR of WAKEFIELD.
Variants:

As above, without period	F5ʳ
The VICAR of WAKFEIFLD. without period K5ʳ	D2ʳ, G2ᵛ,
The VICAR of WAKEFIFLD. v. 2, G2ʳ, K2ʳ.	G1ᵛ, K2ʳ;

Catchwords: None is used though catchwords appear in the third London edition, probably used as copy text.

Type: Text type: Baine's bold or strong-faced long primer roman; (20 lines) body height 69, face height 66; x height 1.5; capital height 2.3. Page (B4ʳ; v.2, B4ʳ), less head and direction lines, 124 x 69 mm, 36 lines to the page, 26 ems to the measure.

Paper: Watermarks: initials IV with countermark TG.

Binding: The two volumes are bound together in contemporary sheep, with five rather broad

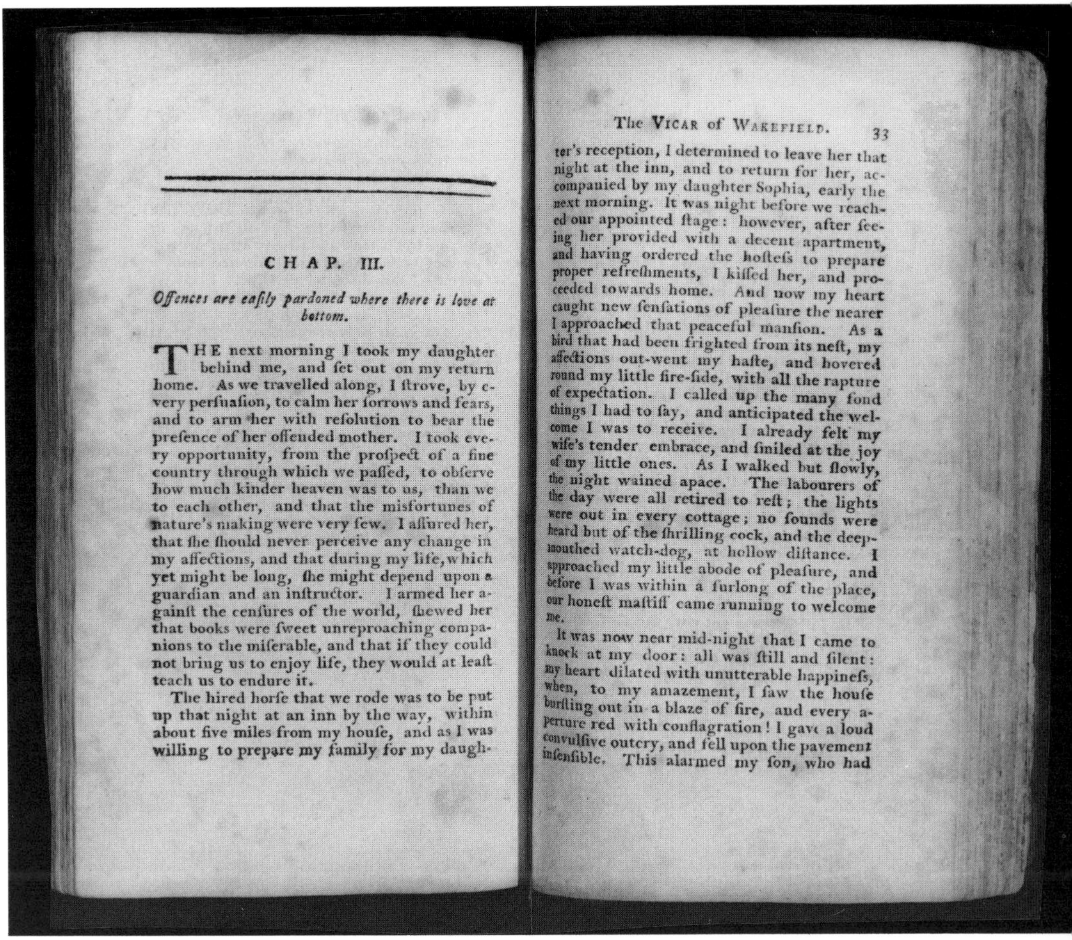

CHAP. III.

Offences are eaſily pardoned where there is love at bottom.

THE next morning I took my daughter behind me, and ſet out on my return home. As we travelled along, I ſtrove, by every perſuaſion, to calm her ſorrows and fears, and to arm her with reſolution to bear the preſence of her offended mother. I took every opportunity, from the proſpect of a fine country through which we paſſed, to obſerve how much kinder heaven was to us, than we to each other, and that the misfortunes of nature's making were very few. I aſſured her, that ſhe ſhould never perceive any change in my affections, and that during my life, which yet might be long, ſhe might depend upon a guardian and an inſtructor. I armed her againſt the cenſures of the world, ſhewed her that books were ſweet unreproaching companions to the miſerable, and that if they could not bring us to enjoy life, they would at leaſt teach us to endure it.

The hired horſe that we rode was to be put up that night at an inn by the way, within about five miles from my houſe, and as I was willing to prepare my family for my daugh-

The VICAR of WAKEFIELD. 33

ter's reception, I determined to leave her that night at the inn, and to return for her, accompanied by my daughter Sophia, early the next morning. It was night before we reached our appointed ſtage: however, after ſeeing her provided with a decent apartment, and having ordered the hoſteſs to prepare proper refreſhments, I kiſſed her, and proceeded towards home. And now my heart caught new ſenſations of pleaſure the nearer I approached that peaceful manſion. As a bird that had been frighted from its neſt, my affections out-went my haſte, and hovered round my little fire-ſide, with all the rapture of expectation. I called up the many fond things I had to ſay, and anticipated the welcome I was to receive. I already felt my wife's tender embrace, and ſmiled at the joy of my little ones. As I walked but ſlowly, the night wained apace. The labourers of the day were all retired to reſt; the lights were out in every cottage; no ſounds were heard but of the ſhrilling cock, and the deep-mouthed watch-dog, at hollow diſtance. I approached my little abode of pleaſure, and before I was within a furlong of the place, our honeſt maſtiff came running to welcome me.

It was now near mid-night that I came to knock at my door: all was ſtill and ſilent: my heart dilated with unutterable happineſs, when, to my amazement, I ſaw the houſe burſting out in a blaze of fire, and every aperture red with conflagration! I gave a loud convulſive outcry, and fell upon the pavement inſenſible. This alarmed my ſon, who had

82. *The Vicar of Wakefield,* fourth edition, Dublin [i.e. Boston] 1767. TCD copy: text set in Baine's 'strong-faced' long primer, vol. II, D4v/5r (page: 17.1 × 10 cm).

raised bands. The title label is missing. The final blank leaf, M4, in volume 2 has been used as the lower paste-down endpaper.

Provenance: The signatures of 'W Sever', and 'James Sever 1811' appear on the title-page. A bookplate, 'Ex libris Robert Sever Hale', signed by the engraver 'J.W. Spenceley, Boston, 1904', is pasted inside the upper cover. The book was bought from a New York bookseller in 1978.

Judge William Sever, 1729-1809, was born in Kingston, Massachusetts, and graduated at Harvard in 1745. His life is treated at some length in Sibley's *Harvard graduates;*[21] he appears to have been an admirable citizen, taking part when called upon in public life but without political ambition and interesting himself in literary pursuits without turning author. He was also pious, charitable, an upright judge and enjoyed 'agricultural amusements and social intercourse'. Sever was returned to the House of Representatives by the town of Kingston in 1766 and promoted to the Council in 1769, and it seems quite possible that while in Boston he bought his copy of *The Vicar* directly from Mein at the London Book store. Three of his sons were graduates of Harvard including James, who presumably inherited the novel after his father's death in 1809. The bookplate shows that the volume was still in the family a hundred years later.

OTHER COPIES[22]

Harvard University (MH). 2v. in 1, rebound and lacking the two final blanks, M3, 4. Paper watermarked with initials IV only.
John Carter Brown Library (RPJCB). Uncorrected running title, v.2., B3r: The VICAR of WAKFEIFLD. 2v. in 1, bound in sheep with red leather label; lacking v.1, I3.4 (pp 89-92), and v.2, M4, blank. Watermarks: initials IV and TG.
Yale University (CtY). Volume 2 only. B3r, running title uncorrected. No watermarks are visible.

NOTES

1. John Eliot Alden, 'John Mein, publisher: an essay in bibliographic detection', *Papers of the Bibliographical Society of America* 36 (1942) 199-214, and 'Scotch type in eighteenth-century America', *Studies in Bibliography* 3 (1950-1) 270-4. I am deeply in John Alden's debt, and would like to thank him, not only for having, in effect, already identified this edition in his earlier papers, but also for a great deal of help in this present case, including information on the book's first owner. He is not, however, to be held responsible for my errors and opinions, and in particular for my speculations on Mein's attitude to British copyright.

2. Isaiah Thomas, *The history of printing in America*, Worcester, 1810, vol. I, pp 362, 365.

3. Thomas, vol. I, p. 362.

4. Thomas, vol. I, p. 361.

5. *Boston New-England. Specimen of Mein and Fleeming's printing types.* Reproduced as plate XIV in Lawrence C. Wroth, *The colonial printer*, 2nd edition (1938), reprinted Charlottesville: University Press of Virginia, 1964.

6. I am indebted to James Mosley of St Bride Printing Library for this information and for his observations on the three specimens referred to here.

7. *A specimen of the printing types and flowers belonging to John Reid, printer.* Edinburgh, 1768. 8⁰. Copy in St Bride Printing Library.

8. Of special interest here is the type's appearance on the title-page of the primary Scots piracy of Goldsmith's *Deserted village*, 1770, which William B. Todd proved was printed at Edinburgh by Walter Ruddiman: *Studies in Bibliography* 6 (1954) 34.

9. Wroth, pp 313-14.

10. John Eliot Alden, 'A note on Tissot's "Advice to the people", London, 1767', *Papers of the Bibliographical Society of America* 34 (1940) 262-6.

11. Bodleian Library, MS Eng. Letters c. 20 (Kincaid and Bell Letter Book, 1764-9), fol. 62.

12. *The Boston Chronicle*, 8 August 1768. The price was given as 6s 8d but on 15 August the novel was offered at two prices, 5s and 6s. According to Mein's practice these may have reflected ordinary and fine paper copies or perhaps different binding styles.

13. Robert D. Harlan, 'David Hall's bookshop and its British source of supply', in *Books in America's past*, edited by David Kaser. Charlottesville: University Press of Virginia, 1966, p. 6.

14. *The Boston Chronicle*, 15 August 1768.

15. *The renowned history of Giles Gingerbread*, 1768, with Mein and Fleeming's imprint, was recorded as a result of his paper by Albert C. Bates in *Papers of the Bibliographical Society of America* 36 (1942) 320. Another title, from the 1768 advertisement, and again with full imprint, is no. 58 in A.S. Rosenbach's *Early American children's books* (1933), New York: Kraus, 1966.

16. Mein's full address has a thoroughly British ring: The London Book-store, second Door above the British Coffee-house, North-side of King-street.

17. William Robertson, *The history of the reign of Charles the fifth.* America: printed for the subscribers, 1770 [-1771]. 3v. The 'Address', prefixed to the third volume, is dated Philadelphia, 4 April 1771. The anonymous imprint, a sop to the inimical incendiaries, is worth noting.

18. First issued in London: printed for G. Burnet, 1764.

19. *Collected works of Oliver Goldsmith* edited by Arthur Friedman. Oxford: Clarendon Press, 1966, vol. 4, pp 9 and 135.

20. Ironically Mentz followed the first authorized edition in his reprint which therefore still contains the earlier text.

21. Sibley's *Harvard graduates.* Boston: Massachusetts Historical Society, 1873- , vol. XI, pp 575-8.

22. I would like to thank Hugh Amory, The Houghton Library, Harvard University, Danial Elliott, The John Carter Brown Library, and Patricia M. Howell, The Beinecke Library, Yale University, who have kindly checked their respective libraries' copies, corrected my errors and made helpful comments.

JONATHAN SWIFT

JAMES WOOLLEY

Before Jonathan Swift (1667-1745) became one of the world's greatest satirists, he was a student at Trinity College. Whether this experience in any direct way led him to write satire continues to be debated.[1] But it has in any case made the College Library the natural repository of documents any Swift scholar must consult — not only Swift's own writings but also biographical documents and writings by Swift's Dublin contemporaries, both friends and foes, that illustrate his own work and make its significance clearer.

Swift entered Trinity from Kilkenny School in 1682, at the age of fourteen. He proceeded through the normal undergraduate curriculum of those days. It is highly unusual for any College pre-eighteenth-century examination records to be preserved, but grades for Easter Term 1683 happen to survive. Swift's record reads as follows:

Ph: male G:L bene Th: Neglig.

That is, he did badly in physics — Aristotelian physics — but well in Greek and Latin; and he was negligent in the *thema* or Latin composition he was required to write.[2] The muniments also record that Swift was occasionally disciplined for such unremarkable offences as missing required chapel services (there were three per day).[3]

83. Death-mask of Jonathan Swift.

In his sixties Swift wrote a brief history of his family and of his own early life [84].[4] This autobiographical fragment was unpublished in Swift's lifetime. Thus the manuscript, which is in the Library, has survived: manuscripts for works Swift himself published seem regularly to have been destroyed. Scholars disagree on when it was written.[5] On Swift's death, the manuscript passed to his cousin and housekeeper, Martha Whiteway. From her it went to her son-in-law and Swift's early biographer, Deane Swift, who printed it in 1755, having already presented the manuscript to the Library in 1753.[6] Here Swift writes as an old man, and his version of events is not always reliable, but the surviving records more or less bear out his claim that as a student he 'had lived with great Regularity and due Observance of the Statutes'. And it is also true that he took

15

So that when the time came for
taking his Degree of Batchelor,
although he had lived with
great Regularity and due
Observance of the Statutes, he
was stopped of his Degree, for
Dullness and Insufficiency,
and at last hardly admitted
in a manner little to his Credit,
which is called in that Colledge
Speciali gratia, ~~which~~ as I am — And this discreditable mark
told, stands upon record in their
Colledge Registry.

The Troubles then breaking
out, he went to his Mother,
who lived in Leicester, and
after continuing there some
Months, he was received ~~[illegible]~~
~~[illegible]~~ by Sr Wm Temple,
whose Father had been a
great Friend to the Family
and who was now retired to
a his House called Moorpark
near Farnham in Surry,
Where he continued for about
two years. For he happened before

twenty

his BA, as he says, *speciali gratia* (by special grace), although his modern biographer, Irvin Ehrenpreis, has concluded that Swift's dour description of this as a 'discreditable mark' was unwarranted.[7]

Not long after earning his BA, Swift left Trinity because the Jacobite war was breaking out. He took an MA at Oxford, but returned to Trinity in 1700 and performed the public disputations required to earn the BD and DD degrees. He had already become a priest of the Church of Ireland, and had probably also finished, or substantially finished, *A tale of a tub*, his brilliant satire on abuses in religion and learning. The book proved detrimental to Swift's church career — that is, to becoming a dignitary of the Church of England. But although in later years he complained to his English correspondents that he was in 'exile' in Dublin, he was happy and productive as dean of St Patrick's Cathedral, a post he was awarded in 1713. His personal sense of possessing unrewarded merit, as well as his resentment that the British government treated Ireland as a colony, proved particularly stimulating and humanizing to Swift as a writer. Such satiric classics as *Gulliver's travels* or *A modest proposal* would probably not have flowed from his pen if he had not had a powerful awareness of himself and his country as victimized.

His ironic and satiric spirit found outlets in many other works as well — even his sermons. It is especially interesting to watch Swift's wit marshall its forces as he revises a draft — as in the Library's manuscript of Swift's sermon 'Brotherly love' [85].[8] This manuscript was first published by Swift's Dublin printer, George Faulkner, in 1754; at that time Faulkner advertised that the manuscript could be seen in his shop, but shortly after publication, the manuscript was donated, presumably by him, to Trinity College Library.[9] Swift records that he finished the manuscript two days before he preached the sermon in St Patrick's in 1717.

84. Extract from autobiographical fragment by Jonathan Swift (MS 1050, fol. 8r).

On the front of the manuscript Swift accurately labels it 'Politicall'. The Tories, with whom Swift had allied himself, had lost power when Queen Anne died in 1714, and in the ensuing years party hatred had reached disturbing heights, particularly so to those who, like Swift, were now out of favour. He addresses himself to his own flock, 'the middle and lower sort' who were — regrettably, he believed — becoming unduly politicized and divided by party strife. He encourages them to lay partisan animosities aside and to remain in close Christian communion with one another.

Swift's conclusion is an admission: 'I have now done with my Text [''Let brotherly Love continue''], which I confess to have treated in a Manner more suited to the present Times, than to the Nature of the Subject in generall'. What had happened, according to Swift's analysis, was that the established Whig government, in order to broaden its natural constituency, had been seeking to enfranchise its allies the Dissenters, and thereby to increase its own power. The slogan for this campaign was 'moderation'. Swift, who in any case strongly supported maintaining the established Church and excluding the Dissenters from the civil life of the nation, argued that the government's campaign for moderation was by no means designed to achieve such truly moderate results as charity toward all or 'liberty of conscience' for all — results he himself supported. Rather, he argued, the campaign was one of shameless political expedience. (The modern disappointment at Swift's illiberal failure to embrace ecumenism is probably anachronistic.) Certainly Swift's sense of being embattled stimulated him to write, and his resentment at the government's successful polarization of his parishioners calls forth his sarcastic description of them as 'able Politicians'. It is in such passages, where Swift is on the attack, that he does most of his revising, honing his irony. In the Library's manuscript, Swift is clearly trying to recopy an earlier foul draft. He had recommended that young preachers speak from a manuscript written in 'a large plain Hand', and that they avoid the 'frequent Blots and Interlineations' that lead a preacher into 'perpetual Hesitations or extemporary Expletives' as he tries to read his sermon to his congregation.[10] Nevertheless, in making his own clear, fair copy from which to preach, Swift cannot avoid this late opportunity to polish his wit further.

Thus, he changes the somewhat indirect 'And they have so far improved' to the ironic 'which Proceeding hath made our People in generall such able Politicians' — thus more effectively ridiculing the way the Whigs and Tories in his congregation have been led by politicians to ostracize one another [85]. The 'wise and mighty' may be humiliated, he jokes, seeing themselves outdone in the arts of the court and the 'publick Assemblyes' [such as the Irish House of Commons?] by 'our meanest Traders and Artificers'. In revising, Swift increases the tone of threat in stating the consequences. He changes 'have been' to 'may perhaps in time prove', thereby maintaining his rhetorical thrust even if his hearer does not agree that the consequences are already dire: very well, they 'may perhaps in time prove' even worse.

The finished version of the passage should thus look like this: 'For so it happens, that instead of enquiring into the Skill or Honesty of those kind of People, the manner is now to enquire into their Party, and to reject or encourage them accordingly [;] which Proceeding hath made our People in generall such able Politicians that all the Artifice, Flattery, Dissimulation, diligence, and Dexterity in undermining each other, which the Satyricall Witt of Men hath charged upon Courts, together with all the Rage and violence, Cruelty and Injustice which have been ever imputed to publick Assemblyes, are with us (so polite are we grown) to be seen among our meanest Traders and Artificers, in the greatest Perfection. All which as it may be matter of some Humiliation to the wise and mighty of this World: So the Effects may perhaps in time prove very different from what I hope in Charity were ever foreseen or intended.'

For a writer from whom so few drafts survive, a manuscript like this which offers even a glimpse at the process of composition must be valued highly. This manuscript also provides some access to Swift's manner as a public speaker. In certain passages, where the ironic emphasis is particularly crucial, Swift places slash marks above the words to be stressed in delivery.[11]

When it comes to printed books, most of the Library's great Swiftian treasures are items not even designed to last and certainly not designed to be treasured. That they have lasted is owing partly to the durability of pre-nineteenth-century papers and partly to whatever collecting instincts led people to bind and save newspapers and broadsides as well as the most ragged and shabbily printed pamphlets. That some of this material has come to be treasured by admirers of Swift reflects, in turn, Swift's characteristic delight in popular events and media, even if he affected to despise them. Thus as a political writer in London he had exploited broadside ballads. There could hardly be a more genuinely popular form; and when he came to Dublin he used, with a mocking twist, broadside elegies, last and dying speeches of condemned criminals, and other popular genres for his satiric purposes.

Among the best and most famous of his ventures into popular pamphleteering in Dublin were the 'Drapier's letters', a series of pamphlets published by John Harding in 1724 at the height of the Wood's Halfpence controversy. The British government, through a licence granted to William Wood, was at-

85. Extract from Jonathan Swift's sermon on brotherly love (MS 1050, fol. 15v).

much more than if he had disparaged his
Neighbor's Goods; or defamed him as a Cheat: For so it happens, that
instead of enquiring into the Skill or
Honesty of those kind of People, the manner
is now to enquire into their Party, and to
reject or encourage them accordingly. ~~And~~
which Proceeding hath made our People in generall such able Politicians ~~they have so few unpractised~~ that all the Artifice
Flattery, Dissimulation, diligence and Dexterity in
undermining each other, which the Satyricall Witt
of Men hath charged upon Courts, together
with all the Rage and violence, Cruelty and
Injustice which have been ever imputed to publick
~~popular~~ Assemblyes, are ~~now~~ with us (so polite
are we grown) to be seen among our meanest
Traders and Artificers, in the greatest Perfection.
All which as it may be matter of some
Humiliation to the wise and mighty of this
world: So the Effects thereof may perhaps in time prove ~~have been~~ very
different from what I hope in Charity were ever ~~in probability were bee~~
foreseen or intended.

2 I will therefore now in the Second Place
lay

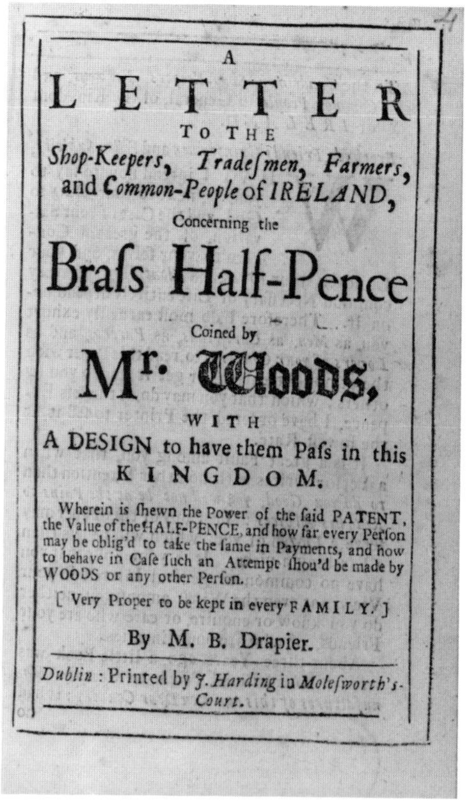
A

LETTER

TO THE

Shop-Keepers, Tradesmen, Farmers, and *Common-People* of IRELAND,

Concerning the

Brass Half-Pence

Coined by

Mr. Woods,

WITH

A DESIGN to have them Pass in this KINGDOM.

Wherein is shewn the Power of the said PATENT, the Value of the HALF-PENCE, and how far every Person may be oblig'd to take the same in Payments, and how to behave in Case such an Attempt shou'd be made by WOODS or any other Person.

[Very Proper to be kept in every FAMILY.]

By M. B. Drapier.

Dublin: Printed by *J. Harding* in *Molesworth's-Court.*

86. The first of the Drapier's letters, by Jonathan Swift.

87 (far right). A unique copy of a broadsheet by-product of *Gulliver's travels.*

tempting to impose on the Irish a coinage that they, spurred on by Swift in the guise of a draper, chose to reject.

The first of the letters the Drapier issued was *A letter to the shop-keepers, tradesmen, farmers, and common-people of Ireland, concerning the brass half-pence coined by Mr. Woods* [sic], *with a design to have them pass in this kingdom* [86]. It employs the simplest, most forceful style, speaking directly to the common people, who are addressed as 'Brethren, Friends, Countrymen, and Fellow Subjects'. The opening paragraph is a fair sample of its direct approach: 'What I intend now to say to you, is, next to your Duty to God, and the Care of your Salvation, of the greatest Concern to your selves, and your Children, your *Bread* and *Cloathing*, and every common Necessary of Life entirely depend upon it. Therefore I do most earnestly exhort you as *Men*, as *Christians*, as *Parents*, and as *Lovers of your Country*, to read this Paper with the utmost Attention, or get it read to you by others; which that you may do at the less Expence, I have ordered the Printer to sell it at the lowest Rate.'

Swift threatens his readers that Wood's money — this 'Filthy Trash' — will drive out all better money from Ireland, leaving the island impoverished and without any convenient way of making payments. An ordinary tenant farmer might require 'Three Horses Load' of the halfpence to pay his semi-annual rent.

Before the government at last capitulated in the face of Ireland's resistance to Wood's money, the 'Drapier's letters' reached a climax in the fourth of the series. Here Swift raised the constitutional issue with dangerous clarity, insisting that the British had no right to impose Wood's money against the will of the Irish: 'For in *Reason*, all *Government* without the Consent of the *Governed* is the *very Definition of Slavery*'. And he insisted that 'by the laws of GOD, of NATURE, of NATIONS, and of your own Country, you ARE and OUGHT to be as FREE a People as your Brethren in *England*'.[12] For this pamphlet Harding was prosecuted and imprisoned.

Gulliver's travels, first published in 1726, took the world by storm. One of the by-products was a set of amusing verses, written by Pope, perhaps in association with Gay or others, to accompany *Gulliver*. One of them, in a kind of truncated dimeter known as Lilliputian verse, purports to be an ode by the poet laureate of Lilliput to Quinbus Flestrin, the Man-Mountain. Others are supposedly by Glumdalclitch, the Houyhnhnms, and Mrs Gulliver. These poems are included in a Dublin broadside of which the Library's is the only known copy: *Poems occasioned by reading The travels of Captain Lemuel Gulliver* [87].

After Harding's death in 1726, his widow,

POEMS occasioned by Reading the *TRAVELS* of Captain Lemuel Gulliver, Explanatory *and* Commendatory.

To Quinbus Flestrin the *Man-Mountain*, An *ODE*.

y *TITTY TITT*, Esq; *Poet-Laureat to his Majesty of* LILLIPUT.

Translated into *English*.

I.
IN amaze
Lost, I gaze!
Can our E es
Reach thy Size?
M y my Lays
vell with Praise!
Vorthy thee!
Vorth me!
use inspire,
l thy Fire!
ards of old
him told,
hen they said
las Head
opt the Skies:
e and belive your
E es!
II.
See him stride
allies wide:
ver Woods,
ver Floods.
hen he treadS,
ountains Heads
roan and shake;
rmies quake,
Let his Spurn
Overturn
Man and Steed;
Troops take heed!
Left and Right,
Speed your Flight!
Lest an Host
B neath his Foot be lost.
III.
Turn'd aside
From his Hide,
Safe from Wound
Darts rebound.
From his Nose
Clouds he blows;
When he speaks,
Thunder breaks!
When he eats,
Famine threats;
When he drinks,
Neptune shrinks!
Nigh thy Ear,
In Mid Air,
On thy Hand
Let me stand,
So shall I,
Lofty Poet, touch the (Sky

The LAMENTATION of Glum- ... Loss of Grildrig. ... RAL.

SOON ... *wretch* mist her pleasing Care,
She wept, she blubber'd, and she tore her Hair,
o *British* Miss sincerer Grief has know,
er Squirrel missing or her Sparrow flew.
e furl'd her Sampler, and bawl'd in her Thread,
nd stuck her Needle into *Grildrig*'s Bed;
hen spread her Hands, and with a Bounce let fall
er Baby, like the Giant in *Guild hall*.
Peals of Thunder, now she roars, and now
e gently whimpers like a lowing Cow.
et lovely in her Sorrow still appears:
er Locks dishevell'd, and her Flood of Tears
em like the lofty Barn of some rich Swain,
en from the Thatch drips fast a Shower of Rain.
In vain she search'd each Cranny of the House,
ach gaping Chink impervious to a Mouse.
Was it for this (she cry'd) with daily Care
Within thy reach I set the Vinegar?
And fill'd the Cruet with the acid Tide,
While Pepper Water-Worms thy Bait suppl 'd,
Where twin'd the Silver Eel around thy Hook,
And all the little Monsters of the Brook.
Sure in that Lake he dropt—My *Grilly*'s drown'd,
he dragg'd the Cruet but no *Grildrig* found.
"Vain is thy Courage *Grilly*, vain thy Boast,
"But little Creatures enterprise the most.
"Trembling, I've seen thee dare the Kitten's Paw,
"Nay, mix with Children, as they play at Taw;
"Nor fear the Marbles, as they bounding flew:
"Marbles to them but roll ng Rocks to you.
"Why did I trust thee with that giddy Youth?
"Who from a *Page* can ever learn the Truth
"Vers'd in Court Tricks, that Mone -loving Boy
"To some Lord's Daughter sold the living Toy;
"Or rent him Limb from Limb in cruel Play,
"As Children tear the Wings of Flies away.
"From Place to Place o'er *Brobdignag* I'll roam,
"And never will return, or bring thee home
"But who hath Eyes to trace the passing Wind,
"How then thy fairy Footsteps can I find?
"Dost thou bewildred wander all alone,
"In the green Thick of a Mossy Stone,
"Or tumbled from the Toadstool's slipp'y Round,
"Perhaps all maim'd, lie groveling on the Ground?
"Dost thou imbosom'd in the lovely Rose,
"Or sunk within the Peaches Down repose;
"Within the King's Cup if thy Limbs are spread,
"Or in the golden Cowslip's velvet Head;
"O shew me, *Flora*, 'midst those Sweets the Flower
"Where sleeps my *Grildrig* in the fragrant Bower!
"But ah! I fear thy little Fancy roves
"On little Females, and on little Loves;
"Thy pigmy Children and thy tiny Spouse,
"The Baby Playthings that adorn thy House.
"Doors, Windows, Chimneys, and the spacious
"Epual in Size to Cells of Honeycombs. (Rooms.
"Hast thou for these now ventur'd from the Shore,
"Thy Bark a Bean shell, and a Straw thy Oar?
"Or in thy Box now bounding on the Main?
"Shall I ne'er beat thy self and House again?
"And shall I set thee on my Hand no more,
"To see thee leap the Lines and travarse o'er
"My spacious Palm? of Stature scarce a Span,
"Mimick the Actions of a real Man?
"No more behold thee turn my Watches Key,
"As Seamen at a Capstern Anchors weigh?
"How wert thou wont to walk with cautious Tread
"A Dish of Tea like Milk-Pale on thy Head?
"How chase the Mite ...
"And keep the rolling Maggot at a Bay?"
She spoke; but broken Accents stopt her Voice,
Soft as the speaking Trumpets mellow Noise:
She sob'd a Storm, and wip'd her flowing Eyes,
Which seem'd like two broad Suns in misty Skies:
O! squander not thy Grief, those Tears command
To weep upon our Cod in *Newfound-Land*:
The plenteous pickle shall preserve the Fish,
And *Europe* taste thy Sorrows in her Dish.

To Mr. Lemuel Gulliver,

The Grateful ADDRESS *of the unhappy* HOUYHNHNMS, *now in Slavery and Bondage in* England

TO thee, we Wretches of the *Houbynhum* Band,
Condemn'd to labour in a barb'rous Land,
Return our Thanks. Accept our humble Lays,
And let each grateful *Houybnhnm* neigh thy Praise.
O happy *Yahoo*, purg'd from human Crimes,
By thy sweet Sojourn in those virtuous Climes,
Where reign our Sires! There, to thy Country's Shame,
Reason you found, and Virtue were the same.
Their Precepts raz'd the Prejudice of Youth,
And even a *Yahoo* learn'd the Love of Truth.
Art thou the first who did the Coast explore;
Did never *Yahoo* tread that Ground before?
Yes Thousands. But in Pity to their Kind,
Or sway'd by Envy, or through pride of Mind,
They hid their Knowledge of a nobler Race,
Which own'd, would all their Sires and Sons disgrace.
You, like the *Samian*, visit Lands unknown,
And by their wiser Morals mend your own.
Thus *Orpheus* travell'd to reform his Kind,
Came back, and tam'd the Brutes he left behind.
You went, you saw, you heard: With Virtue fought,
Then spread those Morals which the *Houyhnhms* (taught
Our Labours here must touch thy gen'rous Heart,
To see us strain before the Coach and Cart;
Compell'd to run each knavish Jockey's Heat!
Subservient to *Newmarket*'s annual Cheat!
With what Reluctance do we Lawyers bear,
To fleece their Country Clients twice a Year?
Or manag'd in your Schools, for Fops to ride,
How foam, how fret beneath a Load of Pride!
Yes we are slaves—but yet, by Reason's Force,
Have learnt to bear Misfortune, like a Horse.
O would the Stars, to ease my Bonds, ordain,
That gentle *Gulliver* might guide my Rein!
Safe would I bear him to his Journey's End,
For 'tis a Pleasure to support a Friend.
But if my *Life* be doom'd to serve the Bad,
O! may'st thou never want an easy Pad!

HOUYHNEM

Mary Gulliver to Capt. Lemuel Gulliver; An *EPISTLE*.

The Captain some time after his Return, being retir'd to Mr. Sympson's *in the Country, Mrs.* Gulliver, *apprehending by his late Behaviour some Estrangement of his Affections, writes him the following expostulating, soothing, and tenderly-complaining* EPISTLE.

WElcome, thrice welcome to thy native Place!
——What, touch me not? What shun a Wife's Embrace?
Have I for this thy tedious Absence born,
And wak'd and wish'd whole Nights for thy Re (turn?
In five long Years I took no second Spouse;
What *Redriff* Wife so long hath kept her Vows?
Your Eyes your Nose, Inconstancy betray;
Your Nose you stop your Eyes you turn away.
'Tis said, that thou shouldst *cleave unto thy Wife*,
Once *thou* didst cleave, and I could cleave for Life,
Hear and relent! hark, how thy Children moan;
Be kind at least to these, they are thy own:
Behold, and count them all; secure to find
The honest Number that you left behind.
See how they pat thee with their pretty Paws:
Why start you? are they Snakes? or have they (Claws?
Thy Christian Seed, or mutual Flesh and Bone:
Be kind at least to these, they are thy own,
Biddel like thee, might farthest *India* rove;
He chang'd his Country, but retain'd his Love
There's Captain *Pannel*, absent half his Life,
Comes back, and is the kinder to his Wife.
Yet *Pannel*'s Wife is brown, compar'd to me,
And Mistress *Biddel* sure is Fifty three.
Not touch me! never Neighbour call'd me Slut!
Was *Flimnap*'s Dame more sweet in *Lilliput*?
I've no red Hair to breath an odious Fume;
At least thy Consort's cleaner than thy *Groom*.
Why then that dirty Stable boy thy Care?
What mean those Visits to the *Sorrel Mare*?
Say, by what Witchcraft, or what Dæmon led,
Prefer'st thou *Litter* to the Marriage Bed?
Some say the Devil himself is in that *Mare*:
If so, our *Dean* shall drive him forth by Prayer.
Some think you mad, some think you are possest;
The *Bedlam* and clean Straw would suit you best
Vain means, alas, this Frenzy to appease!
That *Straw*, that *Straw* would heighten the Disease
My Bed, (the *Scene* of all our former Joys,
Witness two lovely Girls, two lovely Boys)
Alone I press; in Dreams I call my Dear,
I stretch my Hand; no *Gulliver* is there!
I wake, I rise, and shiv'ring with the Frost,
Search all the House; my *Gulliver* is lost!
Forth in the Street I rush with frantick Cries;
The Windows open; all the Neighbours rise.
Where sleeps my Gulliver? *O tell me where?*
The Neighbours answer, "*With the Sorrel Mare.*
At early Morn, I to the Market haste,
(Studious in ev'ry thing to please thy Taste)
A curious *Fowl* and *Sparagrass* I chose,
(For I remember'd you were fond of those)
Three Shillings cost the first, the last sev'n Groats;
Sullen you turn'd from both, and call'd for *Oats*.
Others bring Goods and Treasures to their House,
Something to deck their pretty Babes and Spouses;
My *only* Token was a Cup like Horn,
That's made of nothing but a Lady's *Corn*.
'Tis not for that I grieve; O, 'tis to see
The *Groom* and *Sorrel Mare* prefer'd to me!
These for some Moments when you deign to quit,
And (at due distance) sweet Discourse admit,
'Tis all my Pleasure thy past Toil to know,
For pleas'd Remembrance builds Delight on Woe.
At ev'ry Danger pants thy Consort's Breast,
And gaping Infants squawle to hear the rest.
How did I tremble, when by Thousands bound,
I saw thee stretch'd on *Lilliputian* Ground;
When scaling Armies climb'd up ev'ry Part,
Each Step they trod, I felt upon my Heart.
But when thy Torrent quench'd the dreadful Blaze,
King, Queen and Nation staring with Amaze,
Full in my view how all my Husband came,
And what extinguish'd theirs, encreas'd my Flame
Those *Spectacles* ordain'd, thine Eyes to save,
Were once my Present; *Love* that Armour gave.
How did I mourn at *Bolgolam*'s Decree!
For when he sign'd thy Death he sentenc'd me.
When Folks might see thee all the Country round
For Six pence, I'd have giv'n a Thousand pound.
Lord! when the *Giant-babe* that Head of thine
Got in his Mouth, my Heart was up in mine!
When in the *Marrow bone* I see thee ram'd,
Or on the House top by the *Monkey* cram'd;
The piteous Images renew my Pain,
And all thy Dangers I weep o'er again!
But on the *Maiden's-Nipple* when you rid,
Pray Heav'n, 'twas all a wanton Maiden did!
Glumdalclitch too!——with thee I mourn her Case,
Heav'n guard the gentle Girl from all Disgrace!
O may the King that one Neglect forgive,
And pardon her the Fault by which I live!
Was there no other Way to set him free?
My Life, alas, I fear prov'd Death to Thee?
O teach me, dear, new words to speak my Flame;
Teach me to wooe thee by thy best-lov'd Name!
Whether the Stile of *Grildrig* please thee most,
So call'd on *Brobdingnag*'s stupendious Cost,
When on the Monarch's ample Hand you sate,
And hollow'd in his Ear, Intrigues of State:
Or *Quinbus Flestrin* more Endearment brings,
When like a Mountain you look'd down on Kings
If Ducal *Nardac*, *Lilliputian* Peer,
Or *Glumglum*'s humbler Title sooth thy Ear;
Nay, would kind *Jove* my Organs so dispose,
To hymn harmonious *Houyhnhnm* thro' the Nose,
I'd call thee *Houyhnhnm*, that high sounding Name
Thy Children's Noses all should twang the same.
So might I find my loving Spouse of course
Endu'd with all the *Virtues* of a *Horse*.

FINIS.

Sarah, continued to print for Swift and his circle. She was a printer of limited abilities, and one of her more ambitious undertakings was the *Intelligencer*. This was a single-essay periodical written by Swift and his friend Thomas Sheridan, a Dublin schoolmaster and wit, in 1728 and 1729. Trinity possesses one of only two known complete runs. The Trinity set contains the very rare first of three concealed editions of *Intelligencer* 3 [88]. In this essay, Swift stresses the political implications of John Gay's *Beggar's opera*, then as great a success on the Dublin stage as it was in London. In a reading that Swift's essay helped establish, *The beggar's opera* was interpreted as an attack on the British prime minister, Sir Robert Walpole: 'I mean where the Author takes occasion of comparing those *common Robbers to Robbers of the Publick*; and their several Stratagems of betraying, undermining, and hanging each other, to the several Arts of *Politicians* in times of Corruption'. It was also in this essay that Swift issued one of his most important statements about the nature of satire, admitting that while there was such a thing as satire resting on 'a *Publick Spirit*', and written with the design of 'mend[ing] the World', there was also satire written for its author's 'personal Satisfaction, and pleasure': 'I demand whether I have not as good a Title to Laugh, as Men have to be Ridiculous, and to expose Vice, as another hath to be Vicious. If I Ridicule the Follies and Corruptions of a *Court*, a *Ministry*, or a *Senate*; are they not amply payed by *Pensions, Titles,* and *Power*, while I expect and desire no other Reward, than that of Laughing with a few Friends in a Corner.'[13]

88. A very rare edition of the *Intelligencer* in which Swift considers Gay's *Beggar's opera* and the nature of satire.

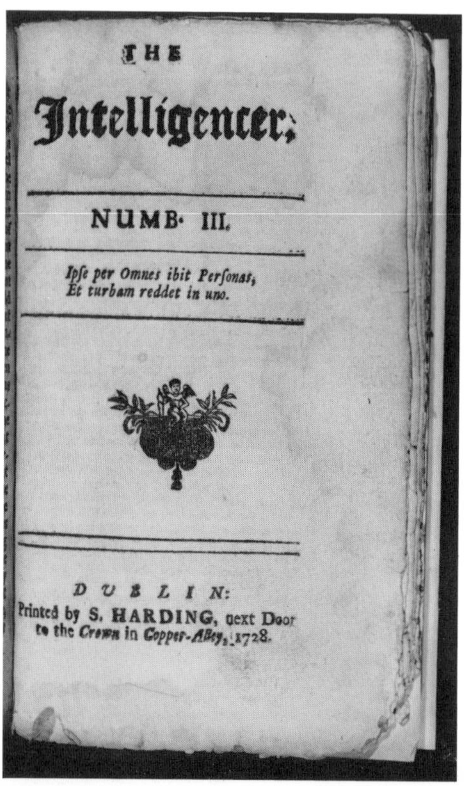
THE

Intelligencer.

NUMB. III.

Ipse per Omnes ibit Personas,
Et turbam reddet in uno.

DUBLIN:
Printed by S. HARDING, next Door to the *Crown* in *Copper-Alley*, 1728.

Sarah Harding's last printing for Swift was *A modest proposal for preventing the children of poor people from being a burthen to their parents, or the country, and for making them beneficial to the publick*, in 1729 [89]. It was issued anonymously, as was the case with virtually all Swift's pamphlet publications, and soon reprinted in London. The brutality of Irish circumstances — three years of famine, dire poverty, infanticide — is balanced against the brutality of the solution, proposed in the 'modest' tones of a contemporary political arithmetician. After all, 'whoever could find out a fair, cheap and easy method of making these Children sound and useful Members of the common-wealth would deserve so well of the publick, as to have his Statue set up for a preserver of the Nation'. Therefore, Swift's projector informs his readers, 'I have been assured by a very knowing *American* of my acquaintance in *London*, that a young healthy Child well Nursed is at a year Old a most delicious, nourishing, and wholesome Food, whether *Stewed, Roasted, Baked*, or *Boyled*, and I make no doubt that it will equally serve in a *Fricasie*, or *Ragoust*'.

Yet the comic outrageousness of such a passage hardly outweighs the pervasive despair about an Ireland where the usual laws of economics seem not to apply and where the more truly reasonable solutions Swift had repeatedly proposed for Ireland's ills had met with no 'hearty and sincere Attempt to put them in Practice'. It would be difficult to exaggerate the importance of this crudely-printed pamphlet — which in the Harding printing is almost unobtainable in the antiquarian market — among Swift's writings. It is today perhaps his best known work, if children's abridgements of *Gulliver's travels* are disregarded.

For reasons not entirely clear, Sarah Harding, who had become identified as Swift's Dublin printer, ceased to be so following *A modest proposal*. Thanks to research carried out in the Library's Department of Early Printed Books, it is now reasonably clear that Swift turned almost immediately to the young Dublin printer George Faulkner (then in partnership with James Hoey). What had previously been known was that a number of Swift's publications at this point appeared in Dublin printings with no printer's name at all. In Early Printed Books, research has for some time been in progress on the various printers' ornaments in use in eighteenth-century Dublin printing, each ornament being carefully catalogued according to what printer used it, insofar as is known. While conceivably printers might sell, lend, or trade their ornaments, it is striking that a number of Swift's works published in the early 1730s include ornaments recorded as having been used, and only used, in other works that George Faulkner printed about the same time.

A case in point is Swift's important poem *A libel on D[r] D[elany]*, identified by no printer's name but bearing an ornament whose homemade ugliness makes it more memorable than most [90]. The fact that this ornament can be firmly identified as Faulkner's means that some more than casual connection between this text of the poem and Swift himself can be presumed. A pattern of relationship between author and printer begins to emerge which, while it must remain conjectural, cannot be ignored by the scholar seeking to say which of the many printings of such a poem are likely to have been backed by Swift's own authority. Other works of Swift have been identified by the same research as coming from Faulkner (or Faulkner and Hoey).[14]

Among the many important and illuminating Dublin broadsides that might be mentioned, *The place of the damn'd* was acquired only recently, as part of the Burgage Collection [91]. It would be tempting to attribute this printing — an extremely scarce item — to Faulkner's press, but in the absence of any printer's name or ornament, it can be said only that this appears to be the first of Swift's publications to identify its author as 'J.S. D.D.D.S.P.D.' (Jonathan Swift, D.D., Dean of St Patrick's, Dublin). This string of initials was used by Faulkner in his editions of Swift's works, and clearly it had Swift's approval as a means of identifying him while preserving at least some wisps of the smokescreen of anonymity he habitually threw up. It would thus not be surprising if

89. Swift's satire at its most savage — fattening children for the table.

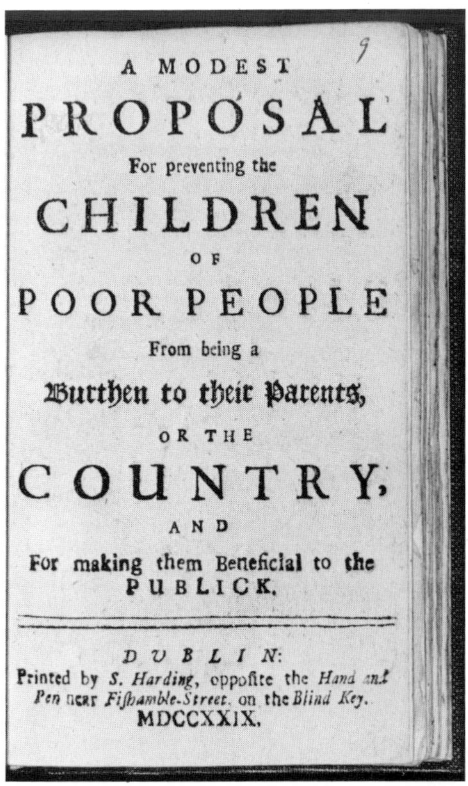
A MODEST PROPOSAL For preventing the CHILDREN OF POOR PEOPLE From being a Burthen to their Parents, OR THE COUNTRY, AND For making them Beneficial to the PUBLICK.

DUBLIN: Printed by S. Harding, opposite the Hand and Pen near Fishamble-Street, on the Blind Key. MDCCXXIX.

this printing were authorized by Swift himself, nor, if that were so, would it be surprising if the job had gone to Faulkner, who by that time was his regular printer. In acquiring the Burgage Collection, the Library also got an apparently unique copy of a grubstreet rejoinder to *The place of the damn'd* called *The devil's gratitude*, which was reprinted in a small edition by the Trinity Closet Press, the Library's laboratory press, in 1980.

Faulkner's enduring fame as a printer and publisher rests on his issuing, in Dublin in late 1734 and early 1735, the '1735' *Works of J.S.D.D.D.S.P.D.* With Swift's cooperation and assistance (though the extent of the assistance cannot be precisely fixed), Faulkner issued four volumes of Swift's writings. This publishing venture could not have been undertaken in London because Britain, unlike Ireland, had a copyright law, and Swift's British copyrights were too widely dispersed among various publishers for such a cumulation to be feasible. Although no legal deposit act required Faulkner to lodge a copy of the new edition in Trinity College Library, he did place the duodecimo edition there, calling attention to his gift on the binding itself [92]. It might be wondered whether this was simple mean-spiritedness, to give the College Library his cheap edition, when he could well have supplied the octavo, or more handsomely yet, the large-paper octavo. His motive seems likelier, however, to have been more creditable. The octavo, which was published first, was plagued by difficulties, particularly in volume 2, which comprised the poems. Not only were many cancels required, but when all the cancelling and replacing was concluded, the chronological order Swift pretty clearly wanted was awry at many points. In short, the duodecimo; though the cheaper edition, was, for the poems, at least, the better; and it seems plausible that this consideration motivated Faulkner's donation.

Very late in his career, in 1736, Swift wrote one of his last and most raucous poems, *The legion club*, abusing the Irish Parliament. This was a poem that never had an authorized edi-

90. The ornament on this titlepage points to it as having been printed by George Faulkner, 'the Prince of Dublin printers'.

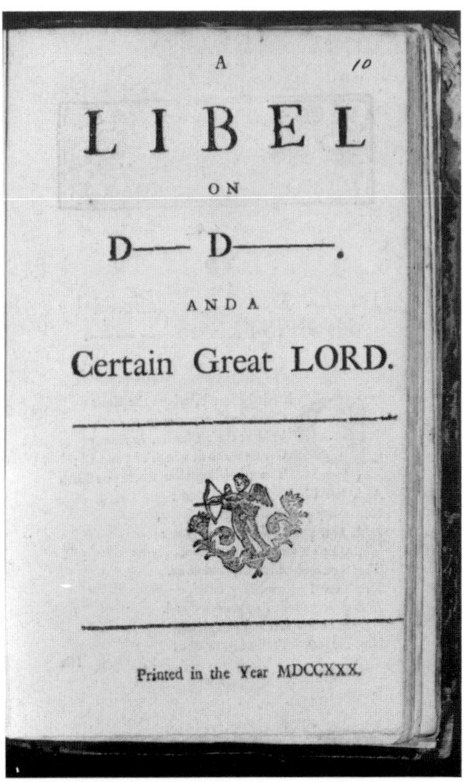
A

10

LIBEL

ON

D—— D——.

AND A

Certain Great LORD.

Printed in the Year MDCCXXX.

91. A broadsheet by Swift under an opaque pseudonym.

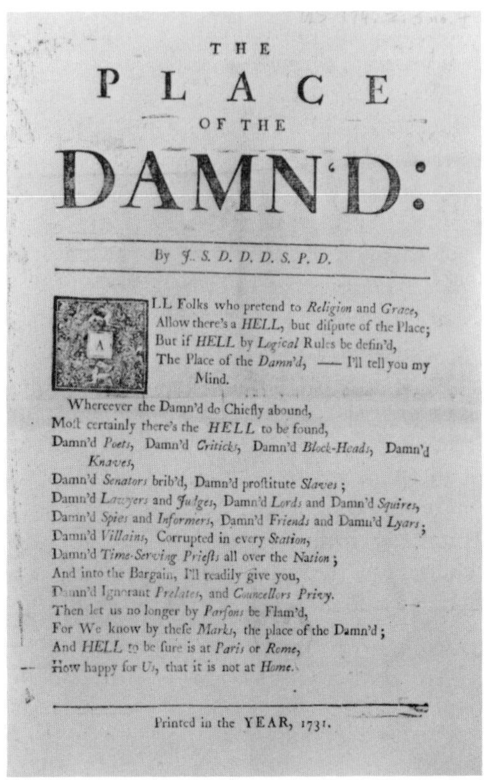
THE

PLACE

OF THE

DAMN'D:

By *J. S. D. D. D. S. P. D.*

ALL Folks who pretend to *Religion* and *Grace*,
Allow there's a *HELL*, but dispute of the Place;
But if *HELL* by *Logical* Rules be defin'd,
The Place of the *Damn'd*, —— I'll tell you my Mind.

Whereever the Damn'd do Chiefly abound,
Most certainly there's the *HELL* to be found,
Damn'd *Poets*, Damn'd *Criticks*, Damn'd *Block-Heads*, Damn'd *Knaves*,
Damn'd *Senators* brib'd, Damn'd prostitute *Slaves*;
Damn'd *Lawyers* and *Judges*, Damn'd *Lords* and Damn'd *Squires*,
Damn'd *Spies* and *Informers*, Damn'd *Friends* and Damn'd *Lyars*;
Damn'd *Villains*, Corrupted in every *Station*,
Damn'd *Time-Serving Priests* all over the *Nation*;
And into the Bargain, I'll readily give you,
Damn'd Ignorant *Prelates*, and *Councellors Privy*.
Then let us no longer by *Parsons* be Flam'd,
For We know by these *Marks*, the place of the Damn'd;
And *HELL* to be sure is at *Paris* or *Rome*,
How happy for *Us*, that it is not at *Home*.

Printed in the YEAR, 1731.

tion, so dangerous was its naming of names, but it circulated in many manuscript transcripts, of which Trinity has a share, and in various printed versions. One of the earliest of these was a compilation called *S---t contra omnes. An Irish miscellany* (1736). Trinity possesses it in the copy once owned by the eighteenth-century traveller John Loveday and in the present century by T. A. Hollick; Trinity acquired the book at the Sotheby's sale of Hollick's books in 1980, using the resources of the Chester Beatty Fund [93].

In *The legion club*, Swift writes of Edward Lovett Pearce's new Parliament House:

As I strole the City, oft I
See a Building large and lofty,
Not a Bow-shot from the College,
Half the Globe from Sense and Knowledge,

. . . .

Tell us what the Pile contains
Many a Head that holds no Brains.
These Demoniacks let one dub,
With the Name of *Legion Club*.

Infuriated by attempts in the Irish Parliament to cut the tithes on pasturage, Swift describes the legislature as a madhouse whose odious inmates raged in hellish squalor.

Were there sufficient space, numerous other resources for the study of Swift might be mentioned. There is, for example, a copy of Ben Jonson's *Works* of 1640 that was in Swift's library — a direct link between Swift and one of the greatest satirists of the previous century.[15] Or there are the manuscript miscellanies such as 'The whimsical medley', in which Swift's work figures importantly. Perhaps the most significant body of material, however, is not any single monument but rather the surprisingly rich collection of eighteenth-century halfsheets, or broadsides, as they are commonly called. Except for a rare latter-day acquisition such as the Burgage Collection, they have been in the Library a long time, which is to say only that they were in the Library when the great nineteenth-century catalogue was published; their previous history is not known. Yet it is these items which afford so rewarding a glimpse into the daily life of eighteenth-century Dublin, where anonymous poems and pamphlets by the nation's greatest living author appeared in ephemeral dress, side by side with trivia. At least some of this ephemeral material is still of interest because it illuminates the writings of Swift himself.

NOTES

1. See John Barrett, *An essay on the earlier part of the life of Swift*. London, 1808; and George Mayhew, 'Swift and the Tripos tradition', *Philological Quarterly* 45 (1966) 85-101.

2. TCD MS 1203 (Examination roll, 1685).

3. Irvin Ehrenpreis, *Swift: The man, his works, and the age*. London: Methuen, 1962-83, vol.1, pp 57-77.

4. TCD MS 1050 (Life of Swift).

5. Herbert Davis, in his edition of Swift's *Prose writings*, Oxford: Blackwell, 1939-68, vol.5, p.xxii, suggests 1727-9; Irvin Ehrenpreis, in his Index to the

92. Dean Swift's 1735 *Works* in the presentation binding given by the printer to the Library.

Prose writings, vol.14, suggests 1738-9; and George Mayhew suggests 1727 in *Philological Quarterly* 48 (1969) 398.

6. Mayhew, *Philological Quarterly* 48 (1969) 398.

7. *Swift: The man, his works, and the age*, vol.1, p.62.

8. TCD MS 1050.

9. Herbert Davis, 'The manuscript of Swift's sermon on brotherly love', in *Pope and his contemporaries*, edited by James L. Clifford and Louis A. Landa. Oxford: Clarendon, 1949, p.155.

10. *A letter to a young gentleman, lately enter'd into holy orders*, in *Prose writings*, vol.9, pp 71-2.

11. The relevant passages are transcribed in Davis, 'The manuscript of Swift's sermon on brotherly love', p.152.

12. *A letter to the whole people of Ireland* [1724].

13. Bibliographical analysis of the concealed editions will appear in an edition of the *Intelligencer* that I am preparing for Oxford University Press.

14. James Woolley, 'Arbuckle's "Panegyric" and Swift's scrub libel', in *Contemporary studies of Swift's poetry*, edited by John Irwin Fischer and Donald C. Mell. Newark: Delaware, 1981, p.209.

15. For this information I am indebted to Hermann J. Real and Heinz J. Vienken.

93. Swift: an attack on the Irish Parliament in *S---t contra omnes*, London [*c.* 1736].

[13]

THE

LEGION CLUB.

v. Swift. VII. 275.

AS I ſtrole the City, oft I
See a Building large and lofty,
Not a Bow-ſhot from the College,
Half the Globe from Senſe and Knowledge,
By the prudent Architect
Plac'd againſt the Church direct;
Making

THE 1798 REBELLION

R.B. McDOWELL

The tumultuous last decade of the eighteenth century, which in Ireland reached its climax in the insurrection of 1798, is represented in the Library's Manuscripts Department by three important collections, the Madden, the Sirr and the Tone.

Richard Robert Madden throughout a very long life in Europe, Asia, Australia and the West Indies as a medical doctor, a traveller, a colonial administrator, a magistrate and Irish civil servant retained a romantic interest in the United Irishmen. He admired their idealism and courage, though himself a respectable liberal who deplored violence, and, working with tremendous energy, he built up 'a vast collection of papers . . . collected . . . amongst the survivors and descendants of the United Irishmen in France, Spain, Portugal, England and Ireland' which he used for his *United Irishmen, their lives and times.*[1] Madden has obvious faults as a historian. He was vehemently partisan and had little sense of form and proportion. On the other hand as a research worker he was indefatigable. With great pertinacity he tracked down sources of information, personal and documentary. He recorded what he was told, and, good humoured and friendly, he sometimes managed to secure letters and papers from their owners. Moreover, whatever might be his defects as a writer, he carefully preserved the material, original documents, communications and notes on which he based his published work. Much of this material, bound in three large volumes, was purchased by James Henthorn Todd, Trinity's devoted Librarian, for sixteen guineas at the sale of Madden's library in 1865.[2]

In 1976 a valuable addition was made to the Madden material when Professor T. W. Moody presented a collection of papers, relating to James Hope, which had been in Madden's possession.[3]

In 1843 the Rev. Joseph D'Arcy Sirr (1794-1868), an evangelical clergyman and author who was a Trinity graduate, presented to the Library a collection of papers relating to the activities of the Irish radicals, which had been accumulated by his father, Major Henry Charles Sirr. Major Sirr, a retired army officer who had become a wine merchant in Dublin, was in 1796 appointed assistant Town Major for Dublin, two years later he was promoted to be Town Major and in 1808 when a new Dublin police act was passed he was appointed a police magistrate. The Town Major had disciplinary responsibilities in a garrison town but in the later nineties the Dublin police force was weak and inefficient, so Sirr, energetic and public spirited, assumed the functions of a political police officer. The Sirr collection[4] comprises reports from informants, and numerous letters, including the correspondence of Thomas Russell, seized by the authorities [94].

The bulk of the Tone collection, the note books containing his diaries, letters and papers, was bequeathed to the College in 1924

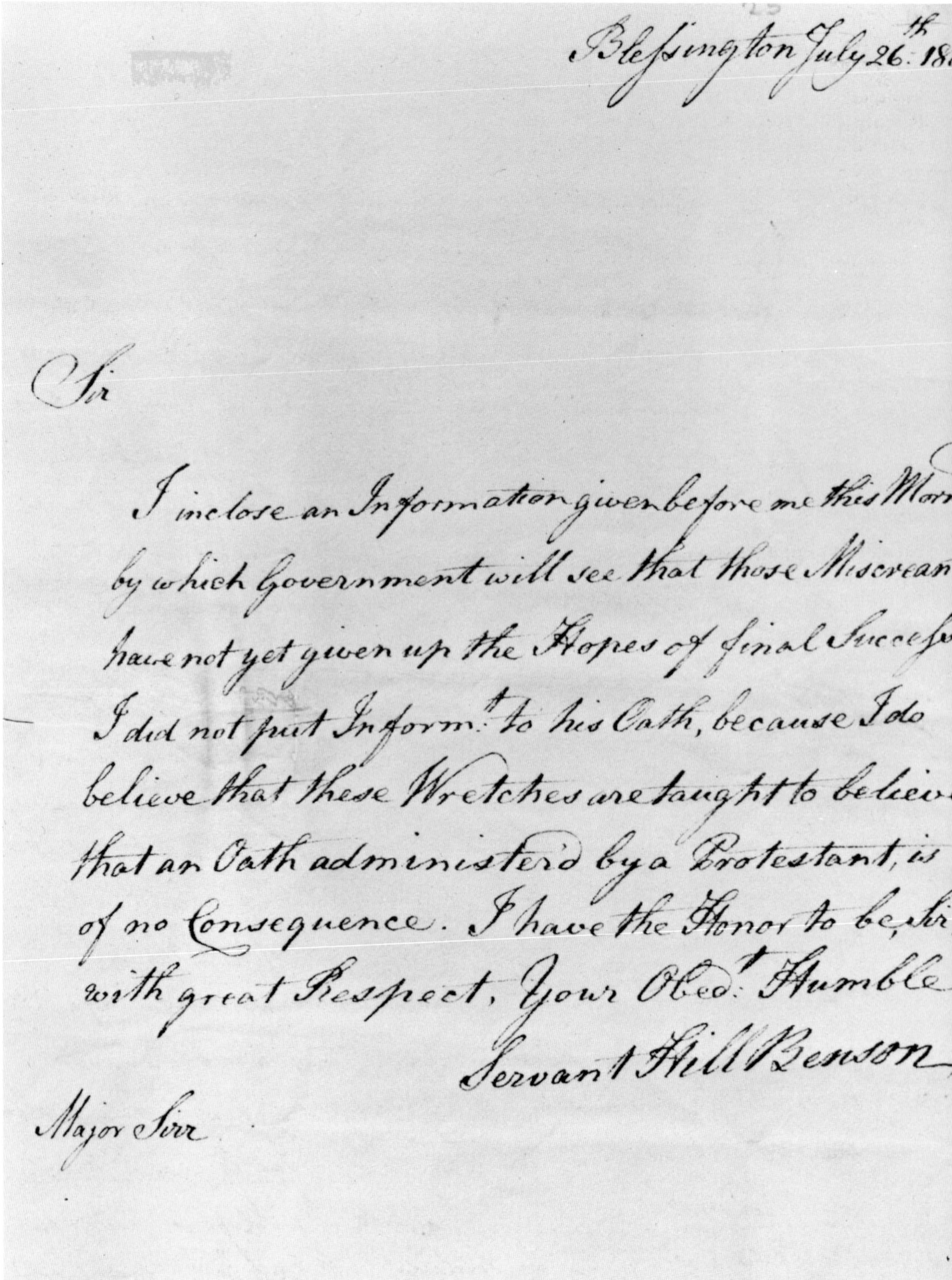

Blessington July 26th 18

Sir

I inclose an Information given before me this Morn
by which Government will see that those Miscrean
have not yet given up the Hopes of final Success
I did not put Inform.t to his Oath, because I do
believe that these Wretches are taught to believe
that an Oath administer'd by a Protestant, is
of no Consequence. I have the Honor to be, Sir,
with great Respect, Your Obed.t Humble
Servant Hill Benson

Major Sirr

94. Letter from Hill Benson, Blessington, to Major Sirr at Dublin Castle commenting on the activities of insurgents, 26 July 1803.

95. Extract from Theobald Wolfe Tone's diary (22 February 1796) outlining his plan to land five thousand French soldiers in Ireland.

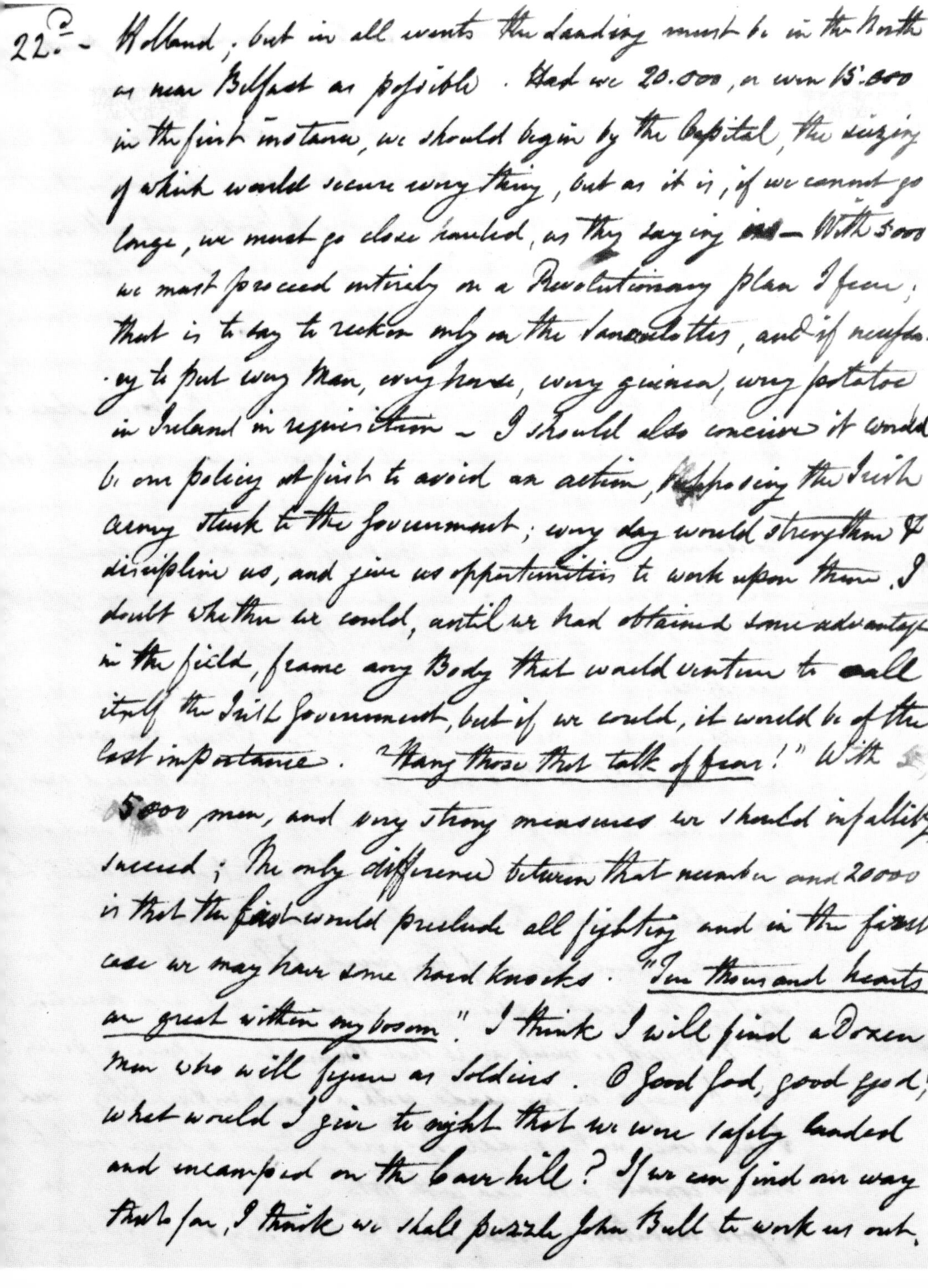

22d. – Holland; but in all events the landing must be in the North
as near Belfast as possible. Had we 20.000, or even 15.000
in the first instance, we should begin by the Capital, the seizing
of which would secure every thing, but as it is, if we cannot go
large, we must go close hauled, as the saying is — With 5000
we must proceed entirely on a Revolutionary plan I fear;
that is to say to reckon only on the Sansculottes, and if necessa-
-ry to put every man, every horse, every guinea, every potatoe
in Ireland in requisition – I should also conceive it would
be our policy at first to avoid an action, supposing the Irish
army stuck to the Government; every day would strengthen &
discipline us, and give us opportunities to work upon them. I
doubt whether we could, until we had obtained some advantage
in the field, frame any Body that would venture to call
itself the Irish Government, but if we could, it would be of the
last importance. "Hang those that talk of fear!" With
5000 men, and very strong measures we should infallibly
succeed; the only difference between that number and 20000
is that the first would preclude all fighting and in the former
case we may have some hard knocks. "Ten thousand hearts
are great within my bosom". I think I will find a dozen
men who will figure as Soldiers. O Good God, good God!
what would I give to night that we were safely landed
and encamped on the Cave hill? If we can find our way
thus far, I think we shall puzzle John Bull to work us out.

by Miss Katherine Anne Maxwell, great-grand-daughter of Theobald Wolfe Tone, and this gift was supplemented by the presentation of a number of similar items[5] by Mrs Livington T. Dickason, Tone's great-great-grand-daughter [95 and 96]. The Tone material is remarkable in one respect. The papers of a middle class radical who, in the last years of his life, moved between Ireland, America and France might be expected to have a poor survival-expectancy, but family feeling — affection and pride — allied to good fortune account for their preservation. Since Tone was a gifted writer, clear, candid and perceptive, in touch with men and affairs, his writings throw considerable light on political and strategic developments as well as providing a very lively picture of life in exciting and critical times.

An outlook very different from that of Tone is reflected in the rebellion diary of Thomas Prior, elected to fellowship in 1792.[6] Another Fellow of the period, Matthew Young, later Bishop of Clonfert, made a verbatim report of a highly dramatic episode, which occurred shortly before the insurrection, the visitation of the College conducted by Lord Clare as Vice-Chancellor of the University.[7]

Legal action in a different sphere is represented by 'Proceedings of Courts Martial, 1798',[8] purchased in 1895, and material that could have been used in prosecuting persons alleged to be insurgents is contained in a volume of sworn informations presented to the Library in 1806 by Sir Richard Musgrave, the strongly conservative historian.[9] Sir Richard also presented to the Library a grim record, 'The bloody Calendar used in Wexford gaol when that town was in possession of the rebels, 1798'.[10] In the summer of 1921 this item, which some months before had been consulted by a reader, was reported to be missing. The Library held a thorough enquiry. The procedures for issuing and replacing a manuscript appeared to be thorough and they seemed to have been strictly observed. However there survives in the Library a list of the prisoners held by the insurgents in Wexford.[11]

NOTES

1. R. R. Madden, *The United Irishmen, their lives and times*. London: Duffy, 1842-6.
2. TCD MSS 873, 1471, 1472.
3. TCD MSS 7252-7257.
4. TCD MSS 868, 869.
5. TCD MSS 3805-3807.
6. TCD MS 3365.
7. TCD MS 1203.
8. TCD MS 872.
9. TCD MS 871.
10. TCD MS 870.
11. TCD MS 870*.

96. A call to arms by General Hardy, commander of the French army, addressed to the people of Ireland.

LIBERTY, EQUALITY, FRATERNITY, UNION.

The General, Commanding the French Army, to the People of Ireland.

IRISHMEN!

YOU have not forgotten Bantry bay! you know the efforts to aſſiſt you which France has already made; her affection for you, her deſire to avenge your wrongs and aſſure your independance, remain ſtill the ſame.

At length, after various attempts, you ſee Frenchmen among you; they come to ſuſtain your courage, to share your dangers, to mix their arms with yours, to shed their blood in common with you, in defence of the ſacred cauſe of liberty; they come to announce to you other Frenchmen, whom you will ſpeedily embrace, as friends and brothers.

Brave Iriſhmen, our cauſe is the ſame; like you, we abhor the rapacious and ſanguinary politics of a tyrannical government; like you, we regard, as imperſcriptible, the ſacred right to be free, inherent in all people who have the courage to reclaim it; like you, we feel that the tranquillity of the world will be perpetually diſturbed, ſo long as the British miniſtry shall be able to traffic with impunity in your labours, your induſtry, and your blood.

Independant of the identity of interets which unites us, we have, beſides, the moſt powerful motives to reſpect, to aid, and to defend you.

Is not France made to ſerve as a pretext for the atrocities which the cabinet of S^t. James's exerciſes daily againſt you? The intereſt which your hearts have all along taken in the grand events of our revolution, is t not imputed to you as a crime? The executioner, the torture, do they not menace every hour, the exiſ-ence of thoſe among you, who are even ſuſpected of being our friends?

LET US THEN UNITE, AND MARCH TO GLORY!

We pledge ourſelves to obſerve the most ſacred reſpect for your properties, your laws, your religion; Be free, be independant, acknowledge no maſter but yourſelves; we wish for no ſucceſs but that which shall e yours, no conqueſt but that which aſſures to you your freedom.

The moment to break your chains is arrived; our victorious armies are on their way to the extremities of he earth, to ſtrike at the root of the wealth, and the tyranny of the common enemy; already the hideous coloſſus is tumbling on every ſide into ruin; where is the Iriſhman ſo baſe and cowardly, as to detach himſelf, n this great occaſion, from the intereſt of his country? If ſuch traitors exiſt, let them be chaſed with infamy rom the ſoil, which they are unworthy to poſſeſs, and let their properties become the patrimony of the children f thoſe gallant men, who fight, and who die, for the liberty of their country.

Iriſhmen, look to the occaſions ſtill recent, where Frenchmen have humbled your enemies to the duſt; look o the plains of Hondschoote; look to Quiberon, to Oſtend; look to America, free from the moment that he willed it; the combat will be short between you and your tyrants.

Friends and allies, let us march together; let our cry of combat be UNION, LIBERTY, THE IRISH REPUBLIC! our hearts, our hands are devoted to your cauſe, our glory is in your proſperity and independance.

HARDY.

'HERE'S FINE WORK! HERE'S FINE SUICIDE, PARACIDE AND SIMULATION'

C. BENSON

The building up of a good collection of drama in English printed before 1820 has been one of the successes of the Library since the 1960s. There is now a collection that is worthy of the succession of great dramatists who have been educated at the College, pre-eminent among whom are William Congreve, George Farquhar, Oliver Goldsmith, Oscar Wilde and Samuel Beckett. The date 1820 is chosen because shortly after that date the inflow of plays under the terms of the Copyright Act of 1801 increased very greatly, and the Library has a large, if imperfectly organized, collection of nineteenth-century plays. It must be said at the outset that consideration of the drama collection involves looking at the holdings of play bills, theatre music, and other works on the theatres and the people working in them, in addition to the plays.

97 (below). Title page to the first edition of William Congreve's *The double dealer,* London 1694.

98 (far right). Title page to William Prynne's attack on the stage, *Histrio-mastix,* London 1633.

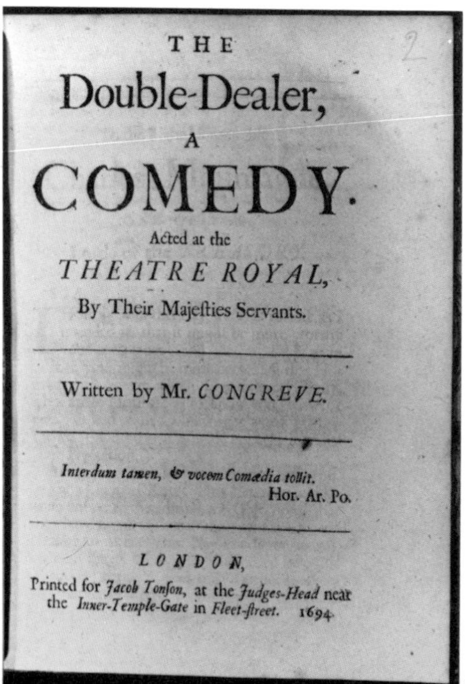
THE
Double-Dealer,
A
COMEDY.
Acted at the
THEATRE ROYAL,
By Their Majesties Servants.

Written by Mr. *CONGREVE.*

Interdum tamen, & vocem Comædia tollit.
Hor. Ar. Po.

LONDON,
Printed for *Jacob Tonson,* at the *Judges-Head* near the *Inner-Temple-Gate* in *Fleet-street.* 1694.

As far as the Library was concerned, drama remained the Cinderella branch of literature until the 1960s. The majority of the plays received under legal deposit were relegated to catalogues that were not available to the public view. Three sizeable collections of plays printed before 1800 had been accessioned, the first of 120 late-seventeenth and early-eighteenth-century quartos, and the second and third containing about three hundred and fifty late-eighteenth-century Irish printed editions. Sundry other editions, many of them important, had been acquired over the centuries, but no policy existed of building a balanced collection. Attitudes changed with the purchase of 400 plays from J. Barry Brown in 1964. These plays were mostly eighteenth-century Irish editions, but with a sprinkling of seventeenth-century English editions, and a good handful of eighteenth-century English and Dutch editions. Since then frequent purchases have been made, within the constraints of limited budgets that have excluded the purchase of the plums of seventeenth-century literature. Particular attention is paid to the collecting of the works of authors educated at Trinity College, of other Irish authors, and of editions printed in Ireland.

HISTRIO-MASTIX.

THE PLAYERS SCOVRGE, OR, ACTORS TRAGÆDIE,

Divided into Two Parts.

Wherein it is largely evidenced, by divers *Arguments*, by the concurring Authorities and Resolutions of *sundry texts of Scripture*; of the *whole Primitive Church*, both under the *Law and Gospell*; of 55 *Synodes and Councels*; of 71 *Fathers and Christian Writers*, before the yeare of our Lord 1200; of above 150 *foraigne and domestique Protestant and Popish Authors*, since; of 40 *Heathen Philosophers*, *Historians*, *Poets*; of many *Heathen*, many *Christian Nations*, *Republiques*, *Emperors*, *Princes*, *Magistrates*; of sundry *Apostolicall*, *Canonicall*, *Imperiall Constitutions*; and of our owne *English Statutes*, *Magistrates*, *Vniversities*, *Writers*, *Preachers*.

That popular Stage-playes *(the very Pompes of the Divell which we renounce in Baptisme,* if we beleeve the Fathers*) are sinfull, heathenish, lewde, ungodly Spectacles, and most pernicious Corruptions; condemned in all ages, as intolerable Mischiefes to Churches, to Republickes, to the manners, mindes and soules of men. And that the Profession of Play-poets, of Stage-players; together with the penning, acting, and frequenting of Stage-playes, are unlawfull, infamous and misbeseeming Christians.* All pretences to the contrary are here likewise fully answered; and the unlawfulnes of acting, of beholding Academicall Enterludes, briefly discussed; besides sundry other particulars concerning *Dancing*, *Dicing*, *Health-drinking*, *&c.* of which the *Table* will informe you.

By WILLIAM PRYNNE, *an Vtter-Barrester of* Lincolnes Inne.

Cyprian. De Spectaculis lib. p. 244.

Fugienda sunt ista Christianis fidelibus, ut iam frequenter diximus, tàm vana, tàm perniciosa, tàm sacrilega Spectacula: quæ, etsi non haberent crimen, habent in se et maximam et parum congruentē fidelibus vanitatē.

Lactantius de Verò Cultu cap. 20.

Vitanda ergo Spectacula omnia, non solum ne quid vitiorum pectoribus insideat, &c. sed ne cuius nos voluptatis consuetudo delineat, atque à Deo et à bonis operibus avertat.

Chrysost. Hom. 38. in Matth. Tom. 2. Col. 299. B. & Hom. 8 De Pœnitentia, Tom. 5. Col 750.

Immo vero, his Theatralibus ludis eversis, non leges, sed iniquitatem evertetis, ac omnem civitatis pestem extinguetis.. Etenim Theatrum, communis luxuriæ officina, publicum incontinentiæ gymnasium; cathedra pestilentiæ; pessimus locus; plurimorumque morborum plena Babylonica fornax, &c.

Augustinus De Civit. Dei, l. 4 c. 1.

Si tantummodo boni et honesti homines in civitate essent, nec in rebus humanis Ludi scenici esse debuissent.

LONDON,

Printed by *E. A.* and *W. I.* for *Michael Sparke*, and are to be sold at the Blue Bible, in Greene Arbour, in little Old Bayly. 1633.

Engraved for Nolan's Theatrical Observ.

MR. TALBOT,
AS
Monsieur Morbleau,

With ease and grace, you shine Sare,
L'agilite combine Sare,
To make The Whole divine Sare,
Bravissimo Monsieur!

The number of editions of plays now amounts to 2600. Of these, 200 were printed in England before 1700, 2000 were printed during the eighteenth century, half in Ireland, the rest in England, Scotland, and the Netherlands, and 400 were printed in the period 1801-20 largely in England. It is convenient to describe them in this order. The pre-Restoration part of the collection is strong in collected editions such as the four Shakespeare folios printed in London in 1623, 1632, 1664 and 1685, the Ben Jonson folios printed in London in 1616, 1640 and 1692, the second Beaumont and Fletcher folio printed in London in 1679, Sir William Davenant's *Works*, London, 1673, and Thomas Killigrew's *Comedies and tragedies*, London, 1664. Among the smaller collections are Thomas Heywood's *Pleasant dialogues and drammas*, London, 1637 containing 'divers *Dramma's*, never before published: Which though some may condemne for their shortnesse, others againe will commend for their sweetnesse', and Thomas Randolph's *Poems, with the Muses looking-glasse*, 2nd ed., Oxford, 1640, and 5th ed., Oxford, 1668. Chief among the editions of individual plays is the unique copy of the interlude *The worlde and the chylde*, London, 1522. There are copies of James Shirley's *The lady of pleasure*, London, 1637, and his *The humorous courtier*, London, 1640, and of Peter Hausted's unsuccessful comedy *The rivall friends*, London, 1632, which suffered the fate of being 'cryed downe by boyes, faction, envie, and confident ignorance, approv'd by the judicious, and now exposed to the publique censure'.

Restoration and late-seventeenth-century playwrights are represented in the Library by some one hundred and fifty quarto editions printed before 1700. The plays of John Dryden, Aphra Behn, Nathaniel Lee and Thomas Otway are particularly well covered. This is the period when graduates of the College began to make their mark on the theatre with such men as Nahum Tate, who adapted Shakespeare's *King Lear* to give it a happy ending, and Thomas Southerne whose development of moral problem dramas in *Oroonoko* and *The fatal marriage* marks a shift away from heroics. William Congreve, who began writing plays in the 1690s, is curiously poorly represented in that only one first-edition of his, *The double dealer*, London, 1694, has been acquired [97]. Of the rest perhaps the most important are the first editions of Sir George Etherege's *The man of mode*, London, 1676, Colley Cibber's *Love's last shift*, London, 1696, and Sir John Vanbrugh's *The relapse*, London, 1697. Music had an important role in late-seventeenth-century theatre and two publications, Henry Purcell's *Orpheus Britannicus,* London, 1698-1702, and Henry Playford's compilation *The banquet of musick* in six parts, London, 1688-92, contain a considerable number of songs performed in the plays of the time.

Much of the writing on dramatic theory was by Dryden in his *Of dramatic poesie, an essay*, London, 1668, and in the prefaces to many of his plays. Other works on this aspect in the Library are François Hedelin's *The whole art of the stage*, London, 1684, and Saint Evremont's *Mixt essays upon tragedies, comedies, Italian comedies, English comedies and opera's*, London, 1685. The seventeenth century also saw some of the most severe attacks ever made on the stage, both on the morality of the plays and on the morality of the actors. It is not surprising that many of these found their way into a College whose ethos was dominated by evangelical (if not downright Puritanical) clergymen. The most notable are William Prynne's *Histrio-mastix. The players scourge, or, actors tragedie*, London, 1633 [98], and Jeremy Collier's *A short view of the immorality, and profaneness of the English stage*, London, 1698. Collier remarks 'to make *Delight* the

99. Montague Talbot as Monsieur Morbleau in W. T. Moncrieff's farce *Monsieur Tonson*. From *The Theatrical Observer*, vol. 8, Dublin 1822.

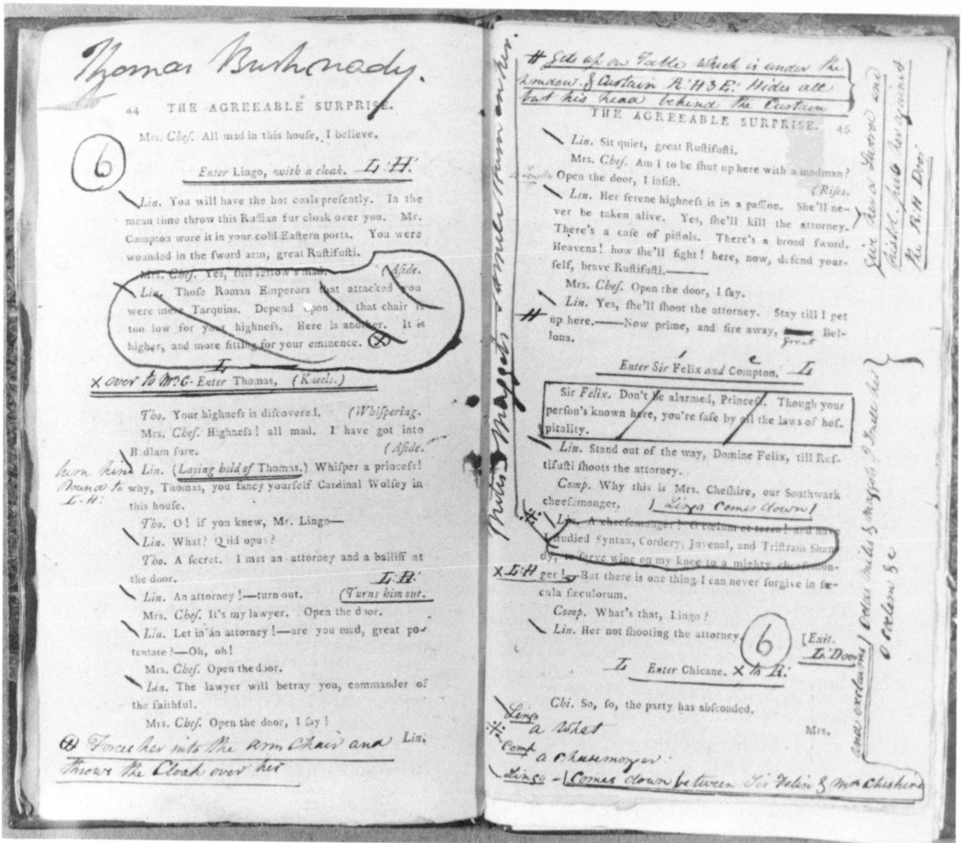

44 THE AGREEABLE SURPRISE.

Mrs. *Cheſ.* All mad in this houſe, I believe.

Enter Lingo, *with a cloak.* L.H.

Lin. You will have the hot coals preſently. In the mean time throw this Ruſſian fur cloak over you. Mr. Compton wore it in your cold Eaſtern ports. You were wounded in the ſword arm, great Ruſtifuſti.

Mrs. *Cheſ.* Yes, this fellow's mad. (*Aſide.*

Lin. Thoſe Roman Emperors that attacked you were mere Tarquins. Depend upon it that chair is too low for your highneſs. Here is another. It is higher, and more fitting for your eminence.

× over to Mrs C· *Enter* Thomas, (*Kneels.*)

Tho. Your highneſs is diſcovered. (*Whiſpering.*

Mrs. *Cheſ.* Highneſs! all mad. I have got into Bedlam ſure. (*Aſide.*

Lin. (*Laying hold of* Thomas.) Whiſper a princeſs! why, Thomas, you fancy yourſelf Cardinal Wolſey in this houſe.

Tho. O! if you knew, Mr. Lingo—

Lin. What? Quid opus?

Tho. A ſecret. I met an attorney and a bailiff at the door. L.H.

Lin. An attorney!—turn out. (*Turns him out.*

Mrs. *Cheſ.* It's my lawyer. Open the door.

Lin. Let in an attorney!—are you mad, great potentate?—Oh, oh!

Mrs. *Cheſ.* Open the door.

Lin. The lawyer will betray you, commander of the faithful.

Mrs. *Cheſ.* Open the door, I ſay! *Lin.*

Forces her into the Arm Chair and Throws the Cloak over her

\# Gets up on Table which is under the window & Curtain R.H.3 E. Hides all but his head behind the Curtain

THE AGREEABLE SURPRISE. 45

Lin. Sit quiet, great Ruſtifuſti.

Mrs. *Cheſ.* Am I to be ſhut up here with a madman? Open the door, I inſiſt. (*Riſes.*

Lin. Her ſerene highneſs is in a paſſion. She'll never be taken alive. Yes, ſhe'll kill the attorney. There's a caſe of piſtols. There's a broad ſword. Heavens! how ſhe'll fight! here, now, defend yourſelf, brave Ruſtifuſti.——

Mrs. *Cheſ.* Open the door, I ſay.

Lin. Yes, ſhe'll ſhoot the attorney. Stay till I get up here.——Now prime, and fire away, great Bellona.

Enter Sir Felix *and* Compton.

Sir Felix. Don't be alarmed, Princeſs. Though your perſon's known here, you're ſafe by all the laws of hoſpitality.

Lin. Stand out of the way, Domine Felix, till Ruſtifuſti ſhoots the attorney.

Comp. Why this is Mrs. Cheſhire, our Southwark cheeſemonger. Lingo Comes down

Lin. A cheeſemonger! ... and have ſtudied Syntax, Cordery, Juvenal, and Triſtram Shandy, to ſerve wine on my knee to a mighty cheeſemonger!—But there is one thing I can never forgive in ſecula ſeculorum.

Comp. What's that, Lingo?

Lin. Her not ſhooting the attorney. [*Exit.*

Enter Chicane.

Chi. So, ſo, the party has abſconded.

Mrs.

Lingo – Comes down between Sir Felix & Mrs Cheshire

100. James Corry's annotations on J. O'Keeffe's *The agreeable surprise,* for a performance at the Kilkenny Private Theatre in 1819.

main business of *Comedy* is an unreasonable and dangerous Principle. It opens the way to all Licentiousness and Confounds the distinction between Mirth, and Madness'.[1] Collier is still more vehement in *Mr Collier's dissuasive from the play-house*, London, 1703, denouncing authors because 'The Lusciousness of double Entendres, and remote Glances wont serve their Turn: To flash a little upon the Imagination, and appear in the Twylight, is not Mischief enough; No: They labour for Perspicuity, and shine out in Meridian Scandal.'[2] Most of the pamphlets responding to Collier's denunciation are in the catalogue. Colley Cibber, reflecting on this period forty years later wrote, 'And it must be farther granted that his calling our Dramatic Writers to this strict Account, had a very wholesome Effect, upon those, who writ after this time. They were now a great deal more on their guard; Indecencies were no longer Wit'.[3] This strain of moral rectitude echoes through the eighteenth century. David Garrick's Advertisement to his *The country girl*, written in 1766, an adaptation of Wycherley's *The country wife*, is a characteristic expression of the sentiment: 'Tho' near half of the following Play is new written, the Alterer claims no Merit, but his Endeavour to clear one of our most celebrated Comedies from Immorality and Obscenity. He thought himself bound to preserve as much of the Original as could be presented to an Audience of these Times without Offence ... For no kind of Wit ought to be received as an Excuse for Immorality; nay, it becomes still more dangerous in proportion as it is more witty.'

What with new plays, new editions of old plays, and adaptations of old plays, the printed output of the eighteenth century in this field alone was enormous. Contemplating the two thousand editions in the Library brought to mind the remarks made by Sherlock Holmes about the owner of the hat in the story *The blue carbuncle*: 'It is a question of cubic capacity', said he; 'a man with so large a brain must have something in it'.[4] The one thousand Irish editions are a match for the holdings in any library in this field. Most of these are reprints of works earlier published in England and there are two principal reasons for this. Firstly, the potentially larger audience in London held out the possibility of substantial gain from the author's benefit nights, and secondly, the lack of any copyright legislation in Ireland meant that literary property was effectively worthless, whereas a play could be sold to a bookseller in London as, for instance, Leonard MacNally sold his *Fashionable levities* to George Robinson for £50 in 1785.[5] However, many reprints, though taking the text of the play from an English edition, do purport to be offering the play as performed at the Theatres Royal in Smock Alley or Crow Street, and may include a Dublin cast list or a prologue specially written for Dublin. Furthermore, there was a succession of plays, all of minor importance, being published for the first time in Dublin right through the century from William Philips's *St Stephen's Green*, Dublin, 1700, James Sterling's *The rival generals*, Dublin, 1722, the anonymous *The scribbler*, Dublin, 1751 (the only play of the period in which the scholars of Trinity College are known to feature), Robert Jephson's *The hotel*, Dublin, 1784 (actually preceded by a pirated edition in Dublin in 1783), and William Preston's *Democratic rage*, Dublin, 1793. There are some Dublin editions of plays that have some claim to textual authority or curiosity such as George Faulkner's edition of Frances Sheridan's *The discovery* in 1763, which he advertises in *Faulkner's Dublin Journal* on 26 February 1763 as 'carefully printed from the Copy sent by the Author to Mr Faulkner and to NO OTHER Person in this Kingdom'. There is some curiosity, at least, in the two editions of Hannah Cowley's *The belle's stratagem*, published in Dublin in 1781, one with the imprint 'Dublin: printed in the year, 1781', the other 'Dublin: printed by T. Bathe, for the Company of Booksellers, 1781'. The texts of these differ from each other, as well as from the first authorized edi-

101. The title page to Michael Kelly's score for Blue-Beard, London 1798.

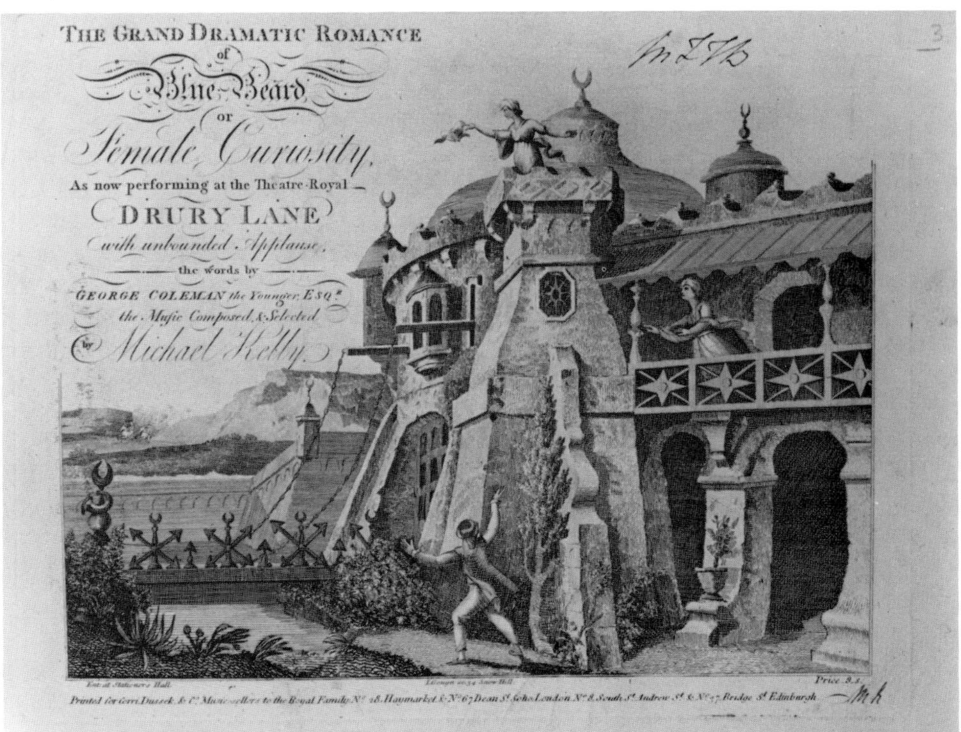

tion published in London in 1782.

The eighty plays published in The Hague by Thomas Johnson between 1710 and 1726 came to the Library in two collections. There were thirty-six printed between 1718 and 1726 in the Fagel collection, and the balance printed between 1710 and 1714, which had belonged to Catherine Bury, Countess of Charleville in 1804, came as part of the Barry Brown collection in 1964. Johnson was a pioneer in the use of the octavo format for plays, replacing the quarto which had been the norm for the preceding century. Many of his imprints are false, alleging London as the place of printing, being no doubt intended for illegal importation into England.

The eighteenth-century holdings are particularly strong in editions of Goldsmith, Sheridan, Arthur Murphy, Richard Steele, Isaac Bickerstaffe, John O'Keeffe, Colley Cibber and Samuel Foote. Among the publishers' series are sets of Robert Dodsley's *A select collection of old plays*, London, 1744 (this copy belonged to the famous theatre historian John Genest), *Bell's British theatre*, London, 1797, *The new English theatre*, London, 1776-7, and *The minor theatre*, London, 1794. The plays printed between 1801 and 1820 are evenly divided between new plays and reprints. The fresh works are dominated by the flood of melodramas, frequently adapted from novels, especially those of Sir Walter Scott as, for example, Charles Farley's *The battle of Bothwell Brig*, London, 1820, based on *Old mortality*. The reprints come principally from the series *The London theatre*, London, 1814-16, edited by Thomas Dibdin, and *The British theatre*, London, 1807-19, edited by Elizabeth Inchbald.

The survival of so many editions points not only to an active theatre existence of the plays but also to the use of plays for entertainment in the home. It seems to have been usual for plays to be read aloud. On 12 May 1759 Emily FitzGerald, Countess of Kildare, and later Duchess of Leinster, wrote to her husband 'Oh, my dear Lord K., what a play *The orphan of China* is! It would kill me were I to see it; I perfectly sobbed at hearing Sarah read it'.[6] Later in the century in 1784 Dorothea Herbert recorded a visit to Castle Blunden near Kilkenny when 'Mr Matthews read Plays to us and Sang Songs till one or two oclock after Supper'.[7] Some plays were written only for reading and others for private acting such as Theodora Louisa Agar's *The reward of constancy*, Dublin, 1818, which 'was originally intended to be acted partially, by private individuals, for the amusement of some select friends'. Amateur acting was a popular activity in the late eighteenth and early nineteenth centuries and it was to an amateur actor, James Corry, that the most important group of prompt copies of plays in the Library belonged. Corry was a stalwart of the Kilkenny Private Theatre from 1808 to 1819. The Kilkenny Private Theatre lasted between 1802 and 1819, though no plays were acted in 1811 and 1813-16, and was a major social attraction. No expense was spared to put the plays on properly, and professional actresses and an orchestra were bought from Dublin. 'The dresses were uncommonly superb. Lord Mountjoy appeared one night in a dress valued at eight thousand pounds', wrote Sir John Carr after a visit in 1805.[8] The actor Charles Mathews wrote to his wife in 1818: 'I arrived here on Saturday night, time enough to see "Macbeth" and "High life below stairs". I have not time to enter into particulars, but have no hesitation in saying, that they are not only the best private theatricals I have ever seen, but that the whole play of "Macbeth" in point of decoration, scenery, choruses etc. was better got up than it would have been at any theatre out of London.'[9]

He goes on to praise Corry as a very fine actor. Of the twenty prompt copies owned by

102. The costume of Tancred in J. Thomson's *Tancred and Sigismunda* from *A collection of the dresses of different nations*, London 1757.

(Habit of Tancred, in the Tragedy of Tancred & Sigismunda.)

Corry some are extremely heavily edited, such as John O'Keeffe's *The agreeable surprise*, performed in 1819 where about one quarter of the play has been cut [100]. In many cases elaborate stage and costume directions are given.[10]

The eighteenth century saw music increasing in importance in the theatre. From having accompanied plays at the beginning of the century, it became a dominant force in the comic operas and melodramas at the end. There was also in England the rise and decline of Italian opera in the first half of the century. The Library is lucky to have over thirty contemporary editions of scores of Handel's operas beginning with *Rinaldo*, in 1711, and running on to *Faramondo*, London, 1740. Attacks on Italian opera began early. Colley Cibber wrote in the preface to *Venus and Adonis*, London, 1715, 'The following Entertainment is an Attempt to give the Town a little good Musick in a Language they understand'. He attacks Italian opera as 'being (if possible) as miserably void of Common Sense in their Original, as the Translation: nay the Tyranny is carried yet farther for the Songs are so often turn'd out of their Places, to introduce some Absurd favourite Air of the Singer, that in a few Days the first Book you have Bought, is reduc'd to little more than the Title Page, of what it pretends to'.

The most spectacularly successful early ballad opera was John Gay's *The beggar's opera*, first produced in 1728, and a continued success into this century. A Dublin edition of the score dating from the 1750s came to the Library with the Townley Hall collection of books and music in 1960. This, the library of the Balfour family, contained a significant amount of music published in Dublin and London after 1760. With the addition of recent purchases the Library now has over forty contemporary scores of English comic operas and melodramas ranging from the scores of Isaac Bickerstaffe's *Love in a village*, London, 1763, *The maid of the mill*, London, 1765, and *Lionel and Clarissa*, London, 1768, William Shield's score for Leonard MacNally's *Robin Hood*, London, 1784, to Michael Kelly's score for George Colman's *Blue-Beard*, London, 1798 [101]. There are as well over seven hundred individual songs taken from operas including the following 'absurd favourite air': Hours of rapture, the celebrated cavatina as sung ... by Miss Forde at the Theatre Royal, Dublin in the 3rd Act of Webers Opera of *Der Freischütz*. Composed expressly for her by Alex^r. Lee. Dublin, I. Willis [*c.*1820].

The announcement of the performance of such a piece in the opera would have been a matter of pride on the playbill of the day. Sadly no such playbill is in our collection. Relatively few playbills have survived for early Irish theatres and those in the Library date with one exception from the end of the eighteenth and beginning of the nineteenth centuries. There is an important group of eight playbills, which constitute the sole known evidence of theatre performances in New Ross in the years 1789-95 [103].[11] These supply abundant evidence of the popularity of theatre in the

103. The earliest known New Ross playbill.

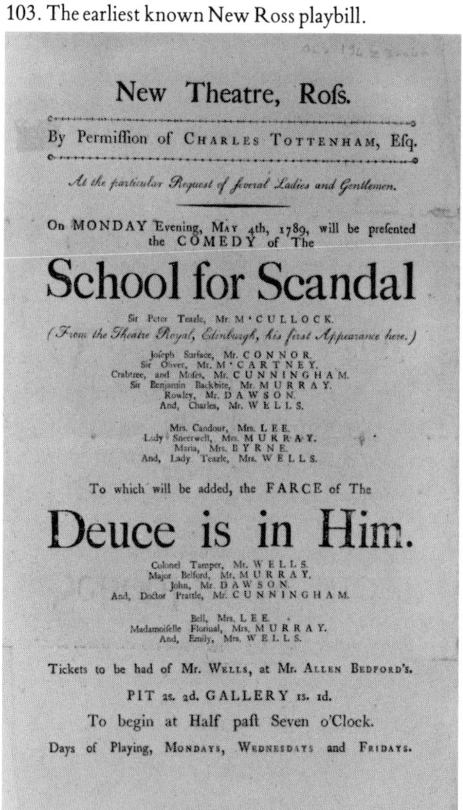
New Theatre, Roſs.

By Permiſſion of CHARLES TOTTENHAM, Eſq.

At the particular Request of ſeveral Ladies and Gentlemen.

On MONDAY Evening, MAY 4th, 1789, will be preſented the COMEDY of The

School for Scandal

Sir Peter Teazle, Mr. M'CULLOCK.
(From the Theatre Royal, Edinburgh, his first Appearance here.)
Joſeph Surface, Mr. CONNOR.
Sir Oliver, Mr. M'CARTNEY.
Crabtree, and Moſes, Mr. CUNNINGHAM.
Sir Benjamin Backbite, Mr. MURRAY.
Rowley, Mr. DAWSON.
And, Charles, Mr. WELLS.

Mrs. Candour, Mrs. LEE.
Lady Sneerwell, Mrs. MURRAY.
Maria, Mrs. BYRNE.
And, Lady Teazle, Mrs. WELLS.

To which will be added, the FARCE of The

Deuce is in Him.

Colonel Tamper, Mr. WELLS.
Major Belford, Mr. MURRAY.
John, Mr. DAWSON.
And, Doctor Prattle, Mr. CUNNINGHAM.

Bell, Mrs. LEE.
Madamoiſelle Florival, Mrs. MURRAY.
And, Emily, Mrs. WELLS.

Tickets to be had of Mr. WELLS, at Mr. ALLEN BEDFORD'S.

PIT 2s. 2d. GALLERY 1s. 1d.

To begin at Half paſt Seven o'Clock.

Days of Playing, MONDAYS, WEDNESDAYS and FRIDAYS.

town, for one manager Ezra Wells led his company there in 1789, 1790 and 1793 in seasons varying in length from at least three to five weeks. A sophisticated repertory was played, ranging from Shakespeare's *The merchant of Venice* and Otway's *Venice preserved*, to Sheridan's *The school for scandal.* The Dublin playbills include a number from Mrs Siddons's tour in December 1793 [104] and January 1794 and some bills for near-circus performances at the Amphitheatre Royal in Peter Street as the century ended.

It remains hard to get a vivid impression of theatre without illustrations, and almost all the Library's illustrations of performers and performances at this period are monochrome engravings. There are a great many of them, from the illustrations of scenes produced for Rowe's edition of Shakespeare's plays in 1709 to the portraits of individuals reproduced in the magazines at the end of the century. A list of over five hundred engravings of named individuals has been compiled from various sources in the Library for the period up to 1800. The only eighteenth-century coloured engravings of costume come from *A collection of the dresses of different nations*, London, 1757 [102].

Any research into theatre history will involve much wider parts of the Library's collections than those solely devoted to theatre, but in what is the essence of theatre, the text for performance, the Library is already rich, and, given reasonable fortune, will be even richer in years to come.

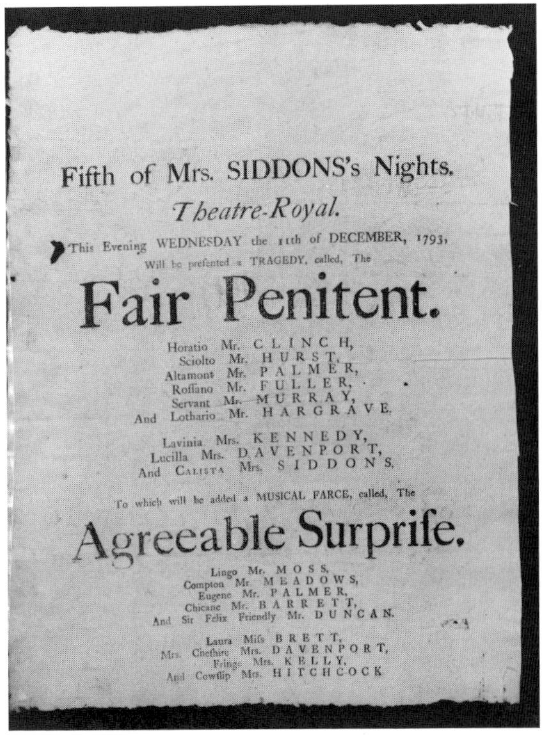
Fifth of Mrs. SIDDONS's Nights.
Theatre-Royal.
This Evening WEDNESDAY the 11th of DECEMBER, 1793,
Will be prefented a TRAGEDY, called, The
Fair Penitent.
Horatio Mr. CLINCH,
Sciolto Mr. HURST,
Altamont Mr. PALMER,
Roffano Mr. FULLER,
Servant Mr. MURRAY,
And Lothario Mr. HARGRAVE.
Lavinia Mrs. KENNEDY,
Lucilla Mrs. DAVENPORT,
And Calista Mrs. SIDDONS.
To which will be added a MUSICAL FARCE, called, The
Agreeable Surprife.
Lingo Mr. MOSS,
Compton Mr. MEADOWS,
Eugene Mr. PALMER,
Chicane Mr. BARRETT,
And Sir Felix Friendly Mr. DUNCAN.
Laura Mifs BRETT,
Mrs. Chefhire Mrs. DAVENPORT,
Fringe Mrs. KELLY,
And Cowflip Mrs. HITCHCOCK

104. A playbill from Mrs Siddons's visit to Dublin in 1793.

NOTES

1. Jeremy Collier, *A short view of the immorality, and profaneness of the English stage*, London: printed for S. Keble, R. Sare and D. Hindmarsh, 1698, p. 161.

2. Jeremy Collier, *Mr Collier's dissuasive from the playhouse.* London: printed for Richard Sare, 1703, p. 7.

3. Colley Cibber, *An apology for the life of Mr. Colley Cibber.* 2nd ed. London: printed by John Watts for the author, 1740, p. 225.

4. Sir Arthur Conan Doyle, *The adventures of Sherlock Holmes.* 2nd ed. London: George Newnes Ltd, 1893, p. 160.

5. G.E. Bentley Jr. 'Copyright documents in the George Robinson Archives: William Godwin and others 1713-1820', *Studies in Bibliography* 35 (1982) 67-110.

6. Emily FitzGerald, Duchess of Leinster, *Correspondence*, ed. by Brian FitzGerald. Dublin: Stationery Office, 1949-57, vol. 1, p. 84.

7. Dorothea Herbert, *Retrospections.* London: Gerald Howe, 1929-30, p. 103.

8. Sir John Carr, *The stranger in Ireland.* London: printed for Richard Phillips by T. Gillet, 1806, p. 427.

9. Anne Mathews, *Memoirs of Charles Mathews.* London: Richard Bentley, 1838-9, vol. 3, p. 23.

10. For a fuller discussion see Charles Benson 'James Corry and the Kilkenny Private Theatre', *Prompts: Bulletin of the Irish Theatre Archive* 3 (1982) 5-9 and 4 (1982) 8-11.

11. Charles Benson 'Wild Oats in New Ross: Theatre in an Irish country town, 1789-1795', *Long Room* 22-3 (1981) 13-18.

THE FAGEL COLLECTION

VINCENT KINANE

Among the hundreds of books called up by readers, and waiting for them on the shelves of the Reading Room of the Library's Department of Early Printed Books, one will find certain groups that visually stand out. Their distinctive coverings of yellow vellum, dark-stained calf or colourful paste paper set them apart from the familiar binding styles of these islands. They are from the Fagel Collection, a large library built up by one of the most powerful families in Holland over the course of almost two centuries.

105 (below). Plate 97 (26 × 21 cm) from vol. IV of *Sammlung verschiedener ausländischer und seltener Vögel,* Nürnberg 1753, a compilation from works in English by Mark Catesby and George Edwards, translated by Johann M. Seligmann.

106 (far right). A late edition of Rembert Dodoens' popular herbal *Cruydt-boeck,* Antwerp 1644, first printed in 1554 (38 × 25 cm).

Tab. XCVII.
Die Somerente des Catesby.
Anas criſtatus, elegans.
N°. 97. IV. Theil.
Le Canard d'Ete de Catesby

The story of its acquisition by Trinity College in 1802 has been told several times before[1] and can be briefly summarized. While Hendrik Fagel, *Greffier* or Chief Minister of Holland, was in England on a diplomatic mission during the winter of 1794-5, his country was overrun by French revolutionary forces, preventing his return to his family and home in The Hague. Initially his property was sequestrated but it was released by mid 1798, and his art collections and library were shipped to London where Fagel, in straightened financial circumstances, had determined to sell them. Through the good offices of John Foster, Speaker of the Irish House of Commons and later described as 'the original proposer of the scheme',[2] money was made available in May 1798 by the Erasmus Smith Charity in Dublin for the purchase of the library for Trinity.[3] There was a delay in putting this scheme into effect and Fagel determined to sell it by public auction, the sale to start on 1 March 1802. The catalogue of almost 10,000 lots, the first part of which was published early in 1802 [107], created a sensation and must have galvanized the Dublin party, for they made a successful bid for the entire library early in February. On 6 March the Erasmus Smith Charity released enough funds to cover Fagel's asking price of £8000 sterling and the cost of transportation.[4]

CRVYDT-BOECK
REMBERTI DODONÆI,
volghens ſijne laetſte verbeteringhe:
Met BIIVOEGHSELS achter elck Capitel,
uyt verſcheyden Cruydt-beſchrijvers:
Item, in 't laetſte een Beſchrijvinghe vande Indiaenſche
ghewaſſen, meeſt ghetrocken uyt de ſchriften
van CAROLVS CLVSIVS.
Nu wederom van nieuws overſien ende verbetert.
REMBERTVS DODONÆVS
T'ANTWERPEN,
Inde Plantijnſche Druckerije
van
Balthaſar Moretus.
M. DC. XLIV.
CAROLVS CLVSIVS
LABORE ET CONSTANTIA

Dr Thomas Elrington, a Fellow and later Provost of Trinity College, was dispatched to London to supervise the packing and shipment of the purchase. He kept a diary in which he recorded details of the six weeks' task, noting the numbers from the sale catalogue of items that went into each packing case, the payments to hauliers and such details.[5] Interestingly, from the figures he provides, it will be found that Elrington, having taken professional advice, insured about three quarters of the cases for a total sum of £8900 sterling; it would appear that the purchase was quite a bargain. On 25 March he took time to estimate the footage of shelving that the collection occupied in the house that Fagel had leased to store it. He calculated that in the parlour, the back parlour, on the first, second and third floors, and allowing for all the volumes on the floor, there were 5300 feet of books; he later revised this upwards to 5528 feet (1.05 miles).

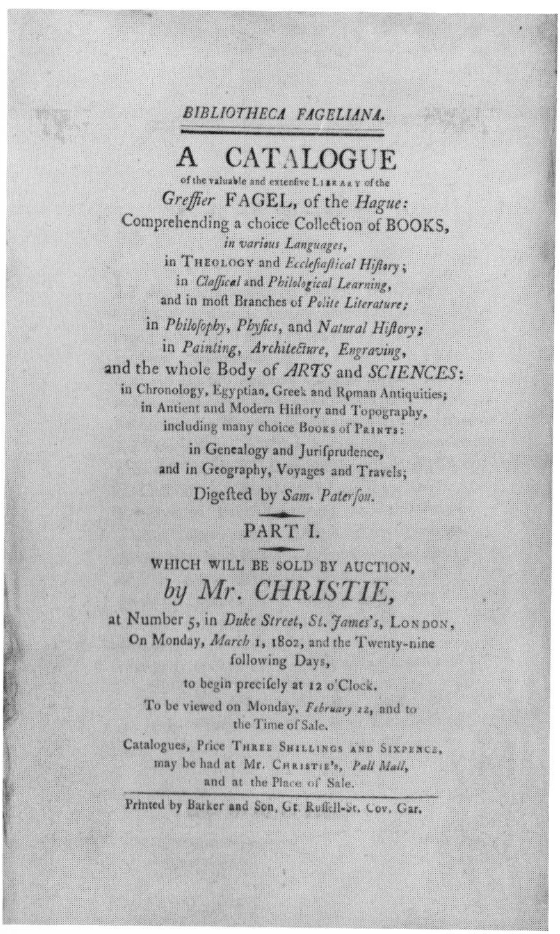
BIBLIOTHECA FAGELIANA.

A CATALOGUE

of the valuable and extenſive LIBRARY of the

Greffier FAGEL, of the *Hague*:

Comprehending a choice Collection of BOOKS,

in various Languages,

in THEOLOGY and *Eccleſiaſtical Hiſtory*;

in *Claſſical* and *Philological Learning*,

and in moſt Branches of *Polite Literature*;

in *Philoſophy*, *Phyſics*, and *Natural Hiſtory*;

in *Painting*, *Architecture*, *Engraving*,

and the whole Body of *ARTS* and *SCIENCES*:

in Chronology, Egyptian, Greek and Roman Antiquities;

in Antient and Modern Hiſtory and Topography,

including many choice BOOKS of PRINTS:

in Genealogy and Juriſprudence,

and in Geography, Voyages and Travels;

Digeſted by *Sam. Paterſon.*

PART I.

WHICH WILL BE SOLD BY AUCTION,

by Mr. CHRISTIE,

at Number 5, in *Duke Street*, *St. James's*, LONDON,

On Monday, *March* 1, 1802, and the Twenty-nine following Days,

to begin preciſely at 12 o'Clock.

To be viewed on Monday, *February* 22, and to the Time of Sale.

Catalogues, Price THREE SHILLINGS AND SIXPENCE, may be had at Mr. CHRISTIE's, *Pall Mall*, and at the Place of Sale.

Printed by Barker and Son, Gt. Ruſſell-St. Cov. Gar.

107. Title-page (17 × 9 cm) of the catalogue for the proposed auction of the Fagel Collection. The sale was abandoned when Trinity offered £8,000 for the entire library.

On 14 April Elrington 'paid Mr Fagel £7,500 at the Bank of Messrs. Coutts & Co.'; it is not clear when the other £500 was paid. Today it is difficult, when £8000 is an average yearly salary, or buys a medium-sized car, to appreciate the magnitude of this sum in early-nineteenth-century Ireland. Some measure of its scale can be had by comparing the annual salary of fifty British pounds paid by the College to the attendant of the Fagel Collection from 1808[6] with the starting salary of IR£5600 paid to library assistants today. Allowing for the exchange rates between the British and Irish currencies then and now, this hundredfold increase would mean that the Fagel Collection cost something like IR£1 million in today's terms.

The arrival of the 115 cases that Elrington had dispatched from London is recorded in the Library Minute Book for 11-14 May 1802.[7] By T.K. Abbott's estimation there were 46,000 volumes in Trinity College Library in 1792,[8] which would indicate holdings of around 50,000 volumes when the Fagel Collection arrived. At a very conservative estimate that collection contains 20,000 volumes (not works — many volumes contain several pamphlets); where was the Library to find a mile of shelving when it was already bursting at the seams? The decision reached was to take the manuscripts from their room in the East Pavilion of the Old Library (on the same level as the Long Room) and to move them to the room overhead, which is now the Early Printed Books Reading Room.[9] The area thus vacated measures in length about 54 feet, in breadth 25 feet and is 16 feet high, which, when shelved, it was calculated would provide the necessary space. A year passed in deciding these plans and in the meantime the books remained in their cases. By mid 1803 however some work was being done towards

108. Visitors to the Fagel Library in the first half of the nineteenth century. From W. B. S. Taylor, *The history of the University of Dublin,* London 1845, plate opposite p. 313.

the eventual arrangement of the collection. The Librarian, Dr John ('Jacky') Barrett, was busy extracting an alphabetical catalogue from the subject arrangement of the sale catalogue.[10] This *Catalogus Fageliana ordine alphabetico dispositus*[11] was eventually delivered to the Library in November 1807.[12]

About the same time as Barrett was starting his catalogue, work had begun on reconstructing the old Manuscripts Room to receive the collection. By the end of July 1803 William Chapman had done enough work to present a substantial bill for over £1000 for 'Carpenter's work done ... in the additional Room to the Library'.[13] It is evident from the account that Chapman had built the major structural framework for the shelving, including the fluted oak pilasters with Corinthian capitals that can be seen in Taylor's illustration [108]. Work on the shelving proper did not begin for almost three years. There were good reasons however for the delay. At a meeting of the Board on 1 May 1802 it was reported that a survey on the safety of the roof of the Library had been inconclusive.[14] Further inspection confirmed the worst and during the years 1805-7 large sums were paid out for strengthening the roof and replastering the ceiling.[15] This crisis must have occupied a large portion of the time of the Librarian and his assistants. During the same period they had to cope with the new influx of books under the terms of the Copyright Act of 1801, which extended to Trinity the privilege of receiving a copy of every work published in these islands. The Library Minute Books show that works were being sent out daily for binding. Little wonder then that the Fagel Room was being neglected.

The shelving project was reprimed in April 1806. Tim McEvoy's account for sundry carpentry work done in the Library includes on the twelfth of that month 'one and a quarter days taking sundry dimensions in Fagal Library to settle books'.[16] McEvoy and his son James presented further bills throughout the following years for work done on the Fagel shelving and their last account was settled on 23 February 1809.[17] George Stapleton submitted a bill for 'plastering the backs of 2 Windows in New Library' in September 1807; these windows were rendered useless by the necessity of placing shelving across their width.[18] In February 1808 and in the first quarter of 1809 he was paid for 'gilding and shading ... large letters [shelfmarks?] in New Library'.[19] Structurally the Fagel Room was now ready.

But what of the books? These had not been neglected. On 16 July 1803 the Board had taken another step towards their sorting by resolving that strict duplicates in the collection were to be put into the Lending Library.[20] The emphasis on 'strict duplicates' was an enlightened decision, as all too often a library's sale of 'duplicates' results in the disposal of textually important earlier editions. The first of many batches of pamphlets

109 (overleaf). One of the more colourful plates from the astronomy section, plate 22 (44 × 52 cm) from Andreas Cellarius, *Harmonia macrocosmica,* Amsterdam 1661.

COELI
CHRISTI
MISPHÆ
Circulus Polaris Sept:
Ecliptica
Æquinoctialis
Hybernus Solstitis
Tropicus
Coluri
S. Iacobus maior
S. Ioannes
Agnus Paschalis
Al. Canis minor
S.Rex Dauid.
Al. Canis maior
Navicula S. Petri
Arca Fœderis
Al. Crater et Corvus
Iordanis
Alias Hydra
Arca Noë
Al. Argo Nauis
S. Abel

STELLATI
ANI HÆ
RIUM PRIUS.
S.Michael
Definitor
TRES
RE
GES
S.Siluester.
Al. Bootes
Tropicus Æstiuus Solstitii
Colurus
Corona XPI Spinea
S.Benedictus
cum Spinis Eiusd.
S.Iacobus minor
Alias Virgo
Æquinoctialis
S.Bartholomæ
Al. Scorpio
Ecliptica
S.Israel
Altare Thymiamatis
Signum Tau
Circulus Polaris Merid.
22

was sent out on 15 August 1804, to be bound up by the College Bookseller and Printer, Richard Edward Mercier. On 6 July 1806 he was also given six copies of the complete auction catalogue to be bound up for presentation to Hendrik Fagel.[21] The placing of the books in the Fagel Room started early in 1807 and a Library Account Book notes the first payment for assistance in that task on 18 March. Various students were paid sums for their help throughout 1808. 'Jacky' Barrett, no longer Librarian at this date, was also involved in the placement; for this, and for his alphabetical catalogue, he was paid £100 on 7 November 1807.[22] His interest in the collection was celebrated many years later in Charles Lever's novel *Charles O'Malley*, published in 1841, where, at the beginning of chapter 16, Barrett appears dressed in 'a gown that had been worn for twenty years, browned and coated with the learned dust of the Fagel'. Michael Logan was engaged throughout 1808 and early 1809 lettering and numbering the volumes *in situ* and in preparing the catalogues.[23] On 1 March 1809, nearly seven years after the purchase of the collection, the Board 'ordered that the Fagel Library be opened forthwith'.[24]

The influx of these 20,000 volumes considerably altered the character of the Library. Hitherto the major strengths had been in the field of religion — theology, biblical exegesis, religious controversy — in works often meant for the scholar and often in Latin. At one stroke the Library had increased its bookstock by about forty per cent, and this portion was much more secular in character. Some idea of its subject coverage can be had by analysing the categories in the auction catalogue. The following table, in rounded figures emerges:

	%
history/topography	37.6
theology	18.1
politics/law	6.4
geography/cosmography/travels	6.3
classics	6.2
literature	5.9
philosophy (including natural philosophy and mathematics)	2.6
natural history	2.6
visual arts	2.5
medicine	.7
military	.6
agriculture/horticulture	.5
economics	.4
miscellaneous	9.6

Music alone is the one glaring gap in this broad, humanistic library.

The preponderance of history, and the substantial holdings of politics/law and geography (including maps) underlies the fact that this was on one level the working library of a family of leading statesmen. The history section is dominated, after works on the Netherlands, by material on her allies/enemies: France, Great Britain, Germany, Italy, in that order. The politics category shows the same orientation. Number 7593 in the sale catalogue alone was estimated by the compiler, Samuel Paterson, to contain 'upwards of 10,000' tracts on the history and politics of every state in Europe. A catalogue in the hand of François Fagel (1659-1746) survives as an index to about eighty per cent of it.[25] The geography section, with its large collection of atlases, single maps and sea charts, provides a comprehensive picture of the world and especially of the Low Countries, and of the colonies and trade routes that sustained them in a position of power and wealth.

Reading through the sale catalogue certain general points about the other categories present themselves. Dutch and English imprints predominate in the section on Theology, and it is, needless to say, Protestant in character. Given that most of the works were printed in the period between 1650 and 1750, Brummel wonders if François Fagel, 'the good old greffier', was the inspiration behind the formation of this portion of the collection.[26] François seems to have taken more interest in the

Library than other members of the family. Not alone did he compile a catalogue of the political tracts but there exists in the Algemeen Rijksarchief in The Hague a manuscript catalogue, which he commissioned, of the library as it existed in his day.[27] The coverage in the classics section is comprehensive, encompassing the seventeenth-century Leiden editions of the Elzevirs through to the eighteenth-century Glasgow editions of the Foulis Press. None of the classics printed at the Dublin University Press are included, which underlines the point made by the late Professor W.B. Stanford as to the essentially insular nature of classical studies in Trinity during the eighteenth century.[28] The literature section is mostly of the eighteenth century. English language material accounts for a third of the works, French slightly less. Reflecting on this in his article Dr J.-P. Pittion remarked that 'the library has caught, frozen in time, so to speak, a major change already taking place in the 18th century: the emergence of English as the successful rival of French in the literary field'.[29] Unfortunately Trinity did not share the Fagels' habit of representative acquisition and many of these literary works, especially the novels, were not deemed worthy of a place on the Library's shelves. Given the understandable dominance of home-country material in the other categories, it is surprising to find that only a sixth of the Literature is Dutch, and most of that, as Brummel notes, is of second-rate eighteenth-century authors.[30]

The breadth of the Fagels' collecting habits is something more often associated with a royal or national library than with a family collection. In considering the collection in relation to the study of French culture Dr Pittion found that it reflected faithfully nothing less than the history of the *ancien régime*.[31] Even in exile Hendrik was assiduously collecting material on the situation in Revolutionary France. Item 6200 in the sale catalogue is an example: *Examen de la constitution de France de 1799* (London 1800).

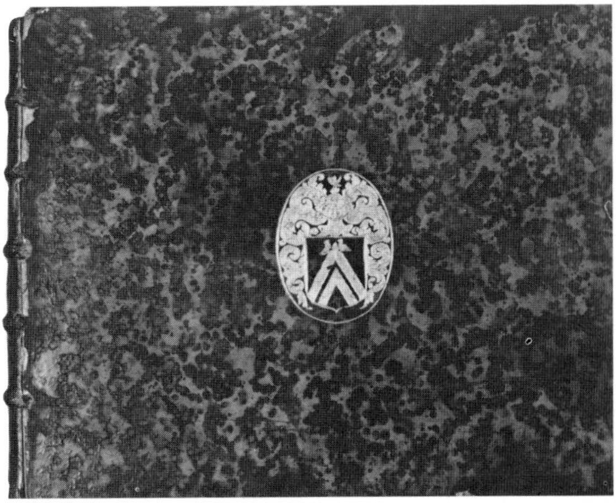

110. The only binding in the Collection showing the Fagel family coat of arms: A. Perelle, *Veües des belles maisons de France,* Paris [*c.* 1680] (31 × 39 cm).

The status of the collection as a working library does not mean that it has no exotic books. The Fagels appear to have wanted to play down their roles as bibliophiles. In a comprehensive bibliographical and historical survey of the collection made in 1962 Dr Ernst Braches found only one volume stamped with the family coat of arms (no. 6302, Fag. K. 2. 1 [110]).[32] The preponderance of plain 'hoorn' vellum and dark-stained calf bindings tends to disguise the riches. But riches there are — in abundance. The section on natural history provides many of the most visually spectacular works in the collection [105 and 106]. In describing these in the sale catalogue (nos 3979-4231), Paterson, normally brief of necessity in his descriptions, resorts time and again to breathless prose to convey their splendour: 'a matchless copy', 'an exquisite copy', 'beautifully illuminated' are recurrent phrases used. Many of these works were drawn together at the time of their arrangement in Trinity and shelved in the glass-fronted cases at locations Fag. GG and Fag. HH. There one will find a copy of the enlarged second edition of Maria Sibylla Merian's *Metamorphosis insectorum Surinamensium,* Amsterdam 1719 (no. 4181, Fag. GG. 2. 10) with many beautifully

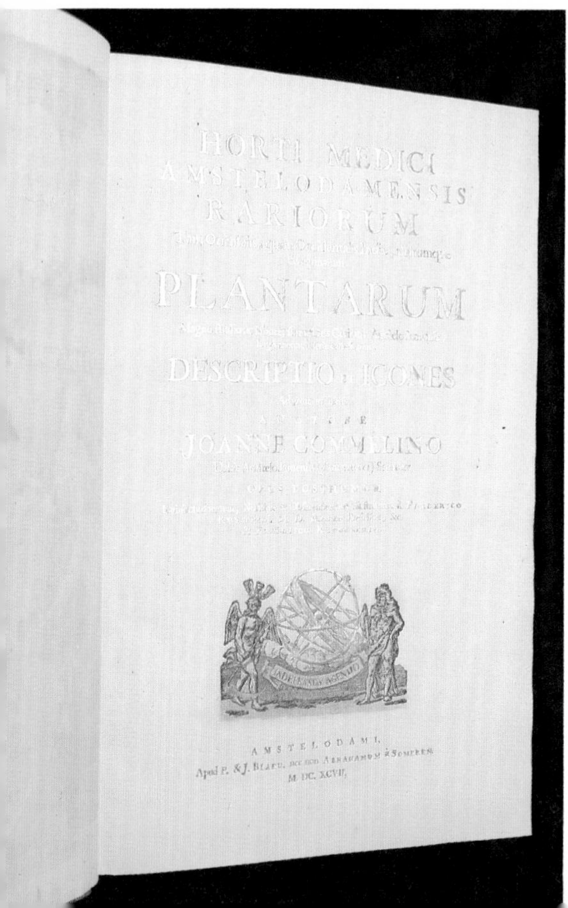

111 (left). Natural history had not yet thrown off the mythological: Matthaeus Merian's illustrations of unicorns in J. Jonston, *Historia naturalis,* Frankfurt am Main [1650], vol. I, plate X (34 × 20 cm).

112 (left). An example from the many lavish, gold-printed titles in the Fagel Collection: Jan Commelin, *Horti medici Amstelodamensis,* Amsterdam 1697 (40 × 26 cm).

113 (above). Plate VI (18 × 19 cm) from one of the scarcest works in the Fagel Collection, Pietro S. Bartoli, *Recueil de Peintures antiques,* printed in an edition of 30 copies, Paris 1757.

114 (right). Plate LVII (34 × 23 cm) from one of the most spectacular books on natural history: Maria Merian, *Metamorphosis insectorum Surinamensium,* Amsterdam 1719.

hand-coloured plates [114]. Merian had spent three years in Dutch Guiana preparing the illustrations for this work; some of the original watercolours on vellum survive in the British Library and in the royal collection at Windsor Castle. Linnaeus and Fabricius were later to acknowledge their indebtedness to this work when compiling their systems of nomenclature.

It is interesting to compare the studied artistic composition and fine execution of Maria's illustrations with those done by her father Mattheus, as for example in J. Jonston's *Historia naturalis de quadrupetibus...*, Frankfurt-am-Main 1650-3 (no. 4100, Fag. M. 4. 51-2). Here artistic considerations are over-ridden by the need to make maximum use of the plate area. The colouring is less accomplished and the inclusion of several illustrations of unicorns undermines one's faith in the veracity of the drawings [111].

At Fag. GG. 3. 16-17 (no. 4065) will be found a copy of Jan Commelin's *Horti medici Amstelodamensis*, Amsterdam 1697 [112], with the following inscription on the front endpaper of volume I (translated from the Dutch): 'The illumination of these plants has been done by Miss Wolters. There are only two specimens like this, of which the other remains with Herr Professor Schwenke. This work has cost 100 ducats.' Another extremely limited edition in the collection is Pietro-Santi Bartoli, *Recueil des peintures antiques*, Paris 1757 (no. 4237, Fag. L. I. 50) [113]. Again a manuscript note explains that this is one of only thirty copies printed. The hand-coloured illustrations are of frescoes from an ancient Roman tomb discovered in the previous century. Bartoli's illustrations had been partially published in 1706 after his death; this completed edition was issued with letterpress explanations by Pierre Jean Mariette and the Comte de Caylus.

Many of these illustrated folios have gold-lettered titles and headings, and are richly bound. One such is Athanasius Kircher, *Mundus subterraneus*, Amsterdam 1678 (no. 4012, Fag. GG. 2. 3). It was bound by Albert Magnus, the most accomplished binder in late-seventeenth-century Amsterdam, for Frederick Willem van Loon, whose arms and monogram appear on the covers [115].[33] Bound in full red goat, it exhibits the 'bird-in-vine' roll, a Magnus hallmark, as the inner of a double roll along the cover borders.[34] There is also a very unusual roll on the turn-ins, which combines musicians with animals and birds. Some other important bindings in the collection have been documented recently in an article by Jan Storm van Leeuwen.[35]

Writing in 1957 Dr Brummel bemoaned the loss to Holland of this important Dutch collection: 'So completely has it vanished, that it is hardly known that the library of Trinity College houses this collection'.[36] This does not take account of the heavy use made of

115. One of the finest bindings in the Fagel Collection: Athanasius Kircher, *Mundus subterraneus*, Amsterdam 1678, bound by Albert Magnus (40 × 26 cm).

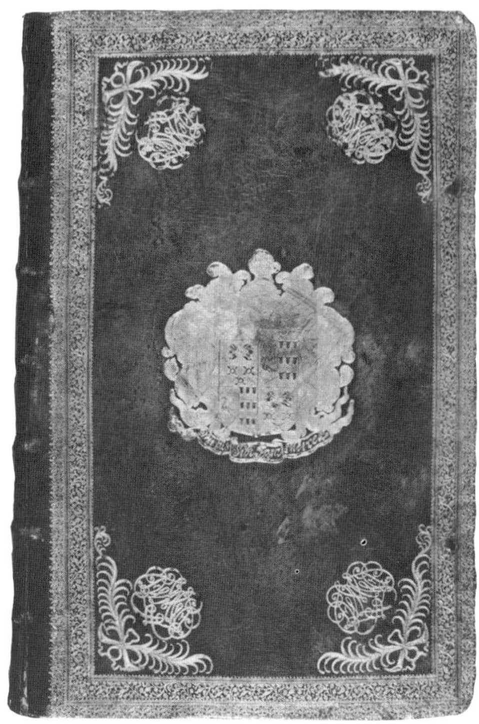

the Fagel by the College; about eight per cent of readers' requests for early printed books are from it and it is a valuable teaching tool for the Departments of French, History, Philosophy and History of Art. But there are depths of riches remaining to be plumbed. In recent times there have been signs of new-found international interest in the collection, and it is to be hoped that this article will stimulate more.

NOTES

I would like to acknowledge the help of Mr David Benson, Dr A.P.W. Malcolmson, Dr Helga Robinson-Hammerstein and Mr Stuart Ó Seanóir in the preparation of this article.

1. R.B. McDowell, 'The acquisition of the Fagel library', *Friends of the Library of TCD Annual Bulletin* 2 (1947) 5-6; L. Brummel, 'The Fagel library in TCD' in his *Miscellanea libraria*, The Hague, 1957; J.-P. Pittion, 'The Fagel collection', *Hermathena* 121 (1976) 108-16.
2. TCD MUN/V/5/5 (Board Register), 13 March 1802.
3. The High School, Dublin, Registry Book no. 3 of the Governors of Erasmus Smith's Schools [1793-1822], 31 May 1798.
4. High School, Erasmus Smith Registry no. 3.
5. TCD MUN/LIB/12/1 (Elrington's Diary).
6. TCD MUN/LIB/11/9/11 (Library Accounts), 23 June 1808 and later to John William O'Neill.
7. TCD MUN/LIB/2/1 (Library Minutes).
8. T.K. Abbott 'The Library' in *The book of Trinity College Dublin, 1591-1891*. Belfast, 1892, p. 156.
9. TCD MS 4960 (T. Elrington's Minutes (personal) of Board Meetings 1801-3), 8 May 1802. Abbott, 'The Library', p. 177.
10. TCD MS 4960 (Elrington's Minutes), 7 May 1803.
11. TCD MUN/LIB/1/21 = MS 1707 (Library Catalogues).
12. TCD MUN/LIB/11/9/5 (Library Accounts).
13. TCD MUN/P/2/187/3 (Buildings).
14. TCD MS 4960 (Elrington's Minutes).
15. TCD MUN/V/5/5 (Board Register), 25 April 1805; MUN/P/2/191-4 (Buildings) bills of Tim McEvoy and George Stapleton.
16. TCD MUN/P/2/191/22 (Buildings).
17. TCD MUN/P/2/193, 194, 197, 199 (Buildings).
18. TCD MUN/P/2/194/39 (Buildings).
19. TCD MUN/P/2/197/78; MUN/P/2/199/62 (Buildings).
20. TCD MS 4960 (Elrington's Minutes).
21. TCD MUN/LIB/2/1 (Library Minutes).
22. TCD MUN/LIB/11/9/3, 5, 17, 19, 20 (Library Accounts).
23. TCD MUN/LIB/11/9/16a, 21a-b; MUN/LIB/11/10/3, 5 (Library Accounts).
24. TCD MUN/V/5/5 (Board Register).
25. TCD MUN/LIB/1/23 = MS 3726 (Library Catalogues).
26. Brummel, p. 230.
27. Fagel Archive 42; lists about 5000 volumes.
28. W.B. Stanford, 'Classical studies in TCD since the foundation', *Hermathena* 57 (1941) 14-16.
29. Pittion, p. 112.
30. Brummel, p. 232.
31. Pittion, pp 112-15.
32. 'The Fagel library: report of investigations made by E. Braches, summer 1962'. Typescript summary in English, with Dutch text. Copy in Early Printed Books Reading Room.
33. H. de la Fontaine Vervey, 'The binder Albert Magnus and the collectors of his age', *Quaerendo* I (April 1971) 158-78; plate V shows a binding in similar style.
34. Mirjam Foot, *The Henry Davis gift* [to the British Library]. London, 1978, vol. 1, p. 245; similar style of spine shown p. 232.
35. J.S. van Leeuwen 'Un groupe remarquable de reliures amstellodamoises...' in *De libris compactis miscellanea,* Brussels, 1984, pp 321-74.
36. Brummel, p. 228.

MAPS AND ATLASES

J. H. ANDREWS

'Our public libraries do not, I fear, contain any materials that would have been of use to you.' This is what Joseph Cooper Walker wrote from Dublin in 1807 to a Scottish friend who had been writing a geography book,[1] and it probably reflects more on the contemporary custodians of Ireland's cartographic heritage than on the maps themselves. Today, at any rate, no one familiar with Trinity College would deny the value of its Library for both modern and historical geography; but because the College's map collection has never been fully described, nothing said about it in the following paragraphs can be quite definitive. One's first impression is that these maps mostly occur in atlases, which is probably understandable in a Library that has never employed a specialist map-curator, and in a College that gave no formal instruction in geography until the 1920s; but this judgment derives from Library catalogues that are primarily devoted to books and manuscripts in general (there is as yet no separate map catalogue), and where cartography is concerned such catalogues are notoriously unhelpful.

In the early years of the Library's history bound and unbound map-sheets were both well represented. Entries in the Trinity 'Particular Book' for the 1600s mention not only three eminent atlas-makers but also 'twelve great maps' and 'many of the lesser'.[2] Maps and a globe also appear in a separate note of Library purchases dating from the same period.[3] But while Ptolemy, Munster, Mercator and many other masters of the atlas are still happily available on the Long Room shelves, nobody seems to know what became of the twelve great maps. Such contrasting fortunes need not surprise us. Sheet-maps are hard to store, awkward to handle, and easily lost or damaged (globes are even worse), whereas an atlas can stand clearly visible alongside other books, can be opened quietly and without fuss, in most cases can fit on to a normal-sized desk, and in general is just as welcome among librarians as any dictionary or encyclopedia.

So there has been no reason why Trinity should not do justice to the variety of this most complex among cartographic media, a variety far beyond the scope of one short essay. Some atlases need no introduction: those of Ortelius and Mercator, for example, may be ranked with the world's most famous achievements in print. But what visitor to the Library has heard of, or wishes to hear of, *Voorne caartboeck van alle de dorpen, en polders gelegen inden lande van oost, ende west Voorne*? Between these extremes lie multi-volume juggernauts from Amsterdam like Joan Blaeu's *Atlas major* (1662), and modest mini-atlases of the kind compiled for Ireland by Francis Lamb (1689) and Bernard Scalé (1776). Subjects can differ as widely as sizes. Some atlas-makers have specialized in counties, like the Elizabethan Englishman Christopher Saxton (1579); towns, as portrayed by Georg Braun and Frans Hogenberg (1618); roads, mapped in a series of narrow strips by John Ogilby (1675) and his imitators; and harbours, first published for English-speaking readers under the title *The mariner's mirrour* (1588). Many atlases are maps and nothing but maps, among them (regrettably) William Petty's *Hiberniae delineatio* (1685). Others have enough text to disarm the most uncartographically-minded of bookmen: a case in point is Henry Hexham's edition of Mercator, which includes among much other descriptive matter on Ireland an early (1636) reference to the 'famous library' at Trinity College Dublin.

A few atlases enjoyed long-lasting and well-deserved success, as witness Trinity's five copies of John Speed's *Theatre of the empire of Great Britaine* (1611-12); others, like Moses Pitt's *English atlas* (1680-3), were blighted by both commercial and critical disaster. The expert's favourite atlases are those that show the greatest 'instability' from one copy to another, a notable instance being Nicolas Sanson's *Cartes générales de toutes les parties du monde* (1670); the ordinary student may prefer his maps without cartobibliographical complications, like those of — but here one hesitates, for how many of the Library's atlases have been pronounced free from anomalies by the latest and most rigorous generation of map-scholars? One claim that does seem fairly safe is that good or bad, interesting or dull, Trinity has at least one copy of all the atlases that might be expected to exist in so venerable an academic library. Or almost

116. The fort and village of Omagh, County Tyrone, a picture-plan acquired by Carew when he led an official inquiry into the progress of the Ulster plantation in 1611.

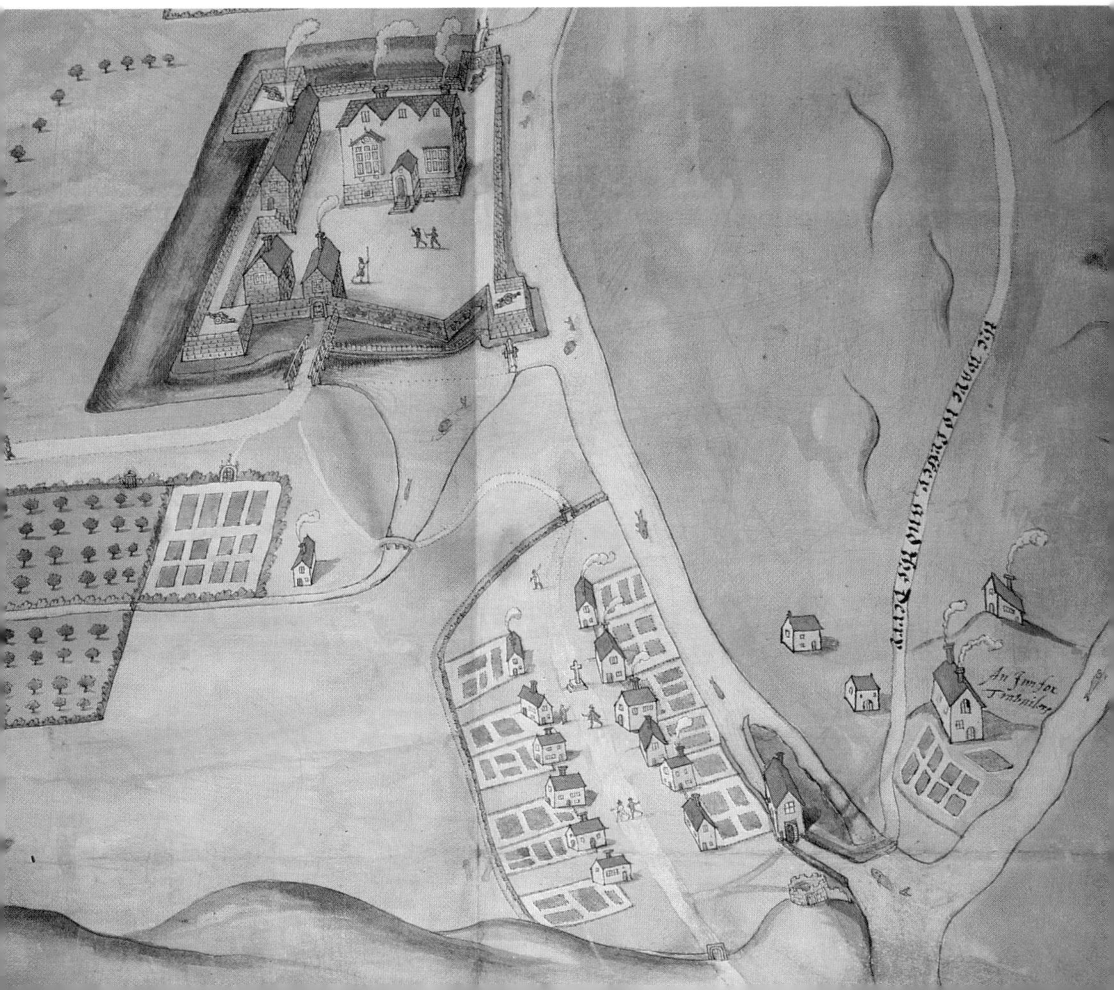

all: because there are just enough gaps, even among the Dublin imprints, to prove how little a fine collection may owe to long-term planning, and how much to a series of happy accidents.

The happiest of accidents is the gift of a complete private library. There are a number of interesting atlases among the books received from William Palliser and Claudius Gilbert in the eighteenth century; to cite only one instance, Palliser's copy of the 1630 Mercator contains an adventitious printed map of Inishowen, County Donegal, of which only two complete impressions have been found in other libraries.[4] The freestanding map is by no means unknown in this kind of benefaction (the uncatalogued sheets donated by J. G. Smyly are an important example, in which the Americas are especially well represented), but there are not so many of them as might have been wished; the kind of collector who endows a public library will probably have anticipated that library's preference for books over sheets. At the same time actual purchases of sheet-maps have never been more than sporadic, and until the twentieth century not many cartographic publishers appear to have been reminded that Trinity's privilege of legal deposit applies to maps as well as books. Nor has the Library ever served as a national archive repository in any official sense, so it has no claim on the outflow of obsolete maps from government sources that has enriched the Public Record Office and the British Library.

Yet Trinity is large enough and old enough for every generalization to have been proved false at some time or other. Its unique sea chart by the Elizabethan pilot William Borough came, of all unexpected places, from 'the family of Primate Henry Ussher'.[5] Among the Library's few records of early map-purchases is at least one major oddity in the map of China bought for twelve guineas in 1812 from 'a person returning from Batavia'.[6] In 1892 the British War Office surprisingly decided to favour the College with a dozen valuable topographical maps, including two important items from the eighteenth century.[7] Nor did every nineteenth-century map-publisher escape the provisions of the Copyright Act, as can be seen from the correspondence of Trinity's two most cartographically-conscious Librarians, J.H. Todd and T.K. Abbott, on the subject of the Ordnance Survey. The first of the Survey's Irish maps were given to the Library very soon after they came out, and were quickly described by one visitor as the most interesting items to be seen there.[8] But in 1863 Todd sharply reminded the authorities of their duty to send him large-scale as well as small-scale Ordnance maps of Britain ('I could easily point out to you the advantage of them to students of history, if that were the question at issue'), to be silenced not long afterwards by a consignment of map-sheets said to number 14,000.[9] A generation later, Abbott successfully applied the same argument to both the revised and the geological editions of the Survey's Irish maps: a highlight of this episode was the Stationery Office's plea that geological maps did not count as a separate publication because they were 'only' the Ordnance maps with colours added.[10]

These various strokes of good luck or good judgement could doubtless be multiplied if the accessions records were more complete and if more map-scholars had worked on them. But still the end-product appears to fall some way short of perfection: certainly the Library's map-sheets are a good deal less representative than its atlases. From a modern standpoint perhaps the least desirable outcome of this long-standing bias towards bound volumes has been a rather patchy coverage of pre-nineteenth-century Ireland on large and medium scales, for such maps were generally published as separate entities or in

117. An advertisement for John Rocque's survey of Dublin issued soon after his arrival in the city. In fact the map as published in 1756 was much more detailed than his earlier plans of London and Paris.

DUBLIN, the 5th of *September*, 1754.

JOHN ROCQUE,

(Chorographer to HIS ROYAL HIGHNESS THE PRINCE OF *WALES*,) Being sollicited by many of the NOBILITY and GENTRY Of the KINGDOM of *IRELAND*, to Survey and publish by SUBSCRIPTION, A MAP of the CAPITAL, in all Respects like those of *LONDON, PARIS*, &c.

IS now executing it, and in great Forwardness, to a Scale of 200 Feet in one Inch: so that the true Ground-Plot of all Public Buildings, Streets, Lanes, Courts, Alleys, *&c.* will be therein expressed, with the Boundary of the City and the other Liberties contiguous. By which the Public, as well as Foreigners, who have been so long at a Loss, may see the beautiful Situation and large Extent of this Metropolis, and be thereby undeceived.

The above Map to be contained in four Sheets of *Imperial* Paper; ~~and to shew to Posterity who were Encouragers of this noble Undertaking, the Subscribers Names shall be Engraved with what they Subscribed for.~~

Likewise, ~~the above four Sheets shall be reduced on one Sheet~~ to the same Scale, ~~on a separate Paper~~ as those of *London*, *Paris*, and *Rome*, Survey'd and published by the said *John Rocque*; ~~and the vacant Parts to be fill'd with~~ the Environs of the City, wherein will be express'd the Plans of the Towns, Villages, *&c.* the just Bendings of the Roads, Rivers, Brooks, and Paths, the exact Situation and Figures of Parks, Gardens, Hedges, Wall Fences, Commons, Heaths, Lakes, Ponds, Hills, Dales, Mills, Ferries, Bridges, Quarries, Mines, *&c.* and the Soundings of the Harbour from *Bullock* to the Hill of *Howth*, which will render it useful, as well as ornamental, ~~will be given in Acres, *&c.* The Divisions of the Parishes, and Names of the Streets, *&c.* will be taken from the Officers of each respective Parish.~~

CONDITIONS.

The Price to Subscribers will be One Guinea, Half to be paid at the Time of Subscribing, and the Remainder on delivery of the two Maps, ~~which will be in eight Months.~~

After the Subscription is closed, none will be sold under Twenty-five Shillings English.

The Subscribers may depend upon being served with the first Impression, in Order as their Subscriptions come in.

SUBSCRIPTIONS are taken in by ~~all the Booksellers in *Dublin*, and their Correspondents Abroad~~; by the said *John Rocque*, at ~~his Lodgings at the Golden Heart~~ opposite *Crane-Lane*, *Dame-Street*, where may be had all his other Works, *viz.*

	l.	s.	d.
His large Survey of London in 24 Sheets	3	3	0
London and the Environ in 16 Sheets	2	2	0
The two reduced on one Sheet each	0	5	0
Paris and the Country adjacent, on the same Scale as the Environ of London, 7 Sheets	1	1	0
Ditto reduced on one Sheet to the same Scale as that of London, by which may be seen the beautiful Situation of those two Rivals, their Extent known, and by how much London exceeds Paris in Acres, Arpans, &c.	0	5	0
Rome in 12 Sheets	2	2	0
Ditto reduced to the same Scale as London and Paris	2	6	0
An actual Survey of the County of Salop, 4 Sheets	0	12	6
City of Paris in one Sheet	0	2	6
Bristol in 4 Sheets	0	10	6
Ditto in one Sheet	0	2	6
Exeter in 2 Sheets	1	1	0
Pontefract	0	10	6
Richmond Garden, 2 Sheets	0	10	6
Wilton, the Seat of the Earl of Pembroke	0	10	6
Chiswick, the Seat of the late Earl of Burlington	0	5	0
Esher, the Seat of the late Rt. Hon. H. Pelham,	0	2	6
Kensington Garden	0	5	0
Claremount Plan and View	0	3	0
The Earl of Lincoln's Garden	0	2	6
Chebucto Harbour and Town of Hallifax	0	5	0
Plan of York	0	2	6
Plan of Geneva	0	2	6
Plan of Calais	0	5	0
British Atlas, or a set of County Maps	0	7	6
Berlin	0	2	6
St. Edmund Bury	0	1	6
View of the Citadel of Plymouth	0	1	6
The Quarter-master Maps, or Cromwell's Map of England, in 6 Sheets, being the best extant	0	10	6
View of Greenwich Hospital	0	2	6
Plan of Constantinople	0	2	0
View of ditto from the Helespont	0	1	0
Plan of the Seraglio	0	1	0
View of ditto	0	1	0
London before the Fire, by Holor	0	1	0
Plan of Nismes	0	2	6
Ditto Montpellier	0	2	6
Ditto Metz	0	2	6
Ditto Thionville	0	2	6
Ditto Madrass and Fort St. George	0	1	0
A Set of 20 Plans of Towns, by Martel	1	1	0
A Set of 15 Views of Towns, by Silvester	0	10	6
A Book of 60 Ornaments, by Brunetti	0	7	6
Twelve Heads after Raphael	0	3	0
Twelve Beasts by Oudry	0	3	0
A Set of Horses	0	1	6
Four Landskips, by Bergham	0	2	0
A new Map of France, in 6 Sheets	0	10	6
The 5 first Sheets of an actual Survey of Berkshire, containing Windsor-Forest, Oakingham, Reading, Newburg, Hungerford, &c. each	0	3	0
Or with the Divisions of the Parishes coloured	0	4	0
A new Topographical Map of the County of Middlesex, in 4 Sheets	1	1	0
And a great variety of Foreign Maps, Plans, Views, Sieges, Battles, &c. which he constantly Imports as soon as publish'd.			

SUBSCRIPTIONS are likewise taken in at his House in the *Strand*, *London*; at *Paris*, by Mr. *Julien*, Geographer to His Most Christian Majesty; at *Amsterdam*, by Mess. *Josué van Duren*; at *Vienna*, by Mr. *Briffaut*; at *Rome*, by Mr. *Joseph Giraud*; and at *Nuremburg*, by Mess. *Homman*, Geographer to the Emperor of *Germany*. &c.

RECEIVED of Half a Guinea, being the first Payment of the above two Maps, which I promise to deliver on receiving Half a Guinea more.

J. Rocque

blocks of not more than half a dozen sheets. That was at a period when the College curriculum had little room for Irish studies, and when it might have been argued that maps of Ireland were no more necessary to students than those of any other country — and no harder to find among contemporary atlases. Only within living memory have Ireland's life and landscape been closely studied in Irish universities on scales that no conventional atlas could be expected to accommodate, and by that time many of the relevant maps had fallen out of print.

Such imbalances — regional versus international, sheet versus atlas — are probably common enough among Europe's older academic institutions. In a brief review confined to one library it seems appropriate to spend most time on maps whose presence could not be taken for granted in a traditional seat of learning. Of the five such collections chosen for more detailed reference, the one most prized by Irish historians is that of George Carew, lord president of Munster at the beginning of the seventeenth century, whose maps formed part of a large and varied personal archive illustrating the history of Ireland up to and including his own time [116 and 118]. Some of them were acquired in the course of Carew's official duties; some seem to have been 'borrowed' from other government employees; some he may have had specially copied. In all they number nearly seventy items, the largest set of original Tudor and early Stuart maps of Ireland surviving anywhere outside the British Public Record Office. Almost all of them are in manuscript, the only published maps of Ireland that Carew showed any respect for being those in John Speed's *Theatre.* Though ranging widely in date (from the 1560s or slightly earlier to the 1620s) and authorship, they are for the most part competently drawn and attractively coloured. Yet far from aspiring to science or scholarship, and displaying not one scale of latitude or longitude in the entire collection, the Carew maps are essentially the byproduct of a military and political conquest. However, as well as forts, defended towns and troop movements, they are rich in placenames, territorial boundaries and a good deal of ordinary landscape detail. The mixture is full of interest for both specialist and general reader, as became evident when a large selection of the maps was exhibited in the Long Room in 1983.

Carew is said to have wanted all his Irish papers to be deposited at Trinity, suggesting a commendably far-sighted view of future academic historiography, though as it turned out most of them finally came to rest at Lambeth Palace in London. Nobody knows when, how or why the maps became detached from the remainder of the collection and found their way to Dublin. They simply turn up in the College records of the late eighteenth century as objects of curiosity to visiting cartographers and antiquarians.[11] It was a non-Trinity historian, James Hardiman of Galway, who first catalogued them in 1821, apparently on his own initiative, and after being bound into a single large volume they became generally known as the Hardiman atlas, and only on formal occasions as MS 1209.[12] By that time their true origin had been forgotten. The credit for its rediscovery belongs to a recent Keeper of Manuscripts, William O'Sullivan, who put the issue beyond any doubt by identifying Carew's hand on many of the Hardiman maps and by collating all their titles and subjects with the original early-seventeenth-century catalogue still at Lambeth.[13]

Not only in name did MS 1209 show the influence of the Hardiman era. Its stout covers proclaimed a characteristic nineteenth-century acceptance of the bookbinder as the ideal conservationist for maps. Assuming

118. From an anonymous map of Ireland in the Carew collection, probably drawn in the 1580s but deriving from a survey completed by the English engineer Robert Lythe in 1570.

IRELANDE
Kerry
Bay of Gaulway
Armagh

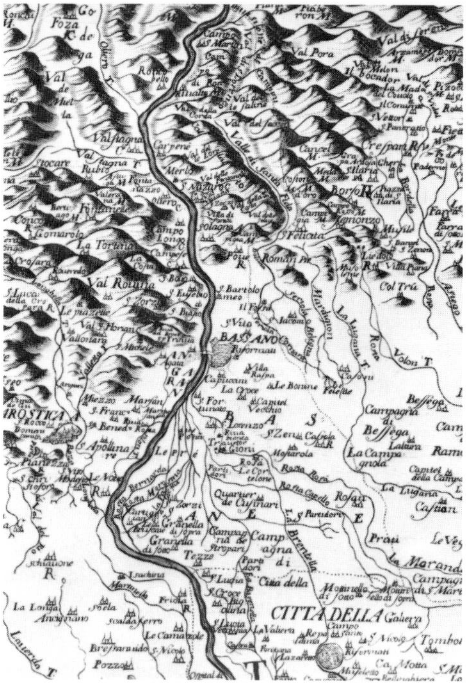

119. From Paolo Bartolomeo Clarici's map of the diocese of Padua in three sheets, published in 1720.

maps to be necessary at all, that is: the College's post-Hardiman expectations in the cartographic field were so modest that at one period this volume was serving as a repository for almost any map not found suitable for the wall of the Librarian's office (the latter a location unconducive to long-term survival, judging from the mortality of those maps once said to have been kept there),[14] the most remarkable of these later insertions being a copy of Baptista Boazio's very rare *Irelande* (1599).[15] Modern covers have been subsequently put on various other College maps; but these retrospective binding campaigns have failed to invalidate our initial distinction between book and sheet; and they have done disappointingly little to encourage a larger intake of separate maps as grist to the binder's mill. In any case binding has now gone out of fashion. The modern expert prefers to encapsulate each map within its own envelope, as was done with the Hardiman atlas in 1982. Readers will have their own opinions of this change. It is always instructive to leaf through a number of maps in quick succession, whatever their subject-matter; but too much variety in one volume can bring its own troubles, such as the need for a judgement of Solomon between library departments when printed and manuscript maps are bound together.

Conquest, confiscation and colonization remained the chief business of Irish cartographers throughout the seventeenth century. Adapting their craft to a wholly peacetime existence was a slow process, not fully complete until Dublin welcomed the famous Huguenot map-maker John Rocque in 1754. Rocque's career had started in London with views and plans of houses and gardens, but by the mid century he was already known for his English county maps as well as for plans of towns in many countries, and his firm had diversified to embrace the whole of cartography from measuring the ground to selling the finished product in its own shop. When he finally returned to London in 1760, Rocque had mapped one of Ireland's largest private estates in County Kildare and published original town plans of Thurles, Dublin, Cork and Kilkenny together with large county surveys of Dublin and Armagh. The topographical vocabulary of these maps was as modern and sophisticated as their ingenious rococo decoration. In the countryside it included roads, land-cover, hills, houses and a selection of cabins; in the city and suburbs of Dublin Rocque recorded every building and every enclosure, on what he advertised as Europe's most elaborate town plan.

Rocque has forty-three entries in the Library's 'pre-1872' printed catalogue, perhaps more than any other cartographer. It would be pleasant to report that he gave or sold these maps to the College himself. In fact they were almost all bought from a certain J. Pim (described in the catalogue as 'bookseller?') in 1855.[16] But at least the Pim purchase may have originated in Ireland at about the time of Rocque's visit. It includes a unique copy of his prospectus issued in Dublin on 5

September 1754 [117], and the same year also marks a watershed among its contents, separating a large number of earlier British and foreign items from a post-1754 component that was almost exclusively Irish. Whatever its exact provenance, this small collection provides a lively cross-section of English Georgian cartography and scenography, from the gardens of Wilton House to the imperial seraglio at Constantinople.

Our third example is on a much grander scale. It is a mass of 1631 loose maps, plans, charts, views and drawings (only four of them wholly devoted to Ireland) with an assortment of atlases numbering about ninety volumes, all of which had belonged to *Greffier* Hendrik Fagel, chief minister of the Netherlands, before being purchased for Trinity in 1802.[17] Despite their bulk these maps form only a small fraction of the whole Fagel library, so here is another happy accident in the sense that the College would obviously have accepted that library even if there had been no maps in it. In breadth of territorial coverage and cartographic subject-matter the Fagel collection can only be described as dazzling: there can have been few map libraries quite so cosmopolitan in the England of 1802 and surely none in Ireland. It appears to have been accumulated during more than one generation, for the period best represented is not Fagel's own lifetime (he was born in 1765) but the late seventeenth and early eighteenth centuries, heyday of the baroque style that gives the collection its almost overpowering aesthetic impact. Its subjects embrace virtually the whole world as known to contemporary Europeans, and its imprints cover almost all the major map-publishing centres of the period — not just those of the first rank like Amsterdam, Paris, London, Vienna, Nuremberg and Augsburg but others less familiar to eighteenth-century Irish readers such as Madrid, Lisbon, Rome, Berlin, Stockholm and St Petersburg [119,121 and 122].

The staple fare of the Fagel portfolios is the kind of straightforward political map that

120. An early thematic map from the Fagel Collection, engraved by the French artist Pierre François Tardieu (1711-71).

their owner could have found in his atlases. He was also well served with historical maps, including reconstructions of the Roman Empire and of the routes followed by famous early travellers like Alexander the Great and St Paul. As might be expected in a Dutch collection there are a wide range of sea charts and a number of maps relating to inland navigation and drainage. Town maps and town views run into several hundreds, most of them with conspicuous Renaissance-style fortifications, supplemented by some interesting wartime news-maps on thin (though well-preserved) paper and by about thirty manuscript drawings, also mainly of military subjects.

Like the Hardiman atlas, then, these maps are dominated by politics and war. The difference is that in a collection as large as Fagel's almost every other type of cartography can be expected to turn up somewhere, and it is probably the 'thematic' or more specialized maps of this period that have most appeal for the modern scholar. Thus physiography is exemplified in a fine portrayal of the mountains and rivers of the Iberian peninsula engraved by P.F. Tardieu [120]. For the urban geographer there are comparative outlines of the world's largest cities brought to a common scale by J.M. Hasius in 1745. Landscape historians will admire the *Specialkarte der Gegend von Mannheim* (1780), which traces the strips and furlongs of the German openfield system with a minuteness common enough on manuscript estate maps but hardly ever seen in print. Even the science of cartography itself — which most of its practitioners would rather keep discreetly hidden — appears in Tobias Mayer's remarkable map of Germany comparing his own outline of 1750 with those of the earlier cartographers Guillaume Delisle and J.B. Homann and specifying the towns for which latitudes and longitudes had been determined astronomically.

121. Europe and Africa symbolically represented in a chart of the Atlantic approaches to Gibraltar by the Dutch hydrographer Joannes van Keulen.

A whole book could, and perhaps should, be written on the Fagel maps, but enough has been said to demonstrate their value as a training ground for some future Trinity map librarian. He or she will have to be largely self-taught, however, for the collection has so far attracted little scholarly interest from inside or outside the College. A noteworthy exception was T.K. Abbott, who in 1900 published a catalogue of the maps that seems to have been compiled some fifty years or more earlier.[18] Abbott deserves thanks, but he showed a typical bookman's ambivalence towards unbound material by burying the Fagel catalogue in a list of College manuscripts where few readers would think of looking for it. (There is no separate catalogue of the Fagel atlases, except for the geographical sections of the original sales catalogue of 1802.) He himself must probably take credit for the fact that in *c.* 1890 several of the maps contributed to an official investigation of the boundary of British Guiana.[19] Since then the only carto-

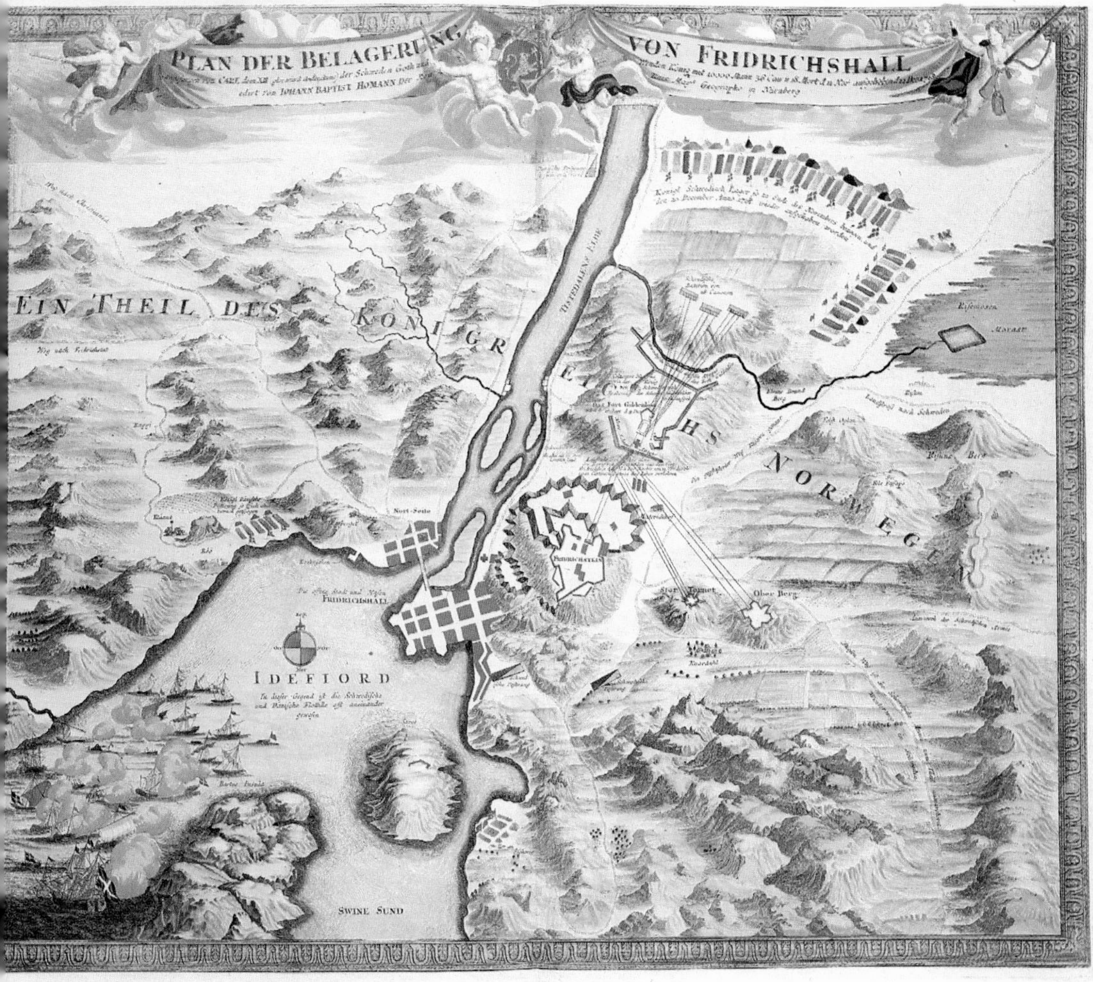

122. A typical war map from the Fagel Collection: the Norwegian frontier town of Fredrikshald under attack by King Charles XII of Sweden in 1718.

graphic specialist known to have opened the portfolios is Professor Gunter Schilder of Utrecht, who soon came upon a map of the Netherlands not recorded in any other library. The whole collection clearly deserves to be better known.

Next in chronological order (still dating each group of maps by the latest map belonging to it) comes a volume that seems to have succeeded the Hardiman atlas as a receptacle for miscellaneous items obtained from various sources over an indefinite period.[20] It carries an index by the well-known archaeologist-historian T.J. Westropp [123 and 124], but the title 'Westropp atlas' is perhaps not to be recommended, though it could hardly add to the confusion that already surrounds this unusual hybrid. The maps in question were bound in 1913, but new sheets continued to be added for many years afterwards. At present there are eighty-six, almost all printed and almost all with Irish subjects, varying in date from the mid sixteenth to the early twentieth century. Despite its unpremeditated origins, the volume makes a useful introduction to Ireland's small-scale cartography, and although most of its contents can be matched in other libraries there is at least one interesting curiosity, a proof impression of William Petty's map of Ulster on which a scale of latitudes has been added by a near-contemporary hand.

Our final case-study is exclusively Irish.

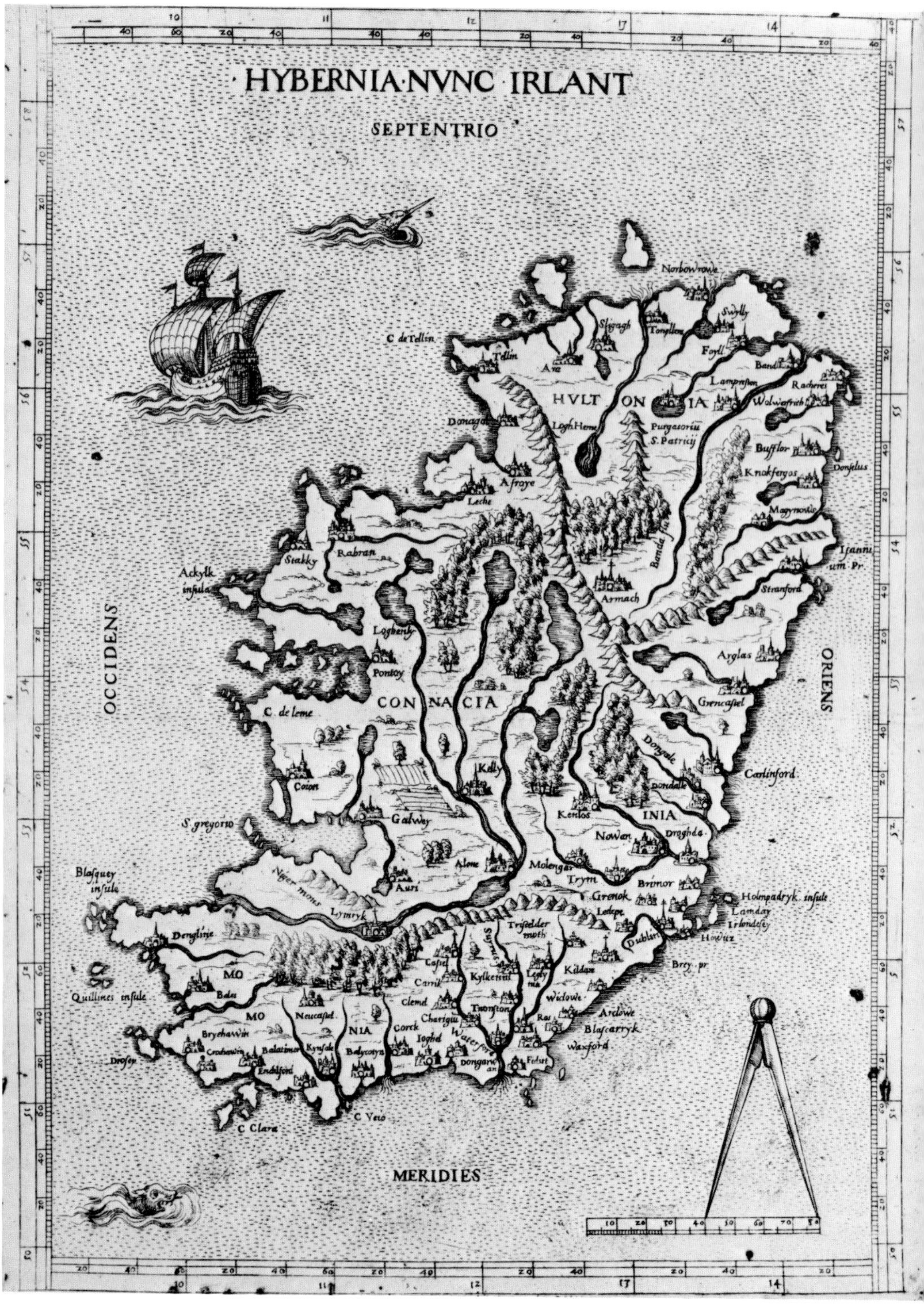
HYBERNIA·NVNC IRLANT
SEPTENTRIO
OCCIDENS
ORIENS
MERIDIES
HVLT ON IA
CON NA CIA
MO MO NIA
INIA
Dublin
Armach
Galway
Lymryk
Waxford
Carlinford
Kildare
Knokfergos
Stranford
Dongarvan
C Clara
C Veto
Niger mons

Some archival institutions have a blind spot about the records of their own behaviour, but this cannot be said of Trinity, where the College muniments, including many maps, have been accessible since about 1970 on the same terms as any other manuscript in the Library. The muniment maps deal with a leitmotiv of modern Irish history, the ownership and occupation of the soil, and in particular of the 200,000 acres that the College itself once owned in Kerry, Donegal, Armagh and elsewhere [125]. Old surveys of this property first became a matter of public interest at the time of the late-nineteenth-century land reforms, when the Assistant Librarian was allowed a small fee to make manuscript maps available 'for purposes of title'.[21] More recently the main value of the maps has been for historical scholarship, especially since an excellent catalogue of them was published in 1964.[22]

Since the College has been owning land for about as long as it has been teaching students, it may appear unlucky or neglectful in having no property maps of sixteenth- or seventeenth-century date apart from a few copies of official plantation surveys.[23] But this is common form in Irish muniment rooms, for it was only after the Williamite confiscation and the government's 'Trustees' Survey' of forfeited estates that cartography made much progress among the country's landowners. At Trinity the breakthrough came with three volumes of large-scale estate maps dating from about 1715. They are drawn and written in a style whose popularity among contemporary Irish surveyors made it virtually anonymous, with much emphasis on acreages and boundaries and very little on the actual appearance of the ground. This was the kind of rather empty-looking map that John Rocque did so much to improve upon in the 1750s. The College never found work for Rocque as a surveyor, though it did eventually buy some of the beautiful maps he drew for the Earl of Kildare.[24] But by degrees his style diffused itself among other practitioners, including several employed on the Trinity estates. Some of its hallmarks appear in the 1770s among the maps of Thomas Sherrard and his partners; others in the more extensive surveys made by Richard Frizell at the same period.

These later surveyors showed a growing interest in houses, roads, land-use and prospects for agricultural improvement, a trend that found even fuller expression in 1824-5 when the Donegal estate was mapped by Thomas Noble. Why Noble should be chosen for this task is not clear: he had only just started practising in Dublin (his previous employer, William Armstrong of Armagh, had no connection with Trinity) and the maps he made for the College are among the earliest that carry his signature. But his careful portraiture of physical and human geography does credit to the Irish map-making tradition at the peak of its achievement, just before that peak was captured by the government's Ordnance Survey department. Like so many of the

123 (far left). Ireland as seen by an Italian cartographer in the 1560s; one of the maps indexed by T. J. Westropp.

124. The destruction of Sodom and Gomorrah, from a map of Palestine by Giovanni Francesco Della Gatta, published in Rome in 1557.

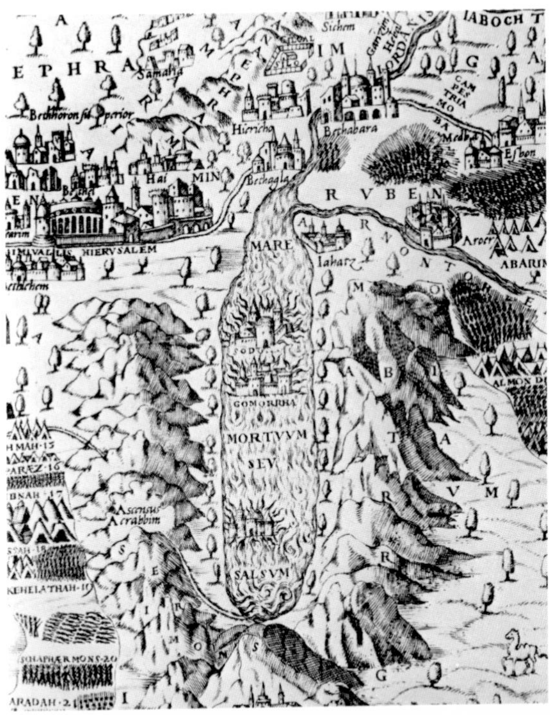

Survey's forerunners, Noble knew how to spring an occasional uncartographic surprise, such as a comment in mid-map on the 'thousands of invalids' who annually visited a well near Letterkenny 'under the idea that its waters are capable of effecting miraculous cures'. But most of his energy went on farms and farmhouses, a topic which began to dominate Irish historical geography in the 1930s and which shows no sign of losing its popularity fifty years later. Noble's contemporaries would never have believed that, for some future academics, an estate map from the bursar's office might seem more 'relevant' than anything in the Long Room or its adjacent pavilions.

NOTES

1. John Nichols, *Illustrations of the literary history of the eighteenth century consisting of authentic memoirs and original letters of eminent persons.* 7. London: J.B. Nichols & Son, 1848, p. 755.

2. J.G. Smyly, 'The old library: extracts from the Particular Book', *Hermathena* 49 (1935) 166-83.

3. TCD MS 358 (catalogue of College Library books, *c.* 1610).

4. J.H. Andrews, 'An early map of Inishowen', *Long Room* 7 (1973) 19-25.

5. TCD MUN/LIB/1/53, fol. 161.

6. TCD MS 1648 (map of China); TCD MUN/LIB/11/7/12; G.N. Wright, *An historical guide to the city of Dublin.* Dublin: Baldwin, Cradock & Joy, 1825, p. 17.

7. TCD MUN/LIB/1/34 (28 April, 2 May 1892).

8. J.G. Kohl, *Ireland, Scotland and England.* London: Chapman & Hall, 1844, p. 164.

9. TCD MUN/LIB/2/4 (11 February 1863).

10. TCD MUN/LIB/2/5, fols 39-40 (August 1889-February 1890); Ordnance Survey Office, Dublin, file 5066 (October-November 1887).

11. TCD MUN/LIB/1/53, iv.

12. TCD MUN/LIB/1/62, published in *Transactions of the Royal Irish Academy* 14 (1824) 55-77.

13. William O'Sullivan, 'George Carew's Irish maps', *Long Room* 26/27 (1983) 15-25.

14. TCD MUN/LIB/2/1 (2 March, 10 March 1788; 13 March 1793), MUN/LIB/13/20 (24 November 1817).

15. J.H. Andrews, 'Baptista Boazio's map of Ireland', *Long Room* 1 (1970) 29-36.

16. TCD MUN/LIB/11/32/15.

17. R.B. McDowell, 'The acquisition of the Fagel library', *Bulletin of the Friends of the Library of Trinity College Dublin* (1947) 5-6.

18. TCD MS 3727.

19. *The book of Trinity College Dublin, 1591-1891.* Belfast: Marcus Ward, 1892, p. 169.

20. Shelfmark 21.u.19.

21. TCD MUN/LIB/2/4 (10 July 1879).

22. F.H.A. Aalen and R.J. Hunter, 'The estate maps of Trinity College', *Hermathena* 98 (1964) 85-96.

23. F.H.A. Aalen and R.J. Hunter, 'Two early seventeenth century maps of Donegal', *Journal of the Royal Society of Antiquaries of Ireland* 94 (1964) 199-202.

24. TCD MS 4278 (estate maps of the manor of Athy, County Kildare, 1756).

125. A map from the Trinity College muniments: land quality, townland boundaries, industrial sites and a prehistoric 'giant's grave' on the College estate in County Donegal, 1824.

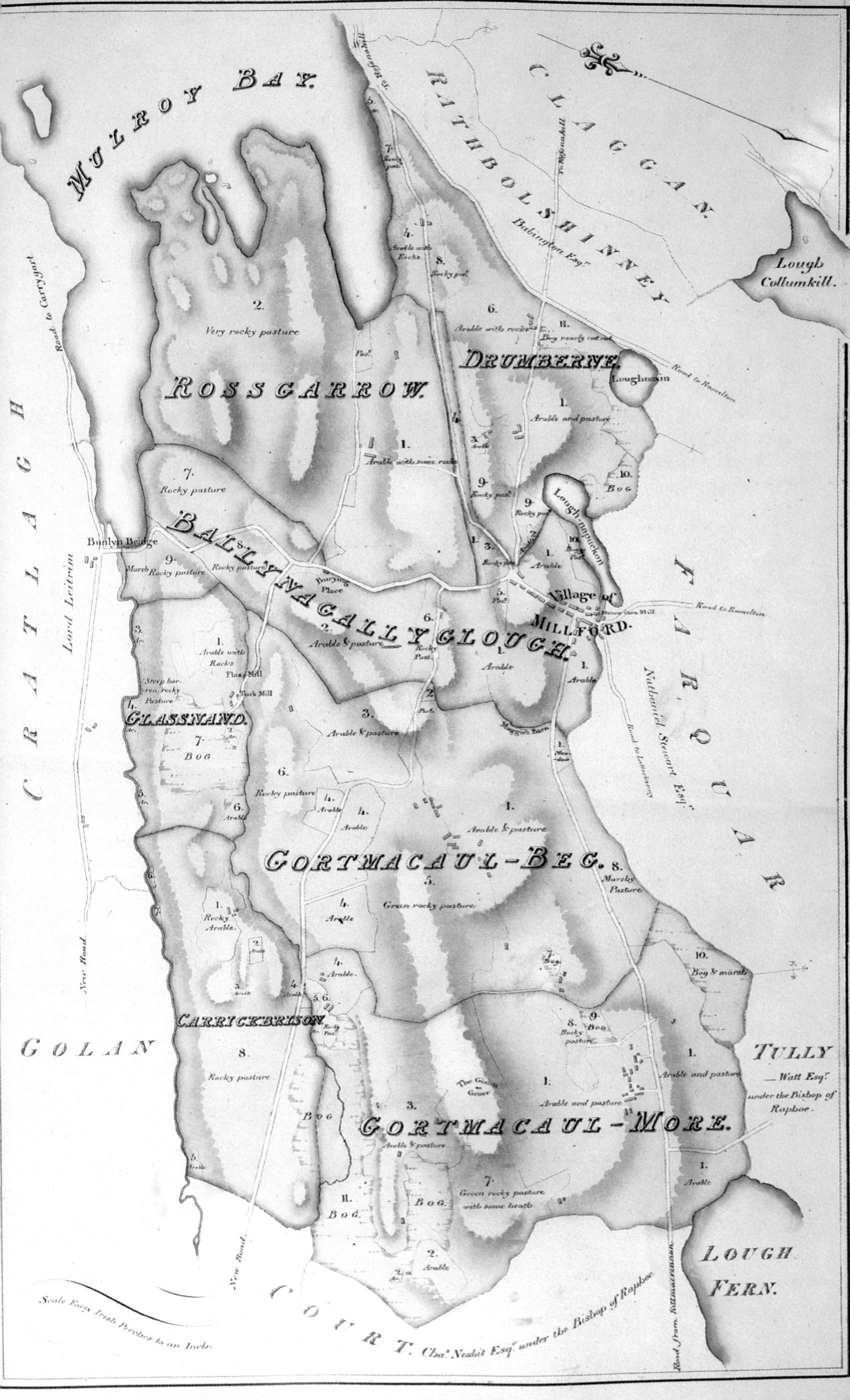

MULROY BAY.
RATHBOLSHINNEY
Babington Esqr.
CLAGGAN.
Lough Collumkill.
Road to Carrygart
2. Very rocky pasture
ROSSGARROW.
DRUMBERNE.
Loughmasin
Road to Ramelton
1. Arable and pasture
1. Arable with some rocks
10. Bog
7. Rocky pasture
Lough-nampuckon
BALLYNACALLYGLOUGH.
Bunlyn Bridge
9. Rocky pasture
Marsh
Burying Place
Village of MILLFORD.
Road to Ramelton
2. Arable & pasture
1. Arable
Lord Leitrim
CRATLAGH
Flax Mill
Tuck Mill
GLASSNAND.
7. Bog
3. Arable & pasture
6. Rocky pasture
Nathaniel Stewart Esqr.
Road to Letterkenny
FARQUAR
GORTMACAUL-BEG.
1. Arable & pasture
5. Green rocky pasture
8. Marshy Pasture
10. Bog & marsh
New Road
CARRICKBRISON
8. Rocky pasture
GOLAN
The Giants Grave
3. Arable & pasture
GORTMACAUL-MORE.
1. Arable and pasture
TULLY
— Watt Esqr. under the Bishop of Raphoe.
7. Green rocky pasture with some heath
11. Bog.
LOUGH FERN.
New Road.
COURT. Chas. Nesbit Esqr. under the Bishop of Raphoe
Road from Kilmacrenan
Scale Forty Irish Perches to an Inch.

BIBLIOTHECA QUINIANA

VERONICA MORROW

One spring day in 1805 a certain wealthy Dublin gentleman by the name of Henry George Quin bought a pistol. A few days later, on 16 February, he shot himself in his bed, leaving a note to say that he was taking his own life because he was tired of living; he was forty-five years of age. Nine years earlier he had made his will, leaving his magnificent collection of books, complete with bookcase, to Trinity College Library.

He was the third son of Professor Henry Quin, MD, an affluent and accomplished Dublin doctor[1] described by Mrs Delany as 'a very sensible, good physician, and an ingenious and agreeable man', and his wife Anne, daughter of Charles Monck and his wife Agneta, née Hitchcock. He followed his elder brothers to Harrow, which he left at the age of sixteen, and then to Trinity, which he entered in 1776, earning favourable mention throughout his college career and graduating with a BA in 1781. Little is known of his activities for the next few years, but it is not surprising that, accustomed as he was to wealth, an established social position and an enlightened and artistic background, he decided to travel abroad in order to further his interest in the arts. Accordingly, he and a friend set out in 1785 on the Grand Tour, returning in the autumn of the following year.

On his travels he kept a most perceptive and entertaining diary, the first volume of which has unfortunately disappeared. The fact that it existed is inferred from volumes two and three. The Library acquired volume two (MS 2261) in 1946 and a microfilm of volume three, which had remained in the family, in 1962. Henry Quin certainly visited Paris in 1785 on his outward journey and bought some books, which he left to be bound by Derome and held for his return. The second volume starts in Savoy; he passed through several northern Italian cities before reaching Rome, where he stayed intermittently nearly three months, leading a very active social life and visiting the architectural and artistic sights [126]. He then travelled northward to reach France via the coastal route. He journeyed through Provence and on to Spain, where the the heat was so intense in Barcelona that he returned to France, making a point of going to Toulouse to visit the splended library of Count MacCarthy-Reagh, which he described as the most magnificent private collection he had ever seen. He reached Paris on 20 July 1785, engaged in considerable bookbuying and binding activity, and stayed at least until 11 August, when the diary ends.

For want of further evidence one must conclude that Quin then returned to Dublin. In 1789 he was appointed Second Chamberlain of the Exchequer, a post he held until his death, and in 1794 he was also appointed to the post of Clerk of the Quit Rents, also in the Exchequer, both sinecures, practically speaking, and both lucrative. He left Ireland on at least two other occasions in pursuit of books. In 1790 he went to Amsterdam to attend the sale

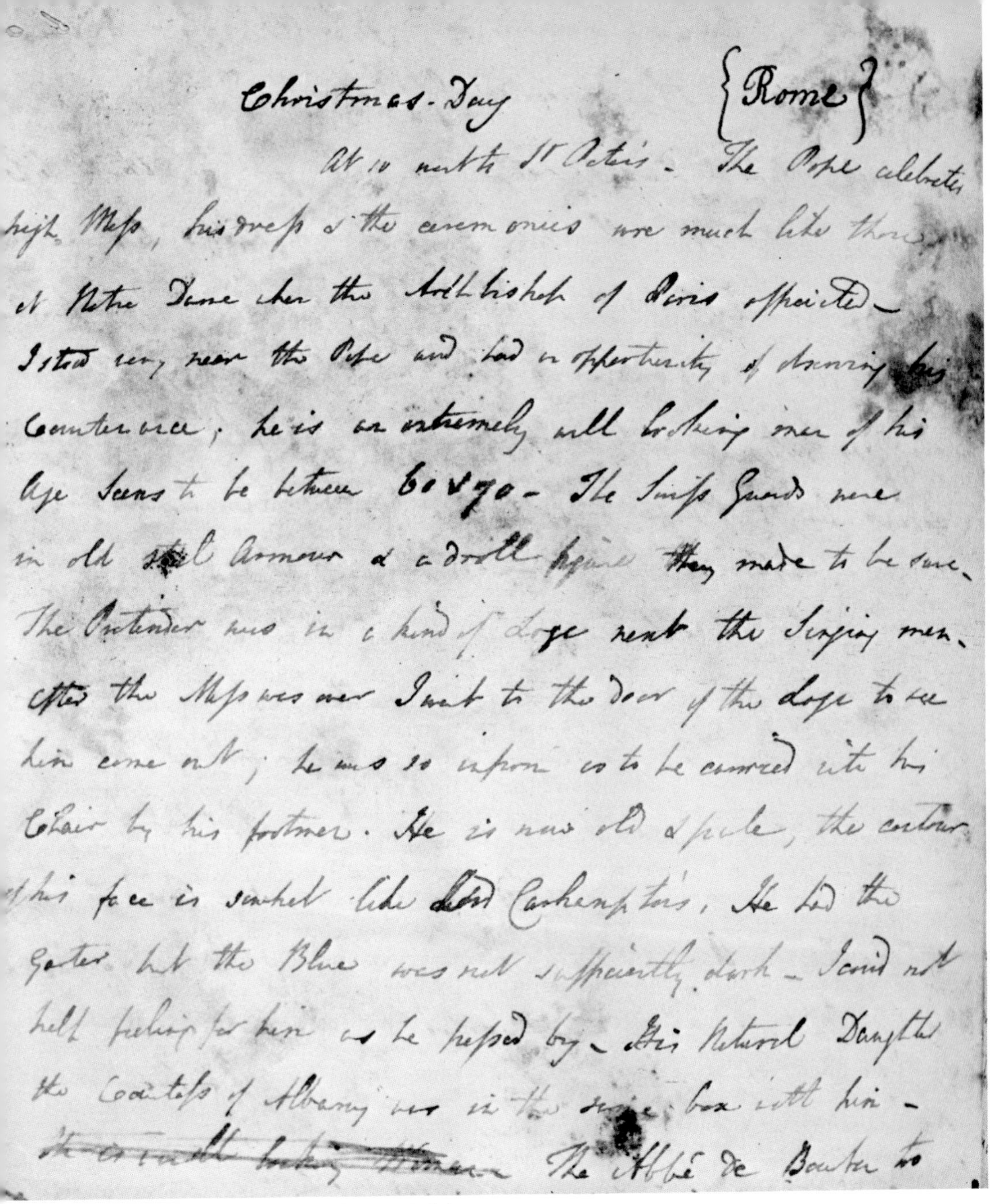

Christmas-Day {Rome}
At 10 went to St Peter's – The Pope celebrated
high Mass, his dress & the ceremonies were much like those
at Notre Dame when the Archbishop of Paris officiated –
I stood very near the Pope and had an opportunity of observing his
Countenance; he is an extremely well looking man of his
Age seems to be between 60 & 70 – The Swiss Guards were
in old steel Armour & a droll figure they made to be sure.
The Pretender was in a kind of Loge next the Singing men.
after the Mass was over I went to the door of the Loge to see
him come out; he was so infirm as to be carried into his
Chair by his footmen. He is now old & pale, the colour
of his face is somewhat like Lord Carhampton's. He had the
Garter but the Blue was not sufficiently dark – I could not
help feeling for him as he passed by – His Natural Daughter
the Countess of Albany was in the same box with him –
The Abbé de Bouter to

126. Quin's diary: on Christmas Day 1785 he attended High Mass in St Peter's, Rome, celebrated by Pope Pius VI.

held by M. Bolongaro-Crevenna. The sale lasted nearly two months, and Quin got some choice editions. He wrote afterwards in his copy of the Crevenna catalogue, which was presented to the Library in 1891, 'I went to Amsterdam on purpose to attend this sale; and indeed my acquisitions there amply repaid my journey. They were the most unsophisticated books I ever saw.'

In March 1791 he attended the sale of the Bibliotheca Parisiana; in its catalogue, also donated to the Library in 1891, he wrote 'I

127. Sixteenth-century Parisian binding made for Henri II of France. 16.1/17.1 × 10.2 × 3.3 cm.

128 (far right). Virgil's *Opera*, printed on vellum (Venice 1470). The hand-painted decoration includes a blank shield intended for a coat of arms. This book fetched the highest price at the Crevenna sale, in recognition of which Quin was awarded the auctioneer's gavel. 22.7 × 33.1 cm.

went to London in order to attend this sale, and intended to purchase the following articles not one of which however I got, all of them being sold at what I thought extravagant prices'.

Upon the death of his father in 1791 he inherited both property and shares, after which little is known of him until his death in 1805. He made his own will in 1794; he left £500 to each of his sisters, £3000 to his brother Charles, and to the eldest brother Thomas the residue of his estate save for his books, as the following extract from his will shows: 'I give and bequeath my large mahogany book-case, together with such of the books and manuscripts as are specified in a catalogue, bound in red morocco leather, written in my own hand, and marked with the letters L.T.C.D., together with the catalogue itself, and the hammer which was presented to me at Amsterdam by Signor Crevenna, I give and bequeath forever to the Provost and Fellows of Trinity College, Dublin, in order that they may be placed in the Library of Trinity College ... and I desire that the words *Bibliotheca Quiniana* in capital letters, two inches in height, and gilt on a dark coloured ground, be put on the top of the two central doors of the aforesaid bookcase, one word on each door ... I desire, likewise, that none of them shall ever be rebound, or any new or additional covering or lettering of any kind shall be put upon them, but they shall always remain precisely in the same state wherein they shall be found at the time of my decease.'

In pre-eighteenth-century Europe books and manuscripts were collected mainly by royalty and others in high office. Later, however, many of the fine libraries collected, inherited or augmented in earlier centuries were dispersed for various reasons, finding their way into salerooms and bookshops and thence into the homes of the antiquarian, the scholar and the wealthy dilettante. In Ireland, book collecting had become a popular pursuit among the more scholarly and enlightened of the nobility, gentry, clergy and professional classes, to judge by the library sales of the many notable collectors of the period.[2] Quin was therefore conforming to custom in collecting books during the last decades of the eighteenth century, and he may have been competing against renowned collectors such as the Earl of Charlemont and Denis Daly, MP, of Dunsandle. The library of over four thousand books belonging to John Carpenter, Roman Catholic Archbishop of Dublin, was sold in 1787, and Quin acquired a treasure from this collection, although he did not purchase it un-

TITYRE. TV PATVLAE
recubans sub tegmine fagi
Siluestrem tenui musam
meditaris auena.
Nos patriȩ fines: & dulcia liquimus arua.
Nos patriam fugimus. tu tityre lentus i umbra
Formosam resonare doces amaryllida siluas.
O meliboee deus nobis hȩc ocia fecit.
Nanq; erit ille mihi semper deus: illius aram
Sȩpe tener nostris ab ouilibus imbuet agnus.
Ille meas errare boues: ut cernis: et ipsum
Ludere quȩ uellem calamo permisit agresti.
Non equidē inuideo: miror magis: undiq; totis
Vsque adeo turbatur agris: en ipse capellas
Protinus ȩger ago: hanc etiam uix tityre duco.
Hic inter densas corylos modo nanq; gemellos
Spem gregis ab silice in nuda connixa reliquit.
Sȩpe malum hoc nobis si mens nō leua fuiss&
De cȩlo tactas memini predicere quercus.
Sed tamen iste deus qui sit da tityre nobis.
Vrbem quam dicunt romam meliboee putaui
Stultus ego huic nrāe similē: quo sepe solemus
Pastores ouium teneros depellere foetus.
Sic canibus catulos similes: sic matribus hȩdos
Noram: sic paruis componere magna solebam.
Verum hȩc tantū alias inter caput extulit urbes
Quantum lenta solent inter uiburna cupressi.
Et quȩ tanta fuit romam tibi causa uidendi?
Libertas, quȩ sera tamen respexit inertem,
Candidior postq̄ tondenti barba cadebat.
Respexit tamen & longo post tempore uenit.
Postq̄ nos amaryllis hab& galatea reliquit.
Nanq; fatebor enim: dum me galatea tenebat
Nec spes libertatis erat: nec cura peculi.
Quis multa meis exir& uictima septis
Pinguis: & ingratȩ premeretur caseus urbi
Non unq̄ grauis ȩre domū mihi dextra redibat
Mirabar quid moesta deos amarylli uocares:
Cui pendere sua patereris in arbore poma.

til 1793, probably from a bookseller: *Pacis querela* etc., Venice: Aldus, 1518 (Quin 114), in a binding made for Jean Grolier, which has an inscription in both Latin and Irish in Carpenter's hand. Quin, who competed on the international market, shared at least one interest with Count MacCarthy-Reagh, whose library in Toulouse has already been mentioned. Dibdin[3] says of the Count: 'his leading passion, in book-collecting (like his late countryman's, poor Mr Quin — who gave 170 guineas for the Spira Virgil of 1470, *in membranis*!) is marked by a fondness for works *printed upon vellum* ... In our country, however, the finest VELLUM LIBRARY in the world might be composed from the collections of His Majesty, the Duke of Marlborough, Earl Spencer, Sir M.M. Sykes, Bart., Mr Johnes, Mr Coke, and the Quin Collection.'

Thus one gets some idea of Quin's standing as a book collector. The books, described in detail elsewhere,[4] which he bequeathed to Trinity represent the nucleus of what had been a much more extensive collection. The two main themes in the present collection are the Greek and Latin classical authors and Italian renaissance literature. There were originally 127 titles in this tiny but choice collection, though only 110 reached Trinity; fourteen were struck out by Quin himself, and the remaining three were never traced. Most of the fourteen he sold at auction, because they did not measure up to his exacting standards. Of one he noted 'this book I returned to Mr Payne because the Price was greater than the Condition of the Copy justified', and of another 'this book I returned to Mr Payne on account of several of the leaves being stained', despite its annotation 'Exemplar Grolierii'.

His library contains books owned by some of the most celebrated collectors of all time, sometimes in their early bindings, in addition to contemporary works for which he himself

129. Sixteenth-century binding made in Paris for Jean Grolier. Green morocco tooled in gold to an interlace design; cypher and coronet on spine added when book passed into ownership of Marquis de Ménars in the seventeenth century. 22 × 14 × 2.5 cm.

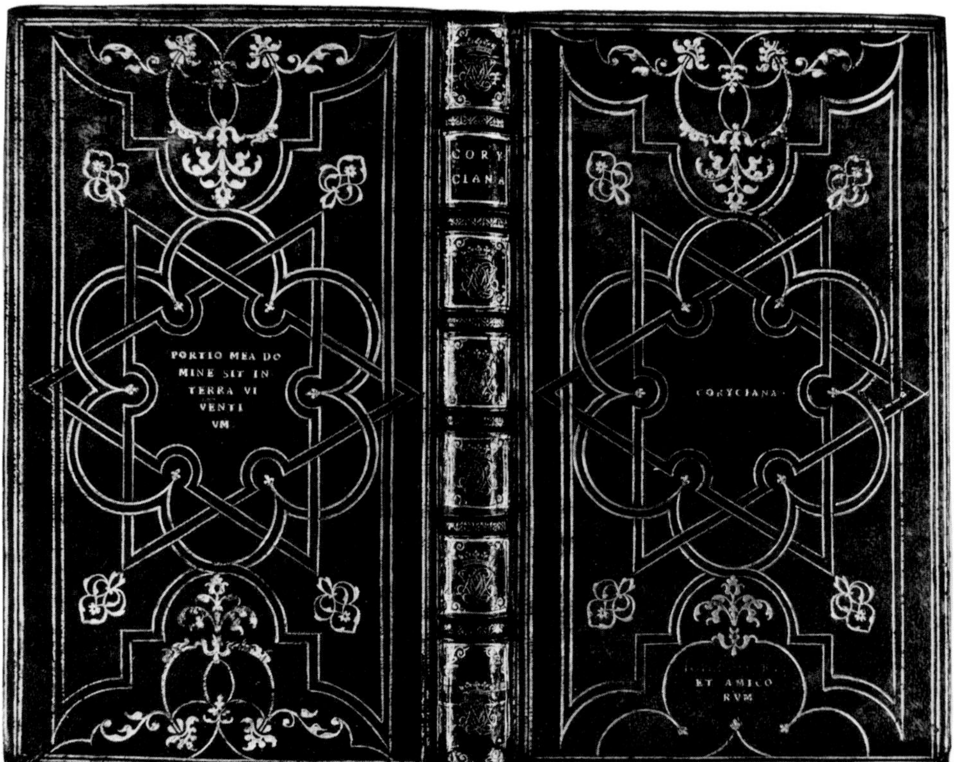

chose the binders. There are seventeen incunables (books printed before 1501). Sixteen books are printed on vellum, and there is one vellum manuscript (the other remaining untraced), Boccaccio *Philostrato* (Quin 74; MS 957) written in a developing humanistic script. One book is printed on white silk, Pindar *Olympia*, Glasgow: Foulis, 1734 (Quin 115). Many of the books are illuminated, including the Virgil *Opera*, Venice: Vindelinus de Spira, 1470 (Quin 64 [128]). This is the book that fetched the highest price — 1925 florins, or £192 10s 0d in Irish currency, including tax and duty — thereby so impressing M. Crevenna that he presented Quin with the gavel which, appropriately inscribed, forms part of the bequest. Quin had the Virgil bound by Roger Payne. Many of the other books are also first editions, including the Dante *Divina commedia*, Foligno: Neumeister, 1472 (Quin 51),[5] which Quin bought in 1789, the year in which he bought the Petrarch *Canzionere*, Venice: Vindelinus de Spira, 1470 (Quin 55), which has painted on it the arms of the Priuli family of Venice. The press with the largest number of books in the collection is that of Aldus Manutius, with twenty-seven titles. There are five from both Bodoni and Didot, three from Baskerville and the Strawberry Hill Press, and two each from Charlewood, Cromberger, Elzevir, Foulis, Giunta, Ibarra, Jenson, Portilia, Typographia Regia, Vindelinus de Spira; the remainder are all represented by single items, including the one example of German high Gothic, Pfintzing *Theuerdank*, Nuremberg: Schoensperger, 1517 (Quin 88), with its 118 wood engravings.

It is not easy, nor is it fair to the collection, to single out individual items for special mention, as each item was specially chosen as being the choicest of its kind. Yet, however interesting the editions may be, in the final analysis the unique element in Quin's books lies in their bindings, whether these were commissioned by him or by other collectors.

130. Sixteenth-century binding made for Marc Laurin of Bruges. Brown morocco over wooden boards, tooled in gold, probably made in Paris by Claude de Picques. 16.8/17.6 × 10.3 × 6.2 cm.

Henri II of France (1519-59) was probably the greatest collector of bookbindings of all time. The Bibliothèque Nationale owns over eight hundred from his library at Fontainebleau, though fewer than thirty genuine, as opposed to presentation, bindings have been located outside Paris, one of these being Quintus Calaber *Derelictorum ab Homero...*, Venice: Aldus [1504?] (Quin 62 [127]). The technical details of the binding are given as an accompanying item in the exhibition showcase; the style is typical of the Greek works in the royal collection. Quin's catalogue and notebook are annotated 'Ex Bibliotheca Henrici II Galliorum Regis et Dianae de Poitiers', but it is now held to be most unlikely that the presence of the crescents and HD monogram on many of the books which almost certainly came from the royal library represent anything as positive as joint ownership between Henri II and his

mistress Diane de Poitiers, duchesse de Valentinois, although the addition of these emblems of Diana may well have been inspired by her. This book, as was customary, has the royal library shelfmark written in ink on the title page, in this case CMMXXXVII crossed through and 649, amended to 655, substituted.

Other prominent public figures collecting libraries and commissioning fine bindings at much the same time as Henri II include Jean Grolier, Thomas Mahieu and Marc Laurin. Grolier (*c.* 1479-1565), who spent most of his life in the service of Henri II and became Treasurer of France, was the greatest of French private collectors. In his early years he patronized Italian binders, but all five in the Quin collection were bound in Paris. These five (Quin 72, 108, 111 [129], 114, 126) are all illustrated and described elsewhere;[6] suffice it to say here that they all bear in the centre of the lower cover Grolier's motto PORTIO MEA DOMINE SIT IN TERRA VIVENTIVM, taken from Psalm 141, verse 6, of the Vulgate, and the ownership inscription 'IO. GROLIERII ET AMICORVM' on the upper cover, across the bottom on four of the books and in a cartouche in the lower part of the design on the fifth. The greater part of Grolier's collection remained in Paris until the early part of the seventeenth century, and eventually the books were dispersed, some

131 (left). Eighteenth-century binding, almost certainly made in Ireland by William McKenzie, the relatively plain covers and the red leather onlays on the richly decorated spine being typical of his work. 29.6 × 23.6 × 3.4 cm.

132. Two small eighteenth-century French mosaic bindings using onlays of different coloured leathers. 13.9 × 8.9 × 1.7 cm and 13.3 × 8.7 × 1.3 cm.

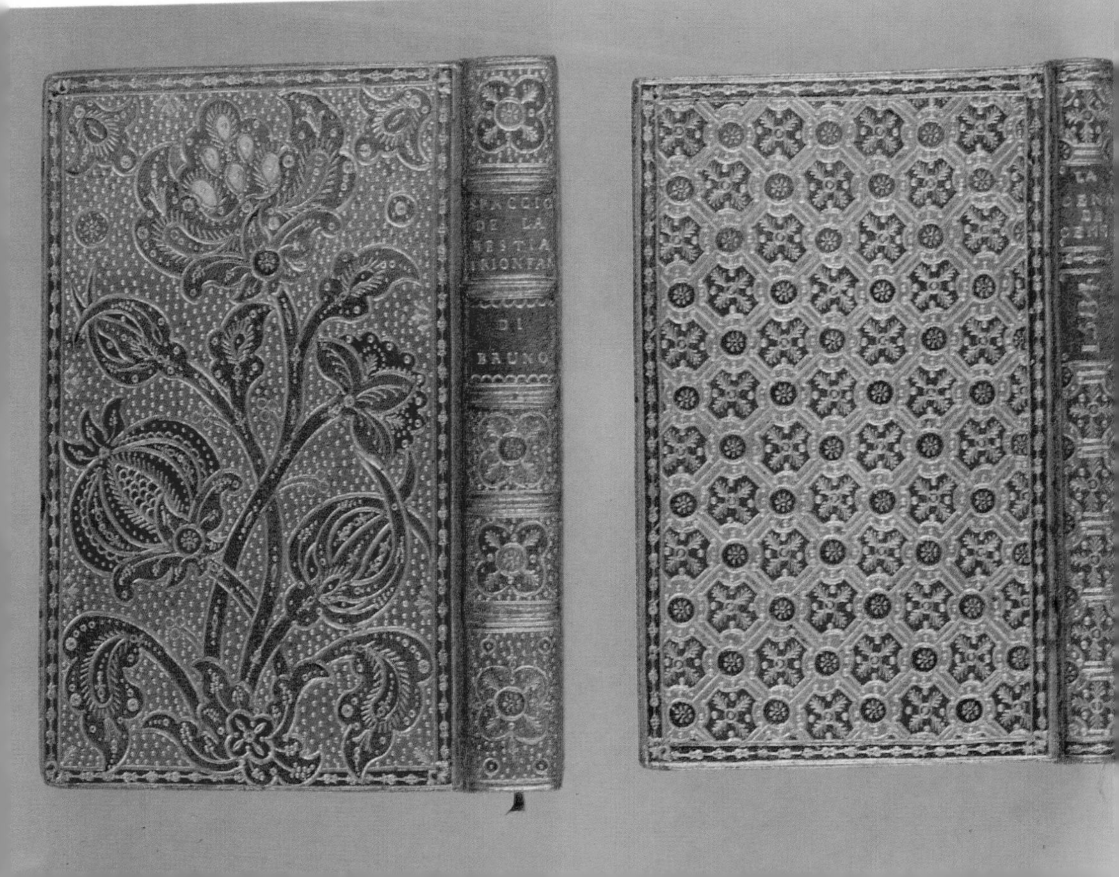

brought to England for sale, many more sold in France during the revolution.

Mahieu's exact dates are uncertain, but he was secretary to Henri II's queen consort, Catharine de' Medicis (whom he may have accompanied from Italy) during the period 1549-60 and was Treasurer of France after 1560. His bindings, which fell into various stylistic groups, resemble some of those made for Grolier. Quin acquired two of his books, the Orus Apollo, Paris: Kerver, 1551 (Quin 91) and the Catullus, Venice: Aldus, 1502 (Quin 124), both of which are bound in golden brown morocco tooled in gold with solid and hatched tools and interlace design, and have Mahieu's motto INIMICI MEI MEA MICHI NON ME MICHI in the centre of the lower cover and his inscription THO. MAIOLI ET AMICORVM at the base of the upper cover. Both are recorded but not illustrated in Hobson.[7]

Marc Laurin, who was born in Bruges in 1530 and died in exile in Calais in 1581, was a contemporary of Grolier and Mahieu. Only thirty of his bindings are recorded, one of them being in the Quin collection, the Euripides *Opera*, Venice: Aldus, 1503 (Quin 99 [130]). Bound in brown morocco over wooden boards, its covers are relatively plain with rectangular panel. The upper cover bears the inscription M. LAVRINI ET AMICORVM near the top, the motto VIRTVS IN ARDVO near the bottom, and has a central design blocked in gold. The spine has a decorative gouged interlace design on studded ground. Like the other 'Greek' bindings made for Laurin, this one was almost certainly made by Claude de Picques, according to Nixon.[8] A copy of this work was sold at the Bibliotheca Parisiana sale in 1791; in his copy of the sale catalogue Quin records 'my Laurin's Copy of this Book is the finest I ever saw'.

133. Eighteenth-century Parisian binding decorated in the dentelle (i.e. lacy) style. Red morocco tooled in gold; blue silk lining. 23.3 × 16.6 × 2.4 cm.

There are three attractive unidentified sixteenth-century Italian bindings, all very different in style, in the collection, which largely bypasses the seventeenth century. Two of the few exceptions are armorial bindings. One belonged to Jacques-Antoine de Thou (1553-1617), royal librarian, historian and diplomat, who left a library of over 1000 manuscripts and 8000 printed books which remained in the family until 1580 when the greater part was purchased by the Marquis de Ménars. It was later bought by the Cardinal de Rohan, passed to his nephew the Prince de Soubise, and finally put on the market just before the revolution; this book bears the arms of de Thou and his second wife Gaspard de la Chastre. Another book formerly owned by de Thou is in the collection, Quin 111. One of the Groliers, it has de Thou's name and the shelfmark in his library, and on the spine it has the coronet and cypher of de Ménars. The other armorial binding belonged to Count Carl Heinrich von Hoym (1694-1736), Polish ambassador to France. Among the eighteenth-century bindings are some made for other collectors whose books he purchased, but Quin himself also features as a collector-patron.

Surprisingly, there are no authenticated

Irish bindings, but there are a few which bear certain signs characteristic of Irish workmanship of the period. The most likely candidate is on the Virgil *Bucolica*, Birmingham: Baskerville, 1757 (Quin 7, purchased in 1785 [131]), which bears all the traces of William McKenzie's style.[9] It is bound in olive green morocco and tooled in gold; the rather plain covers are tooled with roll and floral borders and urns in the angles, and the richly decorated spine has crimson leather onlaid medallions and lettering-pieces.

The Derome family of Paris is represented in the collection. There are three attractive mosaic bindings, all with Crevenna stickers, probably bound by Jacques-Antoine Derome or by his son Nicolas-Denis (Derome le jeune), who certainly bound for Quin. These are Bruno, *Spaccio de la bestia trionfante* and his *Cena de la Ceneri*, Quin 92 and 93 respectively [132] — fictitious imprints, but actually both London: Charlewood, 1584 — and, in a slipcase, Quin 95, Morlini *Novellae*, Naples: de Sallo, 1520; illustrated by Fox[10] and Rau.[11] Numbers 92 and 95 retain the ownership label of Paul Girardot de Préfond and have a flower and fruit design, while no. 93 has a more formal mosaic design. Included among the possibles are two dentelle bindings [133], and of the certainties is the Boccaccio *Decameron*, Florence: Giunta, 1527 (Quin 14), mentioned in his diary and purchased from De Bure in 1785 for 432 livres. This information is all recorded on the book, as is 'relié par de Rome 15 livres', also in Quin's hand, so the Derome le jeune ticket, though present, is not required for corroboration. The book is bound in crimson morocco, with citron lettering-pieces on the spine, and the covers are tooled in gold to a border design.

The remaining identified bindings in the collection were all executed in England, some to his own design. Quin gives some information in his catalogue and on the books themselves and, in addition, seven of the books have the tickets used by Christian Kalthoeber. Six of these are morocco bindings tooled to a rather severe border and panel neoclassical design, though that on the Racine *Oeuvres*, Paris: Didot, 1783 (Quin 25) is more intricate than the others. The seventh, Longus *Pastoralia*, Parma: Bodoni, 1785 (Quin 43 [134]) is much more elaborate. Bound in vellum, with touches of blue and green paint, tooled in gold to an Adamesque design with swags, urns, palmettes and mermaids on the covers, and a flat spine with lettering, urns and a central panel decorated in the French *de présent* style, it has a vivid pink watered silk pastedown and conjugate leaf, tooled in gold with Greek key and decorated border and pineapples in the angles. Quin says of it in his catalogue 'bound and ornamented to my Directions by Kalthoeber', so this is one book for which he chose not only the binder but the style. Yet the design is almost identical to that on a copy of Worlidge's *Antiques,* bound about 1785, in Westminster Abbey;[13] furthermore, the same tools appear on at least half a dozen other works, including the Diettenhofer *Sonatas* in the British Library,[14] bound about 1782, and, as the *Pastoralia* was not printed until 1786, Quin could not have had it bound until after that date, so he can hardly be given credit for the entire design. Still, it is an indication of his taste.

Another firm patronized by Quin was that of Staggemeier and Welcher. Their ticket appears on Tasso *Gerusalemme liberata*, Paris: Didot, 1784-6, which is bound in vellum, tooled in gold and enhanced with blue paint; the covers are tooled to a panel design with Greek key and flower and foliage borders, with dagger-shaped tool in the angles, and the flat spine is decorated similarly to, though less elaborately than, the Kalthoeber just described.

There is one example of an Edwards of Halifax binding, on Shakespeare *Works*, London: Stockdale, 1784 (Quin 35 [135]). In 1785 James Edwards, the London bookseller, took out a patent for rendering vellum

134 (left). Eighteenth-century London binding, vellum tooled in gold and painted. Commissioned by Quin from Kalthoeber, whose ticket it bears. 30.8 × 23 × 2.9 cm.

135 (above). Eighteenth-century English binding by Edwards of Halifax. Transparent vellum, painted on the underside, over white pasteboard; gold tooling. 24 × 16 × 5 cm.

transparent. The method (probably invented by his father, who remained based in Halifax) enabled scenes, usually classical or pastoral, to be painted on the underside; these showed through the vellum with great clarity, and ran no risk of rubbing off with wear. The designs sometimes recurred with variations on other books. The Edwards family was also renowned for another characteristic, the foredge painting, a skill which consisted of painting a scene on the edges of the leaves in such a way that the closed book revealed nothing but when the leaves were fanned the picture appeared. Quin's book has both characteristics; its foredge painting is of Shakespeare's birthplace.

Six bindings in the collection are positively authenticated as having been made by Roger Payne (active towards the end of the eighteenth century in London, died 1797), and there are at least ten others [136] for which there is no proof but which to a greater or lesser degree suggest Payne's tools or workmanship. Not one of the six is signed, nor are there any bills, but five have in Quin's hand on the endleaf a statement to the effect that they were bound by Payne. The sixth, on the Crevenna copy of the Vindelinus Virgil already discussed (Quin 64) has no such annotation, but Quin wrote beside the entry in both his catalogue and his notebook 'Bound by Roger Payne'. It is bound in highly polished olive morocco; the covers are tooled in gold to a panel design with fillets, flowers and lyres, these last repeated on the spine. The very deep turn-ins have gold fillets, lyres and sprays of flowers, there is a brown leather joint, the endpapers consist of a brown paper pastedown and free leaf, and the green headbands are single.

Henry Quin's will was proved in March 1805. It seemed at first as if the Treasury might retain the bookcase on technical grounds, because the position in the Manuscripts Room where he had requested that the case should stand was no longer available, as the Fagel collection, acquired in 1802, occupied the place. The legal difficulties were resolved, however, and Thomas Quin was able to make the final arrangements for the delivery of his brother's bookcase and boxes of books to Dr 'Jacky' Barrett, the Librarian, on 13 September 1805. And the conditions of the will were observed. The books still stand in his 'large mahogany book-case', now on the east gallery of the Long Room and facing, appropriately enough, the Manuscripts Department at the far end of the building; they have not been rebound, nor has any additional material or lettering been put on them, and they are handled with the care and respect he desired. Sadly he did not choose long life to enjoy his books. Once described by Renouard[15] as 'M. Quin, l'un des amateurs actuels qui chérit le plus les livres, et qui s'occupe avec un soin infatigable à embellir son intéressante collection', his epitaph, which appears in the second edition, concludes 'ses livres n'étoient donc pas pour lui *perfugium et solatium*, comme ils le furent pour Cicéron et pour tant d'autres'.

136. Eighteenth-century English binding, tools authenticated as those used by Roger Payne, though documentary evidence lacking. Straight-grain red morocco, tooled in gold. 23.8 × 14.2 × 3 cm.

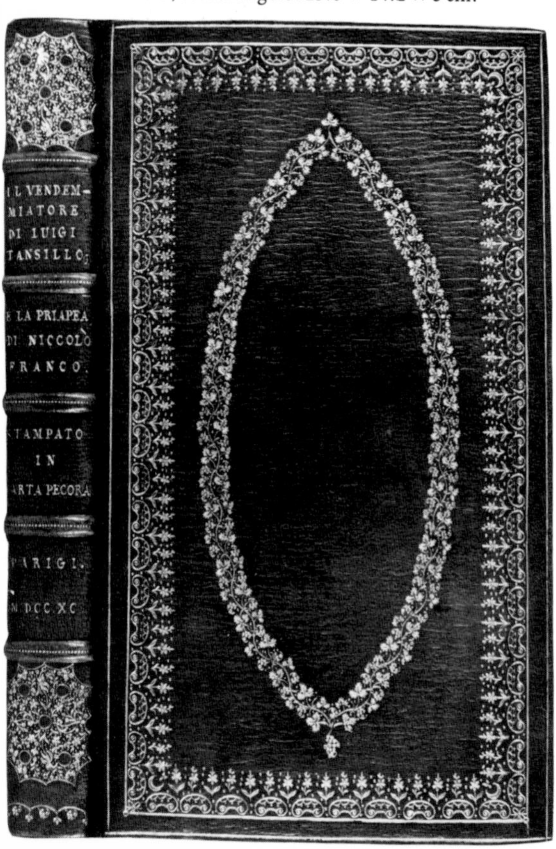

NOTES

1. T.P.C. Kirkpatrick, *Henry Quin, MD.* Dublin, 1919.

2. Walter Gordon Wheeler, 'Libraries in Ireland before 1855'. Unpublished thesis, University of London, 1957.

3. T.F. Dibdin, *Bibliomania; or book madness.* London, 1811, pp 695-6.

4. Veronica M.R. Morrow, 'Bibliotheca Quiniana'. Unpublished thesis, University of London, 1968.

5. Arthur Rau, 'Portrait of a bibliophile XII: Henry George Quin', *Collector* 13 (1964) plate II.

6. *Bookbindings from the library of Jean Grolier: exhibition... British Museum.* London, 1965.

7. G.D. Hobson, *Maioli, Canevari and others.* London, 1926.

8. Howard M. Nixon, *Sixteenth-century gold-tooled bookbindings in the Pierpont Morgan Library.* New York, 1971, p. 138.

9. Maurice Craig, *Irish bookbindings 1600-1800.* London, 1954, p.21.

10. Peter Fox, *Trinity College Library Dublin.* Dublin, 1982, ill. 12.

11. Rau, 'Portrait', plate IV.

12. Howard M. Nixon, *British bookbindings presented by Kenneth H. Oldaker.* London, 1982, no. 21 & ill.

13. Mirjam M. Foot, *The Henry Davis gift: II. North European bindings.* London, 1983, no. 89 & ill.

14. A.A.Renouard, *Annales de l'imprimerie des Alde.* 2e éd. Paris, 1825, vol.1, p.72.

NINETEENTH-CENTURY IRISH SONG CHAPBOOKS AND BALLAD SHEETS

HUGH SHIELDS

Around 1960 it was still possible — if only just — to pick up a recently-printed Dublin broadside ballad on a prize fight. By the mid sixties we find a Trinity College librarian hand-printing 'The cruelty of Barbara Allen. Wicklow version' from the singing of another Trinity librarian. These two phenomena look similar, but they were really quite different. The old 'ballats', as they were called, were in decline, and could not be revived by acts of piety.

The Trinity College broadside is noteworthy, all the same, for the College had no great history of study of popular song, traditional or other. One of its professors of Irish, Canon James Goodman, left the Library his manuscript volumes of tunes noted mainly from Munster pipers of the late nineteenth century: a valuable collection, which may not have to wait much longer for publication.[1] From a generation earlier, some papers of George Petrie also in the Library contain copies of tunes from his collection,[2] though the bulk of this is in the National Library. College alumni have included song-writers ranging from Tom Moore to Percy French. And James Clarence Mangan, who turned Gaelic songs into poetic if not particularly singable English versions, spent a little of his short life in employment in the Library itself, where his failings were probably more evident than his talent.

At a time when Irish folk music was not considered worthy of any attention at all in the university curriculum, it is not surprising that the Library claimed only some of the publications on folk music to which copyright law entitled it. The popular press, for its part, was quite innocent of copyright law. What is surprising, in these circumstances, is that the Library possesses as many as eight collections of nineteenth-century song chapbooks or broadside ballads, which comprise approximately 1600 Irish-printed items. Two other collections, being printed in Britain, fall outside our scope despite the preponderance of Irish songs in one of them; they and the few British items that found their way into the eight Irish collections are excluded from consideration here. The Irish ballads are our subject: prototypes of the hand-printed 'Barbara Allen' which date from an epoch when the rise of mass-produced newspapers was not yet proclaiming the imminent extinction of this diverse and exuberant medium.

Irish ballad sheets go back at least to 1626, when the oldest known Irish ballad, a black-letter text, was printed at Dublin.[3] It was a topical piece of limited interest, like most of those of the later seventeenth and the eighteenth century that are to be found in the Library in appreciable numbers. Not until the 1760s do traditional song-texts in folk idiom begin to appear in quantity in the Irish popular press — to judge at least from extant chapbook copies — but from that time forth they grow abundant. From that time too the chapbook format was preponderant down to about the 1830s, when broadside format again prevailed and chapbooks ceased to appear. The Library contains two volumes of song chapbooks printed mainly in Ireland and dating from the period of chapbook decline (Appendix, Sections **A** and **B**) [137].

Most of these chapbooks contain only song-texts, from two to ten in number; but since chapbooks, and to a diminishing extent broadsides, also admitted other kinds of text, we also find a prose dialogue 'The royal game at cards' (**A** 12) and two chantefables 'Beggars and ballad singers' (**A** 6) and 'The wake of Teddy Roe' (**B** 21). Other features of the collections, both chapbooks and broadsides, may be conveniently discussed after the broadsides have also been briefly set in their historical context. Though they contain a few sheets

137. Title page of a song chapbook of about 1830 (**B** 18). The dramatic subject of the woodcut does not illustrate any of the songs included.

Paddy the Piper.
Cease your Funning.
I'd be a Butterfly.
Saint Patrick was a Gentleman.
See the Conq'ring Hero comes.
Roy's Wife of Aldivaloch.
How oft in Dreams of Bliss.
Lullaby.
DUBLIN:
J. H. NORTH, 7, Old Church-street.

from Belfast, they represent, like the chapbooks, mainly southern towns of which the principal is Dublin. They extend over the remaining decades of the century except the nineties. Broadsides were printed and are sometimes preserved on large sheets containing ten, twelve or even sixteen items for cutting; but the Trinity collections are all of single slips with one or occasionally two song-texts, so that we may guess that they were bought 'retail', probably at fairs or on similar occasions.[4] They are listed in the Appendix in approximate chronology of printing, which brings us to the richest collection first (Appendix, Sections **C** to **H**).

The physical characteristics of the sheets present no surprises to those already familiar with the format: printed one side,[5] black on white, with rare exceptions using colour,[6] with or just as often without the printer's name and/or town, and almost always surmounted by a woodcut that is less likely to have been made specially for the text that follows than to have been part of an existing stock and probably inept: thus the goods train above the macaronic lament for other days 'Kilcash', here entitled 'In praise of Lady Butler' (**C** II 54) [138]. The conservation of old cuts is even more apparent in the chapbooks, where one cut is found passing from printer to printer (**A** 13 = **B** 15, 20), and others look distinctly antique with their eighteenth-century costumes, notably those of Goggin in Limerick (**A** 15-29). Of special interest too are the more contemporary depictions of popular musical practice: a blind fiddler (**B** 21), a blind uilleann piper (**F** 62), a Scots piper (**F** 75), a woman ballad singer with children (**B** 22, **C** II 164) [139], visually evoking a kind of scene given elsewhere in words:

There's Dolly and I, as ballads we cry,
  On a couple of stools see us stand;
The people flock around, as she bawls aloud,
  And I takes my fiddle in hand. — **A** 6

The occasional omission of woodcuts from the chapbooks is likely to have been for a particular reason: for example, to accommodate in **A** 3 (which contains a long 'garland' ballad of eighteenth-century cast, 'The Dublin tragedy') the long 'synoptic' title characteristic of these songs:

THE

Dublin Tragedy,

Or the Unfortunate

MERCHANT'S DAUGHTER,

IN TWO PARTS.

PART. I. Setting forth a brief and authentic account of a rich Merchant's Daughter in the town of Belfast, who was deluded by an Ensign in the army, and for love of him, dressed herself in man's apparel, and sailed with him to England, and were married at Stratford.

PART. II. How she bought a Lieutenant's Commission for him and became an Ensign herself and soon after went to America; also giving an account of their hardships whilst in an American Prison, shewing how after their return to Ireland, she was slighted by her false lover, and afterwards poisoned herself for his sake.

But in the latest collection of broadsides, **H**, it seems more likely that fairly frequent omission of woodcuts signifies nothing else than a decline of the medium. Before that time came, there was a vogue for large pictorial cuts, with or without text, and these are somewhat modestly illustrated here and there in **C** by, for example, the textless picture of a patriot in chains (John Mitchel? — I 172) [140].

The use of text in Irish, on the other hand, is more characteristic of the broadsides than the chapbooks, which have only two garbled Gaelic refrains, one simulating keening (**B** 21; cf. **B** 14). Texts in Irish on the sheets are hardly less garbled, with their crude orthography based on that of English; but they are usually texts of whole songs, or of songs half in Irish and half in English. Though they are far less

54

In praise of Lady Butler

Cod a yean hamede fastha gen Imod,
Is tha dere no goilte er lawr
Is gen tracht er cheelcosh na er a diloch,
Is nee builfur an chriel.go brach,
Mor is ounsude a choniech an di vaa,
Foor gradam agus miere har vna,
Go miech ierlee thairent on vroink oun,
Is an thafferan bieng da ra,
What shall we do now and hereafter
The woods and & groves they'e fallen ,
The elem, the oak, and the hezel,
And the popular straight and tall ;
The ashe that grew very spoutanuous,
Surroundiug its ivy wall
And the people exalting the praises,
Of beautiful Lady Vauus.
Nee clushim onoil lochia na gena un,
Na fhillar a deana eir er chuin,
na fue na masha chon sehar,
Hourach mil agus keare don slue,
Vieh chole bieng villich no nean oun,
Er avork a lea vre weng,
Is a chuheen er vorrie no greave oun,
Do chiroch on seal chon suine.
How lonesome we feel in this Island
Kilkash is lonesome from game,
Where the salmon and trout in season
And th: lambkins did sport and play ;
The back and doe in full chace there,
The mallard the grouse and the stag,
And the cuckoe melodiously chanting,
To lull them to sleep at ease.
A nish o chuig anguir no meen chrave,
Le thanhuve da meen har seul,
Irimshe er vira is er iesa,
Is go dogeshe a riest chiung slawn,
Mor is boirna tha euilaeht da cheene
Fuir srigad bee agus bawn,
Neer van rieve shelieve do vionterach
Toh corrid no veer vucthane,
Now as our Lady went over,
And deserted her native home,
We pray the Lord to restore her'
Again where she was before ;
For her tenauts egret her surely
Her apsence we do deplore,
The widow's and orphans she clothed,
And gave them safe abode.
Do rangiech go duchech she a riest chuing
Do vemist go lare go sauve,
Do vech rionke fodda guale thi ompol,
Clo e fiddle agus tiontha enave'
Do hkemisth cuirth vea hiosur,
A dielcosh so heese go hard,
Is go brach nu go duichech an dielan,
nee eoktee ei a riost er lawr.
If ever she chance to come home.
How happy we'd be at our ease,
With bonfiers & torches a blazing,
We'd congratulate this fair ;
With trumpets loud aeclamations,
And joyfully sound her praise,
And we'll prav to the mighty Johova,
To place her amongst the saint s.

138. A version half in English and half in Irish (spelt as English) of the well-known Waterford Gaelic lament *Cill Cais*: probably printed at Dublin in the 1860s.

numerous than the English texts, the phenomenon of their appearance from about the middle of the century is an interesting one, which must be somehow linked with the rise of national consciousness and the later, more learned, Gaelic revival.

Another kind of mingling that we have noticed in the chantefables of the chapbooks — that of prose and verse — is sustained and varied in the broadsides, some of which move further in the direction of journalism with a prose account of a disaster followed by a song-text on the same incident (**C** I 74-6, three shipwrecks). With them we broach the subject-matter of the song-texts, a brief discussion of which will appropriately conclude this commentary.

The Library's collections, though not abundant, are quite representative of the very varied subjects and styles found in the Irish popular press of the nineteenth century. Texts may be roughly grouped as follows:

1) Traditional songs in folk idiom, usually if at times only lightly retouched in written literary style. These include numerous songs of English or Scottish origin, from a few early ballads to quite recent songs, and a very diverse Irish repertory, some in Irish or macaronic, some translated from Irish, but the majority composed in the English of Ireland. From all these categories many of the broadside songs are still sung in Irish oral tradition today; the example of the 'Bold lieutenant/The fan' will serve to illustrate textual variation in time, space and medium — a broadside text and an oral version juxtaposed [142].

2) Social or political songs of local, newsworthy or ideological interest, such as murder songs — a conventional genre nourished by actual happenings — or the numerous songs that focus on the career or the memory of Daniel O'Connell. This category derives much of its poetic style from the preceding one.

3) Songs of urban origin, British and Irish, stylistically marked by an original theatrical, literary or sub-literary environment, including some songs imitating folk idiom. In this last group, 'Tim Finnigan' (H 63r. b, 'Finnegan's wake') often passes for the 'real thing'. More traditional in style are the poems of William Allingham, which appear in **C** without attribution: 'Lovely Mary Donnelly' (I 12, II 185b), 'Kitty O'Hay' (II 185a) and 'The milkmaid' (III 231), 'first editions' dating from the fifties[7] and in one case, 'Kitty O'Hay', including verses never again printed when the song was made known through a later literary edition. Broadsides rarely indicated authorship, to do which usually signified pretensions not strictly commercial, a feature sometimes underlined by abnormal

139. Ballad sheets on sale sung by the seller and her children: title-page of a song chapbook dating from about 1830 (**B** 22).

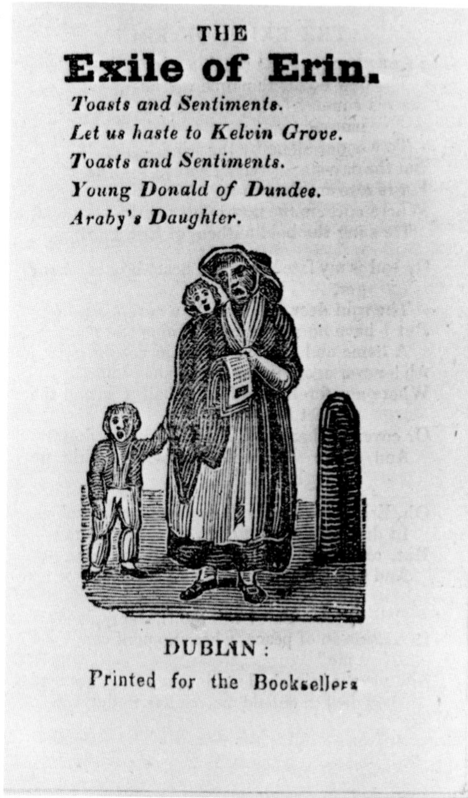

typography or format, as in the 'polite' verses of **F** 1, 2, 100 or **C** I 267 'The ould Tom Cat . . . Henriette M'Lean, Poetress'.

The variety of matter in the texts provides varied opportunities of research, research that has been too long deferred or, up to the present, too sloppily undertaken. Its emphasis may be *historical,* documenting social life more than political events or processes, though often illuminating these by showing a reflection of the popular reaction to them; *literary,* furnishing a socio-cultural background to major writings or major authors of the epoch, and, what is more natural to the medium itself, insights into oral poetry and rare songs or versions of poetic interest; and *ethnological,* indicating the popularity and extension of song types, themes, etc., and the persistence of texts, genres and features.

Little reflection is needed to perceive how thoroughly these branches of research are interrelated and how desirable it is to associate them and to avoid strictly separating song categories on the basis of them. More than most forms of literature, ballad sheets impress on their user the multi-faceted character of the social sciences, as much in what they do not say as in their often deficient statements. We need only think, for an example, of their resounding silence on the performance context of the songs and the component that gave them voice — the missing melodies[8] to which they were performed.

140. An Irish patriot in chains, perhaps John Mitchel.

NOTES

1. TCD MSS3194-7.
2. TCD MSS3262-3.
3. *Catalogue of a collection of printed broadsides . . . of the Society of Antiquaries of London,* ed. by R. Lemon. London, 1866, p. 78, no. 271.
4. See, however, description of **C** for pairs of songs.
5. **C** III 231, 241 are, however, printed on the verso of recycled paper already printed on one side (both Cashel).
6. In **C**, ink red (II 11) or blue (I 182); paper blue (II 61, III 153), green (II 191, III 201) or yellow (III 144): all sheets of Cashel origin?
7. H. Shields, 'William Allingham and folk song', *Hermathena* 117 (1974) 29-31.
8. Tune prescriptions like 'THE STAR OF SLANE./AIR.—"Youghal Harbour."' (**A** 41) are rare, and invoke in any case not just the performance of ballad seller or buyer, but the whole traditional environment.

APPENDIX

In references to printers' addresses, etc., round brackets enclose matter they do not always print, square brackets enclose editorial information or suggestions.

A 'Ballads bought from E.R.McC. Dix 1910 They were printed probably about 1840.', *manu 2a,* pencil, 'mostly [*inserted*] earlier to judge by references to a king and not a queen' — recto of first binding leaf. Bound in faded red cloth with title 'BALLADS' in gilt on the spine (cf. **D**); 106 × 167mm, leaves *c*.93 × 153mm. Sixty numbered eight-page song chapbooks all with title-page woodcuts except nos 3, 5, 12. Dublin: (R. Grace), 3 Mary St. (Cheapside), nos 1-8, (id.), 45 Capel St., nos 9-12; T. Coldwell, 50 Capel St., no. 13; 'for the Booksellers', no. 14 [North? — see **B**]. Limerick: S(tephen) B. Goggin, (15 George's St.), nos 15-29 (each has a second small cut surmounting p. 2). Waterford: W(alter) Kelly, nos 30-53 (46 = 47 except title page). [Omagh]: 'for Flying Stationers', no. 60. Nos 54-9 are British. Dates: 1816?-1843. TCD 66.u.165

B Twenty-three unnumbered eight-page song chapbooks bound in limp dark green board without inscription, 100 × 146mm, leaves *c*.92 × 144mm, all with title-page woodcuts. Dublin: [R. Grace], 45 Capel St., nos 3, 5, 6, 8, [id.], 3 Mary St., Cheapside, nos 9, 12; J.H. North, 7 Old Church St., nos 14-16, 18, 20 (= 15), 23; 'for the Booksellers', nos 17, 19, 21, 22 [North?]. Waterford: W. Kelly, nos 1, 2, 7, 10, 13. Dates: *c*.1828 until after 1837. TCD CC.m.77

C 'Bequeathed by John Davis White Esq [Cashel]' — pasted inside the front cover of vol. 1. A collection rearranged in three volumes *c*.1977 (formerly in two), bound in blue cloth board and inscribed on the spine in gilt 'IRISH BALLADS' followed by the respective volume number. Leaves 285 × 355mm, unnumbered. Items are mounted on rectos, usually two per page, and numbered: I 1-303, II 1-299, III 1-285 (lacks no. 52); numbering occasionally separates two texts that were printed together or unites two items of probable independent origin. Space does not permit as full a description as the collection deserves. Many printers' names occur, those of Haly of Cork and Birmingham of Dublin with special frequency. Belfast: Alex. Mayne, 7½ High St., III 107 etc. and James Moore, 40 Ann St., I 27; Clonmel: O'Flanagan, II 272; Cork: Joseph Haly, 56 Hanover St., I 204 etc. or 59 S. Main St., I 5 etc.; Dublin: W. Birmingham, 92 Thomas St., II 81 etc., P. Brereton, 1 Lr Exchange St., III 232, etc., 'Flying Stationers', III 248, J. Hanvey, Flag Alley, I 180 etc., J. Kirkwood, 13 Upr Ormond Quay, II 193, John F. Nugent, 35 Cook St., I 237 etc. or 88 Francis St., II 87, Ormond Printing House (pictures), III 76 etc., J. Richardson, 1 or 11 High St., III 35, or 63 Cook St., III 84; Johnstown, Kilkenny: T. Harrington, II 141 etc.; Limerick: John Pitt(s), I 26, 285 etc.; Tipperary: Risteard D'Alton, II 18; Waterford: J. M'Coy, Jail St., II 47, O'Keeffe, Patrick St., I 294 etc. or 18 George's St., I 218 etc., and John Troy, 40 Stephen St., II 101 etc.

There is much variety of format, including uncut parallel pairs of songs, often bearing imprints below both: II 39 a-b (Nugent), II 179 a-b (Birmingham) etc. A few sheets are English (II 160, 226, III 82-3, perhaps others). To judge from dates occurring in the texts, the collection was continued from 1848 to 1883; before the rearrangement of the volumes, some songs bore the MS note '1844'. TCD 189.t. 1-3(*ol.* 21.bb. 51-2)

D 'These street ballads were bought in England in spring 1911 for 10s-6d. Their date is about 1870 after which date such sheets became rarer, the issue practically ceasing before the end of the XIXth century' — recto of first binding leaf. Same binding as **A**, with the legend 'BALLADS' running from bottom to top of the spine; leaves 260 × 348mm. One paper folio at each end, 18 card folios, with 2-17 paginated 1-32. Sixty-two numbered sheets pasted down two per page, all with woodcuts except no. 39, some with tailpieces. The printer of all is evidently (P.) Brereton, Dublin: 1 Lr Exchange St., nos 1, 3, 7-11, 13-16, 18, 19, 21, 23-7, 29-31, 33, 38, 39, 41-3, 45, 46, 49, 50, 53-5, 61, 62; (id.), 56 (or 65) Cooke St., nos 17, 34, 35, 37, 40, 51, 57; others n.p.d. Date as above. P. 32 formerly contained several twentieth-century broadsides on Nationalist subjects. TCD OLS. 189.t.4 (*ol.* 82.a.40)

E Thirty uncatalogued and unnumbered loose sheets in an envelope, formerly owned by Denis Johnston and

141. Irish ballad sellers in the seventies: engraving from John Hand's pamphlet *Irish street ballads*, Liverpool, *c*. 1875.

142 (right). 'The bold lieutenant': a ballad sheet probably bought in 1844 (C I 85) with the beginning of a modern oral version (H. Shields, *Shamrock, rose and thistle: folk singing in north Derry*, Belfast 1981, p. 77).

The Bold Lieutenant.

In London city there lived a lady,
Who was possessed of a vast estate;
And she was courted by men of honour,
Lords, dukes, and earls on her did wait.
This lady made a resolution
To join in wedlock with none but he
That had signalized himself by valour,
All in the wars by land and sea.

There was two brothers who became lovers,
They both admired this lady fair,
And did endeavour to gain her favour,
Likewise to please her was all their care,
One of them bore a captain's commission,
Under the command of brave Col. Carr,
The other he was a noble lieutenant,
On board the Tiger man-of-war.

The eldest brother he was a captain,
Great protestations of love did make;
The youngest brother he swore he'd venture
His life and fortune all for her sake.
But now, said she, I'll find a way to try them,
To know which of them the sooner start,
And he that will then behave the bravest,
Shall be the governor of my heart.

She desired her coachman for to get ready
Early by the break of day,
The lady and her two warlike heroes,
To Tower-hill they road away.
When at the tower they had arrived,
She threw her fan into the lion's den,
Saying, he that wishes to gain a lady,
Must bring me back my fan again.

Then out bespoke the faint-hearted captain,
Who was distressed all in his mind,
To hostile danger I am no stranger,
To face my foe I am still inclined;
But here were lions and wild beasts roaring,
For to approach them I dont approve,
So therefore, madam, for fear of danger,
Some other champion must gain your love.

Then out bespoke the youngest brother,
With voice like thunder so loud and high,
To hostile danger I am no stranger,
I'll bring you back, love, your fan, or die.
He drew his sword, and he went amongst them
Those lions fawned and fell at his feet.
And then he stooped for the fan and brought it,
He says, is this it, my darling sweet?

The gallant action it now being over,
And to the lady he took his way;
While the lady in her coach sat trembling,
Thinking he would become the lion's prey.
But when she saw her brave hero coming,
And that no harm to him was done,
With open arms she did embrace him,
Saying, take the prize, love, you have won.

Soon the news to the king was carried,
How his lions they were all slain;
The king being not one bit displeased,
But kindly applauded him all for the same.
He altered him from a third lieutenant,
And made him admiral over the blue,
And to this lady that night got married,
See what the powers of love can do.

26. The fan

The bold lieutenant The lions' den The den of lions The lady's fan The glove and the lions The lover's test The faithful lover, or, the hero rewarded The distressed lady, or, a trial of true love The fairest lady in London city The Bostonshire lady

Eddie Butcher 1966

♩= 150 rubato
1 In sweet Ar · gyll - there - lived a l · a · dy
W · orth ten - th · ou - sand pounds a year
And for - - her w · it and her mild be · hav · iour
Few with this l · a - dy there - - could - com - pare.
This - la · dy she made - a re · so · lu - - tion·e
That she - - would w · ed with no one but he
Who - would pr · ove him·self brave by - val - iour
At·e the war -- by - - lan' or -- sea.
4:1-2
She ar-ose- the next mor·nin'- Ear·ly - by- the break of day
6:5-6, cf.5,8;7:1,8:1
He pulled the scab·bard from off his ree - - fer - And he m·an·ly -
2:7-8
lieu - ten·ant, He bein' head - barr·i·ster of

77

acquired in 1984; *c.*109 × 277mm. MS notes appear on a paper cover: 'Dups. from other collection £1.5.0' (E. R. McC. Dix?); *manu 2a* 'Dub 9-12-38 1-2-6'; *manu 3a* 'Evidently late 60s and early 70s'. They are also evidently all printed by (P.) Brereton — whose address at 1 Lr. Exchange St. alone occurs, cf. **D** — including the items with n.p.d.: nos 4-6, 9, 13, 17, 20, 27. Date as above.

TCD OL

F 127 uncatalogued and unnumbered loose sheets in a folder, mostly printed in Ireland (five or six in England), varying in size, with the text closely trimmed in many; fortuitously assembled? Dublin: (P.) Brereton, 1 Lr. Exchange St., nos 68, 73, 79, 80, 82, 84, 87, 93, 126, (id.), 55 Cooke St., nos 26, 112. [Ireland?], n.p.d.: nos 3-25, 27-38, 41-67, 69-72, 74, 76-8, 81, 83, 85, 88-92, 94-6, 98, 101-111, 113-125. Nos 1, 2, 100 are 'polite' items; nos 99, 127 are Irish handbills. Some duplicates. Dates: 1860s to 1880s (some songs on the informer James Carey, 1883).

TCD OL

G 'Street Ballads, and Cartoons' — paper pasted on to outside front cover. Accession May 1888. Scrapbook bound in faded red marbled boards trimmed with brown cloth over paper and red cloth. 89 grey unnumbered fols, 290 × 380mm. Fol. 1v coloured print; 2r poem; 3r-28r fifty broadside ballads and two newspaper cuttings, two per recto, some duplicates, dates 1867. Dublin: P. Brereton, 56 Cook St., 7b, 8b, 16a; 55 Cooke St., 12b; 1 Lr Exchange St., 9a, 10a, 12a, 14a, 17a; others n.p.d. [W.Birmingham?] 27a; [Nugent?] 3a. 11a, 13b have no cuts. Fols 29-55 rectos, 27 coloured political cartoons signed I.D. Reigh except fol. 45, 1880s (supplements to *Freeman's Journal*?). Fols 56-64 rectos, newspaper cartoons and cuttings, 1887; 65r., *Illustrated Times* 27 March 1858, 'The attack by the police on the students of Trinity College, Dublin'; fols 65-end, blank.

TCD Gall. R. 15.34

H 'A Collection of Irish Street Ballads' — MS, fol. 1r; accession date May 1888. A ledger ruled with blue and red lines, bound in marbled green board trimmed with leather; covers 210 × 332mm, loose. Leaves: unnumbered, here numbered 1-98 excluding the two binding leaves; uneven gatherings indicate removal of several leaves, 32-3 are at present loose. Two hundred and two sheets with two to each recto except that fols 26r, 31r, 94r and 95r have only one, and versos blank except that single, usually wide, sheets are on fols 1v, 27v, 30v, 40v, 41v, 42v, 59v, 61v, 69v, 82v. All with n.p.d., probably all Dublin [Nugent, some Brereton, and others?], 1870s and 1860s. Many sheets probably attributable to Nugent bear stock numbers. Thirty-eight sheets have no cuts or pictorial ornaments.

TCD Gall. R.15.35

143. An irrelevant but decorative Harlequin figure from a ballad sheet probably printed at Dublin around 1870 (**F** 45).

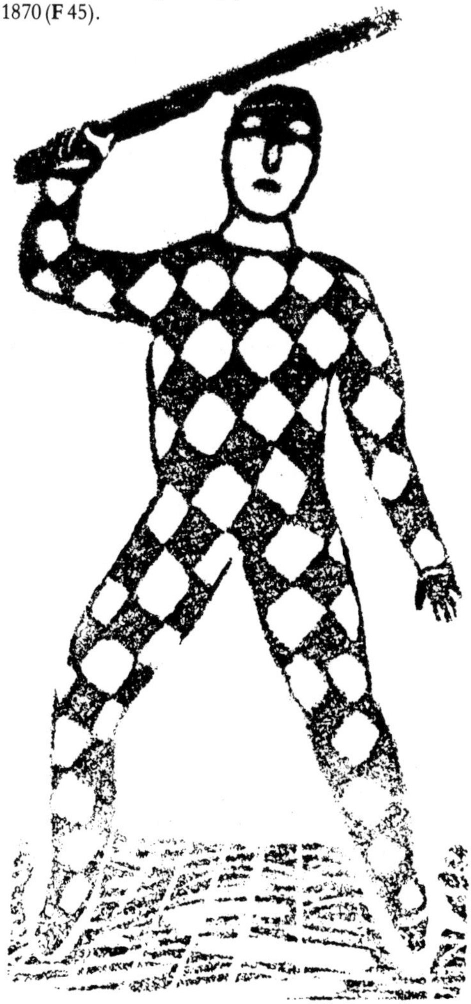

MICHAEL DAVITT'S TRAVELS ABROAD, 1884-1905

FELICITY O'MAHONY

The papers of Michael Davitt[1] (1846-1906) were presented to the Library by his son, Judge Cahir Davitt, in 1982. The collection had originally been put at the disposal of Professor T.W. Moody by the Davitt family during the many years of research for his work *Davitt and Irish revolution, 1846-82* (Oxford, 1981).

Davitt's career was an extraordinary one: founder of the Land League, parliamentarian, international humanitarian, labour leader, social reformer, promulgator of land nationalization, journalist, author, public speaker, traveller, patron of the GAA. The papers — correspondence, diaries, notebooks, press-cutting albums, legal papers, unpublished autobiographical writings, published articles and pamphlets, photographs, and other miscellaneous material — constitute an important, if incomplete, body of evidence for Davitt's career.

It is after 1882, as Davitt gradually distanced himself from the centre of Irish political affairs, that a more complete picture of his life emerges from his writings; there are in fact no original papers existing in the collection before 1870. Professor Moody has drawn largely on the retrospective writings among the Davitt papers but there remains a wealth of material covering the last twenty-four years of his life and, in particular, his travels abroad.

Weary of political agitation and acrimony, Davitt left London in December 1884, under the surveillance of a Scotland Yard detective, to embark on a five month tour to regain his health. As he was to do on all his major excursions abroad, Davitt recorded his experiences in great detail: in this instance he kept a diary (MS 9543) and an accompanying notebook (MS 9544). He spent five days in Paris; it was coincidentally the third New Year's Day he had passed in that city. The opportunity arose during his stay there to pursue his interest in continental revolutionary politics and political refugees. His notebook contains details of an interview on 5 January with a Jewish journalist, 'Moses', who had contact with various continental revolutionary parties. While in Turin, on 24 January 1885, he fulfilled a lifelong ambition when he met his boyhood hero, Louis Kossuth, the Hungarian patriot and political exile, recording in his notebook their discussion on the European political situation and the Irish land question. During his stay in Rome (2 February — 16 March) Davitt was surprised to learn that the French authorities had expelled James Stephens, the founder of the Irish Republican Brotherhood who had fled to Paris after the abortive Young Ireland rising of 1848, on suspicion of involvement in the dynamiting activities of Clan na Gael. He mentions the incident in his diary of 11 March 1885: 'What under heaven can have persuaded French Govt to lift poor old Stephens out of his obscurity & political shroud into the light of martyrdom & publicity ...'.[2] After Stephens's death in 1901 Davitt acquired his papers and they have been incorporated into the present collection as MS 9659d. The weeks spent in Rome allowed Davitt to recuperate and enjoy an unprecedented stretch of relaxation. Ill health was not however the sole reason for his departure from Ireland: a packet of shamrocks sent to him on St Patrick's Day prompted him to write: 'Wish I was there today and no cause for this tour. Have thought manytime since leaving that I was acting wrong to true interests of N[ational] Cause to leave country entirely in hands of P[arnell] Caucus .... It is hard to have to compel oneself to go away on account of the action of a few men whom one has helped to lift out of obscurity and who only seek their ambitious ends in the movement the control of which they have practically captured.'[3]

By 25 March Davitt had reached Alexandria and was savouring his initial experiences of the East. His impressions alternate between disgust at the squalor and clamour of the cities and fascination with the alien culture and vivid landscape. It was unlike anything he had ever experienced before and his notebook is filled with detailed descriptions of all he saw ranging from the picturesque to the bizarre: 'Saw a wretched looking old woman yesterday in Alexandria with the carcasses of three dead sheep in a huge wooden basin on her head!'[4]

He travelled extensively in the Holy Land in the company of a small party of pilgrims guided by a nineteen-year-old dragoman, Yosef, who delighted in running before Davitt's horse crying 'Mr Davitte, God safe Irlant'[5] [144]. He left Port Said on 18 April on his homeward voyage, travelling down the Suez Canal in a 'filthy, narrow, ugly, stinking oil-besmeared, noisy, badly managed abominable old tub . . . ',[6] and rose at daybreak to view De Lessep's great navigational feat.

In August 1886 Davitt arrived in New York to undertake a strenuous lecture tour across the United States and into Canada. He had been to America previously in 1878, 1880 and 1882, but this was the first occasion that he was to use a lecture tour to finance his own career in working for the Irish cause. Throughout the tour he was dogged by ill health and exhausted by endless reception committees, addresses and relentless travel.

His speeches on home rule and the land question received extensive coverage in the American press (MS 9611: press-cutting album) but Davitt was very disparaging about his performances, blaming them in part on the moderate policy he had to enunciate. His itinerary took him through the mid-west and from the Mississippi to San Francisco — territory he had covered in his 1878 and 1880 tours. He was struck by the growth and improvements in the cities since his previous visits. His memorandum book (MS 9547) contains lists of venues that follow one another with startling rapidity. He passed through some breathtaking scenery particularly during his visits to Canada in November, and again briefly in December, where he took a series of snapshots (MS 9649/255-306) [145, 146]. A more difficult aspect of the tour for Davitt, a man who shunned public adulation, was the processions and attendant ceremonies organized by Irish Americans wherever he went. On one occasion, arriving in Seattle at 5 a.m. on 12 October, he was met on board ship by an enthusiastic deputation; he accepted their arrival stoically: 'Poor fellows who could be vexed at such attention though it is a trifle inconvenient'.[7]

The tour did bring him one very great source of personal happiness: he had proposed to Mary Yore on 17 October at Oakland, California, where he had first met her in 1880, and her acceptance was to bring about a great change in his life: 'Thank Heaven there is a prospect now of home life and some peace'.[8] They married on 30 December and Davitt's final engagements in January 1887 closed with a triumphant farewell demonstration at Madison Square Garden before some 10,000 people.

144. Michael Davitt (second rider from right) at the foot of the Mount of Olives near Jerusalem, 11 April 1885 (MS 9649/235).

Davitt returned to America again from May to September 1891, spending much of his time with his wife and family in California as well as taking a health tour in north west Canada. He undertook no public duties but did give interviews to the press (MS 9619: press-cutting album) who were keen to receive his personal views on the Parnell divorce scandal and the rift in the Irish Parliamentary Party as well as his comments on the collapse of his shortlived newspaper, *The Labour World.*

In April 1895 Davitt embarked on a tour of the Antipodes. Another lecture tour, as much as he disliked the prospect, seemed the most ready solution to his pressing financial problems. He was already well known in Australia through his regular column in the *Melbourne Advocate* (MSS 9602, 9613, 9623: press-cutting albums) and could expect a generous response from the large Irish population who had settled in the colonies. On the outward journey, stopping briefly at Ceylon, he received the devastating news of the death of his eldest daughter, Kathleen: 'Here now am I journeying on to this lecture tour with a torn heart & all courage gone out of me. How am I to go through it all?'[9] He had undertaken the journey ultimately for the benefit of his family, and circumstances dictated that he should complete the task; it was a tragic irony that affected him deeply.

The lecture tour (May — November 1895) was a comprehensive one, omitting only the sparsely populated Northern Territory and the northern half of Western Australia. He recorded his experiences in a series of notebooks or diaries (MSS 9562-5), using a memorandum book (MS 9561) for details of his schedule, accounts and lists of snapshots. With characteristic efficiency he collected data on various aspects of Australian and New Zealand life — agriculture, land ownership, Murray River co-operative village settlements, labour politics, prison system, mining, sugar production, exploitation of cheap foreign labour, effects of colonization on the native Aborigines and Maoris — material he would later draw on for his book *Life and progress in Australasia* (London, 1898).

145. Photograph of Manitoba crofters taken by Michael Davitt in 1886 (MS 9649/296).

146. Canadian Indians trying to dodge Davitt's camera, 1886 (MS 9649/304).

Travelling through the mining towns of Queensland and Western Australia Davitt had the opportunity to witness the pioneering spirit at first hand. The towns were generally ramshackle affairs with few decent or even permanent buildings, scant water supply and whiskey in abundance. There are despairing references in his notebooks to drunks disrupting his lectures: on one memorable occasion at Cootamundra, New South Wales, the drunken and belligerent auditor had to be removed by a policeman from the lecture hall.[10] These venues were often only accessible by dirt roads through bush and scrub, travelling in intense heat and dust with the occasional break at a bush hotel such as he describes near the gold mining district of Coolgardie, Western Australia: '... the 50 Mile Criterion Hotel — a typical bush hotel. Material corrugated iron, wood & sacking — the walls inside being all sacking'[11] [147]. As an adjunct to the detailed descriptions in his notebooks he accumulated an interesting collection of photographs throughout the tour (MS 9649/307-459), a considerable number of which he had taken while visiting the gold mining districts.

Leaving Australia on 31 October, on board the 'Mararoa', Davitt prepared for the second leg of his tour in New Zealand. The tediousness of the voyage was alleviated by the discovery that Mark Twain was a fellow

147. Goldrush boarding house, Coolgardie, Western Australia. Photograph taken by Michael Davitt in 1895 (MS 9649/341).

passenger and similarly engaged on the lecture circuit. His schedule of twelve engagements concentrated on the South Island and, as in Australia, the lecture 'Labour Movement of Great Britain' (MS 9651/2: draft script) was in great demand, attracting a considerable number of non-Irish audiences. His seventy-first and final lecture at Auckland on 29 November was greeted with relief: 'May God grant I shall never again be compelled to resort to this hated work for the need of bread and butter'.[12] While sailing to Honolulu on the journey homeward Davitt met a son of J.P. Mahaffy (Provost of Trinity College, 1914-19) travelling to Fiji in agreeable company: 'Told me a chief had given him a daughter to marry *a la* Samoan I suppose, and waxed eloquent over her charms'.[13] He promised personally to assure Mahaffy of his son's good health.

In February 1900 Davitt left for South Africa, commissioned by the *New York Journal* and the *Freeman's Journal* to report on the Boer war. His fervent opposition to the outbreak of the war in October 1899 had been clearly demonstrated by his resignation from parliament after a powerful speech in the House of Commons indicting Britain as the unprincipled aggressor. His withdrawal was a serious loss to the Irish Parliamentary Party but won him widespread acclaim for his political sincerity (MS 9668: press-cuttting album). Letters poured in endorsing his stance (MSS 9418-19); W. B. Yeats wrote in acknowledgement of his idealism: '... I think a speech like yours is just the kind of speech we most need to lift our politics to their old nobility & out of the Depression of the last four or five years. You spoke as Davis or Mitchel might have spoken.'[14] He used his regular column in the *Melbourne Advocate* to deliver scathing attacks on the British government and all those who condoned its action; describing the mass demonstration in Dublin during Colonial Secretary Joseph Chamberlain's visit to Dublin, to receive an honorary LL.D. degree from Trinity in December 1899, he wrote: 'The visit was in every way worthy of the college and of Mr Chamberlain ...'[15] [148].

From the time of his arrival at Pretoria on 26

March until his departure on 14 May Davitt associated almost exclusively with the Boers. He stayed in Boer camps in the Transvaal and Orange Free State, interviewing the generals and their men, filling his notebooks (MSS 9572/1-2, 9573, 9660) with their accounts of military engagements and photographing forts and battle positions (MS 9649/469-497). He wrote to his friend James Collins before heading back to the front: 'I never had a more glorious time'.[16]

It was difficult however to retain the objectivity of an impartial observer as Davitt constantly perceived parallels between the patriotic struggle of the Boers and that of the Irish nationalists. He acknowledged this bias writing in his notebook on 4 April after witnessing the arrival of about four hundred English prisoners in Pretoria: 'I cannot well describe the feeling which the scene created in my mind: a personal sympathy towards them as prisoners: a political feeling that the Enemy of Ireland and of Nationality was humiliated before me and that I stood in one of the few places in the world in which the power of England was weak, helpless and despised'[17] [149].

Davitt continued to voice his indignation against Britain's part in the war on his return to Ireland. He visited America in 1901 and 1902; on both occasions he exploited the extensive press coverage generated by his visits to condemn the war as the 'crime of the century', attacking the British government for waging a dishonourable and barbaric war on the Boer republics (MSS 9668-9: press-cutting albums). The material he had collected during his stay in South Africa was the basis for his book *The Boer fight for freedom* (New York and London, 1902). It was widely hailed as the definitive work on the Boer war by the Irish and American press and not surprisingly was more coolly received in Britain (MS 9672: press-cutting album). His work had by now firmly established him as a journalist of international standing — a reputation that would be further consolidated in the following years.

In May 1903 Davitt was commissioned by the *New York Journal* to report on the recent anti-Semitic pogrom at Kishineff in the Russian province of Bessarabia. As a result of this assignment he wrote his fifth book *Within the pale: the true story of anti-Semitic persecution in Russia* (London, 1903). As an investigative journalist Davitt was at his best, assembling and interpreting evidence with professional

The 'Absent-minded Beggars,'
or
FRIENDS IN ADVERSITY.
DEGREE
T.C.D
CHAMBERLAIN:—"What, my dear Methuen, is the meaning of this! Where is your 'Parade Uniform'?"
METHUEN:—"Being 'absent-minded' lately I had to allow those 'beggarly' Boers to take possession of my luggage—but may I ask you where is your Statesman Costume?"
CHAMBERLAIN:—"Are you not aware that I lost it a few days ago at Leicester, and I am going over to Dublin where I hope to recover it at Trinity College by 'Degrees.'"

148. Newspaper cartoon satirizing Joseph Chamberlain and his award of an honorary degree from Trinity College in 1899 (MS 9669, fol. 43v).

April 4. 9 p.m. Just returned from Railway Station after witnessing the arrival of some 400 English prisoners from the British defeat at Sannahpost. I cannot well describe the feeling which the scene created in my mind. A personal ~~[illegible]~~ sympathy towards them as prisoners. A political feeling that the enemy of Ireland and of nationality was humiliated before me and that I stood in one of the few places in the world in which the power of England was weak helpless & despised. The men looked completely unconcerned at their position. They hung out of the carriage windows in groups gazing at the quiet crowd which received them without a word of insult or a single observation of any kind, a curious inquisitive good tempered crowd. The few Officers who could be seen looked bored & humiliated. One of them with a fine head & face kept his head on his hand most of the time and looked as if he keenly felt his unfortunate position. The Officers were in a first class saloon carriage, while the Tommies who appeared to be a strapping lot skill. He compiled two notebooks (MSS 9577-8) and a series of notes, reports and observations (MSS 9503-5) during his investigations, which were to form the basis of his newspaper reports and, eventually, his book. His efforts to establish the true origins of racial antipathy towards the Jewish populace in Kishineff and to substantiate the rumours surrounding the pogrom were exhaustive. Among his collection of photographs taken in Russia (MS 9649/499-504) are some of those especially commissioned for his newspaper reports on the victims of the violence [151].

The horrifying catalogue of murder, rape and injury that emerged from his research left Davitt profoundly concerned for the future safety of Russian Jews. The only viable remedy as he saw it was outlined in his unpublished article entitled 'The problem of the Russian Jew': 'I have come from a journey through the Jewish Pale a convinced believer in the remedy of Zionism'.[18]

Davitt returned to Russia in June 1904 to report on the civil unrest, which would eventually erupt as the 'revolution of 1905'. Hearst American Newspapers commissioned him to return there in January 1905 to investigate further Russia's internal troubles. His experiences during these two visits are recorded in a series of notebooks and diaries (MSS 9579-83). During January and February 1905 he visited St Petersburg, Moscow, Warsaw and also Helsingfors, Finland, where a working-men's procession took place in February in sympathy with the labour movement in St Petersburg. His investigations led him to believe that the labour strikes were the work of trade unionists rather than revolutionaries and that the government had blundered grievously in retaliating with military force. Moreover the international press had exacerbated the situation by, as Davitt saw it, deliberately exaggerating reports of impending revolution with the intention of undermining Russia's financial credibility in the Russo-Japanese war. His attacks on the British press were the most vitriolic, accusing Britain, as an ally of Japan, of 'warring against Russia on the safer but far less honourable field of calumny'.[19] A storm of protest erupted in the American press during his visit there in April 1904 (MSS 9624, 9673-5): his championing of Russia was denounced not alone for its anti-English bias but as inconceivable from one who had only the previous year criticized the Russian administration for failing to protect its Jewish citizens [150].

The highlights of these last two visits to Russia were undoubtedly his visits to Leo Tolstoy at Yasnia. On both occasions Davitt kept a detailed record of their conversation;

149 (far left). Excerpt from Michael Davitt's Boer War notebook, 4 April 1900 (MS 9572/1, p. 121).

150. Cartoon from *The Lepracaun* portraying Michael Davitt as 'pro-Russian', May 1905 (MS 9673, fol. 20v).

151. Michael Davitt (middle row, second from right) with a group of Russian Jews, Kishineff, 24 March 1903 (MS 9649/499).

firstly on 22 June 1904 (MS 9580: notebook) and again on 2 February 1905 (MS 9524: letter book). Ironically, on their first meeting Tolstoy saluted Davitt as an Englishman, expressing his admiration for the English race and their love of freedom. Davitt in response spoke at length on the Irish stuggle for independence — a cause Tolstoy knew little about and one for which Davitt was anxious to enlist his sympathies. Tolstoy expressed great interest in many of the countries Davitt had visited during his career and regretted the fact that he was now too old to realize his ambition of visiting America. When Davitt urged him to do so, citing his own twenty-six Atlantic crossings as encouragement, he received the response: 'But it cost you very much of your time, and life is short'.[20]

NOTES

1. TCD MSS 9320-9681.
2. TCD MS 9543, p. 70.
3. TCD MS 9543, p. 76.
4. TCD MS 9543, p. 87.
5. TCD MS 9544, fol. 22v.
6. TCD MS 9543, p. 108.
7. TCD MS 9545, p. 285.
8. TCD MS 9545, p. 281.
9. TCD MS 9663b/83v.
10. TCD MS 9564, fol. 100.
11. TCD MS 9565, fol. 32v.
12. TCD MS 9565, fol. 34v.
13. TCD MS 9566, fol. 14.
14. TCD MS 9418/1994.
15. TCD MS 9623, fol. 19a.
16. TCD MS 9659c/75 (xerox copy of letter).
17. TCD MS 9572/1, p. 121.
18. TCD MS 9651, pp 44-5.
19. TCD MS 9509/5547, fol. 4.
20. TCD MS 9580, fol. 63.

THE DILLON PAPERS

STUART Ó SEANÓIR

John Dillon was born in Blackrock, County Dublin on 4 September 1851. He was one of Ireland's leading politicians from 1880 to 1918 and continuously MP for east Mayo from 1885 until 1918.

A full biography of John Dillon has been written by the late Provost of Trinity College, Dr F.S.L. Lyons.[1] A principal source for the biography is the Dillon Papers now in the College Library. These papers occupy about four square metres of shelving and constitute TCD MSS 6455-6909. They descended from John Dillon to his son Professor Myles Dillon who presented them to the Library in November 1975. They had already been exploited by Dr Lyons, in preparation for several of his books, and by some other researchers. When they arrived in Trinity a high priority was given to sorting, arranging, listing and describing them volume by volume and letter by letter, often retaining an arrangement that goes back to John Dillon's time, and making them available to readers in the Manuscripts Department. Eleven volumes of such lists and descriptions are now available.

Dillon's father, John Blake Dillon, was a barrister and co-founder of *The Nation* (1842). He married Adelaide Hart, member of a Dublin barrister family, in 1847. Associated with the 1848 rebellion, he had to escape arrest and go into exile in the USA. John Dillon was born on one of his mother's visits home. After the family returned to Ireland in 1855 and following the subsequent death of his parents, John and his siblings were looked after by the Harts and by a cousin, Anne Deane. John went to the Catholic University, graduated in arts and qualified in surgery in December 1877. He retained a lifelong, often hypochondriacal, interest in medicine, commenting in December 1876 'this belief is so terrible a Demon ... it robs me of Hope' — and he suffered from dyspepsia and other disorders throughout his life [152].

Dillon became involved in the Home Rule League from 1873 and the Tenant Right Association from 1877. He supported the Parnellite group in parliament against Butt and joined the newly formed Land League in 1879, taking a lead in it during Davitt's imprisonment and touring the USA in its support. Elected for Tipperary in 1880 as a Parnellite he was in 1881 twice imprisoned in Kilmainham, once under the Coercion Act and once for sabotaging the Land Act. He resigned his seat in 1882, ostensibly for health reasons, travelled in Europe and stayed with his brother in Colorado, returning in 1885 as Parliament was being dissolved. He joined the Irish National League and won a seat in east Mayo which he was to keep continuously until 1918. He promoted the tenants' cause, or the plan of campaign against the landlords, from 1886 and organized support over the next twenty years. This included fund-raising tours in the USA, Australia and New Zealand and agitation for, and discussion of, new legislation. In 1888 he was imprisoned in

Dundalk for incitement to non-payment of rent but released early for health reasons. He then (1889) went on a fund-raising tour in Australasia. Arrested in 1890 he jumped bail and stayed in the USA until the Boulogne negotiations over Parnell's leadership (following his part in the O'Shea divorce and the Liberal reaction to further co-operation with him). He returned and was imprisoned in February 1891 (released on 30 July).

Now a committed anti-Parnellite he faced within that party a faction led by T. M. Healy. In 1895 Dillon married Elizabeth Mathew (she died in 1907). He became leader of his party in 1896 but in the reunion of the nationalists in 1900 he supported Redmond for leader. Dillon and William O'Brien had been closely tied since early Land League days but they split over O'Brien's acceptance of the 'Land Conference' conciliation policy, which arose from a suggestion of Captain Shawe Taylor in September 1902 and which led to further legislation and funding for the purchase of land by tenants. As second to Redmond — though diverging from him on many points such as his attitude to Ireland's involvement in the Great War and his reaction to the 1916 rising — he was engaged in the party's negotiations for Home Rule legislation in the 1912-16 period and he succeeded Redmond on his death in 1918, only to lose his seat in the October election of the same year when the electorate swung to the abstentionist, new Sinn Féin. Thus by-passed by new political developments, he retired from public life and died in London on 4 August 1927.

152. John Dillon as a young man (MS 6898/31).

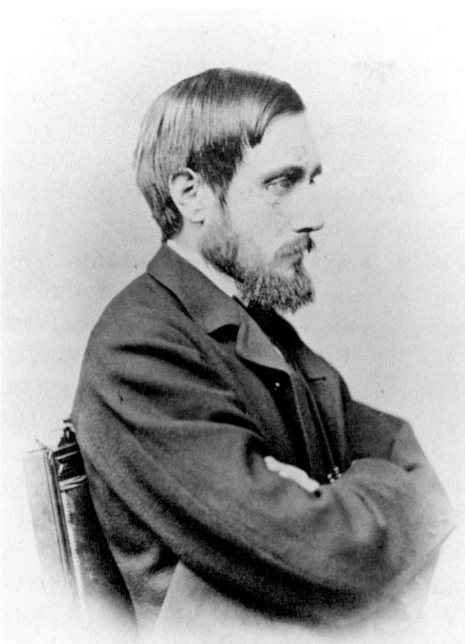

John Dillon stood for a party based on Ireland, nationalism and autonomy. A series of parties, formed around, successively, Daniel O'Connell, Isaac Butt, Charles Stewart Parnell and thereafter (less dominated by single personalities, and split by the controversies over Parnell) led by Justin McCarthy, John Dillon and John Redmond, constituted a bloc in the Westminster House of Commons. They sought not to participate in the government of the United Kingdom and British Empire but to have a parliament in Dublin for an autonomous Irish state under the British crown. Although Home Rule legislation was successfully passed in the Westminster House of Commons, it was, until 1914, rejected in the Lords. The 1912-14 legislation, which became law, had been suspended by amending legislation and was replaced by new legislation in 1920 and 1922. By that time Sinn Féin, a party demanding complete independence for Ireland, preferably as a republic, had won the vast majority of seats (including practically all of the seats outside Ulster) and John Dillon was in retirement. The goal of Home Rule was not achieved, but rather partition, with a mixture of independence for twenty-six counties and Home Rule in Northern Ireland for six counties, an arrangement which endured into our own time.

The failure to achieve their objective and the displacement of the idea of Home Rule by that of an independent republic cast a cloud over the work of these Irish nationalist parliamentarians for the forty years after the gaining of independence. But they have now passed into the fully historical field and not only the standard biographies of Dillon and Parnell but also the standard history of the period[2] have been written.

John Dillon preserved the vast majority of the correspondence he received throughout his life, and the bulk of it survives today. He sometimes kept copies and summaries of letters he wrote to others, especially in the shorthand letterbooks of 1887-97. He kept notebooks (variously described as journals, commonplace books, 'indicators', memo-books and diaries) and at times an annual pocket diary, but not all of these have survived. In addition there were scrapbooks of newspaper cuttings, loose cuttings, financial papers, notes for political speeches. There are also the papers of the previous generation: correspondence of his parents, and of the firm of Hart and O'Hara. A further large section contains the papers he acquired through his involvement in the Irish Parliamentary Party, and in the Evicted Tenants Committee. Dillon's own letters to others survive in such places as the papers of Michael Davitt (also in the Library), William O'Brien and John Redmond.

CORRESPONDENCE

John Dillon's correspondence was voluminous; his surviving incoming correspondence covers several metres of shelving. His principal correspondents were his political colleagues: there are letters from William O'Brien (1100 — all figures are approximate), T.P. O'Connor (1000), John Redmond and his secretary (700), the publishers of the *Freeman's Journal* (350) (and almost as many from its editors), Edward Blake (340), Joseph Devlin, a leading member of the Ulster nationalists who survived the election of 1918 (300), Laurence Ginnell, an office secretary who later joined Sinn Féin (300), and Michael Davitt (300). There is correspondence from most of Dillon's fellow Irish MPs including such political adversaries as Isaac Butt, T.M. Healy, Horace Plunkett and T. Harrington.

In arranging the papers it seemed appropriate to create categories for the (Catholic) clergy, journalists and some lady friends. The clergy correspondence includes Father Denis O'Hara, a relation of Dillon's working in County Mayo (127), Patrick O'Donnell, Bishop of Raphoe and later cardinal (120), and William J. Walsh, Archbishop of Dublin (96). There are some harsh comments from Dillon in this connection and the bishops and clergy usually, in Dillon's view, are on the wrong side. For example on 16 September 1890 he refers to the '"dastardly" attitude of a number of the Bishops and priests. After all is there enough good in the Irish race to redeem it?';[3] on 24 April 1900 to the 'Speech of Card. Logue ... worst class of ecclesiastical politician. This man has done immense mischief in Irish politics'; and on 12 February 1903 'Vitriolic letter from Dr Walsh. He is a strange man'.[4]

There is also correspondence with the United States, Australia and New Zealand, where he travelled. Wilfrid Scawen Blunt (140 items) and Edward G. Browne (90) were the most prominent amongst those who kept him in touch with Britain's policies in Egypt and Persia but there were other informants too (200 letters). In addition there are about 2800 letters from other Irish correspondents and 700 from British correspondents. His most frequent English political correspondents were the Irish Chief Secretaries John Morley and Augustine Birrell (about 120 each). Irish civil servants and law officers (220) also feature. There is an extensive two-way correspondence with his wife (900 items) and other close relatives such as his brothers, William in Colorado and Chicago (500) and Henry (religious name Father Nicholas)

the Sinn Feiners — had
entrenched themselves in
Stephen Green — and
were marching on the Castle
He had followed them
for some distance —
And then when firing commenced
they nearly ran away —
He also told us that
they were in possession
of the General Post Office

(200), his cousin, Mrs Anne Deane (400) and his wife's mother, Elizabeth, Lady Mathew (150) [153].

NOTEBOOKS, JOURNALS

John Dillon liked to, and felt he needed to, record his thoughts in notebooks. Not all his notebooks have survived; there are seventy-nine in this collection.[5] They range in date from August 1876 to December 1926. Some include his personal and political expenses; there are also his foolscap notes from reading, notes in exercise books and on loose leaves. The contents vary over the years: at first numerous entries concern his personal medical problems and his attendant hypochondria but somewhat later his predominant subject is politics [154]. There are some notebooks intended for specific subjects and so labelled ('books'; 'Irish history'; 'politics'; '*Freeman's Journal* business 1892'; 'the South African War'; 'Irish and General politics'), but more general notebooks were being kept at the same time, sometimes two (one for the pocket and one for his 'room', or one for memoranda and accounts and one for his 'journal' and commonplaces).

The fever points of his note keeping were 1888-90 for which there are entries in no less than thirty notebooks and 1876 which appears in seven. Notebooks from before August 1876 were extant when P.J. Hooper was compiling his intended biography of Dillon and copies of entries selected by him are available. No entries for 1879, 1896, 1908-14, or 1927 (the year of his death) can be located. Entries after 1900 are few, though one political notebook for 1892-1904 contains interesting material for those years.

Dillon records his thoughts and particularly reminds himself to buy or to read books, and to reorganize his life (especially his room, his chair, his notebooks, his desk and his papers). He notes questions to which he would like the answers. He makes regular, evidently unsuccessful, resolutions on these and other subjects. He deplores his own state of mind, laziness, state of health and life style. He comments on religion and art, literature and medicine. He records books read — not only in English but also in German, occasionally in French and apparently Italian — on a very wide range of subjects. He gives expression to his feelings, his fight against 'lust', his intellectual enquiries and thoughts, and his hopes to write: he proposes at various times to write a history of 1848, of his own circle, of the reception of the Intermediate Education Bill, of the Isles of Aran, of the 1692-1803 period, of Ireland during the nineteenth century, and an introduction for his brother William's biography of John Mitchel, and he imagines the value of a journal of the 1913-16 period (if only he had been writing a journal at that time!). He was intending also to construct a grammar (of Icelandic apparently). He never managed to write any such works.

COLLECTED PAPERS

More than half of the Dillon Papers are not Dillon's own work but consist of correspondence and the papers that came into his hands through committees or family relationships. Because of Dillon's prominent position in the parliamentary party and in its supporting organizations, he acquired several party minute books for the years 1886 to 1900. The crucial debates over Parnell's situation are not minuted but recorded by using cuttings from the *Freeman's Journal* for 26 November to 6 December 1890. The support organizations included the Irish National Federation and the United Irish League; minute books and letter-books covering 1890-9 and 1902-6 are present. Collections and funds were set up (the Home Rule Fund, the National Fund, the Irish National Fund, the Paris Fund) and also

153. Dillon records the 1916 rising daily for Lady Mathew (MS 9820, fol. 1v-2r).

various special committees (Irish Tenants Defence Association, the Evicted Tenants Committee).

A particularly large section of papers are the dealings of the Evicted Tenants Committee with the Irish National Federation's local committees: there are several thousand letters from tenants, or from local committee members and priests on their behalf, appealing for financial help, and there are records of contributions made by the corresponding parishes to various central funds. 'Parnellite' or Redmondite Irish National League local committees after the split do not feature much here but 194 areas and fifty-one individuals or estates are represented from most parts of Ireland. Almost all the papers cover the period 1893-7 and thus come from after the 'Plan of Campaign' experiment. The administration of the funds fell mainly to Sheehy and J.F.X. O'Brien and the day to day correspondence to J.C. Rooney and Laurence Ginnell (whose comments on some claims for grants are caustic), but Dillon's advice was sought at all times and annotations made accordingly. In addition there is similar correspondence con-

154. Dillon notes a new era: obstructing business in the House of Commons (MS 6551).

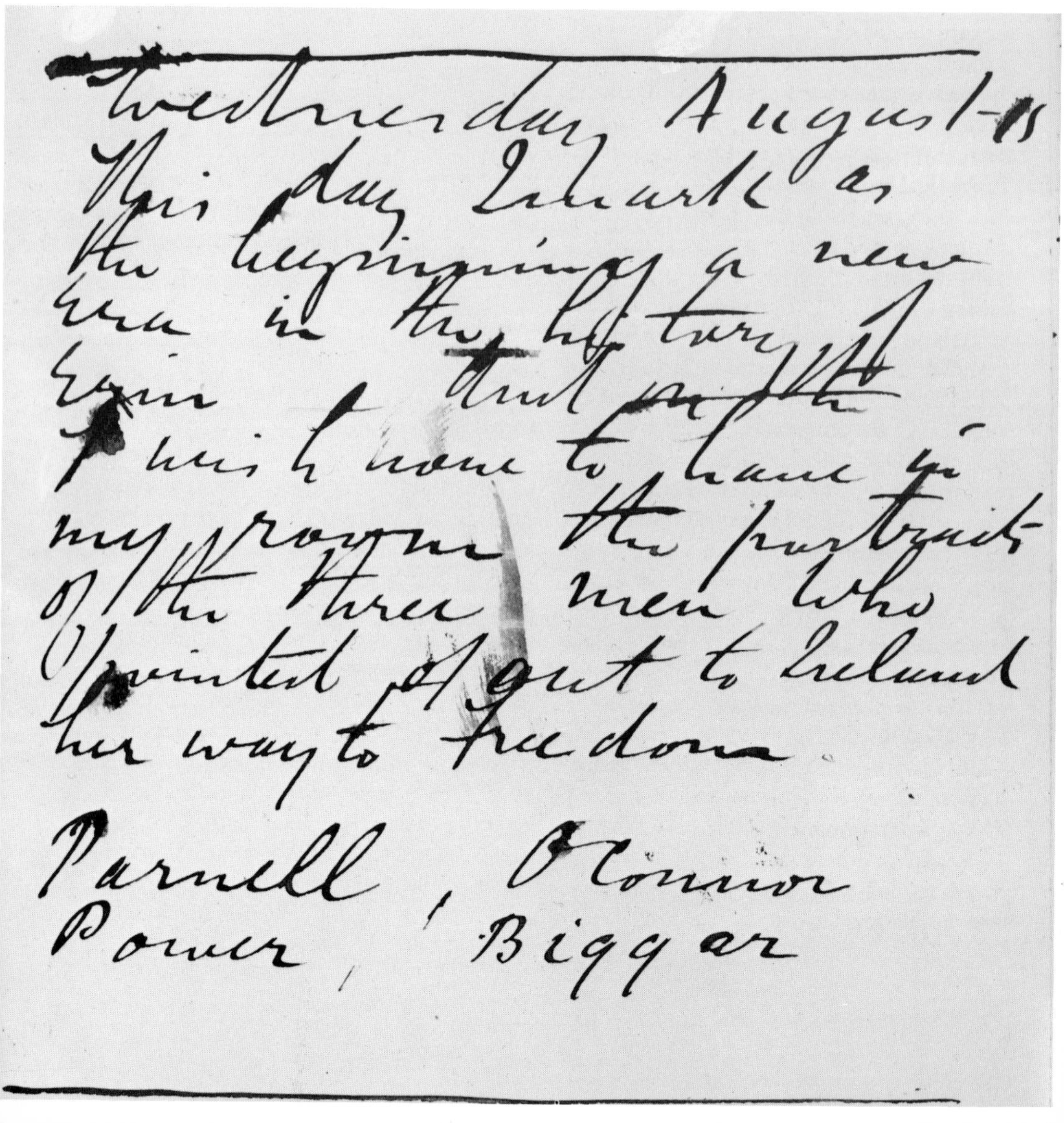
Wednesday August 18
This day I mark as
the beginning of a new
era in the history of
Erin and
I wish now to have in
my room the portraits
of the three men who
pointed out to Ireland
her way to freedom.

Parnell, O'Connor
Power, Biggar

cerning the Smith-Barry estate's town-tenants in Tipperary (fifty-eight files and 350 other items).

Papers of the previous generation of the Dillon (and on the maternal side Hart) family passed into the collection. Dillon occupied the Hart house, 2 North Great George's Street, Dublin, for most of his life. His elder brother William moved to the USA for the sake of his health and his younger brother Henry became a Franciscan monk, but this did not lead to dispersal of the papers. The correspondence of his father, John Blake Dillon, opens shortly before his marriage to Adelaide Hart in 1847 and is much taken up with his letters to her from 1848 to 1855. As a Young Ireland exile he commented on Irish America and the USA generally and on church-state affairs at home in Ireland and on the continent.[6] There are both private and business papers of Charles Hart, and Henry and Robin O'Hara, partners in the legal firm of Hart & O'Hara.

A thirty-eight volume diary of Elizabeth Mathew among these papers covers 1879 to 1904. Much of this precedes her marriage to Dillon (1895 to 1907); there are also her household records during her marriage. Another family member is his cousin, Mrs Anne Deane, née Duff, proprietress of the Monica Duff business at Ballaghadereen, County Mayo. Much of her incoming correspondence, including letters from Elizabeth Dillon (105 items) and from various members of religious orders, religious bodies and charities, and some other papers are in the collection.

The Dillon Papers present us with a portrait of a leading Irish Catholic nationalist politician in the pre-independence, 'Home Rule' era. We see Ireland, however reluctant, in the context of the United Kingdom and British Empire. We have glimpses too of many of Dillon's contemporaries and of the problems of Ireland in the fields of land-tenancy, nationalism, administration and government, and the relationship of politics and religion.

NOTES

1. F.S.L. Lyons, *John Dillon: a biography*. London: Routledge & Kegan Paul, 1968.

2. F.S.L. Lyons, *Ireland since the famine*. London: Weidenfeld and Nicholson, 1971.

3. TCD MS 6566.

4. TCD MS 6542.

5. Two diaries or notebooks covering 1919-21 are known to be in the P. S. O'Hegarty collection in the University of Kansas.

6. For this summary I am indebted to Mr Brendan Ó Cathaoir who is engaged in research on John Blake Dillon.

'ENTRE NOUS': SOME NOTES BY ERSKINE CHILDERS ON THE MAKING OF THE ANGLO-IRISH TREATY, 1921

JOHN BOWMAN

In almost every respect Erskine Childers was atypical of his generation of Irish Republicans. This was especially so in his attitude to written records. Whereas most of his colleagues are unrepresented in the political archives of the country, having failed to deposit, accumulate or perhaps even generate written materials, Childers 'the wordsmith, the rigid logician'[1] has left a voluminous collection of papers, now housed in the Manuscripts Department of the Library.[2]

He was a prolific writer: as a constitutional theorist he worked through a number of drafts of any document under preparation; as a member of any committee he expected his colleagues to conform to orthodox work methods with important matters noted in writing; he himself — whenever time allowed — kept a private diary; and when apart he and his wife Molly were usually in daily correspondence. He was a prodigious worker remembered by his friend Basil Williams as capable of continuing his writing even when friends called on him, 'oblivious to all the talk around him'.[3] Moreover he hoarded his papers [155], and his widow in turn sheltered them from various depradations. Many such collections were broken up following house raids by Black and Tans or later by the security forces of the new state. The collection is one of the most important of any political figure in Ireland during one of the most critical periods in modern Irish history, 1916-22.

Born in 1870 to an English father and Anglo-Irish mother and orphaned as a young boy, Childers was brought up with his cousins the Bartons in Glendalough House in County Wicklow, but his education, at Haileybury and Cambridge, was entirely English. Later he worked as Committee Clerk of the House of Commons from 1894 to 1910. He was also a man of action: he had been wounded in the Boer War; helped ferry guns to Ireland in the Howth Gun Running; and served in the Royal Navy air corps in 1916 earning the DSO. He was a member of the secretariat of Lloyd George's Irish Convention in 1917. It was only as late as 1919 that he

155. Greetings from a friend (Frank Gallagher).

decided that his allegiance would be wholly to Ireland. He was elected to the Dáil, became director of publicity for Sinn Fein and editor of the Republican propaganda paper *The Irish Bulletin*. 'Painstaking, methodical and brilliant'[4] in de Valera's view, he was appointed Secretary to the Irish delegation at the Anglo-Irish talks that led to the signing of the Treaty. Passionately opposed to its terms, his role remained that of propagandist of the Republican side in the Civil War. Arrested and court-martialled for being in possession of a gun he was executed in November 1922 [156].

An unlikely convert to Irish nationalism, his change of allegiance is manifest in his private papers. In March 1919 he wrote to Molly: 'I think much about our future and at present the idea is gaining strength in me that I should work in Ireland. It is far the less easy course in every way and it is for that reason I think that I feel impelled towards it... I think on reflection you are right about the necessity of going the whole hog and becoming Irish.'[5] In her widowhood Molly proved to be a not wholly disinterested custodian of his papers. To the evidence of the letter just quoted may be added the testimony of her son Robert Childers, who recalled her in later years rereading the correspondence. 'When mother was censoring the letters, she came upon a letter from her to father begging him not to come to Ireland and she tore it up to our horror in front of us. We remonstrated and she said: "I've always been blamed for your father being shot. In fact it was the one thing we ever had a quarrel about. I didn't want him to come to Ireland."'[6]

Some few of the letters are cut, others defaced with what would appear to be personal references scored through. It is easy to be critical of such lapses but it is more important to emphasize Molly Childers's achievement in storing this remarkable collection for over forty years before her own death in 1964. Lest it be impounded by the security forces of either the British or later the Irish Free State authorities she had it hidden throughout her house in Bushy Park in Dublin. When she moved house it was necessary for a team of carpenters to take the stairs apart to retrieve parts of it.[7]

156. Erskine Childers.

Molly had the collection placed in a bank vault for ten years after her death. Her sons then gave access to an official biographer, Andrew Boyle. After his life of Childers had been published, the papers were presented to Trinity College Dublin. It was decided that it would be most appropriate to place the papers covering the 1914-18 War in the Imperial War Museum in London, while papers covering the Boer War were deposited in his old college, Trinity College Cambridge. The

Manuscripts Department in Trinity College Dublin holds microfilms of both these series.

It would be impossible in a short article to offer a comprehensive evaluation of this collection. Nor is the present writer qualified to do so, since he is best acquainted with the political papers covering the 1919 to 1922 period. This essay concentrates on material that is rare in Irish archives, political gossip: specifically Childers's inside account of the Irish delegation as reported home to Molly. Readers should bear in mind that Childers as a witness was biassed: he felt omitted from the inner circle, had a personal dislike for Arthur Griffith and was in temperament wholly different from his colleagues.

The history of bilateral diplomacy is not facilitated by records that are exhaustive on one side and meagre on the other. The intensive political bargaining between the Sinn Fein leadership and Lloyd George's coalition government between July and December 1921 provides an example [157]. The making of the Anglo-Irish Treaty was first told in Frank Pakenham's *Peace by ordeal* published in 1935. This book was a rare enough thing: a historian's 'scoop'. Here was the inside story of the negotiations told within fifteen not fifty years and largely based on a private collection of papers that included the official records taken by the British side. Pakenham's account has worn well and is still the definitive account.[8]

In the meantime what additional information has become available has come predominantly from the British side: official records, diaries, memoirs and private papers. The Childers papers derive added importance because they help to redress this serious imbalance. They represent, along with the official Irish records in the State Paper Office at Dublin Castle, the most comprehensive materials for an analysis of policy formulation on the Irish side. Childers's inclination in administering a secretariat was to keep minutes rigorously of all important decisions and meetings. His papers show every sign of this and also of a magpie instinct on his part to save

157. A group photograph of some of the Irish Delegation for the Treaty talks in London. Childers is seated on the right. Others seated, left to right, are signatories, Arthur Griffith, Robert Barton, E. J. Duggan and George Gavan Duffy. Standing on the left is Desmond FitzGerald.

other material not directly related to his office.

It would be difficult to exaggerate the importance of the collection: it would be impossible to express the excitement of any researcher — as happened to the present writer late in researches on de Valera's Ulster policy — at coming on such treasures. The impingement of the Ulster issue on Irish nationalists as they came closer to the negotiating table can be traced in these papers.[9]

The papers have another quality: intimacy. Childers offers us an insider's account of the approach taken by the Irish delegation. His account is highly subjective, but even allowing for bias it remains an important contribution to our knowledge of these critical weeks.

From the beginning it is clear that there is a sharp difference in temperament between himself and some of his senior colleagues. Childers is impatient with the working conditions, reckoning that the London headquarters is 'horribly inconvenient' and full of 'gorgeous useless furniture'.[10] More seriously he complains of his colleagues' work practices, regretting the 'scarcity of men with rigid methods'.[11]

His letters to Molly reveal moments of elation and despair but most often frustration. Along with his diary entries, they offer new evidence for some aspects of the negotiations and any number of hints and clues that should prompt further investigation.

On 8 November 1921 he complains: 'I have a reputation for overwork because I don't go junketing, theatre-going etc. Couldn't stand it and work would suffer anyway if I did. You know how I revel in work and I hate the very idea of merrymaking in this city at this time. There is too much of it *entre nous.*' [12]

Some weeks later on 24 November he confides: 'The week has been pretty tremendous. Personally I have had a knock to-day but it's all one if Ireland is all right and I have fair hope she is. My position here has been extraordinarily difficult.' A portion of this letter was subsequently destroyed, presumably by Molly.[13] By 28 November he admits to being 'callous to crises now, though each less exciting than the last, and more dismal. Oh that I could write to you.'[14] This latter comment — coming after all from a daily letter-writer — is a reminder that even these revelations must be but fragments of what Childers was in a position to know.

On 30 November he writes: 'Everyone is playing roulette but me. This is not purist asceticism on my part, but am I wrong in thinking that there is something in these negotiations that warrants some sobriety of demeanour and habits?'[15] Childers remained deeply frustrated by what he believed was the failure of the delegation's leaders to use his talents fully: there is no empathy with Griffith from the beginning; and Collins is criticized for leaving Childers in the waiting room during one meeting at the Treasury when Collins himself 'did not understand the subject or only imperfectly'.[16]

On 1 December Childers correctly predicts the coming dénouement: 'Everything ... will *probably* be over next week — I mean "temporarily" anyway, permanently perhaps'.[17] And at 1 a.m. on 5 December, he writes of the dilemma facing the delegates: 'Bob (Barton) says all the dead fought for is lost. I say no — the dead died to prevent surrender.'[18]

His original letter telling of the night of the signing of the Treaty is missing, perhaps destroyed. An edited copy typed by Molly in June 1954 is included detailing the awesome pressures that eventually persuaded all delegates to sign: 'I cannot write more but I feel as if my heart would burst'.[19] Molly Childers adds that 'a part of this letter was deleted by Erskine's wish. After his return he said I might keep the rest as an historical record.' She recalled his 'agony of mind' about these events when they again met: had he himself been a plenipotentiary, he would not have signed. 'All this is engraved upon memory.

158 (overleaf). Erskine Childers's last letter to Molly (first and last pages).

Beggars Bush Barracks 20. 11. 22

22 (twenty two pages)

Beloved Wife, I have been told that I am to be shot tomorrow at 7. I am fully prepared ~~([illegible])~~

I think it is best so – viewing it from the biggest standpoint, & perhaps you will agree. To have followed those other brave lads is a great thing, for a great cause. I have belief in a beneficent shaping of our destiny – yours & mine – & I believe God means this for the best; for us, Ireland & humanity. So in the midst of anguish at leaving you & in mortal solicitude for you, beloved of my heart, I triumph, & I know you triumph with me. It is such a simple thing too, a soldier's death, what millions risk & incur, what so many in our cause face & suffer daily. There is this too that living I was tangled with a load of prejudice, unjust, but so heavy that it may be I was even harming our cause. Dead I shall have a better chance of being understood & of helping the cause. – I am, as I sit here, the happiest of men. I have had 19 years of happiness with you. No man ever could claim so great & precious a

Let us unswervingly follow our own righteous ideal & keep the Republic stainless.

It is six. You would be pleased to see how imperturbably normal & tranquil I have been this night, and am. It all seems perfectly simple & inevitable like lying down after a long day's work. That is our precious Christian conviction & I draw it all from you. For me it is easy now, for you the hard road. But you will tread it like the gallant soul you are & with the dear boys beside you.

— II —

And now I am going. Coming to you, heart's beloved, sweetheart, comrade wife

I shall fall asleep in your arms. God above blessing us — all four of us.

Erskine

After his return we discussed every aspect and felt that Dev would have been of like mind.'[20]

Nor should it be assumed that any omissions from the letter of 6 December were exclusively due to Erskine's editing. Many other letters in the collection have been physically cut. Molly's decision to leave only a copy of this document may have involved further editing by herself. Her youngest son Robert recalled the impact that reading Field Marshall Lord Alanbrooke's memoirs had had on his mother: 'Alanbrooke repeated the most appalling things which his colleagues had said in a moment of fatigue or tiredness and mother was horrified. She said: "Well nobody is going to do that with your father's letters" and proceeded to censor them.' She was most concerned with gratuitous cutting remarks or 'when people were quoted when they were off their guard'.[21]

More reliable are Childers's diary notes covering these historic days. His account of the post mortem on the Treaty at the Cabinet meeting of 8 December is important. He reports Barton as strongly reproaching de Valera, saying the crisis was 'due to his "vacillations" from beginning. At last moment had chance of going to London and refused... President talked at great length. Vehemently pressed to come into line he refused, saying he had worked from the beginning for an "association" [de Valera's theory of external association with Britain] which the Cathal party [the fundamentalist Republican wing of the Cabinet led by Cathal Brugha] could just accept and which would not give up the Republic. Now all thrown away without an effort and without permission of cabinet or even consultation. Some one said "Supposing Ulster came in on the Treaty basis, would you agree to it?" He replied that that was the one consideration that might affect his judgement.' To this last comment Childers added: 'This surprised me'.[22]

In assessing Childers's evidence it is important to bear in mind his relatively eccentric approach to work and the mutual antipathy that was now manifest between him and those whom he criticized. Michael Collins on the signing of the Treaty had no further time for Childers: 'The advice and inspiration of C. is like farmland under water — dead... Soon he will howl his triumph for what it is worth....'[23]

Childers opposed the Treaty politically and then militarily, although his role as a strategist in the Civil War was greatly exaggerated by his opponents. Far from being the leader who, in Kevin O'Higgins's words, was 'steadily, callously and ghoulishly . . . striking at the heart of this nation',[24] Childers by October 1922 had despaired of his effectiveness as a propagandist and had set out from Cork by bicycle and on foot to reach his boyhood home at Glendalough House in Wicklow. He had determined to work instead on his political papers and publish his account of the Treaty negotiations.

He was arrested by Free State troops in a raid on the house on 10 November and accused of bearing arms against the state, by then a capital offence. His only weapon was a personal revolver — a gift from Michael Collins in earlier days. He was court-martialled and sentenced to be shot.

From his death cell he put pen to paper for the last time. It was his farewell letter to Molly [158]. She had not been permitted to visit him. Nor was it a private letter: it had to pass the censor. 'Beloved wife, I have been told that I am to be shot tomorrow at 7. I am fully prepared.' These were the opening words of a twenty-two page letter. Childers was resigned. He had 'a belief in the beneficent shaping of our destiny' and believed 'God means this for the best; for us, Ireland & humanity. So in the midst of anguish at leaving you, and in mortal solicitude for you, beloved of my heart, I triumph and I know you triumph with me.'

He saw his as a soldier's death, 'a simple thing', which millions risked and suffered daily. He also comforted his wife with the thought that alive he was weighted with a load of prejudice 'so heavy' that perhaps he was harming the cause of the Republic. 'Dead I shall have a better chance of being understood & of helping the cause. I am, as I sit here, the happiest of men. I have had 19 years of happiness with you. No man ever could claim so great and precious a blessing as that. But for you I should have foundered.' He also surmised that he might have died 'younger possibly, possibly older, but an unhappy man, a dwarfed soul, not understanding love, the secret of all, and not grasping life like a man'. He thanked her for following him 'nobly and loyally into the hard rugged path which has brought me to this cell and death...'.

The letter was not to be delivered to Molly until after his execution. 'I will add to it at the last, therefore, anything I feel that instinct will tell you when the hour comes. At that moment we shall be supremely and eternally one. It came to me yesterday that I would be saying when they fire, "I fall asleep in your arms, God above blessing us". This is only an earthly metaphor expressing our ideal but I caught at it somehow. Till then my spirit was somewhat confused, after that clear, and ever since I have been repeating it to myself and getting little lifts of happiness and security and serenity — serenity yes, I have that at last if never before. *Equanimitas* — what . . . infinity that expresses — faith, hope, holiness, resignation and goodwill to all.'

Childers forgave his executioners and died professing love for his native England and 'passionately praying that she may change completely and finally towards Ireland'.

The final words scribbled on the morning of his execution read: 'You must be pleased to see how imperturbably normal and tranquil I have been this night, it all seems perfectly simple and inevitable like lying down after a long day's work. . . For me it is easy *now,* for you the hard road. But you will tread it like the gallant soul you are with the dear boys beside you... Now I am going, coming to you, heart's beloved, sweetheart, comrade, wife. I shall fall asleep in your arms, God above blessing us — all four of us. Erskine.'[25]

NOTES

1. Andrew Boyle, *The riddle of Erskine Childers.* London: Hutchinson, 1977, p. 21.
2. The Irish papers of Robert Erskine Childers and Mary Alden Childers, including documentation of the Anglo-Irish Treaty 1921. TCD MSS 7781-7931.
3. Boyle, *Erskine Childers,* p. 128.
4. TCD MS 7848/302/2-10, de Valera to Lord Longford, 25 and 27 February 1963 (copy to Molly Childers).
5. TCD MS 7855/1066, Erskine to Molly Childers, 24 March 1919.
6. Author's interview with Robert Childers, Annamoe, Co. Wicklow, August 1985.
7. Interview, Robert Childers.
8. Frank Pakenham, *Peace by ordeal.* London: Jonathan Cape, 1935.
9. John Bowman, *De Valera and the Ulster question: 1917-1973.* Oxford: Oxford University Press, 1982, pp 56-69.
10. TCD MS 7855/1206, Erskine to Molly Childers, 9 October 1921.
11. TCD MS 7855/1217, Erskine to Molly Childers, 22 October 1921.
12. TCD MS 7855/1237, Erskine to Molly Childers, 8 November 1921.
13. TCD MS 7855/1252, Erskine to Molly Childers, 24 November 1921.
14. TCD MS 7855/1255, Erskine to Molly Childers, 28 November 1921.
15. TCD MS 7855/1257, Erskine to Molly Childers, 30 November 1921.
16. TCD MS 7814, Childers, diary, 2 December 1921.
17. TCD MS 7855/1258, Erskine to Molly Childers, 1 December 1921.
18. TCD MS 7855/1260, Erskine to Molly Childers, '4 Dec. or rather 1 a.m. 5 Dec.' 1921.
19. TCD MS 7855/1264, typescript copy by Molly Childers of Erskine to Molly Childers, 6 December 1921.
20. TCD MS 7855/1264, note by Molly Childers.
21. Interview, Robert Childers.
22. TCD MS 7814, Childers, diary, 8 December 1921.
23. Boyle, *Erskine Childers,* p. 302.
24. Boyle, *Erskine Childers,* p. 316.
25. TCD MS 7855/1301, Erskine to Molly Childers, 20-24 November 1922.

MODERN IRISH LITERARY MANUSCRIPTS

NICHOLAS GRENE

In response to a letter from John Quinn, the New York lawyer and literary patron, who had offered to buy the manuscript of *The playboy of the western world* in 1907, J. M. Synge wrote diffidently: 'As to my manuscript, I work always with a typewriter — typing myself — so I suppose it has no value? . . . The MS, as it now stands, is a good deal written over, and some of it is in slips or strips only, cut from the earlier version – so I do not know whether it has any interest to the collector.'[1]

At the time, Quinn's offer was a generous one — he bought many manuscripts in this way, including the famous lost and rediscovered manuscript of *The waste land,* as a tactful way of supporting the writers. And Synge's innocence of the importance of his work to future scholars is natural enough. But in the years to come the worksheets of Synge and of many other major modern Irish writers were to become of more than doubtful value to collectors and libraries. The growing international interest in the literature of Ireland has brought about a 'diaspora' of Irish literary manuscripts throughout the world. In this context, Trinity College Library may be considered lucky to have acquired as much as it has. Among its most significant holdings are the outstanding collection of Synge manuscripts, some very interesting working notebooks of Yeats and of Beckett and, the most recent accession, the papers of Denis Johnston. Between them they afford a whole range of opportunities for studying the genesis of individual works of art and of the imaginative development of the writers. They allow us, as it were, privileged access to creativity in process.

The Yeats manuscripts, donated by Mrs W. B. Yeats on the occasion of a Yeats exhibition in 1956, date from the very beginning of the poet's career.[2] Two working notebooks and some related materials contain drafts of the dramatic poems that Yeats was writing between 1884 and 1886. There are lines for the very early 'Vivien and Time'; there is a sketch for 'The Island of Statues', Yeats's first extended work to be published, which appeared in the *Dublin University Review* in 1885; and most substantially there are several drafts of *Mosada,* which also came out in the *Dublin University Review,* in 1886, and, in its issue as a subscription pamphlet in the same year, became Yeats's first separate publication. All of these belong to the pre-Celtic twilight period of Yeats's career, and at this stage he was still evidently seeking a setting, a local habitation and a name for his other world of the imagination. With 'The Island of Statues', set in a literary Arcadia and *Mosada* in a remote and inadequately realized medieval Spain, we can see how badly Yeats needed the Irish mythology to give distinction and definition to his work.

The manuscripts give us an inkling of the slow and painful business of composition for Yeats. The sketch for 'The Island of Statues', for instance, is remarkably embryonic.[3]

Somewhere between a scenario and a first draft, it contains dialogue that is already in verse, but a rough fragmentary blank verse bearing little relation to the ornate couplets of the finished version. Where there are to be lyrics, Yeats gives only a shorthand indication such as 'the voice sings a song who's chorus is follow follow follow'[4] (Yeats's spelling is shaky throughout and his punctuation is non-existent). We can see dialogue for *Mosada* evolve from drafts of individual scenes in this notebook, through a fair copy with revisions in another [159], to a set of loose sheets with a later draft, and finally a copy of the galley proofs of the *Dublin University Review* printing. All of these dramatic poems are undoubtedly juvenilia, derivative from Spenser and Shelley, tentative in construction and sometimes absurd in expression, but they are striking enough to represent a precocious start — Yeats was only nineteen when the first of the drafts was made, only twenty-one when *Mosada* appeared. But precocity did not take the form of a Popean lisping in numbers. The opulent, fluid and ornate early verse, just like the dense and allusive later poetry, was achieved by patient tenacity and infinitely painstaking craftsmanship. As Yeats was to put it in 'Adam's Curse':

A line will take us hours maybe;
Yet if it does not seem a moment's thought,
Our stitching and unstitching has been naught.[5]

159. W. B. Yeats: draft of the early dramatic poem *Mosada*.

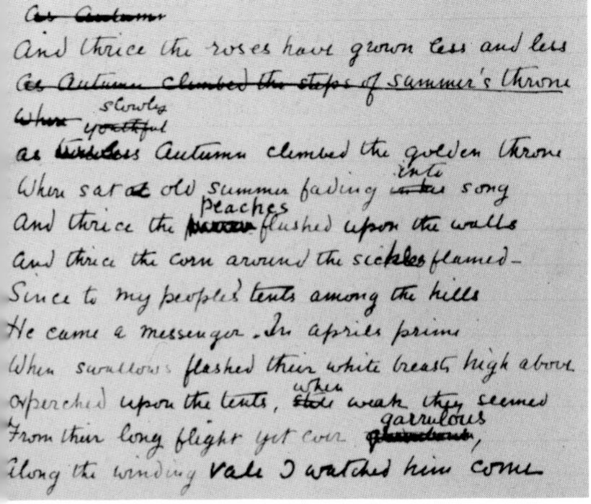
Scene 1
a moorish room in the Village
of Azabra. In the room's center stand a chafing dish upon a tripod
Mosada (alone)
Thrice has the winter come and gone again
And thrice the roses have grown less and less
As Autumn climbed the steps of summer's throne
When slowly youthful
as Autumn climbed the golden throne
Where sat old summer fading into song
And thrice the peaches flushed upon the walls
And thrice the corn around the sickles flamed—
Since to my peoples tents among the hills
He came a messenger. In aprils prime
When swallows flashed their white breasts high above
Or perched upon the tents, when weak they seemed
From their long flight yet ever garrulous,
Along the winding vale I watched him come

After Synge's death in 1909, all his papers were inherited by his nephew and literary executor, Edward M. Stephens, and it was from his widow, Lily M. Stephens, that the Library purchased them in 1969. Mrs Stephens, by her additional generous gift of the large collection of Synge's letters to his fiancée, Molly Allgood, and many other materials of related interest, including the manuscript of Edward Stephens's enormous biography of his uncle, which has never been published in full, helped to make Trinity a centre of unique importance for the study of Synge's work. The manuscripts cover the full range of his career from a bird-watcher's journal, which he kept in 1882, to the drafts of his last play *Deirdre of the sorrows*. In them we can see the gradual and in some ways unexpected emergence of a major dramatist.

It is unexpected in that Synge, unlike Yeats, was anything but precocious. After a solid, if not particularly distinguished degree at Trinity, he went to Germany to study music in 1893. Even after he abandoned the idea of a musical profession and moved to Paris in 1895, it is not clear what literary ambitions he had. In his notebooks and diaries from this period, when he was spending his winters in Paris, his summers with his mother in Kingstown (Dun Laoghaire) and on holiday in Wicklow, we find evidence of very wide reading and fairly systematic language study in French and then also in Italian, but there is relatively little original writing, most of it mawkish and self-absorbed. In 1896 came the historic meeting with Yeats at which, by Yeats's account at least, the decisive advice was given: 'Give up Paris. … Go to the Aran Islands. Live there as if you were one of the people themselves; express a life that has never found expression.'[6] Synge recorded the event

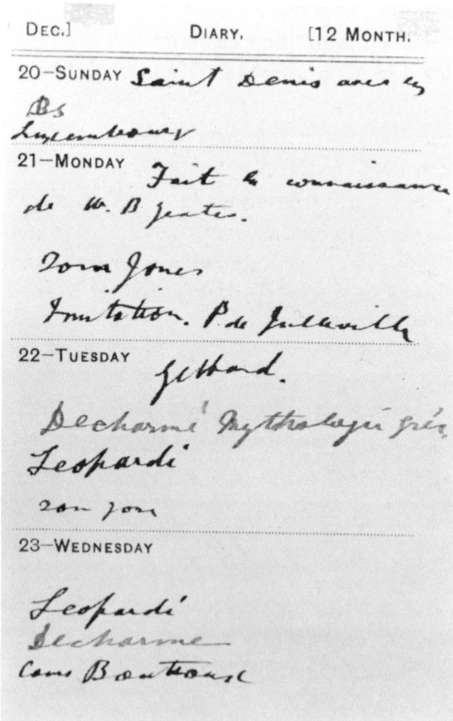

160. J. M. Synge's diary; showing the entry for 21 December 1896 recording his meeting in Paris with W. B. Yeats.

much more laconically in his diary: *'Fait la connaissance de W.B. Yeates'* [160].[7]

It seems doubtful if it was at Yeats's instigation that Synge went to Aran, but his visits there did undoubtedly transform him into a writer. It was by no means an instantaneous transformation: he went to Aran in 1898 and it was not until 1902, at the age of thirty-one, that he wrote his first successful play. But already in the 1898 notebooks we find the sense of awe and wonder that the barren landscape and the primitive life of the people inspired in Synge. By the winter of 1900-1, after his third visit to Aran, he was using his newly-purchased Blickensdorfer typewriter (now in the Library) to type a first draft of his book *The Aran Islands.* It was in writing *The Aran Islands,* as Synge himself later said, that he learned to write the dialect of the plays.[8] Aran supplied him directly with source material both in landscape and stories. A letter in Irish from his closest friend on Aran, Martin McDonough,[9] included the sentence that, literally translated, became Maurya's final words in *Riders to the sea:* 'No man at all can be living for ever, and we must be satisfied'.[10] A tale told him by Pat Dirane, a seanachie on Inishmaan [161], became the basis for *The shadow of the glen.*[11]

The experience of Aran, which he never revisited after 1902, was an enabling one for Synge and from this point on he could make use of other areas of Ireland for his work, including Wicklow, which he had known well from boyhood and where he set *The shadow of the glen,* his first produced play. The experience of having his plays performed and his increasing involvement with the Abbey Theatre, of which he became a director in 1905, was important for Synge's practical stagecraft. In his own printed copy of *The well of the saints,*[12] his first three-act play, we can see manuscript alterations showing changes he made during rehearsals to break up the long concluding speech of the central figure, Martin Doul, and to adjust the balance of feeling between Martin and his wife Mary [162]. For a revival of the play in 1908, Synge further re-wrote parts of the final act. A dramatic text is rarely fixed and final but is necessarily subject to the adaptations and adjustments that staging brings.

In the summer of 1905, Synge was commissioned by the *Manchester Guardian* to do a series of articles on the Congested Districts of Connemara and Mayo with Jack B. Yeats, the poet's brother, as companion to draw illustrative sketches. Jack Yeats was to become a good friend and contributed costume designs for Christy Mahon in *The playboy of the western world* [163].[13] It seems that Synge brought along the camera that he had already used to such good effect on Aran, for there is a splendidly-composed photograph of a fairday at Leenane, County Mayo [164],[14] which must date from this time. It was in Mayo, also, that he was to set *The playboy*, on which he had started work in the autumn of 1904, although the original idea had come from Aran, and much of the dialogue is drawn from idioms noted down in Kerry.[15]

At first planned as 'The Murderer: a Farce',[16] with the emphasis on the mechanical transformation of the parricide by the hero-worship of the villagers, as Synge continued to work on *The playboy* over two and a half years, it became something far more rich and complex and by no means purely farcical. Over a thousand sheets of manuscript material survive to illustrate its protracted development.[17] Each draft of the play was typed, then corrected in manuscript until it was all but illegible, then re-typed as a new draft. Lettering his drafts as he went along Synge reached version *L* for some parts of the play. Although the love

161. J. M. Synge's first typescript draft of *The Aran Islands* with the tale which became the basis for *The shadow of the glen*.

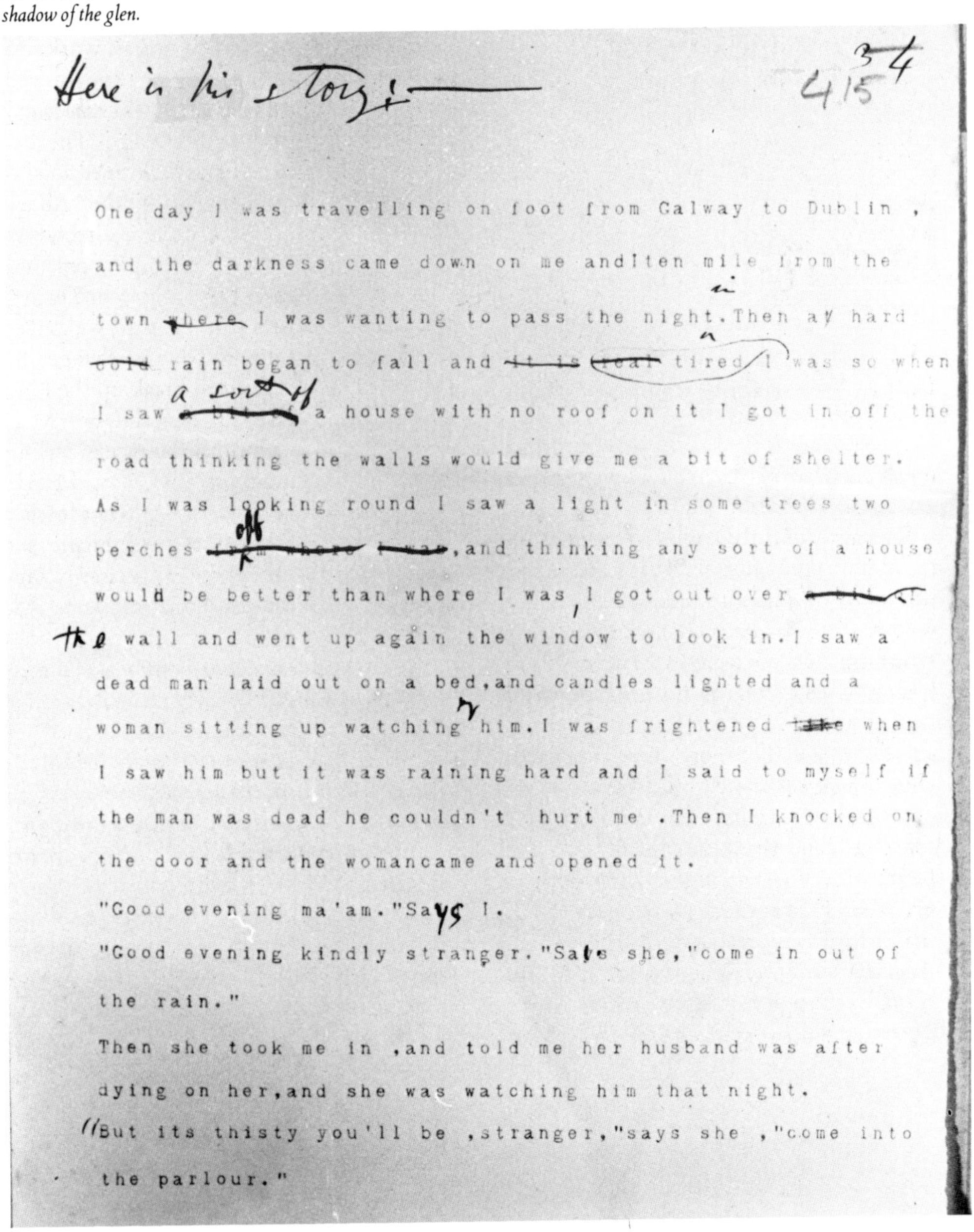
Here is his story:—

415

One day I was travelling on foot from Galway to Dublin , and the darkness came down on me andIten mile from the town where I was wanting to pass the night.Then a hard cold rain began to fall and it is tired I was so when I saw a sort of a house with no roof on it I got in off the road thinking the walls would give me a bit of shelter. As I was looking round I saw a light in some trees two perches off from where I was,and thinking any sort of a house would be better than where I was,I got out over the wall and went up again the window to look in.I saw a dead man laid out on a bed,and candles lighted and a woman sitting up watching him.I was frightened when I saw him but it was raining hard and I said to myself if the man was dead he couldn't hurt me .Then I knocked on the door and the womancame and opened it.

"Good evening ma'am."Says I.

"Good evening kindly stranger."Says she,"come in out of the rain."

Then she took me in ,and told me her husband was after dying on her,and she was watching him that night.

"But its thisty you'll be ,stranger,"says she ,"come into the parlour."

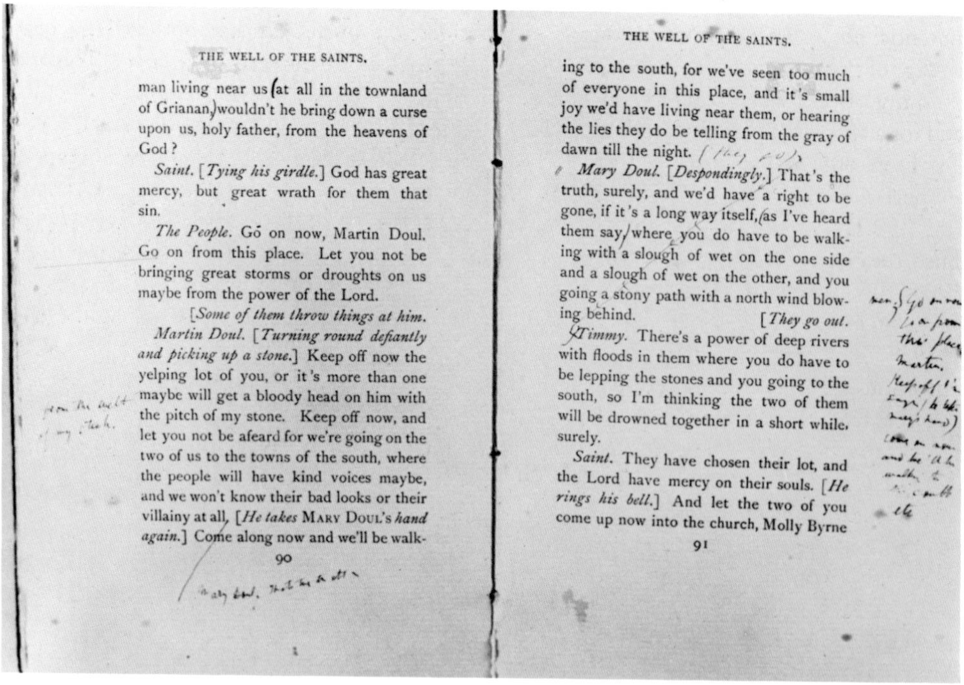

THE WELL OF THE SAINTS.

man living near us at all in the townland of Grianan, wouldn't he bring down a curse upon us, holy father, from the heavens of God?

Saint. [*Tying his girdle.*] God has great mercy, but great wrath for them that sin.

The People. Gō on now, Martin Doul. Go on from this place. Let you not be bringing great storms or droughts on us maybe from the power of the Lord.

[*Some of them throw things at him.*

Martin Doul. [*Turning round defiantly and picking up a stone.*] Keep off now the yelping lot of you, or it's more than one maybe will get a bloody head on him with the pitch of my stone. Keep off now, and let you not be afeard for we're going on the two of us to the towns of the south, where the people will have kind voices maybe, and we won't know their bad looks or their villainy at all. [*He takes* MARY DOUL'S *hand again.*] Come along now and we'll be walk-

90

THE WELL OF THE SAINTS.

ing to the south, for we've seen too much of everyone in this place, and it's small joy we'd have living near them, or hearing the lies they do be telling from the gray of dawn till the night.

Mary Doul. [*Despondingly.*] That's the truth, surely, and we'd have a right to be gone, if it's a long way itself, as I've heard them say, where you do have to be walking with a slough of wet on the one side and a slough of wet on the other, and you going a stony path with a north wind blowing behind. [*They go out.*

Timmy. There's a power of deep rivers with floods in them where you do have to be lepping the stones and you going to the south, so I'm thinking the two of them will be drowned together in a short while, surely.

Saint. They have chosen their lot, and the Lord have mercy on their souls. [*He rings his bell.*] And let the two of you come up now into the church, Molly Byrne

91

162. Synge's copy of the first edition of *The well of the saints* (1905) with manuscript changes made during rehearsals.

interest between Christy and Pegeen Mike was prominent from an early stage, Synge remained uncertain until quite late on in the process of composition as to how to end the play. In one version, Christy and Pegeen are at the chapel about to be married when Old Mahon intervenes; in others Old Mahon marries the Widow Quin or Christy himself marries her. As well as these major structural alterations, the drafts illustrate the minute changes Synge constantly made to perfect the poetic cadences of the dialogue, as we can see, for instance, with Christy's famous speech about the Lady Helen of Troy [6].[18] What Synge finally created was a play so multi-faceted, so subtle and ironic in theme and form, that it may have been partly out of bewilderment at its strangeness and force that the 1907 first-night audience rioted.

Synge's last two years of life were dominated by his relationship with Molly Allgood and his efforts to write his last play, *Deirdre.* Synge had become engaged to the nineteen-year-old actress in 1906 and the almost daily letters he wrote her from then on reveal both his deep love and the difficulties that surrounded them.[19] They were divided by age, class and religion; their relative positions as director and actress at the Abbey, the unspoken disapproval of Yeats and Lady Gregory, Synge's jealousy and growing illness all made for an uneasy relationship. The letters, with Synge's constantly deferred hopes of an early marriage, make moving but sad reading. Illness and other distractions also interrupted work on *Deirdre.* Although he continued to work on the play until he went into hospital for the last time, he did not succeed in finishing it to his satisfaction, and he died of Hodgkin's disease in March 1909. *Deirdre* in its unfinished state, with its worksheets showing Synge frenetically working against time, stands as a monument to the lost potential of the great playwright who died at the age of thirty-seven.

Samuel Beckett, a distinguished graduate and for a time a lecturer in French at Trinity, has been one of the College's most loyal supporters over the years. Approached by the late R.B.D. French, whom he had known since they were together in College in the 1920s, Beckett generously agreed to donate some of his manuscripts to the Library in 1969.[20] These include drafts of work and notebooks containing unfinished or abandoned pieces from the 1950s and early 1960s. Part of an early discarded scene of *Fin de partie,* dating from 1953-4, is important as it shows that Beckett was working on the play well before December 1955 when it was actually written.[21] There is useful material for the study of Beckett as a bilingual writer with samples of his work as self-translator both ways: drafts of the translation of *Malone meurt* and of *Textes pour rien* I into English,[22] and of *Words and music* into French.[23] Perhaps most interesting of all are the fragmentary pieces that contain the germs of later publications. An 'abandoned play' dated 'Ussy 15.8.58', written in French, for three characters identified only as A, B and C appeared finally in English as 'Theatre II' in *Ends and odds* (1977).[24] A notebook from 1963 reveals several ideas that were to provide the basis for much later drama. One fragment called 'Kilcool' is a monologue for 'Woman's face alone in constant light' who 'talks of herself in 3rd person'.[25] This was to be developed into the even more extreme metonymy of the mouth in *Not I* (1973), but the central conception was obviously already there.

Even more striking in terms of the gap in time between conception and execution is the draft headed 'J.M. Mime' [165].[26] Here Beckett can be seen trying to work out an extremely complicated pattern of movement for two figures within a square playing area. He seems rapidly to have dropped the idea of it as mime and wrote some dialogue for the two figures, a son and mother, both wearing coats but naked underneath their coats. This was abandoned, but in 1982 with the television play *Quad* Beckett at last found a vehicle for his image of the permutations and combinations of movement within the square space, though with the added complication of four players and no words. In this 1963 notebook we can see Beckett in a transitional phase between the semi-representational mode of his earlier drama and the much more abstract formalism of his later work. It is illuminating to discover that with Beckett, as with other creative artists, images and ideas may have to be stored for years before they can at last find appropriate expression.

Denis Johnston (1901-84) had a long and eventful life, a life of many different careers. Coming from a distinguished legal family, he qualified as a barrister and continued to work as a lawyer through the 1920s and early 1930s while writing some of his best known plays such as *The old lady says no!* and *The moon in the Yellow River,* besides acting and directing with the Dublin Drama League, the Abbey and the Gate theatres. In 1936 he joined the BBC where

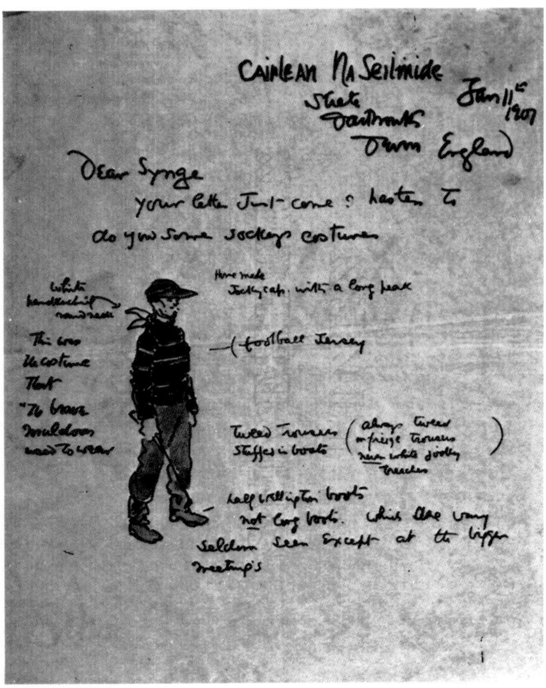

163. Letter from Jack B. Yeats to Synge with costume sketches for *The playboy of the western world.*

164. Fair day at Leenane, County Mayo. Photograph taken by J. M. Synge about 1905.

he worked as a producer and programme director both before and after the war. During the war itself he was BBC correspondent in North Africa and Europe, experiences described in his autobiographical *Nine rivers from Jordan* (1953). In the 1950s he launched into a new profession as university teacher in the United States at the New England colleges of Mount Holyoke and Smith. He returned to Ireland in the 1970s where he continued to work in a full and active retirement until his death in 1984. In 1985 Denis Johnston's family took the extremely generous decision to donate all their father's remaining papers to Trinity College Library. At the time of writing the collection has not yet been fully catalogued and much of the material is therefore not yet accessible, but it is already obvious that it is a very important collection indeed.

Among the plays, the fullest worksheets are those for *The old lady says no!* A notebook, apparently dating from 1925-6, originally used for law notes, contains an outline plan for the play and some snippets of dialogue. The first full draft, which Johnston marked 'Ur Alpha', already has the basic pattern of the final work, the sentimental patriotic play about Robert Emmet interrupted when the actor playing Emmet gets a knock on the head, followed by his delirious wandering round the streets of 1920s Dublin in the character of the young rebel. In the first version there are some scenes later discarded, such as a farcical one in which the Speaker/Emmet causes havoc by appearing in Dáil Éireann. Some sharp and detailed criticism by Yeats, who read the play for the Abbey in a second version 'Ur Beta', led to major revisions. From the beginning Johnston had planned the dance of the shadows of great figures from Ireland's past as a key moment in the play — *Shadowdance* was its working title. But as he re-wrote it, he included more and more quotations and echoes of past Irish writers. The opening Robert Emmet playlet, originally a simple parody of the romantic nationalist style, became a grotesque patchwork of nineteenth-century Irish poetry. The figure of the old flowerseller, the Old Lady of the final title, became explicitly identified with Cathleen Ni Houlihan, with lines from Yeats's patriotic play to clinch the point. By means of this extraordinary collage of quotation, Johnston went beyond a satiric and disillusioned view of post-Treaty Ireland;

165. Samuel Beckett: 1963 notebook with an unfinished sketch (later used in *Quad*) in which Beckett tries to work out a complicated pattern of movement for two figures within a square playing area.

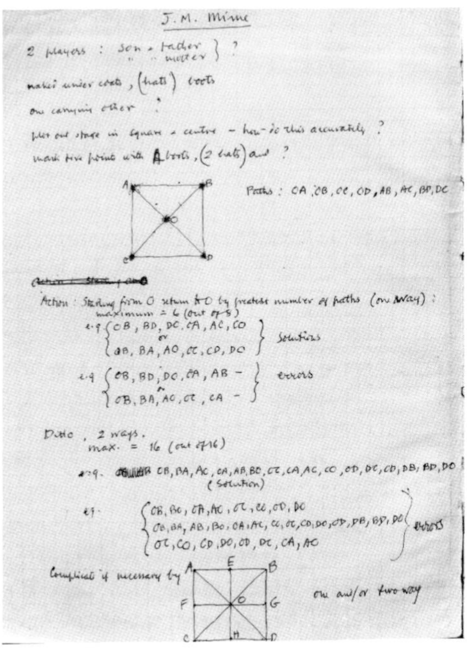

he sought to explore a whole city, a whole nation with its past and present, its myths and realities in confused collision.

The play was re-submitted to the Abbey and turned down again. In a preface in his *Collected plays,* Johnston told the story how, at this point, the play got its title, 'written by somebody on a sheet of paper attached to the front of the first version, when it came back to me from the Abbey'.[27] The clear implication is that the old lady who said no was Lady Gregory, and by turning the rejection into a title Johnston brilliantly identified her conservative opposition to the play's experimentalism with the conservatism of the 1920s Cathleen Ni Houlihan. Sure enough, a title page of one of the manuscript versions, 'Ur Delta', does bear the words 'Sorry *The Old Lady says No!*' [166]. However when this is investigated more closely it becomes apparent that the 'Sorry' has been added, and that *The Old Lady says No!* is in fact written in the hand of Art Ó Murnaghan, who composed the incidental music for the play and was stage manager at the Gate Theatre where it was first produced in 1929. One is tempted to the conclusion that Johnston, in mischievous mood, doctored one of his own manuscripts to authenticate the anecdote. It is a pity to spoil a good story, but all the evidence suggests that it was Yeats rather than Lady Gregory who was the decisive voice in rejecting the play.[28]

For later plays there are scripts for radio and television in which we can see Johnston using his professional skills to adapt his own work for broadcasting. There is a vast amount of other material in the archive as well, drafts of his many non-dramatic works, reviews, letters, prompt scripts and photographs. Most outstanding of all are the private diaries, which Johnston kept from 1918 to the early 1980s and which have never been publicly accessible before. The Library's collection will no doubt prove an invaluable mine of material for the fascinating biography of Denis Johnston that remains to be written.

The study of literary manuscripts can seem to some an arid, a trivial or a parasitic employment, recovering what was intended to be discarded, pedantically noting changes and deletions, the epitome of unproductive scholarship. But for many of us there is an absorbing interest in being able to see how a familiar work of art came into being. What emerges from all of the manuscripts in the Library's collections considered here is the long, difficult and unpredictable nature of the creative process. Yeats was something like a born writer, but he had to work for every line of poetry he wrote. Synge, so unpromising a beginner, in the experience of Aran found a subject, a medium and an inspiration for the startlingly original drama he was to create. In the minimalism of Beckett's late drama we can find images that had already been with him as much as twenty years before. Johnston, like Yeats an inveterate reviser of his own work even after it was published, dated the final version of *The old lady* in his 1977 *Dramatic works*, 'Bloomsbury 1926 – Dalkey 1976'.[29] To study the manuscripts of these writers is to go some way towards understanding the working of the literary and dramatic imagination. It can never be explained.

166. Denis Johnston: title page of the typescript version of *The old lady says no!*

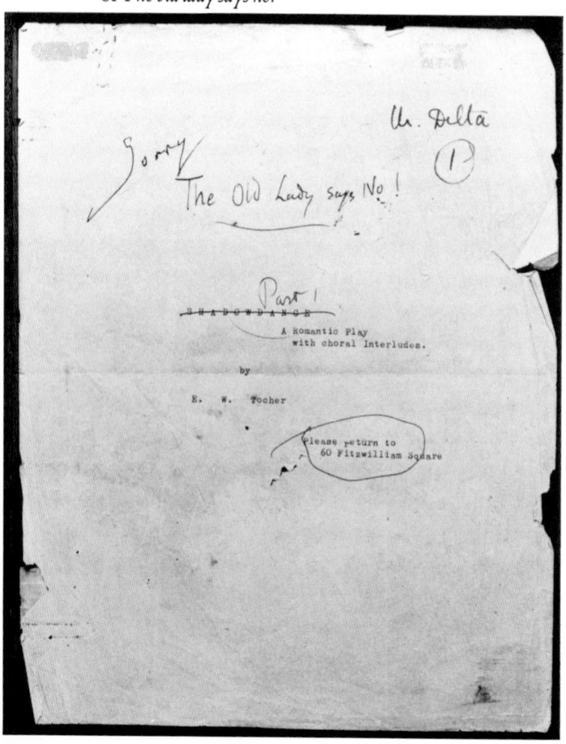
The Old Lady says No!

Part I

~~SHADOWDANCE~~

A Romantic Play
with choral Interludes.

by

E. W. Tocher

Please return to
60 Fitzwilliam Square

NOTES

1. J.M. Synge, *Collected works*, IV: *Plays*, book II, edited by Ann Saddlemyer. London: Oxford University Press, 1968, pp xxxii-xxxiii.
2. TCD MS 3502.
3. TCD MS 3502/2, fols 13v-30v.
4. TCD MS 3502/2, fol. 20v.
5. W.B. Yeats, *Collected poems*. London: Macmillan, 1950, p. 88.
6. Synge, *Collected works*, III: *Plays*, book I, p. 63.
7. TCD MS 4417, fol. 46v.
8. Letter to Leon Brodzky, TCD MS 3460. Quoted in J.M. Synge, *Collected works*, II: *Prose*, edited by Alan Price. London: Oxford University Press, 1966, p. 47n.
9. TCD MS 4429/109. Quoted in Declan Kiberd, *Synge and the Irish language*. London: Macmillan, 1979, p. 205.
10. Synge, *Collected works*, III, p. 27.
11. TCD MS 4344, fol. 415.
12. TCD MS 6408.
13. TCD MS 6225/1.
14. Reproduced in Synge, *Collected works*, II, facing p. 336.
15. See TCD MS 4391, 4401-4, 4407.
16. TCD MS 4395, fols 1-1v.
17. TCD MS 4331-3.
18. TCD MS 4331-3, fol. 797.
19. TCD MS 4429.
20. TCD MS 9793/2/1-16.
21. TCD MS 4662, fols 1-4.
22. TCD MS 4662, fols 15v-27, 4663, fols 1-12.
23. TCD MS 4664, fols 20-23.
24. TCD MS 4661, fols 1-33.
25. TCD MS 4664, fol 10.
26. TCD MS 4664, fols 1v-2r.
27. Denis Johnston, *Dramatic works*, vol 1. Gerrards Cross, Bucks.: Colin Smythe, 1977, p. 16.
28. See Christine St Peter, '*The old lady:* in principio' in *Denis Johnston: a retrospective*, edited by Joseph Ronsley. Gerrards Cross, Bucks.: Colin Smythe, 1981, p. 20.
29. Johnston, *Dramatic works*, p. 75.

THE DOLMEN PRESS COLLECTION

CHRISTINE NUDDS

The desire to provide an outlet for new Irish writing prompted Liam Miller to found his Dolmen Press. Since its foundation in 1951 the Press has become a major Irish publishing success, with 324 books published and over 120 private printings. This success has not only had a profound effect on Irish book design but has also gained international reputations for many of those writers whom Miller set out to serve.

Press policy has always insisted on some Irish input for its publications. In a recent conversation Miller stated, 'We take a book on an Irish subject from any author regardless of nationality and we take a book on any subject from an Irish author — when Arland Ussher wanted to explore his thoughts on Grimm's Fairy Tales and Tarot cards we published those without any hesitation and when Hirobashi in Japan wanted to expound on Yeats's drama in relation to the Noh we published her book — that's really the guiding philosophy.'[1]

Trinity College Library has a rich collection of Dolmen Press material, acquired both through legal deposit and in the Michael Freyer collection purchased in 1979. Freyer describes how his interest in the Press was inspired: 'From the moment I handled those first Dolmen publications I got a feeling of pleasure, excitement and anticipation which has increased with each new issue from the Press'.[2] Freyer's collection, made between 1951 and 1973, contains approximately 346 Dolmen Press publications and a hundred private printings, and includes copies of every publication in every format with one exception (although the Library's legal deposit run neatly fills this gap). In addition there are a few reprints and re-issues, proof copies, Dolmen catalogues and single book prospectuses, with related ephemera, posters, greeting cards, theatre programmes, etc. Also included is an unpublished bibliography compiled by Freyer, and articles and newspaper cuttings relating to the Press. The legal deposit collection contains an almost complete set of publications from 1951 (although without all the variants), twenty private printings and some proof copies. The Library also has copies of job books (1964-79), account books (1964-72) and estimate books (1964-74), and archives for a few privately printed items.

PRINTING AND PUBLISHING HISTORY

For his first exploration into printing Miller acquired an 11 in. × 7 in. Adana flatbed press and a fount of Caslon type. Dolmen's first book, *Travelling tinkers,* was issued in August 1951 from Miller's home in Sion Hill Road, Drumcondra, Dublin. The small press allowed only two pages of type to be printed simultaneously and so Miller was pleased to accept Cecil ffrench Salkeld's loan of the wooden handpress used at his Gayfield press. This handpress, although temperamental, allowed four pages of text to be printed together. A move to Glenageary in late 1954 provided garage space and in 1955 three further presses were acquired: an 8 in. × 11 in. Adana platen, an Albion handpress and an Arab treadle press, later converted to power. The Press moved to Upper Mount Street, Dublin, in 1958 when Miller finally made publishing and printing his full-time occupation. The staff was then increased by three and a Heidelberg platen was acquired. Later cylinder presses used by Dolmen were a Falcon (acquired 1965), a Mercedes (acquired 1969) and a Heidelberg.

The first type used at the Press was Caslon twelve point, augmented by a fount of Bodoni which came with the Gayfield press. Initially acquisition of type was slow, sixteen point Poliphilus being added in 1953, eighteen point Caslon in 1954 and twelve point Plantin in 1956. From 1957 two or three founts were added annually until the mid 1970s when the Press possessed sixteen typefaces, ten in a range of text sizes, with twelve display founts. At first the most heavily used were obviously Caslon and Poliphilus; Caslon was still favoured in the early 1960s, but by the mid 1960s Gill Pilgrim was the most popular, appearing in forty-four of the 119 publications produced by Dolmen that decade, and Times Roman, used nineteen times, was second choice. In the 1970s, however, Times Roman rivalled Pilgrim, appearing forty-four times against the forty-eight of Pilgrim in a total of 118 publications. Baskerville was heavily used (twenty times) towards the end of the decade.

The Press policy has always been to use Irish materials wherever possible. Swiftbrook Paper Mills, Saggart, County Dublin, provided paper for a number of early volumes and also made paper to the Press's own specifications when necessary. Vellum made by N. Elzas & Zonen at Celbridge was used for ten copies of *Faeth fiadha: the breastplate of Saint Patrick* (1957) [8].

In 1966 the Press established a publishing office at Herbert Place, Dublin, which eventually moved with the printing division to North Richmond Street in 1973. Towards the end of the 1970s Dolmen decided that to compete financially it would be necessary to add offset lithography equipment to their letterpress operation. Sadly, however, the print unions could not agree to let the same crew operate both offset and letterpress equipment and it was decided to close down Dolmen's printing works. Prior to closure the two presses in use were Heidelberg platen and cylinder presses and the staff numbered ten.

Dolmen's annual output grew steadily from the two books issued in 1951 to an average of six by the late 1950s. The 1960s saw a great increase — twenty-two were published in 1968 — culminating in what Miller calls their 'best efforts' in 1969 with the publication of *Riders to the sea* and *The Táin.* Numbers dropped during the mid 1970s to about a dozen new issues per year and in 1980 only five new books appeared, possibly a result of the printing works closure and transfer of the publishing office to Miller's home in Mountrath, County Laois. In 1984 eleven new books appeared and several new editions of earlier publications were issued.

Edition size varied between 100 and 500 in the early days but by the early 1960s Dolmen produced some editions to compete commercially with those published in London and New York. Thomas Kinsella's *Downstream* (1962) was published in an edition of about 2500 copies and more recently, for example, *An duanaire* . . ., Irish poems arranged by Seán Ó Tuama with translations into English by Thomas Kinsella (1981), was printed in an edition of 12,500 and still needed to be reprinted.

Most of the earlier books were issued in

167. *The XXII keys of the Tarot,* by Arland Ussher; designs by Leslie MacWeeney. 1957. Trial setting in Pilgrim type (top) abandoned when the sheets were printed as the face seemed too light for the designs. Reset in twelve point Poliphilus (bottom).

Adolescence (the 9 germination-years of the mature self). The first 13 Cards of the Tarot (by this reckoning) are *human* symbols, the remaining 9 are *cosmic* ones. The Fool is pure Contingency, Impulse completely undetermined and free as air, both Will and Destiny and neither: he is aboriginal Chaos, primary Matter in which the dry and the earthy have not yet been parted from the wet and the oceanic. He is the traveller who tosses up at every crossroads, and, because he has no goal, cannot lose his way; or one might say that of him the aphorism of Kafka is true, "There is an end, but no way—what we call the way is a shilly-shallying." In this sense he seems an allegory, not only of humanity, but of the Gipsy race itself. We meet him again in the Hanged Man—his reversed image, the reflexion he throws on Time's stream. In this Card he pauses on the brink of that stream, looking not downward but backward—heedless of the drop in front of him—and his dog, like a fate, presses him from behind. In some versions the dog is a tiger or panther—the "pard," it may be, of the fool Dionysus; and a crocodile (perhaps that of Egyptian mysteries) waits to devour him. This Card is also called "the Mate" (il Matto, the Mad).

are *human* symbols, the remaining 9 are *cosmic* ones. The Fool is pure Contingency, Impulse completely undetermined and free as air, both Will and Destiny and neither: he is aboriginal Chaos, primary Matter in which the dry and the earthy have not yet been parted from the wet and the oceanic. He is the traveller who tosses up at every crossroads, and, because he has no goal, cannot lose his way; or one might say that of him the aphorism of Kafka is true, "There is an end, but no way—what we call the way is a shilly-shallying". In this sense he seems an allegory, not only of humanity, but of the Gipsy race itself. We meet him again in the Hanged Man—his reversed image, the reflexion he throws on Time's stream. In this Card he pauses on the brink of that stream, looking not downward but backward—heedless of the drop in front of him—and his dog, like a fate, presses him from behind. In some versions the dog is a tiger or panther—the "pard",

special and ordinary editions. By the 1960s, with the need to compete commercially, more books were issued in unlimited editions in the mainstream of trade publishing, but in 1966 a desire to get back to the original aims of the Press prompted the start of the 'Dolmen editions'. Miller recently explained, 'I wanted to print things as I saw them and so Kinsella's sequence *Wormwood* was designed and printed on . . . mouldmade paper with all the care and attention we could give it. . .'.[3] Twenty-eight 'Dolmen editions' appeared between 1966 and 1979, all in limited editions, mostly of between 750 and 1000 copies.

From 1961 until 1975 Oxford University Press acted as Dolmen's general distributors from London and several Dolmen books were actually co-published with them. In Ireland two of Thomas Kinsella's books were co-published with Peppercanister, Kinsella's own imprint. An arrangement with Cadenus Press allowed Dolmen to publish trade editions of two volumes in their series 'Irish writings in the age of Swift' originally published in limited editions. In 1977 Dolmen registered the 'Five Lamps Press' imprint for privately printed material. The Library's collection contains copies of the four books issued with this imprint. From 1963 to 1971 Dufour Editions Inc. were Dolmen's general distributors in the USA and Canada before Humanities Press Inc. took over. Dolmen's latest publishing venture has been into children's literature. Four volumes appeared in 1984 and 1985 under the new imprint, Brogeen Books.

168. *The ballad of Jane Shore,* by Donagh MacDonagh. (Dolmen Chapbook 1.) 1954. Title page with handcoloured cut by Eric Patton.

DESIGN

In *A prospect of Dolmens* Miller stated that 'Centuries before the invention of printing Ireland was the greatest producer of books in the world . . .' and that 'although primarily a writer's press, we hope to achieve something in the way of book production and decoration which may, in time, form a small contribution to Ireland's heritage in the world of books'.[4] Miller's architectural training provided him with a disciplined approach to the complicated task of designing a visually pleasing book. He always believed in the importance of the text: 'We aim to produce each work in a manner inspired by the text. . . . This involves more experimental setting and matching of type, paper, illustration and binding. For instance *The XXII keys of the Tarot* had gone through many trial stages and had been set in Gill Pilgrim face, but when the sheets were printed, the face seemed too light for the designs and so we reset in Poliphilus'[5] [167].

These principles were those rekindled by the private press movement of the late nineteenth century, and Miller in describing *The sons of Usnech* (1954) admits that the illustrative style drew not only on the artist's

Celtic tradition but also on the printer's obsession with the Press books of the 1890s.[6] In attempting to marry text and typography Miller has even gone to the lengths of involving the authors: 'I've always tried also to work very closely with the writers and embody their wishes and desires in the design of the books wherever possible. In our very early years, in fact, we trained several poets to set type and so help get their books out'.[7] Two of these poet typesetters were Thomas Kinsella and Francis Barry.

Early experiments in typography and format led to the ballad sheet and chapbook series. Nine ballad sheets were issued between 1951 and 1958. The 'Dolmen chapbooks', issued in twelve parts between 1954 and 1960, contained short texts with illustrations using various type formats and techniques within a uniform page size [168]. The Library's collection contains ordinary and special editions of all the ballad sheets and chapbooks with related ephemera.

Illustrations were used wherever necessary and young Irish artists such as Leslie MacWeeney [167], Bridget Swinton and Frank Morris benefited from the Press's early patronage. Various illustrative techniques have been featured including wood engravings by Elizabeth Rivers [169], woodcuts and linocuts by Tate Adams [7], line drawings by Ruth Brandt and ink brush drawings by Louis Le Brocquy [172].

Dolmen have received a number of design awards, in particular the first Irish Book Design Award, awarded by CLÉ/The Irish Book Publishers' Association and sponsored by the Kilkenny Design Workshops, which went to *Dolmen XXV: an illustrated bibliography* (1976). The East German awards for 'The most handsome books from all the world' selected Dolmen's edition of *Holinshed's Irish chronicle 1577* (1979). The bronze medal and commendation were presented at the Leipzig Spring Fair in March 1981.

SUBJECT CONTENT

The Dolmen Press, founded primarily as a poets' press, also reflects Miller's other interests. He says himself, 'our list has grown out of my personal curiosity, taste, judgment or whatever you'd like to call it'.[8]

Dolmen's first major project, Brian Merriman's long poem *The midnight court,* translated by David Marcus, was published in 1953 in an edition of 200 [170]. Printed in black and red, with linocuts by Michael Biggs (his first illustrations for the Press), it was launched with Dolmen's first literary luncheon. The small amount of Irish Petrie type was lent by Dublin University Press. Copies 7 and 41, plus 'publication delay' notice, launching invitation and *Irish Times* review are in the Library's collection.

Poetry has certainly formed the bulk of Dolmen's publications with forty-six per cent of the output to date. Amongst these are twenty-six first collections, not least Thomas

169. *Out of Bedlam, XXVII wood engravings* by Elizabeth Rivers, with texts from Christopher Smart. 1956.

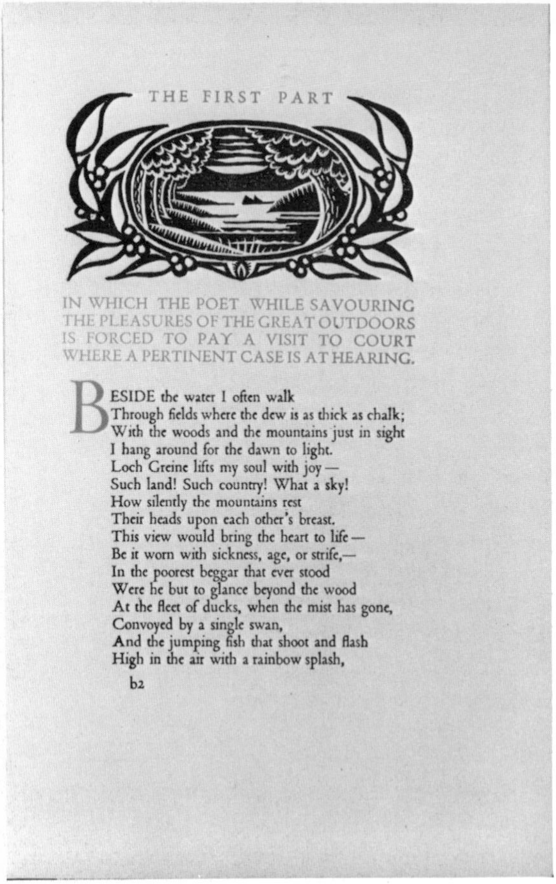
THE FIRST PART

IN WHICH THE POET WHILE SAVOURING THE PLEASURES OF THE GREAT OUTDOORS IS FORCED TO PAY A VISIT TO COURT WHERE A PERTINENT CASE IS AT HEARING.

BESIDE the water I often walk
Through fields where the dew is as thick as chalk;
With the woods and the mountains just in sight
I hang around for the dawn to light.
Loch Greine lifts my soul with joy—
Such land! Such country! What a sky!
How silently the mountains rest
Their heads upon each other's breast.
This view would bring the heart to life—
Be it worn with sickness, age, or strife,—
In the poorest beggar that ever stood
Were he but to glance beyond the wood
At the fleet of ducks, when the mist has gone,
Convoyed by a single swan,
And the jumping fish that shoot and flash
High in the air with a rainbow splash,

b2

170. *Cúirt an mheadhon oidhche: The midnight court,* by Bryan Merriman, newly translated into English by David Marcus; linocuts by Michael Biggs. 1953.

Kinsella's first collection (1956) and John Montague's first collection, *Forms of exile* (1959). The Library's holdings include one of the few proof copies of the latter, ordinary and special copies, review, postcard announcement and display notice.

The Dolmen venture was also welcomed by established writers: Padraic Colum wrote from New York to offer his poetry when he heard of the Press's existence. From 1961, with the publication of Austin Clarke's *Later poems,* the Press published all of his poetry, plays, and a novel, bringing him to the attention of a wider English and American public.

The *Dolmen miscellany of Irish writing* no. 1, which included poetry and prose, was published in 1962 but lack of public support prevented its continuation. Another attempt at a periodic publication was a revival of the *Poetry Ireland* magazine founded by David Marcus in Cork in the 1940s. Eight numbers were issued between 1962 and 1968 and the Freyer collection contains a complete set, an invitation to the launching and related newspaper cuttings, which are initially optimistic but by the third issue in 1964 bemoan the public's indifference suggesting that the 'Irish prefer to beg magazines rather than buy them'.[9] The journal was succeeded by a series of 'Poetry Ireland editions', which published collections or long poems by individual poets. Fifteen were issued between 1968 and 1972, all in similar format. One project, which unfortunately never came to fruition, was *The Dolmen book of Irish verse,* to be issued in several volumes with Irish text and parallel translations. In the Library are specimen pages. It was being planned with David Greene and Frank O'Connor, but on the latter's death was passed to Macmillan, who published it in one volume as *The golden book of Irish verse.* The ideas behind the Dolmen book were not incorporated, but the concept was recently revived in *An duanaire* (1981).

The Press has received numerous literary awards since Kinsella's *Another September* (1958) became the first book published outside Britain to be chosen by the Poetry Book Society of London. The Library's collection

171. *A Gaelic alphabet,* by Michael Biggs. (Dolmen Chapbook XI.) 1960. Proof copy printed in an edition of twenty-five copies in 1954. Published in 1960 as Dolmen Chapbook XI, with a note on Irish lettering by Liam Miller.

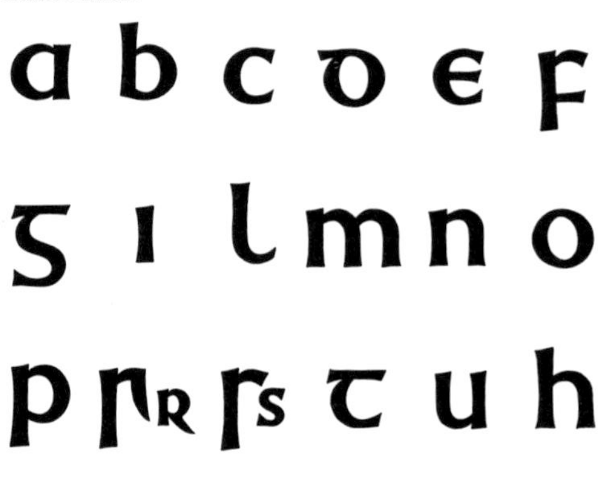

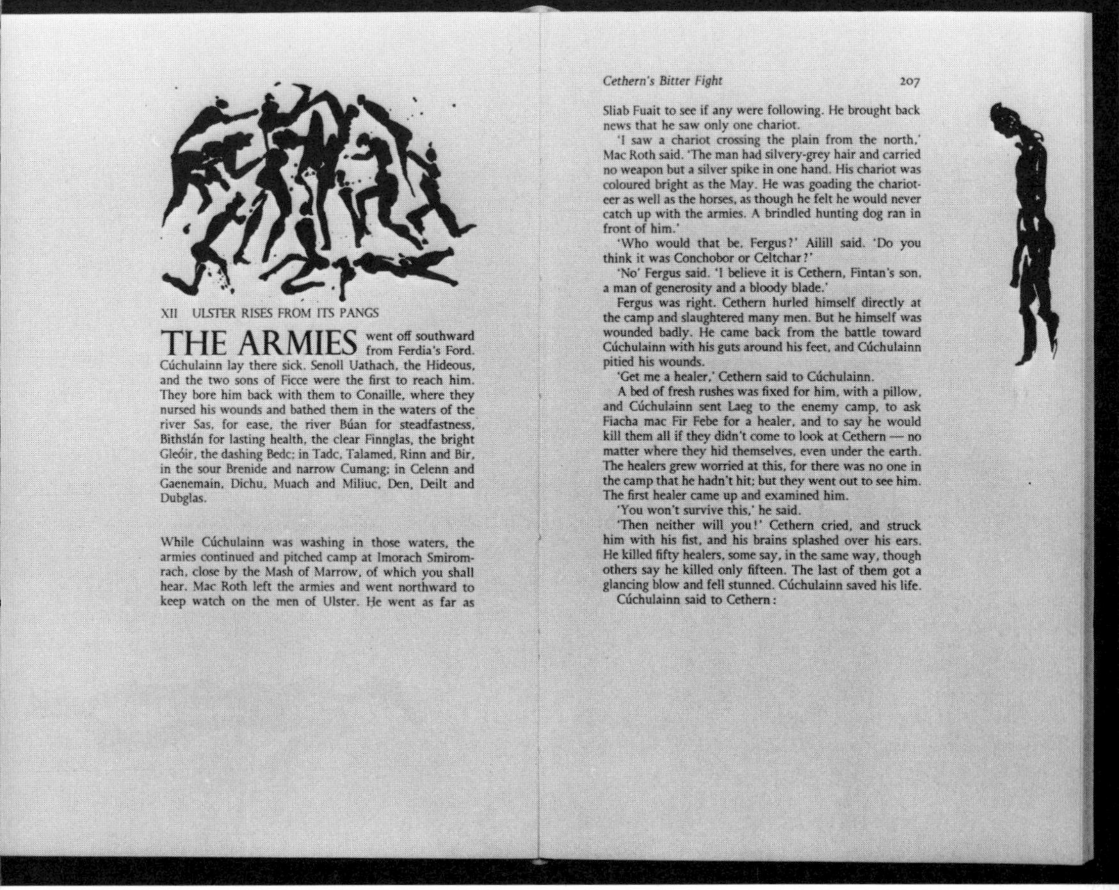
XII ULSTER RISES FROM ITS PANGS

THE ARMIES went off southward from Ferdia's Ford. Cúchulainn lay there sick. Senoll Uathach, the Hideous, and the two sons of Ficce were the first to reach him. They bore him back with them to Conaille, where they nursed his wounds and bathed them in the waters of the river Sas, for ease, the river Búan for steadfastness, Bithslán for lasting health, the clear Finnglas, the bright Gleóir, the dashing Bedc; in Tadc, Talamed, Rinn and Bir, in the sour Brenide and narrow Cumang; in Celenn and Gaenemain, Dichu, Muach and Miliuc, Den, Deilt and Dubglas.

While Cúchulainn was washing in those waters, the armies continued and pitched camp at Imorach Smiromrach, close by the Mash of Marrow, of which you shall hear. Mac Roth left the armies and went northward to keep watch on the men of Ulster. He went as far as

Cethern's Bitter Fight 207

Sliab Fuait to see if any were following. He brought back news that he saw only one chariot.

'I saw a chariot crossing the plain from the north,' Mac Roth said. 'The man had silvery-grey hair and carried no weapon but a silver spike in one hand. His chariot was coloured bright as the May. He was goading the charioteer as well as the horses, as though he felt he would never catch up with the armies. A brindled hunting dog ran in front of him.'

'Who would that be, Fergus?' Ailill said. 'Do you think it was Conchobor or Celtchar?'

'No' Fergus said. 'I believe it is Cethern, Fintan's son, a man of generosity and a bloody blade.'

Fergus was right. Cethern hurled himself directly at the camp and slaughtered many men. But he himself was wounded badly. He came back from the battle toward Cúchulainn with his guts around his feet, and Cúchulainn pitied his wounds.

'Get me a healer,' Cethern said to Cúchulainn.

A bed of fresh rushes was fixed for him, with a pillow, and Cúchulainn sent Laeg to the enemy camp, to ask Fiacha mac Fir Febe for a healer, and to say he would kill them all if they didn't come to look at Cethern — no matter where they hid themselves, even under the earth. The healers grew worried at this, for there was no one in the camp that he hadn't hit; but they went out to see him. The first healer came up and examined him.

'You won't survive this,' he said.

'Then neither will you!' Cethern cried, and struck him with his fist, and his brains splashed over his ears. He killed fifty healers, some say, in the same way, though others say he killed only fifteen. The last of them got a glancing blow and fell stunned. Cúchulainn saved his life.

Cúchulainn said to Cethern:

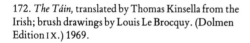

172. *The Táin,* translated by Thomas Kinsella from the Irish; brush drawings by Louis Le Brocquy. (Dolmen Edition IX.) 1969.

contains one of about ten advance proof copies with the title *Baggot Street deserta* (printed for the Society's Selection Council), a proof of the final edition, an ordinary copy and special copy no. 12. Three other Dolmen books have been the Poetry Book Society choice with eight receiving recommendations. Miller says, 'That we have succeeded with, say, the major poetry society outside Ireland, proves to me that once you open a channel of communication, then the status of the publisher in Dublin is as good as anywhere in the world'.[10] In 1976, 1977 and 1978 the Patrick Kavanagh Poetry Award went to Dolmen volumes.

Miller's concern for the past has resulted in seventeen volumes of early Irish texts. He encouraged Kinsella and others to translate from old Irish, and has always emphasized the glories of the Irish heritage. Miller's own particular interest in Gaelic led him very early on to ask Michael Biggs to design an alphabet [171]. Twenty-five proof copies were printed in 1954 and in March 1960, with a brief essay, it became part XI of the 'Dolmen chapbooks'. A special edition of fifty copies was also issued and a revised version appeared in August 1960. The Library's collection contains copies of all issues, plus a single sheet proof printed in 1959, which indicates the alphabet was cut on lino.

The Táin [172], translated by Thomas Kinsella, appeared in 1969 as 'Dolmen edition IX', in an edition of 1750 copies. The production of this book, which is undoubtedly the most famous issued by the Press, involved many years of planning, dating from

Kinsella's first interest when he translated *The sons of Usnech* (1954). There were a number of trial settings: eight trial pages in fourteen point Pilgrim entitled *The great Táin* were printed in an edition of fifty copies in 1965; single pages were set in fourteen point Pilgrim (December 1966 and January 1967) and fourteen point Bembo (December 1966); the section *Cuchulainn's boyhood deeds* was printed in an edition of fifty copies in fourteen point Pilgrim for private circulation in 1968. The book was designed in very close consultation with the illustrator Louis Le Brocquy. Swiftbrook was commissioned to produce four tons of a special paper loaded with kaolin to avoid the black images showing through on the verso of the page. Miller envisages the opening words of the chapters in tall capitals to signify an old story teller's catching attention at the start of a tale. No expense was spared on the production and the book just about paid for itself. A reading of *The Táin* by Kinsella was given at the Peacock Theatre on 31 August 1969. A publicity leaflet giving details of a small exhibition of 'The development of the edition' held in Hodges Figgis Bookshop at the time of the publication and a prospectus were issued by the Press. The Freyer collection contains some proof copies and various ephemera. A trade edition of *The Táin* was co-published with Oxford University Press in 1970, reproduced in a reduced format by

173. *The history and topography of Ireland,* by Giraldus Cambrensis, translated from the Latin by John J. O'Meara; drawings by Susan Hayes after MS 700 in the National Library of Ireland. (Dolmen texts 4.) 1982. Title page (with lettering by Timothy O'Neill) and frontispiece, of special edition of seventy-five handcoloured copies.

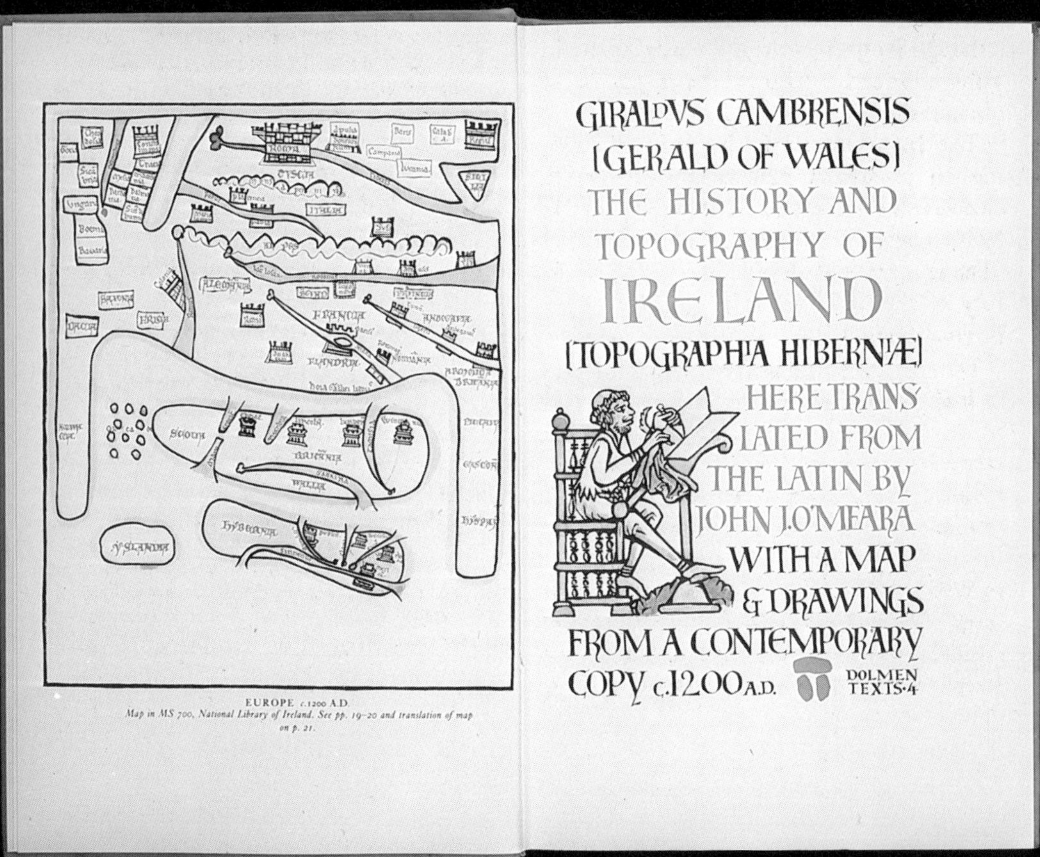

photolithography, including thirty of the original 130 illustrations. *Der Rinderraub,* a translation into German by Susanna Schaup was published in 1976. A new 'library edition' including all the illustrations was issued in July 1985.

Miller's love of the theatre has resulted in eleven volumes of plays. Synge's *Riders to the sea,* edited by Robin Skelton, appeared in 1969 as 'Dolmen edition VIII', in a limited edition of 750 copies [7]. The edition had been planned since 1958 when Tate Adams made the first experimental linocuts. The whole text was set in fourteen point Pilgrim, with colour printing to distinguish the characters' names and stage directions. A trial setting of one page of text and one linocut was printed in twenty-eight or twenty-nine proof copies in 1963; the Freyer collection contains a copy. A sheet of the linocuts with the title was also proofed. The character 'Cathleen' is so called in the trial setting, but in the final version is called 'Cailteen'. Austin Clarke in his *Irish Times* review stated that 'there is no such word or name as Cailteen in Irish'[11] and that although Synge did write the word Cailteen in a note to an early version of the play it was an obvious slip of the pen for Cathleen.

The 'Irish theatre series' began in 1970 aiming to provide a comprehensive survey; twelve volumes were issued between 1970 and 1984. Volume 6 was the first of a sub-series, 'The modern Irish drama', providing a history of the Irish theatre since the Literary Revival of the 1890s.

Dolmen publications have often filled gaps in Irish publishing. Robin Skelton says that Miller 'has looked for cases of inadequate recognition or downright neglect and made it his business to see that justice was done'.[12] For example, Miller's publication in three volumes of the complete plays of George Fitzmaurice, plus a volume of short stories, was inspired by his long-held belief that Yeats had treated Fitzmaurice badly, and led to a revived interest in Fitzmaurice and the showing of his plays once more at the Abbey Theatre.

Miller's obsession with W.B. Yeats was first evident in 1962 with Sheelah Kirby's guide *The Yeats country,* published to coincide with the Sligo Yeats Festival. In 1965 the first series of 'Yeats centenary papers' began, of which twelve parts appeared by 1968, followed by a collected bound volume. The 'New Yeats papers' numbered I-XX appeared between 1971 and 1981.

The success of the Dolmen Press is undoubtedly due to the driving force of its founder. Luke Peter, editor of *Enter certain players* (1978) acknowledges Liam Miller, 'whose enthusiasm for this project, whose skill as a publisher and whose impeccable taste as a designer has given us this handsome volume'. Dolmen has given us many handsome volumes and Trinity is fortunate to have such a fine collection of this Press.

NOTES

1. Liam Miller, tape transcript of a recent conversation, February 1985 (copy available in the Department of Early Printed Books, Trinity College Library).
2. Michael Freyer, 'The Dolmen Press . . .', *The Private Library* 3 (1960) 10-14.
3. Miller, tape transcript.
4. [Liam Miller], 'A prospect of Dolmens', *Ireland's press and printing* (June 1953).
5. Hal Speer, 'The Dolmen Press . . .', *The American Book Collector* 9/2 (1958) 21-3.
6. Liam Miller, *Dolmen XXV: an illustrated bibliography . . . 1951-1976.* Dublin: Dolmen Press, 1976, p. 20.
7. John Unterecker, 'Interview with Liam Miller', in *Modern Irish literature: essays in honor of William York Tindall* edited by Raymond J. Porter and James D. Brophy. New York: Iona College Press, 1972, p. 25.
8. Unterecker, 'Interview', p. 29.
9. *Sunday Independent,* 12 April 1964.
10. Unterecker, 'Interview', p. 26.
11. *Irish Times,* 1 November 1969.
12. Robin Skelton, 'Twentieth-century Irish literature and the private press tradition: Dun Emer, Cuala & Dolmen Presses 1902-1963', *The Massachusetts Review* 5 (1964) 368-77.

A SELECT BIBLIOGRAPHY OF THE LIBRARY

ANN O'BRIEN

This bibliography is arranged chronologically within each section and is confined to a selection of representative works on the Library and guides to the content of the collections. The numerous books and articles on individual manuscripts and printed books are omitted.

PERIODICALS

Annual Report: Library, 1972/3-.

Annual Bulletin of the Friends of the Library of Trinity College Dublin, 1946-57 [abbreviated to *Annual Bulletin* below].

Long Room (Friends of the Library of Trinity College Dublin), 1972-.

Newsletter (Friends of the Library of Trinity College Dublin), 1984-.

GENERAL WORKS ON THE LIBRARY

X.D., 'Trinity College Library', *Irish Penny Journal* (1841) 340-2.

W.B.S. Taylor, *History of the University of Dublin from its foundation to the end of the eighteenth century.* London: printed for T. Cadell and J. Cumming, Dublin, 1845.

D.C. Heron, *The constitutional history of the University of Dublin.* Dublin: James McGlashan, 1848.

'Lending libraries and copyright', *Hibernia* (1882) 179-80.

'The Library Association at Dublin', *The Library Chronicle* (1884) 161-4.

J. Kells Ingram, *The Library of Trinity College Dublin: being an address delivered at the seventh annual meeting of the Library Association of the United Kingdom, September 30, 1884.* London: Chiswick Press, 1886.

T.K. Abbott, 'The Library', in *The book of Trinity College Dublin 1591-1891.* Dublin: Hodges Figgis, 1892.

W.M. Dixon, *Trinity College Dublin.* London: Robinson, 1902. (College histories.)

J.P. Mahaffy, 'The Library of Trinity College Dublin: the growth of a legend', *Hermathena* 27 (1902) 68-78.

J.P. Mahaffy, *An epoch in Irish history: Trinity College Dublin, its foundation and early fortunes, 1591-1660.* London: Fisher Unwin, 1903 (reprinted 1970).

E. Sullivan, 'The Library of Trinity College Dublin', *Book Lover's Magazine* 7 (1908) 1-12.

C.E. Maxwell, *A history of Trinity College Dublin 1591-1892.* Dublin: University Press, 1946.

H.W. Parke, 'Mr Timothy Casey's robberies: an episode from the Library Minutes', *Annual Bulletin* (1949) 7-9.

H.L. Murphy, *A history of Trinity College Dublin from its foundation to 1702.* Dublin: Hodges Figgis, 1951.

W. O'Sullivan, 'The Library before Kinsale', *Annual Bulletin* (1952) 10-14.

R.B.D. French, *The Library of Trinity College Dublin: a great library and its needs.* Dublin: Colm Ó Lochlainn at the Three Candles, 1954.

Building for books. Documentary film, colour. 1959.

R.B.D. French, 'Great Library of Trinity College Dublin', *Library Journal* (1959) 3533-5.

M.B. Bennett, *Trinity College Library Dublin.* Palm Springs, Calif.: privately printed by the Welwood Murray Memorial Library, 1959.

H.W. Parke, *The Library of Trinity College Dublin: a historical description by the Librarian.* Dublin: 1961.

F.J.E. Hurst, 'The College Library', *Kosmos* (1967) 20-1.

A.R.A. Hobson, *Great libraries.* London: Weidenfeld & Nicholson, 1970. [Trinity: pp 174-85.]

W. O'Sullivan, 'The eighteenth-century rebinding of the manuscripts', *Long Room* 1 (1970) 19-28.

P. Brown, 'Trinity College Library', *Protean* (Winter 1972) 24-7.

C.J. Benson, 'A friend of the Library', *Long Room* 9 (1974) 40.

R. Bell, 'Legal deposit in Britain', *Law Librarian* 8 (1977) 5-8, 22-6.

E.F.D. Roberts, 'Trinity College Library, University of Dublin', in *Encyclopedia of library and information science,* vol. 7, pp 308-14.

M. Buschkühl, 'Die Bibliothek des Trinity College in

Dublin'. Unpublished thesis. Bibliothekar-Lehrinstitut des Landes Nordrhein-Westfalen, Köln, 1980.

P. Fox, *Trinity College Library Dublin.* Dublin: Eason, 1982. (Irish heritage series.)

R.B. McDowell & D.A. Webb, *Trinity College Dublin 1592-1952.* Cambridge: University Press, 1982.

R.J. Chepesiuk, 'Great libraries of Dublin: a scholar's delight', *Wilson Library Bulletin* 57 (1983) 657-61.

MANUSCRIPTS

Catalogi librorum manuscriptorum Angliae et Hiberniae. Oxford, 1697.

E. Hincks, *Catalogue of the Egyptian manuscripts in the Library of Trinity College Dublin.* Dublin: Milliken, 1843.

J.H. Todd, *Books of the Vaudois: the Waldensian manuscripts preserved in the Library of Trinity College Dublin.* Dublin: Hodges Figgis, 1865.

J.T. Gilbert, *Facsimiles of national manuscripts of Ireland.* Dublin: Public Record Office, 1874-84.

T.K. Abbott, *Catalogue of the manuscripts in the Library of Trinity College Dublin; to which is added a list of the Fagel Collection of maps in the same library.* Dublin: Hodges Figgis, 1900.

Don L. Gougad, 'Répertoire des facsimiles des manuscrits irlandais', *Revue celtique* (1913) 14-37.

M. Esposito, *Inventaire des anciens manuscrits français des bibliothèques de Dublin.* Paris: Champion, 1914-21.

R.H. Murray, *A short guide to some manuscripts in the Library of Trinity College Dublin.* London: SPCK, 1920.

T.K. Abbott & E.J. Gwynn, *Catalogue of the Irish manuscripts in the Library of Trinity College Dublin.* Dublin: Hodges Figgis, 1921.

J.G. Smyly, 'Notes on Greek manuscripts in the Library of Trinity College', *Hermathena* (1933) 163-95.

R.O.D. Dougan, *A descriptive guide to twenty Irish manuscripts in the Library of Trinity College Dublin, with an appendix of five early Irish manuscripts in the Royal Irish Academy.* 2nd ed. Dublin: University Press, 1955.

M. Garau Aunós, 'Manuscritos españoles de la biblioteca del Trinity College de Dublin', *Il Biblioteconomia* (1965) 52-8.

R.J. Hayes, *Manuscript sources for the history of Irish civilisation.* Boston, Mass.: G.K. Hall, 1965. *First supplement 1965-75.* 1979.

The Synge manuscripts in the Library of Trinity College Dublin: a catalogue prepared on the occasion of the Synge centenary exhibition 1971. Dublin: Dolmen Press, 1971.

E. Maconchy, *Ina Boyle: an appreciation with a select list of her music.* Dublin: printed for the Library of Trinity College Dublin at the Dolmen Press, 1974.

List of the collections of modern papers, 18th-20th century, in the Library of Trinity College Dublin. London: Royal Commission on Historical Manuscripts, 1975.

L. Shields, 'Medieval manuscripts in French and Provençal', *Hermathena* 121 (1976) 90-100.

J.J.G. Alexander, *A survey of manuscripts illuminated in the British Isles. Vol. 1: Insular manuscripts from the sixth to the ninth century.* London: Harvey Millar, 1978.

M.L. Colker, *A descriptive catalogue of the medieval and renaissance Latin manuscripts in the Library of Trinity College Dublin.* [Forthcoming.]

PRINTED BOOKS

Catalogus librorum in Bibliotheca Collegii Sanctae et Individuae Trinitatis Reginae Elizabethae juxta Dublin. Dublinii: typis et impensis Johannis Hyde, [*c.* 1715?].

Catalogus librorum quibus aucta est Bibliotheca collegii SS. Trinitatis reginae Elizabethae juxta Dublin anno exeunte Kal. November MDCCcIII. Dublin: Typis Academicus, 1854.

A catalogue of the books in the Lending Library of Trinity College Dublin. Dublin: printed at the University Press by M.H. Gill, 1861.

Catalogus librorum impressorum qui in Bibliotheca Collegii Sacrosanctae et individuae Trinitatis Reginae Elizabethae juxta Dublin adservantur... Dublinii: E. Typographeo Academico, 1864-87. 8 vols. Supplementum addenda et corrigenda, 1887.

Libri in publica Collegii Bibliotheca 29 Febr. anno 1600: entry no. 49 in the Particular Book, Trinity College Dublin. Facsimile with introduction and appendices by J.P. Mahaffy. London: T. Fisher Unwin, 1904.

T.K. Abbott, *Catalogue of fifteenth-century books in the Library of Trinity College Dublin, in Marsh's Library Dublin, with a few from other collections.* Dublin: Hodges Figgis, 1905.

List of current and recent foreign periodicals, 1906.

A.A. Luce, 'List of editions of the works of George Berkeley in the College Library', *Annual Bulletin* (1946) 11.

D.A. Webb, 'Broadsides relating to Swift', *Annual Bulletin* (1946) 8-11.

I. McPhail, 'A short list of Elizabethan books in the Library', *Annual Bulletin* (1958) 3-7.

V.M.R. Morrow, 'Bibliotheca Quiniana: a description of the books and bindings in the Quin collection in the Library of Trinity College Dublin. Unpublished thesis. University of London, 1970.

E. Gleeson, *Union list of current legal periodicals held in Dublin law libraries.* Dublin: Trinity College, 1978.

N.R. Jessop & C. Nudds, *Guide to collections in Dublin*

libraries: printed books to 1850 and special collections. Dublin: Reprint, 1982.

Eighteenth-century short title catalogue. London: British Library, 1983-.

Nineteenth-century short title catalogue . . . extracted from the catalogues of the Bodleian Library, the British Library, the Library of Trinity College Dublin, the National Library of Scotland and the university libraries of Cambridge and Newcastle. Newcastle-upon-Tyne: Avero, 1984-.

A directory of rare book and special collections in the United Kingdom and the Republic of Ireland ed. by M.I. Williams. London: Library Association, 1985.

BUILDINGS

'Alterations of library building, Trinity College Dublin', *Dublin Builder* (1860) 196.

E.H. Alton, 'Some notes on the Library and the cost of its building', *Annual Bulletin* (1948) 10-12.

W. O'Sullivan, 'The new Manuscripts Room', *Annual Bulletin* (1958) 12-13.

International architectural competition for a new library building. Dublin: Hely's, 1960.

[International architectural competition] *Decisions and report of the jury of award.* Dublin: University Press, 1961.

F.J.E. Hurst, 'Trinity College Dublin proposed new library', *Library Association Record* (February 1961) 45-8.

'The Library, Trinity College Dublin', *Architect and Building News* (11 October 1967) 611-18.

A. Colquhon, 'Library, Trinity College Dublin', *Architectural Review* (October 1967) 265-77.

P. Delaney, 'Trinity College Library Dublin', *Architectural Design* 37 (1967) 459-68.

J. Donat, 'Magic box: Trinity College Library in Dublin', *Architectural Forum* (October 1967) 78-85.

M. Brawne, *Libraries: architecture and equipment.* London: Praeger, 1970, pp 108-11, 148, 173.

W. O'Sullivan, 'The new Manuscripts Room', *Long Room* 5 (1972) 23-5.

A. Crookshank, *The Long Room.* Dublin: Gifford & Craven, 1976.

CONSERVATION LABORATORY

A. Cains, 'Book conservation workshop manual, pt 1', *New Bookbinder* 1 (1981) 11-25.

A. Cains, 'The work of the Conservation Laboratory', *Trinity College Gazette* (10 March 1983) 5-6, 11.

TECHNICAL SERVICES

H.D. Hutton, *Impressions of twelve years cataloguing in a great library.* London: Chiswick Press, 1886.

N. Harris, 'Pilot projects using variable length library records', *Program* (1968) 13-16.

A.M. Tucker, 'Experiences with MARC based systems at Trinity College Dublin', in *International Seminar on the MARC Format and the Exchange of Bibliographical Data in Machine Readable Form, Berlin 1971: proceedings.* München-Pullach: Verlag Dokumentation, 1972, pp 157-71.

E.B. Ceadel, *Adaptation of computer programs for catalogues for use in another library.* Cambridge: University Library, 1977. (British Library research & development report 5352.)

PICTORIAL REPRESENTATIONS OF THE LIBRARY

C.H. Oldham, *Trinity College pictorial account of the foundation of the College: a tercentenary souvenir.* Dublin: Thom, 1892.

W.H. Benyon, Portfolio of Trinity College Dublin: a series of illustrations, photogravure, etc. from original negatives, 1901.

Clarté: art et art decoratif, n.9 (septembre 1935) [includes an illustrated account of the Library].

A.N. Jeffares, *Trinity College Dublin founded 1591: 34 drawings and descriptions.* Dublin: Thom, 1944.

MISCELLANEOUS

Novae bibliothecae SS Trin. Coll. Dub. descriptio, poema. In duabus partibus. Ad calcem accesserunt nonnulla varii argumenti epigrammata. . . Dublinii: ex typographe R. Reilly; impensis Thomae Thornton, 1735.

'In the Library', *TCD: a College Miscellany* (9 March 1904) 44. [Dramatic vignette.]

'To the gent who snored in the Library the other day: an ode' (by K.H.B.), *TCD: a College Miscellany* (25 November 1908) 167.

'The Library' (by Pip), *TCD: a College Miscellany* (15 December 1921) 65. [Sonnet.]

'Obiit tranquillitas', *TCD: a College Miscellany* (27 October 1927) 8. [Poem on the pleasure of silence in the Library.]

'Songs of the College 4: the Library', *TCD: a College Miscellany* (31 May 1928) 183. [Poem.]

[M. Pollard] *The architects' and builders' new song; addressed to the New Library from the ruins of the Old.* Dublin: St Sepulchre's Press, 1967. [Broadsheet ballad.]

INDEX

Figures in square brackets indicate illustration numbers.